Buddhist Literature and Art

These articles have been published in the Indian Historical Quarterly and the details of the articles is given below for reference:

Issue	Year of Pub.	Page Nos.	Page Nos. in the present book
Vol. 9 (1-2)	1933	227-236	1-10
Vol. 9 (1-2)	1933	567-576	11-20
Vol. 12 (1-4)	1936	109-120	21-30
Vol. 8 (1-2)	1932	93-110	31-48
Vol. 8 (1-2)	1932	342-350	49-56
Vol. 7 (3-4)	1931	740	57-58
Vol. 8 (3-4)	1932	790-793	59-62
Vol. 7 (1-2)	1931	259-286	63-86
Vol. 37 (1-4)	1961	287-292	87-90
Vol. 3 (1-2)	1927	412-417	91-98
Vol. 7 (1-2)	1931	377-379	99-102
Vol. 2 (3-4)	1926	563-574	103-116
Vol. 39 (1-4)	1963	1-12	117-126
Vol. 32 (1-4)	1956	352-353	127-128
Vol. 35 (1-4)	1959	274-275	129-130
Vol. 34 (1-4)	1958	187-192	131-136
Vol. 32 (1-4)	1956	170-178	137-144
Vol. 39 (1-4)	1963	69-79	145-154
Vol. 9 (1-2)	1933	417-419	155-158
Vol. 19 (1-4)	1943	1-11	159-168
Vol. 11 (1-4)	1935	199-210	169-180
Vol. 34 (1-4)	1958	1-5	181-184
Vol. 7 (3-4)	1931	669-673	185-190
Vol. 8 (1-2)	1932	332-341	191-200
Vol. 6 (1-4)	1930	1-30	201-224
Vol. 32 (1-4)	1956	286-289	225-228
Vol. 2 (3-4)	1926	698-709	229-238
Vol. 2 (3-4)	1926	495-508	239-250
Vol. 17 (1-4)	1941	196-206	251-262
Vol. 13 (1-4)	1937	610-616	263-268
Vol. 2 (3-4)	1926	657-662	269-274

Facets of Buddhist Thought and Culture: 4

Buddhist Literature and Art

Collection of Articles from the Indian Historical Quarterly

Compiled by
Dr. Mahendra
P. Mittal

Introduction by
Prof. S. R. Bhatt

Originals
(an imprint of Low Price Publications)
Delhi-110052

Distributed by
D.K. Publishers Distributors (P) Ltd.
4834/24, Ansari Road, Darya Ganj,
New Delhi-110002
Phones: 51562573, 51562575, 51562578
e-mail: dkpd@del3.vsnl.net.in
visit us at: www.dkpd.com

Articles first Published in the Journal from 1925-1963
First Published as a book
With an Introduction 2004
ISBN 81-88629-28-6

Published by
Originals
(an imprint of Low Price Publications)
A-6, Nimri Commercial Centre,
Near Ashok Vihar Phase-IV,
Delhi-110052
Phones: 27401672, 27452453
e-mail: lpp@nde.vsnl.net.in
visit us at: www.lppindia.com

Printed at
D K Fine Art Press P Ltd.
Delhi-110052

PRINTED IN INDIA

in translations and can be retrieved. It will be a huge but highly significant task to restore the lost literature, but it should be attempted by world scholarship as it would be valuable asset to human culture.

The basic Buddhist literature grew up on Indian soil in Pali and Sanskrit languages and has shaped the intellectual climate of India in ancient times. Soon it spread out to other Asian countries and reformed their psyche. In modern times Buddhist literature is being produced all over the world mostly in expository form. For the ancient literature there are several catalogues like that of Tanjore, Gilgit, Nanjio and some good bibliographic histories like that of Taranatha. A classified and comparative account of the entire Buddhist literature produced so far is a need of the times. It will be a gigantic work to be undertaken by a team of scholars.

The Buddhist literature is mainly concerned with biographies of Śākya Muni, the Buddha, his previous births and future incarnations, the Bodhisattvas and their noble conduct, teachings of the Buddha, disciplinary codes for the Samgha, expositions of philosophical, epistemological, moral, religious and eschatological ideas, beliefs and practices.

From 3rd century B.C. to 3rd century A.D. there was a phenomenal growth of Buddhist art and literature in India. Since Buddhism emphasised corporate life, many caityas, viharas, stupas, temples etc. were built. Alongwith them the arts of architecture and painting were developed. A specific Buddhist art imagery came into existence which was known as Gandhara. Buddhist mode of tantra was also developed and Buddhist arts and tantra were brought closer to the arts and tantra practised in other religious sects of India of those times.

In the stupas the highest objects of adoration were the Buddha, the Dharma and the Samgha known as triratnas. The relics of the Buddha and other holy persons were preserved and worshipped. The relics were śārīrika or corporeal, uddeśikas or memorial and pāribhogikas or articles used by Buddha and others. Hair relics, tooth relics, bone relics etc. are still preserved in some of these stupas. Some of the stupas also known as pagodas in Burma, Java, Ceylon and Nepal are majestic in size and shape and are masterpieces in architecture.

Along with stupas there are sculptures and bronze which have great aesthetic merit and iconographic value. The images of Buddha in elegant form and with radiant spiritual ecstasy, expressing wisdom and compassion are noteworthy. There are stone and metal images which are of great artistic and spiritual worth.

Introduction

Art and artistic pursuits constitute the very essence of a culture. A culture is known and evaluated in terms of its achievements in the fields of Arts apart from Science and Technology. Multiple arts and varied art-forms provide richness to a culture. It gets refinement and sophistication through development of Arts which cater to finer sensitivities of the human being.

Human mind has an innate necessity to express its thoughts, feelings and emotions through bodily gestures, languages and other symbolic modes of expression. When the highly subtle, complex and sublime thoughts, feelings and emotions cannot get exhibited through ordinary human language, human mind resorts to arts of different variety. Human mind cannot remain confined to itself. On the one hand it impels actions, and on the other it gets expressed in literature and arts.

Indian culture during its vast spatio-cultural canvas has evolved various types of arts and has achieved high degree of advancement. Indian art traditions have very ancient and long history and have been marvels in the world culture and civilization. Right from the Vedic times Indian mind has excelled in artistic creativity.

In the total stock and storehouse of art treasures the contribution of Buddhism has been immense and intense. Buddhist artists have expressed through various media all the noble ideas and ideals, beliefs and practices, mythologies and religiosity enunciated and inculcated in the Buddhist fold. The pursuit of arts in Buddhist circles had received great heights when Buddhism stepped outside the Indian territory. Buddhist arts acquired newer forms and newer dimensions in the countries it was spread over outside India. It got mingled with local morass and refined sensitivities of the people.

Buddhist literature is amazingly vast. It has been produced at all points of time in ancient, medieval and modern times in India and outside all over the world. Buddhist literature can be classified time-wise, language-wise and country-wise. Unfortunately a large amount of ancient literature could not be preserved and has been lost in oblivion. Some of it has been lost in original but some of it is available

There are quite a good number of paintings in caitya halls and in caves which reveal the subtlity of ideas and depth of feelings. Solemn dignity, poise and detachment, spiritual sublimity and religious piety are the hallmarks of classical Buddhist paintings in India. Thanka paintings of Ladakh are well-known for their display of vigour, grace and vitality. Likewise, Gandhara art tradition finds its expression on book covers of Gilgit manuscripts. These paintings depict stories from Jatakas and Avadanakalpalata. Paintings at Ajanta, Ellora, Bagh etc. are world famous and they attract both scholars and tourists from all over the world.

Apart from paintings there are terracotta figures, exquisite ivory carvings and sculptures which have fine display of artistic skills. Here we find finest figures of the Buddha and the Bodhisattvas in human form. Their appearance is not only soothing but also bliss-giving. The Buddhist mythologies get full representation in Buddhist art.

Tantric influence of the Vajrayāna variety is quite prominent in Buddhist art. All the tantric deities which are common to Buddhism and Hinduism have received a place of prominence in the Buddhist paintings. These paintings reveal the four Noble Truths, concepts of Prajñā or śunyatā and karuṇā with super-human qualities, feats of adventure and miraculous performances of Buddha and Bodhisattvas. Some of the paintings also reveal awe and reverence for the Buddha and the Dharma. Buddha has been quite often represented as a Kalyāṇa Mitra, a spiritual guide and liberator. He is also represented as Bhaiṣ ajya Guru who is always willing to help the suffering humanity.

Apart from sculpture and painting the Buddhist art is also expressed through music, dance and drama which are important components of the mode of expression of religiosity. Music and dance in particular have tantric influence, overtone and bearing. They help in heightening of religiosity and spiritual enlightenment. They are the outcome of intense forethought, contemplation and concentration. They elevate mind to a state of total freedom, calmness and tranquillity so as to receive the inflow of divine grace.

Another form of Buddhist art is the inscriptions of the Buddhist rulers who have depicted the rules for noble conduct and ideal behaviour. Some of these inscriptions are in Brahmi characters and some of them are in script which was evolved later. All inscriptions convey a message of peace, universal well-being and orderly behaviour. They begin with obeisance to Lord Buddha, invoke his grace and enjoin people to follow the path shown by the Buddha.

The Buddhist art occupies a very significant position in the totality of Indian art traditions. Though distinctive in ideas and thematic descriptions, it is in line with the general Indian art traditions. The Buddhist art went outside India alongwith the spread of Buddhism and it assumed newer forms in the countries of its locale. It is a remarkable event in world history to witness Buddhist art in veriegated forms in the countries of Asia. For example, the Pagoda at Barabudur in Java, at Anuradhapuram in Ceylon and the Swayambhu Nath Temple in Nepal are artistic marvels which provide richness to world culture and civilisation.

Contents

List of Plates

Chapter - 1
The Buddhist Manuscripts at Gilgit

N. Dutt

The third manuscript that has been examined by me is, as is the case with the other two manuscripts,[1] written on birch-bark in Cursive Gupta characters of the 6th century A.D. Considering the period it was under earth, it is surprising to find that the glaze of the ink still remains and can be easily revived bya slight wiping with a damp piece of soft cloth.

The title of the Ms.

The title of the book, as given in the last leaf of the Ms., is

सर्वतथागताज्ञान-बोधिसत्त्वभूमिक्रमणम् and

सर्वतथागताधिष्ठान-सत्त्वावलोकन-बुद्धक्षेत्रसन्दर्शनव्यूहम् ।

The second name has been adopted in the Tibetan version, in which the Sanskrit title is given thus (MDO, Kha, 395a):

आर्यसर्वतथागताधिष्ठान-सत्त्वावलोकन-बुद्धक्षेत्रनिर्देशनव्यूहनाम महायानसूत्र and its Tibetan rendering is as follows:

*Ḥ*phags. pa.de. *b*shiṅ. gśegs. pa. thams. cad. kyi. byin. gyis. *br*labs-sems. can. la *gz*igs.śiṅ-saṅs. *rg*yas.kyi. shin. gi. *bk*od. pa.kun. tu. ston. pa.shes. bya. ba. theg. pa. chen. poḥ. *m*do. On restoration it would be आर्यसर्वतथागताधिष्ठान-सत्त्वावलोकन-बुद्धक्षेत्रव्यूहसन्दर्शननाम महायानसूत्र।

Csoma Körösi translates the title thus: "Description of the province of Buddha, on which, for the sake of all beings, all Tathāgatas have bestowed their benedictions" (*As. Res.*, XX, p. 425).

---

1. For the accounts of the previous tow mss. see *IHQ.*, VIII, pp. 93-100, 312-350.

In this connection In must thank Mr. Ramchandra Kak, who realises the value of the finds, for taking the necessary care of the mss. and giving me all the facilities to deal with them.

The Chinese text, which has been taken byNanjio as a version of this Sūtra, contains only a small fraction of the whole Sūtra, and is entitled Fo-shuo-chuang-yen-wang-to-lo-ni-ching (for Chinese characters, see next page, 1.1), and its Sanskrit form would be बुद्धभाषित व्यूह राजधारणीसूत्र। but in 11. 5-6, the full title of the Sutra is given thus: *i'ch'ieh-ju-lai-so-hu-kuan-ch'a chung-sheng-shih-hsien-fo-ch'a-chung-yen-wang-to-lo-ni* (For Chinese characters, see next page, 11. 5-6).

Nanjio has reproduced the Sanskrit ittle as transliterated in Tibetan characters in the xylographs, but the exact restoration from the above Chinese expression should be सर्वतथागताधिष्ठान-सत्त्वावलोकन-बुद्धक्षेत्रव्यूह-राजधारणी।

Its translation in the light of the Chinese rendering would be: "The Dhāraṇī for a beneficent watch over the beings of the excellent Buddha-land, to whom all Tathāgatas vow their protection."

The Chinese and Tibetan versions

The Tibetan translation of this work has been made by Surendrabodhi, Śīlendrabodhi, and Jinamitra with the Tibetan monk Ye-shes-de. The translation is as literal as possible and hardly needs any comment.

The Chinese translation of I.tsing, printed in the Taisho edition is equally literal, making allowances of course for the insurmountable difficulties presented bya non-alphabetic language. On a comparison of the Chinese version with our Ms., it appears that the Chinese text contains the essential portion of this Sūtra i.e. the actual *dhāraṇī,* and not the supplementary *dhāraṇīs* and the accounts of their efficacies. Perhaps the Chinese version represents the earliest form of the *Sūtra,* which, in course of time, attained by additions its present form as found in our manuscript and the Tibetan version.[1] The Chinese text (see 1. 2 of the Chinese characters), as restored into Sanskrit begins thus:

---

1. Cf. the beginning of the Sanskrit ms. and the Tibetan text, infra, p. 236.

1 佛說莊嚴王陀羅尼呪經

2

3 如是我聞。一時薄伽梵。在布怛洛迦山。爲諸

4 人天一切大衆演說法要。遍觀十方以妙音

5 聲。告觀自在菩薩妙吉祥菩薩言。善男子有

6 經名一切如來所護觀察衆生示現佛刹莊嚴

7 王陀羅尼。我昔初發心時。於花光顯現如來

所。與九十俱胝衆生。一聞此法皆得如來智

[2] एवं मया श्रुतम्। एकस्मिन् समये भगवान् पोतलकपर्वते विहरति स्म। सन्ति बहवो [3] देवमनुष्या: सर्वे महाव्याख्यानधर्मकामा:। [अथ] दशदिशमवलोक्य वल्गुमनोज्ञस्वरै [4] अवलोकितेश्वरं बोधिसत्त्वं आमन्त्र्य मञ्जुश्री: बोधि-सत्त्वोऽवोचत्। अस्ति कुलपुत्र (lit. सत्पुरुष) [5] सर्वतथागताधिष्ठानसत्त्वाव-लोकन-बुद्धक्षेत्र-व्यूह [6] राजधारणी नाम सूत्रम। मया पूर्व प्रथमचित्तोत्पादकाले सुकुसुमज्योति:सन्दर्शतथा-गतस्यान्तिकात् श्रुतम्। येषां [7] नवतीनां सत्त्वकोटीनां तद् धर्म श्रुतं तेषां तथागतज्ञान-प्रङ्किङ्क

A comparison of this with the Sanskrit text shows that an addition of a long passage covering 4 leaves has been made after the words विहरति स्म and before दशदिशमवलोक्य. In the Chinese text, there is the first line of the Sūtra as found in Sanskrit, i.e. the name of the place where Buddha was staying but not the names of the Bodhisattvas, gods and other beings that assembled to hear him. It then skips over 4 leaves of the Sanskrit Ms. corresponding to 3 (395-397) leaves of the Tibetan xylograph, and then comes to the 5th leaf of the Sanskrit Ms. corresponding to leaf 398a of the xylograph. The Chinese text henceforth keeps quite close to the Sanskrit original up to leaf 132a, 1. 2.

In the Chinese version as also in the Tibetan, the *dhāraṇīs* or *mantrapadas* are not translated but transliterated, and compliment must be paid to the Chinese for the great skill that has been shown in the reproduction of Sanskrit sounds.

The concluding passage of the Chinese version is given below along with its Sanskrit restoration. The last three lines (5-7) are not found in the Sanskrit Ms.

[1] मरणकाले बुद्धबोधिसत्त्वदर्शनं भविष्यति। [2] कायमुत्सृज्य सुखावत्यां लोकधातौ पुनरुत्पत्तिं लप्स्यष्यते। आयुर्वर्णवलसमन्वागतः भविष्यति (परिपूरिं गमिष्यति)। सर्वेशत्रवः [3] शमिताः सत्त्वाः प्रमुदिताः। अस्यां धारणयां भाष्यमाणायां षष्टीनां च प्राणिसहस्वनां अनुत्पत्तिकेषु धर्मेपु [4] क्षान्तिप्रति-लम्मोऽभूत् सवोवरणाविनिमुक्तः सर्वाभिप्रायपरिपूर्णाः।

[5] एवं खलु लोकज्येष्ठेन भाषितं तत् सूत्रम्। अव-लोकितेश्वरः बोधिसत्त्वः मंजुश्रीर्बोधिसत्त्व [6] सर्वो महासंघश्च प्रमुदिताः सुप्रतिपन्नाः॥ [7] बुद्धभाषित-व्यूहराजधारणी सूत्रम्।

1 臨命終時觀佛菩薩，捨身之後必得
2 往生極樂世界，壽命色力悉皆具足，一切怨
3 讎並生歡喜，說此呪時六萬有情得無生法
4 忍，永除諸障所願滿足
5 爾時世尊說此經已，觀自在菩薩妙吉祥菩
6 薩，一切大衆聞佛所說歡喜奉行
7 佛說莊嚴王陀羅尼呪經

The above extract indicates a natural end. In view of the fact that after this a new Dhāraṇī is being recited, it may be easily concluded that the rest of contents of the manuscript is a later addition.

The Tibetan version is a *verbatim* rendering of the whole of the Sanskrit Ms. and hence it is much larger in size than the Chinese. Nanjio has not taken note of this fact in his *Catalogue*.

Date of the Work

The safest data for ascertaining the time of composition of the ms. are the dates of the Tibetan and Chinese translations. The Tibetan translation was made in the ninth century while the Chinese in the seventh (about 701 A.D.). Hence there can be no doubt about the existence of this work in the sixth century or some time before this. Though the Chinese translator had, as his basic text, an original different from the present one, there need not be any doubt about the work belonging to the sixth century A.D., as the script of the present ms. testifies. Again, if it be held that the Chinese translators worked with a Sanskrit original, which is earlier in date than the present one, then its date may be pushed further back, say, by a century, and we may safely conclude that this text was written as early as the 5th century A.D.

Résumé of the Contents*

Section I—The text opens as usual with an account of Buddha's residence which is here located at Potalaka, the abode of Avalokiteśvara, and his audience consisting of gods, men, bodhisattvas and other beings. There, at the request of all these beings Buddha delivered the Sūtra containing the principal Dhāraṇī.

Section II—What follows after Section I is really superfluous. It is only another dhāranī called *Abhayatejam*, delivered by Vajrapāṇi Bodhisattva; the only reason for its inclusionis perhaps that it is also a *Buddhādhiṣṭhāna* and that the merit acquired by learning this *dhāraṇī* is similar to that conferred by that of the previous one.

Section III—After the conclusion of this *dhāraṇī* and followed by an account of a ceremonial, Mañjusrī appears on the scene and asks why the present sūtra is called *Sarcatathāgatādhiṣṭhāna-sattvāvalo-kana-buddhakṣetrasandarśana-vyūha* (leaf 134b), and then puts a few other incidental questions, which Buddha answers, by uttering some gthās.

Section IV—Ārya Avalokiteśvara comes with another *dhāraṇī* called *Vyavalokana-prātikārya*; the reason for its inclusion is that it speaks of *sattcādhiṣṭhāna* or *sattvāvalokana* and that by reading and writing this *dhāraṇī* all the merits described before by the Tathāgatas are acquired (*sarcān etān tathāgata-bhāṣitān guṇān pratilabhante*—leaf 139b, 1. 4).

Section V—The *Vyavalokana-prātihārya* is followed by three other *dhāraṇīs* with descriptions of their respective rites given by Anopamā Mahāyakṣiṇī, Śaṅkhinī Mahādevī, and Bhīmā Mahādevī. All these are meant to confer benefits, or protect those beings who will read, write or propagate this Sūtra.

Section VI—Lastly comes the section dealing with the merits acquired by studying and propagating the Sūtra, and the suitability of its title.

Various Points of Interest

Of the various points of interest to which attention should be drawn, the first is the Indian Buddhist system of writing two or more books in one volume with running pagination, and the adoption of that system by the Tibetan translators.

* For want of space the full summary cannot be published in this number. It will appear in *IHQ*., IX. 2.—Ed.

When Sāhityācārya Śivanātha Śāstrī, the learned paṇḍit of H.H. the Maharaja of Kashmir, commenced in collaboration with myself the transcription of this ms., our first impression was that 123 leaves of the ms. had been lost, as the page number began with 124. On a comparison, however, of this Ms. withits Tibetan version, it appeared that the ms. lacked only two leaves, i.e., nos. 122 and 123. From the numbering of the leaves i.e. from 122 and not from 1, it seems that the present ms. was a copy prepared at the instance of a certain upāsaka from another ms. which bore these page-numbers, and that the preceding leaves of this ms. viz. from 1 to 121 were left out as they evidently contained other books. Our ms. represents the last part (leaves 395-426) of the second (kha) volume of the Tibetan Kanjur mDo. This Tibetan bundle contains four sūtras, of which the first is the *Lalita-vistara* (1-329), the second *Mañjuśrī-vikrīḍita nāma mahāyāna-sūtra,* the third *Mañjuśrīvikurvāṇa* and the fourth *Sarva-tathāgatādhiṣṭhāna-sattvāvalokana-Buddha-kṣetra-nirdeśana-vyūha.* On the basis of the division of the volumes as made by the Tibetans and the page-numbering of the present ms., the opinion may be hazarded that the Tibetans adhered to the divisions as made by the Indians, who, as is the practice in writing mss. both among the Indians and the Tibetans, included 3, 4 or more books in one bundle, writing the last words of one book and the first words of another in the same line, leaving a little space between them. It is very likely that the *Lalitavistara*, being very extensive, was not given a place in this volume, and that the original bundle, from which the present ms. was copied, contained the last three books of the vol. *kha* of mDo.

The second point of interest is the name of the donor, Śulivajra, at whose instance this ms. was copied. The name occurs thrice in the ms., every time it being mentioned in the concluding line of the Dhāraṇī, by which invocation is made for the protection and well-being of the donor. The name of the person and, probably, that of his *gotra* are non-Sanskritic, indicating thereby the non-Indian nationality of the donor. It may be that he was a Hūṇa, about whom we read so much in Kalhaṇa's *Rājataraṅgiṇī*. The Dhāraṇī (Ms. 130b; Tib. 402b) is worded thus:[1]

1. This mantra is collated with its Tibetan and Chinese transliterated texts. The devanāgrī figures indicate the numbers given in the Chinese text, and the footnotes show the differences in reading.

१ २ ३ ४ ५
नमः सर्वतथागतानां। तद् यथा बुद्धे सुबुद्धे बुद्धमते*। लोके विलोके
६ ७ ८ ९ १०
लोकातिक्रान्ते। सत्त्वा-वलोकने सर्वतथागताधिष्ठिते।** सर्वाशापरिपूरणे द्युतिन्धरे
११ १२ १३ १४ १५ १६
नरदेवपूजिते+ तथागतज्ञानदे तथा-गताधिष्टाने सर्वलोकं सुखीभवतु। पूर्वकर्म क्षपय।++

मम [नात्सेहं मारपति शूल्क्षिणास्य आर्यदिक महाश्राद्धौपासक शूलिवज्रस्य±]
१७ १८ १९
रक्षा भवतु। सर्वभयेभ्यः तथागताधिष्ठानेन स्वाहा॥

The third point of interest is that the Dhāraṇīs in the ms. are found transliterated and not translated in the Tibetan and Chinese versions, pointing thereby to the belief current among the Buddhists, both Indian and non-Indian, of the 6th or 7th century A.D. about the efficacy of the mantras by their proper intonation.

Lastly, it is of interest to note the remark occurring in leaf 153a that this Sūtra will become popular in the south and not in the north, east or west, where the people will not give it its due honour and as a result will go to hell. The author of this Sūtra never dreamt that it would gain popularity more in the north than in the south and that an inhabitant of the farthest north would be instrumental in propagating its copy in the 20th century.

The scene of this Sūtra is located at Potalaka as is the case with many other Dhāraṇīs (see, e.g. *Dhāraṇī-Saṅgraha*, ASB. Ms. 1. 11b). Yuan Chwang refers to this mountain as a place of great sanctity, being the abode of Avalokiteśvara Bodhisattva. He locates it on the east of the Malaya mountain, the scene of the well-known Mahāyāna sūtra, *Laṅkāvatāra*.[1] It was very near the sea, and a stream of water after a long winding course flowed into the sea from the

---

* Ms. सुद्धमते; Chin. omits it.

** Ms. सर्वतथागताधिष्ठानाधिष्ठते

\+ Ms. नरके च पूजिते

++ Tib. सर्वकर्म क्षपयतु

± The Chinee, as restorcd into Sanskrit, gives मम अमुकस्य स्ववर्ण स्वनाम; for this Tibetan gives here nothing. The Ms. in another place mentions this name which may be read thus:

नात्सेहं मारपति शूल्क्षिणस्य आघ्घदिक शुलिव्यज्रस्य।

1. *Laṅkā.*, p. 1.

lake on the Potalaka mountain. The port of India from which people sailed to Ceylon was on its north-east. If we take Dhanuṣkoṭī to be that port, Potalaka should be located somewhere between the Malaya mountains and Dhanuṣkoṭi. In the *Gaṇḍavyūha* (leaf. 28b) occurs the name *Śāgara nāma Laṅkāpatham* and in leaf 27a *Sāgaramukha,* a place suitable for meditating upon the vastness of the sea. It seems that these forsaken places near the border of the sea and amid the mountains became the haunt of the meditating monks, and many Mahāyāna sūtras came into existence in those places. Watters (II, p. 230) dismisses away the Malaya mountain as a 'poetical creation' but Nundolal Dey gives ample evidence to show that it really existed and constituted the southern part of the Western Ghats (see his *Geographical Dictionary,* p. 132). He further states that one of the summits of these mountains bore the name of Pothigei, the Bettigo of Ptolemy, the abode of Agastya, and was also called Agasti-kūṭa or Poṭiyam, which was the southernmost peak of the Annamalai mountains where the river Tāmra-parṇī has its source (see *Ibid.*, Map.). Can this Poṭiyam be our Potalaka?

The tradition recorded by Tāranātha about the location of Potalaka, the abode of Avalokiteśvara, also points to its existence somewhere in the southernmost corner of India. The upāsaka Śāntivarman[1] wanted to go to Potala from Śrīdhanakaṭaka caitya,[2] the identification of which has been placed beyond doubt by the finds at Amarāvatī and Nāgārjunikoṇḍa. He had to traverse a long perilous way over uninhabited regions and had to cross rivers, forests, lakes and so forth. Superstitious as the people must have been at that time, Śāntivarman, for safety while travelling, invoked Tārā, Bhṛkūṭī, Hayagrīva, Ekajaṭī and lastly Avalokiteśvara all well-known names of gods in the later Buddhist literature to aid him in his tour over the wild uninhabited region. In the account there is no indication that the route lay across the vast sea to an island like Madagascar, where Prof. Tucci[3] would have us look for the location of the Potalaka, the abode of Avalokiteśvara on the basis of an account of the travels of

---

1. See Schiefner, *Geschichte etc.*, p. 132.
2. It is located in Dhanaśrīdvīpa. The Tib. word is *Dha.na.sri.i.gliṅ, glin* being usually restored as Sanskrit *drīpa*. According to S.C. Das's Dictionary, it may also mean "an isolated large monastery." Tāranātha, I think, as used the word *gliṅ* in the sense of a 'monastery.' In that case, Dha.na.śrī.i.*gliṅ* would refer to the huge monastic establishment at Amarāvatī or Nāgārjunikoṇḍa.
3. See *IHQ.*, vol. VII, pp. 695-6.

Buddhagupta. It may be contended that in p. 157 of Tāranātha's *Geschichte* while describing the the route of Candragomin from Nālandā to Potala *via* Dhanaśrī-gliṅ (gliṅ=*rihāra* and not *drīpa*), it is said that he travelled in a boat which was wrecked, and that he was saved by the goddess Tārā. This also does not suggest that we are to look for Potala in Madagascar, for it is quite natural that in those days, when the land-routes were generally infested with wild animals and robbers, and when there were the difficulties of crossing rivers and mountains and obtaining food and shelter on the way, it was safer and more comfortable to travel by the river-routes or coastal sea-routes, and that this was preferred by the Indians is amply proved by the *Jātakas* and such other literature. In this case, I think, Candragomin went in a boat along the eastern coast up to Amarāvati and thence to Potala or Potalaka. In view of the fact that the scene of the present work is laid at Potalaka, and the statement that the work will become popular in the south, it behoves us to look for its location somewhere near the southern extremity of India, where it will not be too much to expect that we shall, in no distant future, hear of the discovery of ruins of as great an antiquity and importance as those at Nāgārjunikoṇḍa.

We shall conclude this preliminary note by reconstructing from the Tibetan xylograph the Sanskrit text which was written on the first two leaves of the Ms. nos. 122 and 123 that are lost. It is as follows:

एवं मया श्रुतमेकस्मिन् समये पोतलकपर्वते आर्यावलोकितेश्वरायतने दिव्यमणिरत्नश्रीइन्द्र-नीलमये पुष्पसंस्तृते देवसिंहासने भगवान् सार्द्ध महता भिक्षुसङ्घेन पञ्चमात्रैर्भिक्षुशतैः सर्वैरर्हद्भिः क्षीणास्त्रवैः चेतौवशिताप्राप्तैः सद्धर्मपारंगतैश्च सार्द्ध बोधिसत्त्वैः सर्वैः महाकरुणाज्ञानप्राप्तैः सर्वैः एकजातिप्रतिबद्धैः द्विजातिभ्यां च त्रिजातिभिर्दशजातिभिर्विंशतिजातिभिस्त्रिंशतिजातिभिः शत-जातिभिर्वा प्रतिबद्धैः सर्वैः अष्टफलप्राप्तैर्दशभूमिस्थितैः तद् यथा आर्यावलोकितेश्वरेण मंजुश्रिया विमलकेतुना रत्नश्रिया वज्रकेतुना विमलप्रभेण चन्दनेन अमृतकेतुना एवंप्रमुखैः सप्तशतैः बोधि-सत्त्वैः सार्ध उपासकोपासिकाभिः सर्वैः च व्याकृतैः समाधिप्राप्तैः नानालोकधातुभिः सन्निपतितैः पञ्चसहस्त्रैः सर्वैः गन्धर्वशतसहस्त्रैः पूर्वबुद्धपर्युपासितैः तथागतप्रातिहार्यदृष्टैः साघं सर्वाभिः महायक्षिणीभिः बोधिसत्त्वज्ञानप्राप्ताभिः व्याकरणप्राप्ताभिरवैवर्तिकाभिः अनौपम्यया विमलप्रभया च प्रभावत्या भीमश्रिया यक्षिणया च एवं प्रमुखाभिरशीत्या महायक्षिणीभिः। शतक्रतुब्रह्म-वेश्रवणवृतराष्ट्र-विरूढकविरूपाक्षमणिभद्रपुत्रपूर्णाभद्राः एतैश्च लोकपालैः सार्धं निवगणोऽभूत्।

अथ तैः सर्वैः तथागतं सिंहासनं निवगणां ज्ञात्वा स्वकस्वकैः कुशलमूलेस्तथागतं दिव्या-लंकारवस्त्रपुष्पमाल्यधूपविलेपनवाद्यशब्देन मानितः पूजितः शतसहस्त्रकोटिशः प्रदक्षिणीकृत्य अर्चितश्च। तेन खलु पुनः समयेन भगवान् सर्वसत्त्वमहाकरुणाज्ञानस्थितं नाम समाधि समा-पन्नोऽभूत। तेन समाधिधारणबलेन त्रिसाहस्त्रमहासाहस्त्रलोकधातवः आभया अवभासिता अभूवन्। सर्वरूपाणि स्फुटितानि। ये च सत्त्वा जात्यन्धाः चक्षुषा रूपाणि पश्यन्ति स्म। वधिराः श्रोत्रेण शब्दान् शृणवन्ति स्म। रोगष्पृष्टा विगतरोगा भवन्ति स्म। नग्नाश्च वस्त्रावृता बभूवुः। उन्मत्ताः स्मृतिं प्रतिलभन्ते स्म। होनकायाः परिपूर्णेन्द्रिया बभूवुः। दरिद्रा धनानि प्रति-लभन्ते स्म। सत्त्वानां यः खलु धनवस्तुभोगविहीन आसीत् स धनवस्तुभोगसम्पन्नोऽभूत्। सर्वसत्त्वाः सर्वसुखसमर्पिताः सर्वाशापरिपूर्णा अभूवन्। त्रिसाहस्त्रमहासाहस्त्रलोकधातौ ये केचित् सत्त्वा अनुशासनधर्मश्रवणाय येन भगवान् तेनांजलिं प्रणाम्य उपसंक्रान्ताः। ये सत्त्वाः देवभूताः ते सर्वे देवसुखं संप्रहाय बुद्धानुस्मृतिं कृत्वा धर्मश्रवणाय येन भगवान् तेन उपसंक्रान्ताः। ये सत्त्वा मनुष्यभूताः ते च मनुष्यसुखं परित्यज्य धर्मश्रवणकामाय येन भगवांस्तेन उपसंक्रान्ताः। ये सत्त्वा नागयक्षराक्षसप्रेतपिशाचभूतास्ते बुद्धानुस्मृतिं प्राप्य सर्वसत्त्वेषु मैत्रचित्ता भूत्वा काय-चित्तमुखं लब्धा धर्मश्रवणाय येन भगवान् तेनोपसंक्रान्ताः। ये सत्त्वा यमलोके अन्धतमिस्त्रायां जातास्तेऽपि बुद्धानुभावेन एकक्षणां स्मृतिं लब्वा परस्परं परिजानन्ति स्म। ते महातमिस्त्राभ्यः परिमुक्ता बभूवुः। सर्वे सत्त्वाः परस्परं मैत्रचित्ताः बभूवुः। तेषामुपक्लेशाः क्षीणा अभूवन्। तेन खलु समयेन महापृथिवी षड्विकारं प्रकम्पते उन्नमति अवनमति स्म। अथ तस्यां पर्षदि मंजुश्रीकुमारभूतः सन्निषणणाः सन् बोधिसत्त्वं महासत्त्वमार्यावलोकितेश्वरमेतदवोचत्। कुलपुत्र, महाबोधिसत्त्वपर्षदि अवभासितायां महापर्षदः पूर्वनिमित्तं परिस्फुटम्। अनेकबोधिसत्त्वकोटि-नियुतशतसहस्त्राणां च व्याकरणं प्रकटितम्। धर्ममहावाक्यस्य [Leaf. 124 पूर्वनिमित्तं संदृश्यते। कुलपुत्र अनेकानां च बोधिसत्त्वकोटि-नियुतशतसहस्त्राणां सर्वाशापरिपूरिमहाज्ञानप्रतिलम्भो भविष्यति। तत् कुलपुत्र सत्त्वानां कारुणयमुत्पाद्य हिताय सुखाय यावदनुत्तरस्यां सम्यक्-संबोधौ प्रतिष्ठापनाय तथागतं परिपृच्छ।]

Chapter - 2
The Buddhist Manuscripts at Gilgit

N. Dutt

In the previous issue (*IHQ*., IX. I, pp. 227-236), an account has been given of the third manuscript entitled *Sarvatathāgatasattvāvalokana-buddhakṣetra-sandarśanavyūha*.

The first two leaves of this Ms. are lost, and so in the previous issue they were restored into Sanskrit from Tibetan. The object of this paper is to offer a translation of the text contained in the two leaves lost and summarise the contents of the remaining portion of the manuscript.

(Summary)

Thus have I heard. Once Bhagavā was dwelling on the Potalaka mountain in the abode of Ārya Avalokiteśvara and was seated on a be-jewelled throne strewn with flowers with 500 bhikṣus, who were all arhats, free from āsravas, having full control over their minds and mastered the good Law, with 700 bodhisattvas, who were endowed with great compassion and knowledge and who were to become Buddhas after one, two or (at the most) one hundred births, all of them, were in the possession of eight fruits and established in the ten *bhūmis* (stages of spiritual progress), the prominent among them were Avalokiteśvara, Mañjuśrī, Vimalaketu, Ratnaśrī, Vajraketu, Vimalaprabhā, Candana, etc., with 5000 male and female lay-devotees, all of whom had been predicted (to become Buddhas), were meditators, and assembled from the various lokadhātus; with 100,000 Gandharvas who had previously served the Buddhas and witnessed the miracles performed by them; and with the 80 Mahāyakṣiṇīs, who had obtained the Bodhisattva knowledge, and had been predicted to become Buddhas without the chance of retrogression, the foremost among them being

Anopamā, Vimalaprabhā, Prabhāvatī, and Bhīmaśrī. Knowing that Buddha had taken his seat on the throne, all those (assembled) worshipped him in accordance with the meritorious power of each, with divine clothes, ornaments, flowers, garlands, incense, unguent and music, and then circumambulated him innumerable times. Then Buddha entered into a meditation called the *Sarvasattva-mahākaruṇā-jñāna-sthita*. By the power of this *samādhi*, light shone forth in all the *trisāhasra-mahāsāhasra* worlds. Everything became visible, the born blind began to see objects, the deaf heard sounds, the diseased were freed of their diseases, the naked were covered with clothes, the insane got back sanity, the physical defects of the defective were removed, the poor became rich, and beings, who were without wealth and property, became endowed with them, in short, all beings became happy and all their hopes were fulfilled. All beings whether of *Devaloka* or *Manuṣyaloka*, sacrificing their own enjoyments, approached Buddha for hearing the religious discourse; even the Nāgas, Yakṣas, Piśācas, by remembering Buddha, became friendly to all beings and approached Buddha for hearing the discourse. By the power of Buddha, those beings who were ever in darkness in he Yamaloka got back their memory for one moment and came to know each other; they became friendly when they were rescued from the pitch dark state and freed from their troubles. At that time, the earth quaked six times. In that assembly was seated Mañjuśrīkumārabhūta. He said this to Avalokiteśvara: "O Kulaputra, the premonitory signs of the great assembly are visible, innumerable Bodhisattvas have received predictions (about their attainment of Buddhahood), and similar signs of a great discourse are also visible. Countless Bodhisattvas are to obtain knowledge which will fulfil all their hopes. Out of compassion to them, for their good, and for establishing them in (the path leading to) the highest *sambodhi*, O Kulaputra, request the Tathāgata (to deliver the discourse). In future, there will be beings who will commit sins, be poor and destitute, possess discoloured bodies, suffer from old age and disease and have limited enjoyments. They will be unrestrained in the use of the senses, possessed of short life and poor intellect, and subject to attachment, hatred and delusion. It is for them, that you, O Kulaputra, should solicit the Tathāgata for delivering a discourse, and by doing so, you will be conferring lasting benefit and happiness on beings, saving them from evils, diseases and sins, and helping them in the fulfilment of their wishes including the attainment of the highest *nirvāṇa*. At this, Ārya Avalokiteśvara looked around in ten directions, remembered the countless Tathāgatas, and after due salutations, said: "There will be, in future, O Bhagavan, beings afflicted byold age, disease, misery and death; (they will be) poor and short-lived, unrestrained in the use of the senses, given to fighting among themselves on account of mutual jealousy and ill-feeling, depriving one another of their wealth and property, finding pleasure in frivolous amusements, labouring under the misconception that things of the world are good and permanent. These beings will be born in the various lower spheres of existence including hells, and it is for their welfare, for their rescue from evils and fulfilment of desires including the attainment of the Tathāgata-knowledge that I pray you, O Bhagavan, to deliver a discourse. To you there is nothing unknown and unheard; many are the monks and nuns, male and female lay-devotees, denizens of heavens and other spheres, who are wise, and worshipped the previous Buddhas; they have assembled here to listen to your discourse. Let them not be disappointed. Then all those assembled endorsed in one voice the request of Avalokiteśvara. When Bhagavān was thus requested thrice, he looked around the ten corners of the world, and with a ringing sweet musical voice addressed Avalokiteśvara as follows: "There is, O Kulaputra, a Samādhi (meditation) called *Sarva-tathāgatādhiṣṭhāna-sattvāvalokana-buddha-kṣetrasandarśana-vyūha*, which I heard, after I had obtained the first *Bodhicitta*, from the Tathāgata Sukusumajyoti-sandarśa, and the moment it was heard, it was practised by innumerable beings, resulting in 90 koṭis of them attaining the Tathāgata knowledge, and the rest including myself hearing the prediction (*vyākaraṇa*) as to the attainment of Buddhahood. And I now remember through my Tathāgata-knowledge that 30,000 Tathāgatas delivered this discourse for the benefit of beings, and in every case, yourself and Mañjuśrī were the supplicants. The assembly of Bodhisattvas and lay-devotees, similar to the one present here, evinced their veneration (to this text), and thereby again, countless being heard the prediction as to their attainment of Buddhahood in future and gained mastery over many Bodhisattva-meditations. All their desires were fulfilled. They became free from all diseases. Their merits matured, and their hindrances were removed. They obtained pleasing, lovely bodies, and their treasuries and store-houses were filled with wealth and corns. They were respectfully treated by the kings, ministers, and the beings in general. They became possessed of wisdom and the power of recollection, and developed faith in Buddha, Dharma, and Saṅgha. They were blessed in every way, viz., with long life, noble birth, strong physique. They had not to suffer separation from the dear ones. Such will be the fruits of those who will worship this Text (*dharmaparyāya*) with flowers, incense, scents, garlands, unguents, flags and festoons, uttering *namo Buddhāya*, and praise it, remember it, deliver it or have it delivered, write it or have it written, or respectfully listen to its delivery by a Dharmabhāṇaka. In this life, they will derive all the benefits mentioned above, viz., beautiful and healthy physique, wisdom and intelligence, honour from kings, ministers and the people generally, and wealth and property. Their breath will give out sandal scent and their eyes will be like the blue lotus. By day and night they will visualize Buddhas and Bodhisattvas, and all their hindrances (to emancipation) will be removed. They will be protected by the gods, and at the time of death, they will see the Bodhisattva. Their minds will be undistracted and free from envy. After death, they will be reborn in the Sukhāvatī lokadhātu. All of them have been predicted to become Buddhas, and one need not have any doubt about same. If any one commits this treatise to memory, write it or have it written with due veneration, all his mental and physical troubles, be they regarding their physique, property, intelligence, dear ones, kingdom, disease, food, or dress, will cease through the power of this Samādhi. But he should confess (*pratideśana*) all the sins that he might have committed during this and previous lives, develop firm faith in Buddha, Dharma, and Saṇgha. By doing so, he will be absolved from all sins and he will have ample wealth and will never be born in any evil sphere of existence. Such is the merit of this Samādhi. The immense benefits can be derived by listening to, committing to memory or writing the *Dhāraṇī-mantrapadas*. On the delivery of this discourse the earth quaked six times and there was on the Tathāgata a shower of flowers, cloth etc. Then what are the *Mantrapadas*? They are:

नमः सर्वतथागतानाम्। तद् यथा बुद्धे सुबुद्धे बुद्धमते* । लोके विलोके लोकातिक्रान्ते। सत्त्वावलोकने सर्वतथागताधिष्ठिते† सर्वाशापरिपूरणे द्युतिन्धरे नरदेवपूजिते+ तथागतज्ञानदे तथा-गताधिष्टाने सर्वलोकं सुखीभवतु। पूर्वकर्म क्षपय++ । मम [नात्सेहं मारपति शूल्क्षिणस्य आर्यदिक महाश्राद्धोपासक शूलिवज्स्य] रक्षा भवतु। सर्वभयेभयः तथागताधिष्टानेन स्वाहा॥

* Ms. सुद्धमते; Chin. omits it.

† Ms. सर्वतथागताधिष्टानाधिष्टित

+ Ms. नरके च पूजिते

++ Tib. सर्वकर्म क्षपयतु

These *Mantrapadas* were uttered by 30,000 Tathāgatas and I am also doing the same for the benefit and protection of all beings, for the checking of all diseases, and for the future appearance of these beings in Buddhakṣetras."

If anyone be anxious to know how to acquire the merits enumerated by the Tathāgata, he is advised to develop loving and compassionate mind and get rid of envy, pride, deceit and anger; then with concentrated mind he is to worship Buddha and cogitate over the merits of the Tathāgatas, perform 108 *japas*, and offer one flower to every Tathāgata. That will make him prosperous and he will see the Tathāgata even in dream and at the time of his death. He will be reborn in the Sukhāvatī heaven, and there he will be endowed with long life, strength and beauty and all his hopes will be fulfilled. On the utterance of this *Dhāraṇī*, 60,000 beings obtained insight into the non-origination of all things, had their hindrances removed and their hopes were fulfilled.

II

Then Vajrapāṇi, looking around the ten corners, said: "There is, O Bhagavan, the *Dhāraṇī* called the *Abhayateja*, which I heard from the Abhayavyūharāja Tathāgata. Whoever hears this *Dhāraṇī*, all his afflictions disappear, I wish to impart this *Dhāraṇī* to those who recites, or listen to (the previously stated sūtra), or those who worship or remember it." The Mantra is as follows:

नमः सर्वबुद्धानां± सर्वबोधिसत्त्वानामर्हतानाम्±± । तद् यथा । ओम् वज्रधर वज्रकाय वज्रबल वज्रतेज । हुं हुं वज्रपाणि तथागताज्ञां पालय । स्मर प्रतिज्ञाम् । सर्वव्याधि सर्वपापाणि नाशय । देहि मे यथेप्सितं वरम् । मम [नात्सेहं मारपति शूलक्षिणस्य आर्यदिक शुलिवज्रस्य] यं यमेवाभियाचाम तं तमेव समृध्यतु । हे हे तुरु तुरु§ आगच्छागच्छ । मा विलम्ब । दर्शय वज्रकायम् । दर्शय वज्रकायम्§§ । बुद्धाधिष्ठानेन स्वाहा ॥

On the utterance of this mantra the earth moved, all the Yakṣ as, Rākṣasas, gods and men praised him. Then Vajrapāṇi dilated on the merits acquired by the utterance of this mantra. If anyone wishes to have wealth and property, kingdom, Vidyādhara-hood, long life and strength, he is to set up an image of Vajradhara of sandal-wood,

---

± Tib. तथागतानां

±± Ms. ०मर्हन्तानाम्

§ Ms. रूरू रूरू

§§ Ms. does not repet it.

adorned with all the ornaments and with a face bursting into a *aṭṭāṭṭ a* laugh. Then he is to worship it with certain rituals (the details are passed over here). After this Vajrapāṇi is again praised and nobody entertains any doubt about the efficacy of the mantras.

III

Then Mañjuśrī asked: "Why O Bhagavan, this Samādhi is called *Sarvatathāgatādhiṣṭhāna-sattvāvalokana-buddhakṣetra-sandar-śana-vyūha.*" Bhagavān said: "Because it leads to the attainment of the Tathāgata practices (*adhiṣṭhāna*) constituting all the *Samādhis* and *Dhāraṇī-mukhas* resorted to by the Bodhisattvas, to the knowledge of beings' thoughts (lit. contraction and expansion of mind and mental powers), to the development of, in the minds of gods and other bȩings, faith in Buddha, Dharma and Saṅgha. It dissuades beings form committing evils, removes their envy, hatred etc. and establishes them in the path to Bodhi. These beings become faithful and will never have any suffering. It is for this reason, O Kulaputra, this is called *Sarva-tathāgatādhiṣṭhāna* etc., by hearing which one becomes a non-retreating (*avaivartika*) Bodhisattva." Then, it is asked, why the readers, writers or hearers of this *Sūtra* are predicted about their attainment of Buddhahood. What must be their merits, what are the difficult tasks accomplished by them? In reply Bhagavān said: "By listening to, writing and preaching this *Sūtra*, one acquires merit far more than that accumulated by the completion of the *pāramitās*. To remember, write,.........this sūtra is also a very difficult task, because people are given to evil deeds, worldly enjoyments of eating, drinking etc., subject to desire, anger and so forth, surrounded by evil friends. They suffer and repent only at the time of death when the whole world appears to them as a cemetry. They lack faith and desire for good actions. They have not seen the Tathāgatas nor they are aware of the prediction about their future attainment of Buddha-hood. It is very difficult for such persons to worship,.........this *sūtra* and its preacher." Then all those assembled said: "We shall, O Bhagavan, honour those who will preach, or listen to, this *sūtra*, and shall propagate it so that it may endure long." Bhagavān endorsed their wish but warned them that for honouring and propagating the *sūtra* and for furnishing the *sūtra*-preachers with their necessities, they will have to stand with abuses, beating etc. and so for that reason, they must be careless about the sufferings of their body and mind."

Then Bhagavān uttered the following verses:

श्रृणुत कुलपुत्र अप्रमत्त
मा पश्चकाले परिताप्यु भेष्यतः।
बुद्धस्य उत्पाद्यु कदाचि लभ्यते
कल्पेन कोटीभि शतैः सहस्त्रैः॥
गुणाश्च श्रृणवत्यभिश्रद्दधेत
न दुर्लभा तेषु समाधि भेष्यति।
कल्पेन कोटी यथा गंङ्गावालिका
यो दानु दद्या द्विपदोत्तमेषु॥
धनं च धान्यं तथा वस्त्रभूषणां
गन्धं च माल्यं विलेपनं च।
यश्चैव सूत्रं अभिश्रद्दधित्वा
श्रुणेय वाचेय लिखापयेत।
न तस्य पुणयस्य प्रमाणु विद्यते
ता चाप्रमाणां सूगतेन देशितम्॥
रणयं च सेवेत सदाप्रमत्तो
ध्यान च ध्यायेतु सदान्यचित्तः।
दानं च दद्या प्रियपुत्रधीतरा
हस्तौ च परित्युजेत यथैव॥
सूत्रस्य धारेति कश्चि अयं
ततो पुणया विशिद्धु प्रासु यते।
अर्थस्य दाता वरसूत्रमेतत्।
सर्वस्यापाय सदावर्जितस्य॥
धनस्य धान्यस्य च दायको ह्ययं
गुणाश्च सर्वेपि न तस्य दुर्लभ।
आयुर्बल वीर्य न तस्य दुर्लभं
धारेति सूत्रं य इमं विशुद्धम्॥
द्रक्ष्यन्ति बुद्धं अमिताभुनायकं
मयापि स व्याकृतु बुद्ध बोधौ।
न तस्य पापं पि कदाचि विद्यते
सुखावतीं द्रक्ष्यति लोकधातुं॥
यं चापि तस्य सद र्क भेष्यति
सर्वक्षयं यास्यति चित्तनीड़े।
कायस्य शूले तथ शीर्षतापे
न तस्य जातु विनिपातो भेष्यति॥
सांद्दष्टिकाश्चापि गुणां स लप्स्यते
सर्व यथा चित्तितु प्रार्थितं च।
तस्माभि तेभिषद भिक्षुभिक्षुणी
उपासकोपासिका राजाभिषदाः॥
इदं च सूत्रं सद धारितव्यं
संत्करू नित्यं च कर्तव्यधारके।
गन्धैश्च माल्यैश्च विलेपनैश्च
सत्कह कृत्वा च लिखापयेत॥
गुरु गौरवं कृत्वा च धर्मभाणके
यथा नरेन्द्रस्य तथागतस्य।
मा पश्चकाले जरव्याधिपीड़िता
अनेक आयाससहस्त्रव्याकुला॥
नरकेषु तिर्यञ्च परिभ्रमणा
शणडश्च पणडाश्च जुगुप्सनीयाः।
य जात्यन्धभूता कुणपाश्च गन्धिन
स जास्यते नीचकुलेषु स्त्रीषु॥
ईर्ष्यालुकस्य सद पापचारिण
क्रोधाभिभूतस्य च मत्सरिष्य।
बुद्धेषु धर्मेषु करित्व गौरवं
इमेषु जातीषु प्रपतते सौ॥
तत्रैव दुःखानि च वेदमाना
मा पश्चकाले परिताप्यु भेष्यतः।
तस्माभि तेहि सद पूजितस्य
यश्चैव धारेत प्रकाशयेत॥
?श्चैव परिभाषणु तस्य कुर्वते
जुगुप्सना ताडन बन्धनश्च।
मयैव च तेन परिभाषणकृता
मयैव सत्करु करित्वा धारके॥
तस्मात्तैर्हि सद धर्मभाणके
यश्चैव धारेत लिखेत वाचये।
सत्कुरु तैश्च सद नित्यु कुर्या
स्निग्धाश्च वाचां मधुरा भणेत॥

IV

Ārya Avalokiteśvara then saluted Bhagavān and said, "I remember the *Dhāraṇī* called *Vyavalokana-prātihārya*, which I heard from the Jñānaketuprabhākara Tathāgata. Memorising, hearing and preaching of this *Dhāraṇī* bear all the fruits mentioned by you. All the wishes of a being are fulfilled, the hindrances due to his *karma* are destroyed, he obtains *samādhi* and becomes free from disease and visualises Buddhas and Bodhisattvas. Then at the request of Bhagavān, he utters the *mantrapadas,* after which he gives a detailed account of the ceremony of worshipping images and the merits acquired thereby.

V

Then comes Anopamā Mahāyakṣiṇī, who saluted Bhagavān and siad, "I acquired a *mantra* while dwelling at Ghoṣilārāma in Kauśābī. I know the inner mind (*hṛdayam*) of all Vidyādharas and that I want to communicate it to you for the benefit of all beings." Then she utters the mantrapadas, followed by a detailed account of a ceremony of worshipping the *Tathāgata-pratimā*, and the merits acquired thereby.

After this appears Śaṅkhiṇī Mahādevī, who utters a *mantrapada*,—this mantra is addressed to herself and is meant for the protection of Tathāgata's religion and the dharma-preachers and listeners. It is followed by a short account of the ceremonies of an image-worship.

In the same way Bhīmā Mahādevī utters a mantra addressed to herself followed by an account of the ceremony of an image-worship.

VI

Then follows an interlocution between Avalokiteśvara and Bhagavān about the merits of reading, writing, remembering, preaching and worshipping the *Sūtra*. The merits, as usual, are said to be unsurpassable by anything else and the beings are therefore instructed to worship it in some form or other.

Then it is said that this *dharmaparyāya* will spread in the south (Dakṣiṇāpatha) and not in the north, east and west where the people are not so religious and given to wordly pleasures.

Again the merits are expatiated upon and Bhagavān winds it up by the following gāthās:

Ms. folio 137b-138a (a tentative reading).

गृह्णाहि आनन्द इमं समाधि
या भाषिता पूर्वभवेषु नायकैः।
यश्चैव त्रैधातुकदानु दद्या
सप्तान् रत्नान् च पूरयित्वा॥
बुद्धेषु धर्मेषु सदाप्रमत्तः
यश्चैव सूत्रस्य धरेति कश्ची
अयं ततो बहुतरु पुणयु भेष्यते॥
यश्चैव बुद्धस्याभिश्रद्दधित्वा
विहार कारापयि चैत्तिकानि।
इमस्य सूत्रस्याभिपूजयित्वा
उपमापि तस्य न स भोन्ति दानम्॥
यश्चापिएक क्षिपयेत पुष्पं
वस्त्रं च माल्यं च विलेपनं तथा।
यश्चापि कार्षापणु दानु दद्या
इमस्यसूत्रस्य च पूजनार्थं।
जनित्वा बोधाय च मैत्रचित्ते
अयं ततो बहुतरु पुणयु प्राप्तु या॥
यश्चापि सत्त्वेषु इमं समाधि
प्रकाशये देशयि बोधिसत्त्वः।
प्रतिपादये बोधिमनुत्तरे तथा।
उपमानि पुणयापि न तस्य भोति॥
तस्मापि सूत्रं इमु धारयेत
लिखेत वाचेत तथा प्रकाशये।
इमं च श्रुत्वा तथ आनुशंसा
कृत्वा मैत्रं तथ सर्वसत्त्वैः॥
मा पश्चकाले परिताप्यु भेष्यथ
उपपद्यमानं नरकेषु प्रेतयो।
जख्याधिमृत्यु परिताप्यु पीड़ित
स मृत्युकाले भयभीतमानसो।
अभीक्ष्ण उश्वासन उश्वषन्तः
मुखे मुखं प्रेक्ष्यति बालबुद्धिः॥
कोऽस्माभि त्राणं भवते परायण
यस्माभि पूज्यं न कृतं तथागते।
बौद्धं च धार्म्यं च तथ सांधिकं च
हरिष्य नेष्ये यमलोकि दारुणे।
न तस्य त्राणं सद कश्चि भेष्यति
न पुत्रदारं न च मित्रबान्धवं॥
न चापि राष्ट्रं न च हास्यलास्यं
धनं न धान्यं न च वस्त्रभूषणाः॥
सर्वं जहित्वा पुनरपि दुःखदारुणं
अनुभेष्यते वालु तथापिदारुणो।
को बालबुद्धी न जने प्रसादं
इमु दुःखु इमु अनुशंसा॥[^^]
तस्माञ्च तैर्हि सद भिक्षुभिक्षुणी
उपासकोपासिका राजभिसदा।
इमं च सूत्रं सद धारितव्यं
सत्करु नित्यं च कर्तव्यधारके॥

Ms. fol. 154a-155a (a tentative reading).

Then Ānanda appears and promises to commit this *Sūtra* to memory and Bhagavān emphasises on the necessity of remembering and propagating *Sūtra*. On the delivery of the *sūtra*, minds of 60,000 beings obtained emancipation from *āsravas*, 700 Bodhisattvas attained Bodhisattva-samādhi and 500 were predicted to be able to visit the Buddha-kṣetras and 90,000 were freed of their *kleśas*.

Then on enquiry Ānanda learns that the title of the *Sūtra* is to be *Sarvatathāgatajñāna-bodhisattvabhūmikramaṇam* or *Sarvatathā-gatādhiṣṭhāna-sattvāvalokana-buddhakṣetrasandarśanavyūha*.

Chapter - 3
The Buddhist Manuscripts at Gilgit

N Dutt

This is the fourth Gilgit manuscript examined by me in Kashmir.[1] It is a very small ms. consisting of 22 leaves written on birch-bark in clear upright Gupta characters of the sixth century A.D. The condition of the ms. is good. The scribe must have been a poor Sanskritist for the ms. bristles with numerous mistakes even in spelling. The treatise contains two dhāraṇīs. The first is entitled एकादशमुखं नाम हृदयम् (vide leaf 1 b, 1. 4) which in the Tibetan translation appears in a fuller forms as आर्य अवलोकितेश्वर एकादशमुखं नाम हृदयम् with the following Tibetan translation:

འཕགས་ པ་སྤྱན་ རས་གཟིགས་
དབང་ ཕྱུག་ཞལ་ བཅུ་གཅིག་པ་ཅེས་ བྱ་བའི་གཟུངས །

(Kanjur, rgyud, pha, f. 410 b).

The Tibetan version follows our text up to verse 11(a) and after a few concluding remarks closes the *Dhāraṇī*. Our text also puts here the words एवं मूलमन्त्र: । Evidently the mantras appearing after these words were additions made later on, and they look like general ritualistic directions to be carried out after the utterance of the main mantra. They are स्नानोपस्पृशनवस्त्राभ्युक्षिपण-मन्त्र:; धूपदीपनिवेदन-मन्त्र:; गन्धपुष्पदीपनिवेदनमन्त्र; वलिनिवेदनमन्त्र:; होममन्त्र: । Then follows the second dhāraṇī entitled हयग्रीवविद्या which in Tibetan is entitled अवलोकितेश्वर-हयग्रीवधारणी। As we propose to deal with this dhāraṇī in detail in a future issue, we have reproduced here the Sanskrit text only just as it appears in the ms.

In Nanjio's *Catalogue*, two texts are mentioned with the title Ekādaśamukham, one (No. 321) a translation of Yaśogupta (A.D. 557-

581) and the other of Hiuen-tsang (A.D. 656). In the Tokyo edition of the Tripiṭaka, these two appear in vol. XX, under the titles:

No. 1070: 十 一 面 觀 世 音 神 呪 經

No. 1071: 十 一 面 神 呪 心 經

The Chinese texts also follow theTibetan in extent, closing the text with the *mūlamantra,* which appears in these in Chinese transcript.

From the Chinese rendering of the word *dhāraṇī* by 神 呪 it is evident that it meant *ṛddhimantra*, a magical charm. The *dhāraṇī,* as the term implies, was, in fact, a mantra written on a brich-bark or palm-leaf and put within an amulet to be worn by a person to avert evils. This interpretation is fully supported by the present ms., verse 19b, 1. 1.

The edition offered here is wholly a tentative one with a view to acquaint the readers with the contents of a ms. which otherwise would have remained locked up in the Kashmir Secretariat.

एकादशमुखम्

1 (a)

१ ओं नमः सर्वबुद्धबोधिसत्त्वेभ्यः ॥ [1]एवं मया श्रु[तमेक-]

२ समये भगवांच्छ्रावस्त्यां विहरति स्म करी[रीम-]

३ ण्डले च[1]। अथ खल्वार्यावलोकितेश्वरो बोधिस[त्त्वो]

४ महासत्त्वोऽनेकविद्याधरकोटीनियुतशतसह[स्रेण]

(b)

१ परिवृतो[2] येन भगवांस्तेनोपसंक्रामदुपसंक्रम्य भगव-

२ तः पादौ शिरसा वन्दित्वा भगवन्तं प्रदक्षिणीकृत्वा[3] [ए]का

३ न्ते न्यसीद[4] भगवन्तमेतदवोचत्। इदं मम भग-

४ वन्नेकादशमुखं नाम [5]हृदयमेकादशभिः [कल्पको][6]

1...1 Tib. has no corresponding passage. Cf. *Dīgha Nikāya,* II, p. 1: Ekaṃ samayaṃ Bhagavā Sāvatthiyaṃ viharati Jetavane Kareri-Kuṭikāyaṃ...Kareri-maṇḍala-māḷe.

2. རིག་ སྔགས་ འཆང་ དུ་ མས་ ཡོངས་སུ་ བསྐོར་ ཏེ

3. བཅོམ་ལྡན་ འདས་ཀྱི་ཞབས་ས་ ལ་ ལན་ སུམ་ etc.,=भगवतः पादौ त्रिष्प्रदक्षिणीकृत्वा

4. འདུག་ སྟེ= निषद्य

5. སྙིང་པོ་ གདོང་ བཅུ་ གཅིག་ པ་ ཞེས་ བགྱི་ བ

6. བྱ་ བ་ ཕྲག་ བཅུ་ གཅིག་ གིས་ གསུངས་ པ་ ལགས་ ཏེ

2 (a)

१ टीभिर्भाषितम्। अहं चेत्तर्हि भाषिष्यामि सर्व [सत्त्वाना-]

२ मर्थाय हिताय सुखाय[१] सर्वव्याधिप्रश[म-]

३ नाय सर्वपापालक्ष्मीदु:स्वप्नप्रतिनिवारणा-

४ य सर्वाकालमृत्युप्रतिनिवारणाय अप्रसादानां

(b)

१ प्रसादनाय सर्वविघ्नविनायकानां[२] प्रशमनाय। ना[हं]

२ भगवन् समनुपश्यामि सदेवके लोके समारके

३ सब्रह्मके सश्रमणब्राह्मणिकाया: प्रजाया

४ यदनेन हृदयेन रक्षे कृते[३] परित्रे[४] परिग्र[हे शा]

3 (a)

१ न्तिस्वस्त्ययने[५] दण्डपरिहरे शस्त्रपरिहरे विष[प्रहा][६]

२ णे कृते य: कश्चिदतिक्रमे[तू] न प्रशमे[तू] न्नेदं [स्था]

३ नं विद्यते[७] स्थाप्य पौराणां[८] कर्म विपच्यते। [९]तद-

४ स्य च कल्पयतोऽभिश्रद्दधत: सर्वेण सर्वं न भवि-

(b)

१ ष्यति[९]। [१०]सर्वबुद्धस्तुत: समन्वाहृतोऽयं हृदयं सर्वत-

२ थागतानुमोदितोऽयं हृदयम्[१०]। स्मराम्यहं भगवं

३ गङ्गानदीवालुकासमानां कल्पानां परेण [११]श-

४ तपद्मनयनचूडा प्रतिहतरङ्गवेलाकिरण [राजा]

---

1. སྨན་པ་ Tib. omits हिताय सुखाय
2. བགེགས་ དང་ ལོག་ འདྲེན་ རྣམས་ cf. S.C. Das, Tib. Dict., p. 1223.
3. སྲུང་ བར་ བགྱི་བ་
4. ཡོངས་སུ་ བསྐྱབ་ པ་ = परित्राणे
5. ཞི་བ་ དང་ བདེ་ལེགས་ འགྱུར་ བར་ བགྱིས་པ་
6. དག་ གཞིལ་ བ་ བགྱིས་ པ
7. य:...न विद्यते = གང་ ལ་ ལ་ ཞིག་ འགལ་ བར་ བགྱིད་ པ་དེ་མ་མཆིས་ དེ །
8. སྔོན་ གྱི་ ལས་ ཀྱི་རྣམ་པར་ སྨིན་ པ = पूर्वकर्मणां विपाकं

9...9 It is not in Tib.

10...10 སྙིང་པོ་ འདི་ ནི་ སངས་ རྒྱས་ བཅོམ་ ལྡན་ འདས་ ཐམས་ ཅད་ ཀྱིས་ བསྟོད་ ཅིང་ དགོངས་ པ་ ལགས་ སོ །

11. སྦྲུན་ གཙུག་ གིས

4 (a)

१ नाम तथागतस्य। मया तथागतस्यान्ति [के]

२ श्रु तमयं हृदयं उद्गृहीतं [च]।[1] सह प्रतिलंभे[न]

३ दशसु दिक्षु सर्वतथागताः सुमुखीभूता अनुत्प-

४ त्तिकधर्मक्षान्तिप्रतिलब्धाः। एवं बहुकरोयं हृ-

(b)

१ दयं तस्मात्तर्हि श्राद्धेन कुलपुत्रेण वा कुलदुहित्रा वा

२ सत्कृत्यायं हृदयं साधयितव्यम्। अनन्यमनसा नि-

३ त्यं साधत्तिव्यम्। कल्यमुत्थाय अष्टोत्तरवारशतं

४ प्रवर्तयितव्यम्। दृष्टधर्मिका गुणा दश परिगृही[तव्याः]।

5 (a)

१ कतमे दश। यदुत निर्व्याधिर्भवष्यिति। सर्व[तथागतैः]

२ परिगृहीतश्च भविष्यति। धनधान्यहिरण्या[भर-]

३ णमस्य अक्षयं भविष्यति। सर्वशत्रवो वश्या

४ अवमर्दिता भविष्यन्ति। राजसभायां प्रथममालपि-

(b)

१ तव्यं मंस्यति। न विषं न गरं न ज्वरं न शस्त्रं काये क्रमिष्य-

२ ति। नोदकेन कालं करिष्यति। नाग्निना कालं करिष्यति।

३ नाकालमृत्युं नाकालञ्च करिष्यति। अपरे चत्वारो

४ गुणानुशंसा उद्ग्रहीष्यति। मरणकाले तथा[गतद-]

6 (a)

१ र्शनं भविष्यति। न चापायेषूपपत्स्यते न [विघ्ना-]

२ परिहारेण कालं करिष्यति। इतश्च्युतः सुखा-

३ वत्यां लोकधातावुपपत्स्यते। स्मराम्यहं भग-

४ वन्नित दशानां गङ्गानदीवालुकासमानां कल्पा-

---

1. གཅེས་ བདག་ གི་ སྙིང་ པོ་ འདི་ ནི་ དེ་ བཞིན་ གཤེགས་ པ་ ཐམས་ ཅད་ཀྱིས་ རྗེས་སུ་ཐུགས་ རངས་ པར་ མཛད་པ་ ལགས་ སོ།

(b)

१ नां ततः परेण परतरेण मन्दारवगन्धो नाम तथाग-
२ तोऽभूत्। तत्र मया[1] गृहपरिभूतेनायमुद्गृहीतम्। च-
३ त्वारिंशत् कल्पसहस्राणि संसारान्[2] पश्चान्मुखी-
४ कृतानि। एष च मया हृदयं प्रवर्तित्वा स[र्वस्मि-][3]

7 (a)

१ न् करुणायनज्ञानगर्भबोधिसत्त्वविमोक्षं प्र[तिल-]
२ ब्धम्। ये बन्धनबद्धा ये बध्यप्राप्ता
३ ये उदकाग्निविविधदुःखाभ्या-
४ हता तदनेनाहं सर्वसत्त्वानां लयनं त्राणं श-

(b)

१ रणं परायणं भवामि। यत्[4] सर्वदुष्टयक्षराक्षसाना-
२ मनेन[5] हृदयेण कर्षित्वा मैत्रचित्ता[न्][6] दयाचित्तान्
३ कृत्वानुत्तरायां सम्यक्संबोधौ प्रतिष्ठा-
४ पयामि एवं महर्द्धिकोयं[7] मम भगवन् हृ[दयं]

8 (a)

१ एकवेलां प्रकाशित्वा[8] चत्वारो मूलापत्तयः क्ष[यं]
२ गच्छन्ति पञ्चानन्तर्याणि कर्माणि निरवयवं तन्वी
३ चरिष्यन्ति। कः पुनर्वादो[9] यथाभाषितं प्रतिपत्स्य-
४ न्ति। अनेकबुद्धशतसहस्रावरोपितकुशल-

---

1. ཁྲིམས་པར་གྱུར་པས་
2. Ms. संसारा
3. ཐམས་ཅད་ཀྱི་སྙིང་རྗེ་འཛེག་པ = करुणायन
4. Ms. यः
5. Ms. मनया
6. Ms. ० चित्ता
7. Tib. རྫུ་འཕྲུལ་ཆེ་བ
8. ལན་ཅིག་བརྗོད་པས
9. The meaning becomes clear if the words तेषां ये are inserted after पुनर्वादो.

(b)

१ मूलं भविष्यति ये श्रोष्यन्ति प्रागेव जपसाधनादिभिः। स-
२ र्वमनोरथं परिपूरयिष्यामि यश्च[1] चतुर्दशीपं-
३ चदशी[2] मामुद्दिश्य [3]उपवसति। चत्वारिंशकल्पस
४ हस्राणि संसारान्[4] पश्चान्मुखीकरिष्यन्ति। तेन ना[मधे-]

9 (a)

१ यमपि ग्रहणेन भगवन् सह सोयं बुद्धकोटीनियुत[शतस-]
२ हस्रातिरेकसमम्। मम नामधेयग्रहणेन [स-]
३ र्वसत्त्वा अवैवर्त्तिकत्त्वं प्रसवन्ति। सर्वव्याधिभिः [प-]
४ रिमुच्यन्ते। सर्वावरणेभ्यः सर्वभयेभ्यः सर्वकायवा-

(b)

१ ङ्मनोदुःश्चरितेभ्यः परिमोक्ष्यन्ते। तेषामेव करतलगता बुद्ध-
२ बोधिर्भविष्यति। भगवानाह। साधु साधु कुलपुत्र यत्
३ सर्वसत्त्वानामन्तिके एवंरूपा महाकरुणा शक्ष्य-
४ सि त्वं कुलपुत्रः अनेनोपायेन सर्वसत्त्वाना[मनुत्तरा-]

10 (a)

१ यां सम्यक्संबोधौ प्रतिष्ठापयितुम्। उद्गृहीतं च [मया]
२ हृदयमनुमोदितम्। भाषध्वं कुलपुत्र। ततः ख-
३ ल्वार्यावलोकितेश्वरो बोधिसत्त्वो उत्थायासनादे-
४ कांसमुत्तरासङ्गं कृत्वा भगवतश्चरणयोः प्र-

(b)

१ णिपत्य इदं हृदयमावर्त्तयति स्म॥
नमो रत्नत्रया-
२ य नमो वैरोचनाय[5] तथागताय[6] नम आर्यावलो-
३ कितेश्वराय बोधिसत्त्वाय महासत्त्वाय महा-
४ कारुणिकाय[7] नमः अतीतानागतप्रत्युत्प[न्नेभ्यः]

---

1. It would have been better if यश्च could be replaced by तेषां ये च.

2. In Sanskrit it should be चतुर्दश्यां पञ्चदश्यां.

3. བདག་གི་ སྙིང་ དུ

4. Ms. संसारा

5. Tib. नम आर्यज्ञानसागरवैरोचनबुद्धराजाय

6. Tib. adds अर्हते सम्यक्संबुद्धाय—नमः सर्वतथागतेभ्यः अर्हद्भ्यः सम्यक्संबुद्धेभ्यः

7. Tib. adds तद्यथा ॐ.

11 (a)

१ सर्वतथागतेभ्योऽर्हद्भय: सम्यक्संबुद्धेभ्य:ॐ [धर धर धिरि धिरि][1]

२ धुरु धुरु इट्टे विट्टे चले चले प्रचले प्रचले [कुसुमे][2]

३ कुसुमवरे इलि मिलि विटि[3] स्वाहा॥

एवं मूलमन्त्र:[4]॥

४ नमो रत्नत्रयाय। नम आर्यावलोकिते-

(b)

१ श्वराय बोधिसत्त्वाय महासत्त्वाय। तद् यथा हा [हा हा] हा

२ हमे तिले चिले भिले खिले स्वाहा॥ स्नानोपस्पृशन

३ वस्त्राभ्युक्षिपणमन्त्र: सप्तजापेन॥

नमो रत्नत्र-

४ याय। नम आर्यावलोकितेश्वराय बोधिसत्त्वा[य म-]

12 (a)

१ हासत्त्वाय। तद्यथा टुरु टुरु हा हा हा हा स्वाहा॥ धू [पदी]-

२ पनिवेदनमन्त्र:॥

नमो रत्नत्रयाय। नम आर्या-

३ वलोकितेश्वराय बोधिसत्त्वाय महासत्त्वाय।

४ तद्यथा थिरि थिरि धिरि धिरि स्वाहा॥ गन्धपु-

(b)

१ ष्पदीपनिवेदनमन्त्र:॥

नमो रत्नत्रयाय। नम आर्यावलो-

२ कितेश्वराय बोधिसत्त्वाय महासत्त्वाय महाका-

३ रुणिकाय। तद्यथा सादे सादे सिदि सिदि सुद्ध सु-

४ द्ध स्वाहा॥ वलिनिवेदनमन्त्र एकविंशतिजापेन॥ न-

13 (a)

१ मो रत्नत्रयाय। नम आर्यावलोकितेश्वराय [बोधिस-]

२ त्वाय महासत्त्वाय महाकारुणिकाय। तद्यथा

३ मसिद्धसि चरि हुरु इचुरु: सुरु:मुरु: स्वा-

४ हा॥ होममन्त्र:॥ अनेन मण्त्रेण ज्ञातीनाष्टै (?) रग्नि प्रज्वा-

---

1. Supplied from Tibetan.
2. Supplied from Tibetan.
3. Tib. चितिज्वलमवनय
4. The Tibetan rendering finishes up the text here by a few concluding remarks about the merits of the mantra, mentioning the title at the end.

(b)

नमो रत्नत्रया-

३ य नम आर्यावलोकितेश्वराय बोधिसत्त्वाय महा-

४ सत्त्वाय महाकारुणिकाय। तद्यथा इलि मिलि

14 (a)

१ तिलि तिलि हिलि स्वाहा॥ दिशाबद्ध उदकने [× ×]

२ [र्वा] भस्मना वा सप्तजापेन॥

नमो रत्नत्रयाय। न-

३ म आर्यावलोकितेश्वराय बोधिसत्त्वाय महास-

४ त्त्वाय महाकारुणिकाय। तद्यथा पिटि पिटि तिटि ति-

(b)

१ टि विटि विटि गच्छ गच्छ भगवानार्यावलोकितेश्वर स्वभव-

२ नं स्वभवनं स्वाहा॥ उदके सप्तवारा परिजप्य चतु-

३ दिशं क्षिपे आर्यावलोकितेश्वर गच्छ स्वभवनम्॥

हयग्रीवविद्या

४ नमो रत्नत्रयाय। नम आर्यावलोकितेश्व-

15 (a)

१ राय बोधिसत्त्वाय महासत्त्वाय महाकारुणिकाय।

२ नमः सर्वसत्त्वव्यसनघातिने। नमः सर्वसत्त्वभय-

३ प्रशमनकराय। नमः सर्वसत्त्वभयोत्तारणा-

४ कराय। नमः सर्वविद्याधिगताय। नमः सर्वविद्या-

(b)

१ विधिगतमूर्तये महाकारूणिकाय। नमो महाविद्या

२ राजप्राप्तये महायोगिने। तस्मै नमस्कृत्वा इ-

३ दमार्यावलोकितेश्वरमुखोद्गीर्णं वज्रधरमहीयं

४ हयग्रीवं नाम परमहृदयमावर्तयिष्यामि [स]

16 (a)

१ र्वकर्मार्थसाधकं असह्यं सर्वभूतानां यक्षाणां च [ना]

२ शकं अमोघं सर्वकर्मणां विषाणाम्। यद्यथा

३ ॐ तरुल तरुल विरुल विरुल सर्वविषघा-

४ तक ज्वलितविस्फुलिङ्गाट्टहास केसराटोपप्रवृद्ध-

(b)

१ वेग वज्रखुरनिर्घातक चलितवसुधातल निःश्वसितह-

२ सितमारुतोत्क्षिप्तधरणीधर परभृतगणसमूह-

३ विक्षोभणकर परविद्यासंभक्षणकर सर्वग्राहो-

४ न्मादनकर परमशान्तिकर सर्वग्रहप्रशमनकर

17 (a)

१ बुध्य बुध्य धाव धाव च भगवा हयग्रीव खाद खाद प[रमं]

२ त्रां रक्ष रक्षक्षमस्व क्षमस्व म

३ याभिहितां मन्त्रां सिद्धि मे दिश आविश आविश

४ घोरपिशाच सर्वग्रहेष्वप्रतिहतोपम वरवज्र-

(b)

१ दंष्ट्र किं चिरापयसि इदं दुष्टग्रहं दुष्टसत्त्वं दुष्टपिशा-

२ चं वा अधुन विधुन कम्प कम्प मथ मथ प्रमथ प्र-

३ मथ। तथागताज्ञां पालय बुद्धधर्मसंघानुज्ञा-

४ तं मे कर्म शीघ्रं कुरु कुरु मा विलम्ब हयग्री[वा]-

18 (a)

१ य फट् वज्रखुराय फट् वज्रदंष्ट्राय फट्॥ वज्रद

२ त्फट् भयभैरवाय फट्॥ परविद्यासंभक्षणाय

३ फट्॥ परमन्त्रविनाशकाय फट्॥ सर्वग्रहो-

४ त्सादकाय फट्॥ सर्वविषघातकाय फट्॥ सर्व-

(b)

१ ग्रहेष्वप्रतिहताय फट्॥ वडवामुखाय फट्॥ सर्व-

२ ग्रहपिशाचान् मे वशामानय। यावन्तो मम

३ अहितैषिणः तान् सर्वान् वडवामुखे

४ न निकृन्तय फट्॥

नमो नम आर्यावलोकितेश्वराय

19 (a)

१ बोधिसत्त्वाय महासत्त्वाय। सिध्यन्तु मम

२ स्या मंत्रपदा हयग्रीवो भगवां आज्ञा [प]

३ यति स्वाहा॥ अयं हयग्रीवविद्या आज्ञापित

४ सिद्धः उपचारः आत्मरक्षाजापेन पररक्षा पंच

(b)

१ रंगी सूत्रं एकविंशतिग्रन्थाय कृत्वा बन्धितव्यं यावजी-

२ वं रक्षा कृता भवति डाइनीग्रहगृहीतस्य प्रति-

३ कृतिं कृत्वा पिण्डशस्त्रेण छेतव्या सर्वपरकृता मंत्रा-

४ श्छिन्ना भवन्ति सर्वशत्रुस्तंभनं मनसा व्यवहारे सु-

20 (a)

१ खं मुखे कृत्वा विद्या जप्तव्या उत्तरायति स्पृष्टावेशन

२ स्नातं शुचिवसॅत्रप्रावृतं शुचौ प्रदेशेषु मनसा [ ]

३ बद्धा आवेशये शुक्लवलिर्यथालंभेन॥ चन्द्रग्र-

४ हे सूर्यग्रहे घृतं ताम्रभाजने कृत्वा ताव जपेद्या

(b)

१ वचन्द्र मुक्तो भवति तं घृतं पिवे मेधावी भवति एकेनो

२ द्देशेन श्लोकशतमुद्गृह्णाति॥ पद्मां (?) जुहेधतम

३ क्षयं भवति॥ अथ साधितुमिच्छेत्। तृणमयं लो-

४ केश्वर प्रतिमा कर्त्तव्या दक्षिणेनार्यवज्रधरः वा[मे]

21 (a)

१ नार्यावलोकितेश्वरः त्रिमूर्त्ति कार्याः सर्वोपरि वडव

२ मुखः परविद्या संभक्षण॥ तस्याग्रतः अयं

३ हयग्रीवो विद्या राज्ञा अष्टसहस्त्रं जपेत्। ततः

४ सर्वकर्माणि कुर्या[द]ष्टावेशनं गुग्गुलधूपेन स-

(b)

१ ततजापेन सर्वकार्या शीघ्रं भवति सर्वडाइनी दृष्टमा-

२ त्रा वशीभवन्ति भस्मना सर्षपेण उदकेन सप्त

३ जप्तेन रक्षा कर्त्तव्या सीमाबद्धः कृतो भवति सर्व

४ मुद्रामोक्षणं उदकेन वशीकरणं फलपुष्पाद्यः

22 (a)

१ अयं पठित सिद्धा असाधित [एव सर्व कर्मा[णि कु]

२ रुते॥०॥

ANOTHER DHĀRAṆĪ

नमो बुद्धाय संघाय। नमश्च ॐ वज्रपाण

३ ये महायक्षसेनापतये। तद्यथा उग्राय स्वाहा॥ अति उ

४ ग्राय स्वाहा। उग्रप्रियाय स्वाहा। [अति] उग्रप्रियाय स्वाहा॥

(b)

१ उग्रक्रोधनाय स्वाहा अत्युग्रक्रोधनाय स्वाहा वज्ररोषणाय

२ स्वाहा। रोषप्रशमनाय स्वाहा। प्रहरणी वज्रह-

३ वणी अट्ये वट्ये वह्ने निहसे स्वाहा महारक्षय।

---

1. For the previous ms., see *IHQ.*, vol. IX, pp. 567-575.

Chapter - 4
A Buddhist Manuscript at Gilgit*

N. Dutt

The note published by Sir Aurel Stein in the *Statesman* of Calcutta and, later on, in he *JRAS*. (1931, October) and in the *IA*. (1932, March) on the *Archæological Discoveries in the Hindukush* created a stir in the world of Buddhist scholars. In October last, the authorities of the Calcutta University realising its importance wished that a preliminary survey of the manuscripts found at Gilgit should be made, and requested the authorities in the Kashmir State to give me the necessary facilities to examine them. The communal trouble was just then at an ebb; so I ventured to proceed to Srinagar, where I was very kindly received by Sir Zafar Ali Khan, who gladly complied with the request of the Calcutta University by giving me a week's time to examine the mss. As most of the mss. were still lying at Gilgit, an almost unapproachable place in October and November, I had to satisfy myself with the dxamination of five mss, that had been brought to Srinagar.

Introductory

The manuscripts are all in a bad condition and damaged in many places. Two of the manuscripts are incomplete, while the remaining nearly complete. They are all written on birch-bark in Gupta characters of the 5th or 6th century A.D. in the calligraphic style, and the characters have in many cases similarity with those of the Bower Manuscript and of the inscription of Yaśodharman.

---

* This article contains valuable information collected from a class of finds examined by an Indian scholar for the first time. My best thanks are due to Sir Zafar Ali Khan, a lover of Indian culture, for giving the writer the necessary facilities, and also to my friend Mr. Syamaprasad Mookerjee, M.A., Bar-at-law, Fellow of the Calcutta niversity, for taking the initiative to enable the writer to ascertain details about the Mss.—Editor.

The first manuscript, that has been examined by me and of which I propose to give here a detailed summary, contains 41 leaves and is entitled the *Ajitasena-vyākaraṇa-nirdeśa-nāma-mahāyāna-sūtra*. From the colophon it appears that the present ms. was written by one Ārya Sthirabuddhi with the help of the dharma-bhāṇaka Narendradatta. The only clue to the date of the ms. is the palæographic evidence supplied by its characters, which can be dated in the 5th century A.D. at the earliest.

The importance of the ms. lies in its (a) language, (b) the light thrown by it on the Aṅga (division of Buddhist literature) called *Vyākaraṇa*, (c) the form of Buddhism, envisaged by its contents, and (d) the whereabouts of the Arhat Nandimitra.

In language and style, it bears a close resemblance to the *Lalita-vistara*. Like this work it relates an incident or gives a prayer first in easy and correct Sanskrit and then repeats it in broken Sanskrit, called the Gāthā dialect by the late savant Dr. R.L. Mitra. The shortening of vowels, indiscriminate use of *u* in word-endings, disregard of grammar, contraction of words for the exigencies of metre are as frequent as we find in the gāthā portions of the *Lalitavistara* and other *Mahāyāna* work.

The treatise is undoubtedly a Mahāyāna-sūtra but it represents, as I have said in my *Aspects of Mahāyāna Buddhism* (pp. 36-38), the semi-Mahāyānic form of Buddhism. The reason for this opinion will be found in the fact that the *Sūtra* contains only as edifying story admonishing the people to give alms to the Buddhist monks, develop faith in Buddha as the saviour of mankind, and thereby attain Buddha-hood in all its glory. In the story, there is clearly an admixture of both the Hīnayānic and Mahāyānic ideals. It will be seen at page 107 that the king's son who attained Arhathood was capable of visualizing all the Buddhakṣetras. The conception of innumerable Buddhas presiding over their respective Buddhakṣetras is foreign to the Hīnayānists, while Arhathood has no place in the spiritual stages of the Mahāyānists. The admixture of the two conceptions appears to me to indicate the stage of Buddhism in which Hīnayāna was just incorporating the Mahāyānic ideals without, however, its philosophy of *Dharmaśūnyatā*; or in other words, when the *Pāramitās* only were being included in the ethical code of the Hīnayānists.

On account of its frequent references to the infinite virtues of Buddha, the immeasurable merit acquired through gifts to monks and the inconceivable suffering caused by refraining from making such gifts, it can be called a Mahāyāna-sūtra of the Mahāvaipulya class.

Of the 9 or 12 divisions (*aṅgas*) of the Buddhist literature it shows, both by its title and contents, that it belongs to the division called *Vyākaraṇa*. So far the Buddhist scholars as also Buddhaghosa were not quite sure as to which portions of the *Tripiṭaka* should be placed under the *Vyākaraṇa* class. Buddhaghosa, probably quite unaware of the existence of a literature to which the present ms. belonged, said that the whole of the *Abhidhamma-piṭaka*, all *suttas* in which there are no verses, and all other *Buddhavacanas* not included in the remaining eight divisions should be called Veyyākaraṇa (*Sumaṅgala Vilāsinī*, p. 24). An interpretation like this seems on the face of it a laboured one. The Mahāyānic interpretation of the *Vyākaraṇa* division of literature is more to the point. According to it, the sūtras like the *Gaṇḍavyūha, Samādhirāja,* and *Saddharma-puṇḍarīka* come under the *Vyākaraṇa* class (see *Aspects of Māhāyāna Buddhism*, p. 9). All our doubts, however, about the *Vyākaraṇa* class of Buddhist literature are set at rest by the present ms. It shows that those *Sūtras,* the chief object of which is to make a prophecy about the attainment of Buddhahood by one or more devotees, belongs to the *Vyākaraṇa* class. In this sense, the *Nidānakathā* of the *Jātakas* may well be called a *Vyākaraṇa* as it relates the story of Sumedha Brāhmaṇa, and the prophecy made by Dīpaṅkara Buddha about his future appearance as the Buddha Śākyamuni. The sixth and ninth chapters entitled the *Vyākaraṇaparivarta* and the eighth chapter *Pañcabhikṣuśatavyākaraṇaparivarta* of the *Saddharmapuṇḍarīka* is distinctly of the *Vyākaraṇa* type, and the same may also be said of the *Gaṇḍavyūha* which depicts the career of Sudhana until his attainment of Buddhahood, he having been foretold on many occasions about the certainty of his ultimately becoming a Buddha. (See also *Śatasāhasrikā*, p. 309).

Of other matters of religious interest, I may refer to the mention of the infinite merits acquired by those who read, preach and preserve the preent treatise along with the anathema pronounced upon its revilers or destroyers,[1] and to the mention of the begging-bell, the headdress, and the custom of assembling monks by striking a gong.

---

1. Such anathemas are also given in other Mahāyāna treatises, e.g., in the *Saddharmapuṇḍarīka*, pp. 226, 268, 337, 386, 414 etc., *Aṣṭasāhasrikā Prajñāpāramitā*, pp. 181ff; *Lalitavistara*, pp. 88-89; *Kāśyapa-parivarta*, pp. 226ff.

The last mentioned practice is still found in many Buddhist countries. At Chittagong, ther is still to be found the practice of carrying a bell (of bell-metal) by a śramaṇa accompanying a bhikṣu while going on the begging rounds. The practice of carrying a stick with small bells is noticed among certain non-Buddhist ascetics of the present day. The head-dress, I surmise, was sanctioned specially for the monks living in cold countries like Kashmir.

Of particular importance are the principal figures of the story, king Ajitasena and his spiritual guide Nandimitra, and the name of the capital of Ajitasena.

Mr. Watters supplies us with some information about Nandimitra from the Chinese work: *Ta A-lo-han Nan-ti-mi-to-lo so-shuo fa-chu-chi* (The record of the duration of the Law, spoken by the great Arhat Nandimitra) (*JRAS.*, 1898, p. 331). This has been supplemented by a fuller account given by Profs. Sylvani Lévi and Eduard Chavannes in their paper: *Les Seize Arhat Protecteurs de la Loi* (published in the *Journal Asiatique*, 1916, pp. 5ff.) which gies the French translation of the important portions of the Chinese text.

In the Introduction to the Chinese book, the following information is given about the author Nandimitra:

800 years after the *Parinirvāṇa* of Buddha there was in the capital of Sheng-chün (勝 軍) in the Chih-shih-tzu (執 師 子) country an arhat called Nandimitra. He had obtained the eight *vimuktis* (vimokṣas?), three *vidyās* and six *abhijñas*. He was free from impurities (araṇā), could know the aims and objects (*praṇidhi-jñāna*) (of beings), and had obtained the highest *samāpatti*. He had a great spiritual power which spread his fame far and wide. By the power of his *Praṇidhijñāna*, he could ascertain the feelings and actions of all living beings of the world. When his rebirth and its cause had terminated, and he was going to attain Parinirvāṇa he collected all the monks and nuns, and recounted to them the great merits realised by him personally and all that he had done for the benefit and joy of living beings. He then told them that he would be no more, and asked them to put questions in order to remove their doubts. At this, the monks and nuns beganto lament and one of them spoke out thus,

"The Buddha Bhagavā has long since entered into Nirvāṇa, the five disciples of his also are gone. The world is now void of any true leader. At present you are the only Venerable who are the eyes of gods and men. Why should you wish to have your turn to abandon us. Have pity on us and live some time more."

Nandimitra consoled them saying, "It is not proper for you to weep, O good men, you know the law of the world that whatever is born must have decay. The Buddhas who had vanquished the four demons and who possessed the power to fix the length of their lives conformed to the laws of the world and realised Nirvāṇa. How it will benefit you if I live permanently. Suppose I comply with your request, it will not bẹ of any proit to you. You should understand it and not be sorry."

On hearing this they all began to weep more. After some time they said, "We do not know how long yet the most excellent Law of Bhagavā Śākyamuni will last?"

The Venerable said, "Listen attentively, the Tathāgata has already preached the sacred *sūtra* on the duration of the Law."

Then he told them briefly how Buddha Bhagavā had entrusted the most excellent Law to sixteen great Arhats and their followers and asked them to protect it so that it might not be destroyed.[1]

Schiefner in his *Geschichte des Buddhismus* (p. 62) mentions one Nandamitra as a bhikṣu who realised the Truth when Aśvagupta was in charge of the Teaching at Pāṭaliputra and when a son of king Kanishka was ruling at Puṣkalāvatī, while the Tibetan work *dPag. bsam. ljon. bzaṅ* (pp. 48, 51) mentions one *dgaḥ-baḥi bśes-gñen* restored by Mr. S.C. Das as Ānandamitra (by Profs. Lévi and Chavannes as Nandimitra), and relates the cause of the disappearance of the excellent religion (*bstan. pa. nub. pāḥi rgyu. ni*).

The present treatise furnishes us with a clue to the identification of the Mahāśrāvaka Nandimitra with the Nandimitra of the Chinese work. In the latter, it is stated that the Arhat Nandimitra lived in a garden in the capital of king Sheng-Chün (勝 軍) in the Chih-shih-tzu (執 師 子) country. Watters was not very confident about the restoration from the Chinese words *Sheng* and *Chün*. Following Nanjio he suggested either Prasenajit or Jayasena, for *Sheng* means "to conquer, to get the victory" while *Chün* means "army, troops" (Williams, *Syllabic Dictionary of the Chinese Language*), and he preferred the first, as the name is well-known in the Buddhist history. Profs. Lévi and Chavannes, in the absence of any other known name, accepted his suggestion (*JA.*, 1916, p. 27-28). The present ms. throws some light on this doubtful restoration. The two Chinese wors may

1. See *JA.*, 1916, pp. 6-10.

be restored as Jayasena or Ajitasena, though strictly for *Ajita* we should expect in Chinese the two additional letters preceding sheng, viz., *wu-neng* 無能 Ajitasena may not be an historical person, but the fact that his name is associated with Nandimitra may be taken as a valid reason for restoring Sheng-chün as Ajitasena.

Now let us examine the restoration ofthe name of the capital of Jayasena or Ajitasena where Nandimitra lived. In Chinese it is called *Chih-shih-tzu* and is located in Magadha. It is a pity that the ms. does not give the Sanskrit name of the capital. Mr. Watters rightly suggested (though in the fn., see *JRAS.*, 1898, p. 332) that it should be restored as Siṃhadvīpa, but as no town of importance is known by this name, he hesitatingly followed Nanjio's suggestion that it meant Siṃhaladvīpa, i.e. Ceylon, but he was inclined to look for a place of this name within Magadha and he traced also one in the *Mūlasarvāsti-vāda Vinaya* (*Bhaiṣajyavastu*, Tok. XVII, 4, 29b, col. 17), where Buddha once stopped on his way from Śrāvastī to Rājagṛha. Profs. Lévi and Chavannes preferred Siṃhala (Ceylon)[1] and adduced reasons for the same, without seriously minding the anomaly presented by the time, place and name of the king. The present ms. proves clearly that one should take Watters' suggestion, viz., that Chih-shih-tzu referred to a place, known as Siṃhadvīpa or by some such name in Magadha situated between Śrāvastī and Rājagṛha, for in the ms. also we see that Buddha was at Śrāvastī and asked Nandimitra to go eastwards to Magadha to convert Ajitasena and his son.

Our object therefore should be to look for a place in or near Magadha having *siṃha* as a part of its name. A careful study of the *Mahāvaṃsa* yield very interesting results. The ancient name of Ceylon as given in the *Mahāvaṃsa* is either Tambapaṇṇi or Laṅkā, and nowhere do we find mention of Siṃhala. The introductory verse of chapter ix of the *Dīpavaṃsa*,[2] if literally translated, would be: "there was the Laṅkādīpa (inhabited by) the Sīhala people so called after *sīha*. The story of the conversion of Ceylon which is as follows also shows that Ceylon was originally called Laṅkādīpa but later on came to be known as Siṃhala after the Sīhala people of eastern India.

There was the king of Vaṅga in the city of Vaṅga in the kingdom of Vaṅga. He made the daughter of the king of Kaliṅga his

1. "L' indication geographique est plus precise; le royaume de Tche-che-tseu est certainement Ceylon"—*JA.*, 1916, p. 27.

2. Laṅkādīpo ayam ahū sīhena sīhalā iti.

queen. She lost herself in the forest of Lāḷaraṭṭha, and lived with a lion. She had a son and a daughter called respectively Sīhabāhu and Sīhasīvali. After some time she returned to Vaṅga with her children. Her son Sīhabāhu was offered the throne of Vaṅga for killing the lion. He accepted it but gave it away to the 'husband of his mother.' He took his sister and went back to the forest of his birth and bulit a city called Sīhapura and the kingdom reclaimed by him from forests was known as Lāḷaraṭṭha.[1] His eldest son was Vijaya who colonised Ceylon. He gave the new name Tambapaṇṇi-dīpa to the place which had hitherto been known as Laṅkādīpa. The people who accompanied him were called Sīhalas as they were connected with the king Sīhabāhu who received the appellation of Sīhala for killing the lion.

This story clearly shows that Sīhabāhu, father of Vijaya, had nothing to do with Ceylon. His capital was called Sīhapura and the people of his realm the Sīhalas. The Chinese words *Chih-shih-tzu* may well, therefore, refer to this Sīhapura. Dr. P.C. Bagchi suggests that *Chih-shih-tzu* should literally mean "one who holds the lion" from *chih* meaning "to hold," and *shih* the "lion," i.e., in Sanskrit it should be Siṃhadhara. It will be seen in the *Mahāvaṃsa* (vii, 42) that Sīhala is also derived exactly in the same way, viz., because of Sīhabāhu catching the lion, he was called the Sīhalo (*Sīhabāhunarindo so sīhaṃ ādinnavā ti Sīhalo*). Mr. Watters and Profs. Lévi and Chavannes, I think, would not object if *Chih-shih-tzu* be restored as Sīhala and identified with a place in Magadha, I mean, Sīhapura of the *Mahāvaṃsa* tradition. Unless and until some positive evidence is found aboutthe historicity of the town, it may be treated as a town known in legends and fiction, and though the Chinese travellers mention it, that does not go to prove its historicity. The fact is that the faithful Buddhists of the early Christian eras knew some place in or near Magadha as Sīhapura without probably knowing its exact location. In the *Mahāvastu*,[2] Siṃhapura is in one place located in Kaliṅga and elsewhere it is treated as a capital as prosperous as Hastināpura and not very far from it. A previous Śākyamuni Buddha is said to have entered the town of Siṃhapura for alms and thereby had converted many. In the *Cetiya Jātaka* (No. 422) Sīhapura,

1. *Mahāvaṃsa*, vi, 34, 35:

   So rajjaṃ sampaṭicchitvā datvā *mātupatissa taṃ*
   Sīhasīvalim ādāya *jāti-bhūmiṃ* gato sayaṃ.
   Nagaraṃ tattha māpesi, āhu Sīhapuram ti taṃ
   ....
   Lāḷaraṭṭhe pure tasmiṃ Sīhabāhu narādhipo

2. *Mahāvastu*, II, p. 95; III, pp. 238, 432.

Hatthipura etc. were said to be cities founded by sons of the king of Ceti. All these evidences tend to show that the Chinese words Chih-shih-tzu, the dwelling place of Nandimitra, referred to Sīhala or Sīhapura near Magadha. It may therefore be concluded that the ancient name of Ceylon was Laṅkadīpa or Tambapaṇṇi-dīpa but the people of the country were called Sīhalas (Simhalese) after the name of the conquering people who accompanied Vijaya.

Nandimitra's dread for the city of Ajitasena and unwillingness to go there is quite interesting. It also points to a border country of Magadha, people of which place were rough and evidently were not in favour of Buddhism. (See page 104).

King Ajitasena, as we have alrady hinted, was a mere local chief, and as such, his name was not of sufficient importance as to find place in history. If we rely on the bare name, we may identify him with the Ajitasenarājā mentioned in the *Mahāvastu* (I, p. 170) who is said to have attained the ninth *Bhūmi*. In the *Record of the Duration of the Law* preached by Nandimitra one Ajita is mentioned as the fifteenth Arhat to guard the Law. His place of residence was at Gṛdhrakūṭa (Rājagṛha).

I have not so far been able to trace any Tibetan version of the present ms., but I hope some scholars will find it out after going through this summary and will enlighten me about it.

Summary of the Contents of the Ms.

Salutation to the Omniscient! Thus have I heard. Once Bhagavā was dwelling at Śrāvastī in the hermitage of Anāthapiṇḍada with a large congregation of monks, 12500 in number, viz., Pūrṇa Maitrāyaṇīputra, Vakkula, Śāriputra, Ājñāta Kauṇḍinya, Mahānāma, Revata and others. Then to him, while at Jetavana, came a large number of Bodhisattvas, viz., Anik iptadhūra, Maitreya, Avalokiteśvara, Mahāsthāmaprāpta andsuch other 32000 Bodhisattvas, and after saluting him, they stood on one side.

After putting on his morning robe Bhagavā wanted to enter into the great city of Śrāvastī for alms. He asked Ānanda to fetch his almsbowl, begging-bell and head dress which were at once brought to him. Ānanda then addressed to him, with folded hands, the following verses:

यदा त्वं प्रविशसि पिण्डपातिक

विमोचयेयं हि प्राणिनाम

उत्तारयेयं वहवं हि सत्वा

नरकभयजातिजरामरणभय-

संसारदुःखकलिलमहाभयात्

विमोचयेयं तदा.........

महानुभावि वरदक्षिणेयो

विमोचयित्वा वहव हि सत्त्वा

संसारदुःखकलिलमहाभयाः

[When you will enter (into a city) as a collector of alms, -you will rescue many beings from fear of hell, birth, old age, and death and from the great evils and sufferings of the world. O the grat-souled, deserving the most excellent gifts, who has rescued the beings from the dread of the sufferings of the world].

When Bhagavā was not very far from the great city of Śrāvastī, many miracles took place and the citizens were at a loss as to what could be the cause of the appearance of suchh good omens. At that time, an old man of many centuries removed the doubts of the citizens by telling them that the cause of the omens is that Śākyamuni Tathāgata, possessing knowledge and good conduct, the knower of the world, the incomparable, the teacher of men and gods, who is now dwelling at Jetavanna-vihāra is about to enter into the city for alms. Then the people wondered how virtuous must be Śākyamuni at whose entrance into a city such miracles could happen. On hearing this, the old man said in verses:

"If one merely utters the name of Śākyanātha, he will be delivered of great misery and will never go to hell. He will go to heaven quickly. He, who hears only his name uttered, will become a Bodhisattva and will never be born in any lower region or go to hell, and will become a king or emperor. He who remembers his name will be cleansed of all his past sins, and enjoy happiness for ages, and visit all the Buddha-kṣetras and can never go to hell."

When the old man had just concluded his praises, Bhagavā entered into Śrāvastī through the city-gate. At the gate appeared 12 koṭis of lotus flowers, and on each lotus flower was seated a Bodhisattva, cross-legged and with hands folded in adoration. The moment Bhagavā entered the city, 99 koṭis of beings were established in the Sukhāvatī lokadhātu[1] and 84 koṭis in the Abhirati lokadhātu—the Buddha-kṣetra of Akṣobhya Tathāgata.

Bhagavā accompanied by Ānanda went to the house of the city-sweeper (?). On hearing the sound of the begging-bell, the daughter of the city-sweeper was astonished because no monk so far had visited her house for alms. As she had nothing to give, she shed tears, cursed her povertyand even was about to kill herself by a sharp sword. Then a god of the Suddhāvāsa heaven came to know of this situation, and so, putting on an invaluable pearl necklace, he instantly appeared before the girl with a hundred kinds of sweet food and Kāśikā cloths. He then requested the girl to wear the Kāśikā cloths and adorn herself with the pearl-necklace and then offer the food to Bhagavā. She did as she was bidden by the god.

Bhagavā then asked her to make the offering as she had done formerly to Vipaśyi, Śikhi, Viśvabhuk, Krakutsanda, Kanakamuni, Kāśyapa and other Tatlrāgatas, and said that by this offering, her femininity and poverty would be at an end. When she followed him to some distance, Bhagavā asked her to return and promised to tell her her past birth-stories. The girl fell at his feet and prayed thus in verses:

"Be compassionate to me, and rescue me from the misery of old age, disease and death. Be my refuge, and in accordance with the vow taken by you, save me as well as all those beings living in the ten corners of Jambudvīpa from the ocean of misery, and make them happy."

Bhagavā then told her the cause of her poverty. He aid, 'she once came out of her house to give alms to a begging monk but went back, thinking that she would not give alms to one shaven-headed. It was by this refusal that she was reborn in indigent circumstances and suffered immensely from poverty for 12,000 kalpas. But by one meritorious act, she received the *Bodhi-vyākaraṇa* (i.e., the prophecy that she would become a Buddha). As she received it (by this gift), she would become after many ages the Tathāgata Nagaradhvaja, possessed of knowledge and good conduct, the controller of men, the knower of the world and the teacher of gods and men.' Then she circumambulated the Bhagavā thrice, and enquired

1. The Buddakṣetra of Amiṭābḥa. Cf. *Saddharmapuṇḍarīka*, pp. 419, 458; also ch. VII.

as to the nature of the Buddha-kṣetra she would have when she became the Buddha. Bhagavā satisfied her curiosity. She became much pleased and was about to return to her house. At this moment, Bhagavā told her that she would die on the seventh day and would be reborn in the east in the country of Magadha as the son of king Ajitasena and this would be her last existence. He then left the city by the western gate and went back to his Jetavna hermitage.

Ānanda once more appeared before Bhagavā and after saluting him and circumambulating him thrice, said in verses:

"O the great Being endowed wit all the 32 signs of great men! When you go round for alms, you save all beings and establish them in happiness by the exercise of your *maitribala* (power of love), but what will happen when your religion will disappear after your demise, and there will be none to remember the sūtras."

On hearing this Bhagavā asked him to strike the gong (*gaṇḍī*) and said that he would start on his round for alms in the company of the monks. Ānanda being curious regarding the merits of hearing the sound of the gong asked Bhagavā about it. Bhagavā said:

"Whoever hears the gong-sound, gets absolved from the five deadly sins (*ānantaryāni kṛtyāni*) and becomes a never-returning Bodhisattva destined to attain bodhi."

Ānanda then struck the gong slowly and repeatedly. On hearing the sounds, all the great disciples (*mahāśrāvakas*) assembled, took their respective seats and commenced taking their meals. Among them was seated the Mahāśrāvaka Nandimitra. Bhagavā addressing him said, "Go, O Nandimitra, to the east to the country of Magadha, the kingdom of Ajitasena, and be the king's spiritual guide (*kalyāṇamitra*)." Nandimitra replied, "No, O Bhagavan, I shall not be able to go to that part of the land, for the people there are hard to manage and they will take my life." Bhagavā answered, "There is not a being who can destroy your hair, not to speak of your life."

Then Nandimitra donned his golden robe early in the morning, started eastwards for Magadha and reached the capital of Ajitasena. The king was much pleased to hear of his arrival and sent one of his ministers to escort him to the palace. But Nandimitra declined to come to the king at the bidding of the minister. On hearing this the king sent 500 ministers but they too failed to make him to come to the king. Then the king himself approached the Mahāśrāvaka and entreated him with folded hands to enter into his capital. Taking him by the right hand, the king led him into the palace and made him sit on the throne.

When Nandimitra had explained to the king thhat monks and recluses live on alms only, the king offered him food. Nandimitra took the food and expatiated inverses on the merits of giving alms, and on the rare qualities of the Teacher. He said,

'The giver of the alms to the order of monks, who are rarely found, can never suffer at the hands of demons and such other wicked beings, and are freed from old age, disease and sufferings; those who utter the name of the Teacher never go to hell."

Nandimitra then expressed his willingness to accept the food-offerings of the king. When he was served by the king with food, hard and soft, he enquired of the latter if there was any garden hard by and on hearing that the king had one very beautiful, he wanted to see it. He found it suitable for his dwelling as it had all the necessary equipments, viz., a cold water tank for summer, and a tank for the rainy season with water, neither very hot nor verycold, both having golden steps running down into the water; Aśoka, Mucilinda, Pāṭali and such other flower-trees giving out scents; Śuka, Śārikā, Cakravāka, Mayūra, and Kokila birds singing sweet songs; golden lotus flowers and so forth. As soon as king Ajitasena learnt from him that he liked the place, he struck the drum; on hearing the sound his ministers assembled and enquired of him about the reason for making the sound. He asked them to make ready his chariots drawn by horses and elephants, as he wanted to go to the garden. In company with the Mahāśrāvaka, the king came tothe garden and asked him as to the kind of cottage (*kuṭikaṃ*) needed by him. The Mahāśrāvaka replied, "O king, build one according to your heart's content and regard for me." The king then ordered his chief minister to build a hermitage 30 yojanas long and 6 yojanas wide well-decorated with jewels, and pearls, having a terraced walk 4 yojanas long and 2 yojanas wide. He then offered it to Nandimitra, saying in verses:

"The hermitage and a dry and beautiful walk have been completed, now rescue the beings; it was a great resolution made by you that you would preach the dharma."

He then returned to his capital leaving Nandimitra in the garden-hermitage.

When Nandimitra entered into meditation, his hair, eyes, hands, chest, stomach, legs—all limbs became quite different (*anyena keśā anyena nayanā anyena bāhūni anyena hṛdayaṃ anyena udaraṃ*...). For seven days the king eulogised him but the words did not reach the ears of the Mahāśrāvaka. After some time the king came with his son to the hermitage and found him as a mere lump (of flesh). Seeing this, he became very remorseful, and was going to cut himself asunder by a sharp sword, when his son with folded hands said thefollowing verses:

मा शोकचित्तस्य भवे तृपेन्तु।
मा वेदयी वेदनमीदृशानि॥
आत्मघातं करित्वा तु निरये गमिष्यसि।
रौरवं नरकं चापि गमिष्यसि सुदारुणं॥
दक्षिणीयो अयं लोके जरव्याधिप्रमोचकः।
दुर्लभो दर्शनं अस्य वोधिमार्गस्य दर्शकः॥

[Do not grieve, be happy, do not suffer such apain; by committing suicide you will go to hell. You will go to the frightful Raurava hell. In this world, the saviour of beings from old age and disease is worthy of gifts; difficult it is to have a look at one who shows the path leading to Bodhi].

By such words, the son prevented his father from slaying himself, and told him that the Mahāśrāvaka was engaged in meditation and asked him to retire till the Mahāśrāvaka would rise from same. As soon as the Mahāśrāvaka rose from meditation, he asked the king to come near him. The king, seeing the bhikṣu (Mahāśrāvaka), took off his crown and placed it on his son's head with the words, "let the kingdom be yours, govern it righteously and not unrighteously." The son replied, "I have performed innumerable kingly duties but never had satisfaction, so let the kingdom be yours, father, I have no desire for kingdom, wealth and power, rule the kingdom righteously."

The Mahāśrāvaka then dwelt on the merits of offering gifts to monks and advised the king to do so.

At this, the king ordered his ministers to make his chariots readyfor going to Jetavana vihāra to see and worship Śākyamuni and hear from him the dharma. When the king was nearing Jetavana in his bejewelled chariot, Śākyamuni collected his monks and asked them to enter into the meditation which would make them appear as a garland of flames (*jvālāmālaṃ bodhisattva-samādhi*). The king seeing this garland of flames asked Nandimitra what it meant. Nandimitra told him that it was there where Śākyamuni Tathāgata lived and preached his doctrines, and practised meditation. The king then alighted from the chariot with his son and approached Bhagavā, around whose body he saw a golden flame two cubits long moving about. After ascertaining who Śākyamuni was,the king fell at his feet. He was raised by the outstretched hands of Śākyamuni with the words, "O king, you have for innumerable kalpas seen this body; what is your object in falling at my feet?" The king saluted him uttering in verses:

"I bow down my head to the leader of the world, endowed with the excellent signs, having long arms and golden body—one who saves beings from old age and disease, and stops the passage of beings into hell."

He then expressed his desire to retire from the world. At this Bhagavā was exceedingly pleased and said that his conversion would be a great gain to the religion as the religion would spread widely (*vaistārikī*). He asked the king to go back to his kingdom and promised to go there after seven days. The king greatly delighted returned to his capital preceded by his spiritual guide (*kalyāṇamitra*). He then ordered his ministers to have the streets cleansed, ask the people to hoist flags in their houses and put bejewelled pitchers of water at the door of every house. When all these were done, just on the seventh day, the Tathāgata with a large number of monks headed by Śāriputra, Maudgalyāyana, Ānanda, Pūrṇa Maitrāyaṇīputra reached the capital. The king Ajitasena, preceded by his spiritual guide, received Bhagavā with a basket of flowers and sprinkled the flowers on him, and prayed that by that meritorious act might all beings attain the highest *sambodhi*. Mats were then spread for all and Bhagavā was seated on the throne. Bhagavā delivered his teachings from the throne and the king satisfied him and his disciples by giving them various kinds of food. Then the king's son was presented before Bhagavā. He sought for ordination before the king and was at once ordained by Ānanda by Bhagavan's direction. As soon as he was ordained, he attained *Arhathood* (*pravrajita mātreṇa arhattvaṃ samprāptaṃ abhūt*) and saw all the Buddhakṣetras (*sarva-buddhakṣ etrāṇi paśyati sma*). Then the son hovered in the sky and addressed the following verses to his father:

मा विलंवं कुरु तात
मा खेदं किंचि यस्यासि।
अहो सुलब्धं सुगतान दर्शनं
अहो सुलब्धं सुगतान लाभं॥
अहो सुलब्धं परमं हि लाभं
प्रव्रज्यालाभं सुगतेन वर्णितं।
संसारमोक्षः सुगतेन वर्णितं
प्रव्रज्य शीघ्रं मा विलंव तात॥
मा खेदयी लोकविनायकेन्द्रं
सुदर्लभं लब्धं मनुष्यलाभं।
सुदर्लभं दर्शनु नायकानां
शीघ्रं च प्रव्रज्य मया हि लब्धं॥
प्राप्तं मया उत्तममग्रबोधिं।
श्रुत्वान राजा तत् पुत्रवाक्यम्।
निष्क्रामी प्रव्रजि शासनि नायकस्य

[Do not delay, O father, (to take ordination), you will not experience any trouble. It is a great gain to see and meet the Sugata. Retirement frfom the world has been praised by Bhagavā, so also emancipation from the world of transmigration. Take ordination quickly and do not delay and do not cause grief to the lord of leaders. Difficult it is to be born as man, difficult (also) to meet the Leader; quickly have I retired from the world and quickly have I attained the highest knowledge. Hearing these words of his son the king retired and embraced the doctrine of the Leader].

The king was much pleased at his son's words and spent 30 koṭis for building monasteries. The 1000 women of the harem were all transformed into men and they all took ordination.[1] Bhagavā after ordaining them returned to the Jetavana-vihāra.

---

1. It fully endorses the view mentioned in the *Saddharmapuṇḍarīka*, p. 264 that the following five positions cannot be attained by a woman: Brahmasthānaṃ, Sakrasthānaṃ, Mahārājasthānaṃ, Cakravartisthānaṃ, and Avaivartika Bodhi-sattvasthānaṃ. It further says that a woman may fulfil the *pāramis* but can never become a Buddha.

Ānanda asked "O Bhagavā, what will be the result of these meritorious acts of king Ajitasena?"

Bhagavā replied, "You have done well, Ānanda, that you have asked me such a question. After countless ages, this king Ajitasena will become Ajitapralokanātha-tathāgata having knowledge and good conduct etc."

Ā: What will be the results of the good deeds of Nandimitra Mahāśrāvaka, the spiritual guide of the king?

Bh.: He will become at that time Mandiprabhanāma-tathāgato.

Ā: How will their Buddhakṣetras be called?

Bh.: Their Buddhakṣetras will be called Aparimitaguṇa-sañcaya (a collection of innumerable merits).

Ā: What will be the merits of him who will in future promulgate (*prakāśayiṣyati*) this religious treatise (*dharmaparyāyam*)?

Bh.: They will attain Bodhi just as much as I have done through incalculable acts which are hard to perform (*duṣkara*). He, who listens to a gāthā of 4 pādas, will become non-returning (avaivarttika) Bodhisattvas.

Ā: What will be the merits of those *dharma-reciters* (*bhāṇakas*) who will preach this *dharma-paryāya*?

Bh.: Those who will preach the whole of this *dharmaparyāya* will become kings or emperors, lords of the four continents (*dvīpa*) and will ultimately be emancipated from birth, old age, disease, grief and death.

Ā: What will be the fate of those who will speak ill of this *dharmaparyāya*?

Bh.: Enough, Ānanda, do not ask me about the great sins that will be incurred by them; I cannot enumerate them, nor can the koṭ is of Buddhas.

Ā: Tell them, O Bhagavā, O Sugata.

Bh.: Then listen, Ānanda, they will undergo immense sufferings for ages by having their birth in the great hells of Raurava, Hāhaha and Avīci, or in the Yamaloka, animal-world or spirit-world. If they are born as human beings, they will have long and dry palate and throat (*dīrgha-śuṣka-tālukaṇṭha*), their tongues will be 12 yojanas long, and with their aid they will declare that those who will speak ill of the *dharmaparyāya* will fare like them.

Ā: How will this excellent dharma be destroyed?

Bh.: In future, there will be some who will rebuke, speak ill of and even injure the reciters or repositories of the *sūtras*, to whom they will bear hatred. Their demerits will be much more than those who extract the eyes of all the beings of the three thousand worlds. So also will be the demerits of those who will bear hatred towards the repositories or reciters of the *sūtras*.

Ānanda then said that many *sūtras* had been heard by him but none like this. Then in verses he said, "I shall remember and preach this sūtra and protect it from the hands of the revilers."

Then the Mahāśrāvakas Kāśyapa, Sārīputra, Pūrṇa Maitrāyaṇīputra uttered verses eulogizing the *sūtra* and its preacher the Buddha, and promised to preach it. They were followed by Brahmā Sahampati, who also took the vow to protect the *sūtra*. This is the *Ajitasena-vyākaraṇa-nirdeśa-nāma-Mahāyāna sūtram*. This (ms.) is written by Ārya Sthira-buddhi (and recited) by the *dharmabhāèaka* Narendradatta.

Chapter - 5
The Buddhist Manuscripts at Gilgit

N Dutt

The Title of the Ms.

The second manuscript examined by me is written in the calligraphic Gupta characters very similar to those in thefirst manuscript.[1] The characters are much more legibly written, though their size is comparatively smaller. It is also a birchbark manuscript containing 41 leaves and on each leaf there are 5 lines. The title of the book as stated at the end of the ms. is *Bhaiṣajyaguru nāma mahāyānasūtra* (leaf 40 b). In the *Sikṣāsamuccaya* it is called *Bhaiṣ ajyaguru vaidūrya-prabha-rāja-sūtra*, while in its Tibetan version (Rgyud. Tha., pp. 470ff), the Sanskrit title is *Ārya-Bhagavato-Bhaiṣ jyaguru-Vaidūryaprabhasya Pūrvapraṇi-dhāna-viśeṣa-vistara nāma mahāyāna-sūtra* (phags. pa bcom. ldan ḥdas. smon-gyi bla vai. du. ryaḥi ḥod-kyi sṅon-gyi smon-lam gyi khyad. par rgyas. pa shes. bya. ba theg. pa chen. poḥi mdo). The Tibetan title though too long for the title of a book is not without a basis for we have on leaf 2 the following passage, in which Mañjuśrī requests Buddha to deliver the sūtra:

देशयतु भगवांस्तेषां तथागतानां नामधेयानि पूर्वप्रणिधानविशेष विस्तरविभङ्गम्।

(Preach O Bhagavan, in full details, the excellent resolutions that were made previously by the Tathāgatas).

The object of the whole work is to relate the great resolutions (*mahāpranidhāṇas*) made by each of the seven Buddhas, and the effect of such resolutions. This section deals with the resolutions of the Buddha called Bhaiṣajyaguru-vaidūrya-prabharāja. In the *Saddharmapuṇḍarīka*, (p. 470), Bhaiṣajyarāja and Bhaiṣajyasamudgata are

1. For an account of the first Ms., see *IHQ.*, VIII, pp. 93ff.

described as sons of king Śubhavyūha and are repeatedly mentioned as highly meritorious bodhisattvas, but it is difficult to say whether any of these bodhisattvas became later on the Buddha Bhaiṣajyaguru-vaidūrya-prabharāja, for in the Chinese version of this *sūtra* the former names appear as bodhisattvas. If these Bodhisattvas have been elevated to Buddhahood, it must have been done posteriọr to the time of compilation of the *Saddharmapuṇḍarīka*, the date of which may be placed in the 1st century A.D.

In a paper contributed to the *Bulletin de l'Ecole Française d' Extreme-Orient,* vol. III, 1903, pp. 33-37),[1] Prof. Paul pelliot has dealt with the Chinese versions of this work. He writes:—"The Bhaiṣ ajyaguru is one of the most popular Buddhas in China, Japan and Tibet. His name in Chinese is *Yao-che lieou-li-kouang-jou-lai*, (Bhaiṣ ajyaguruvaidūryaprabha). The restoration of the original name is guaranteed by the dhāraṇī transcribed phonetically in the *sūtra* consecrated to the glory of Bhaiṣajyaguru. The Sanskrit text of the sūtra has not been discovered, but it exists in more than one translations in Chinese."

Its Chinese Translations

From the Chinese and Tibetan translations we learn that the present work is the last chapter of the book dealing with the great vows (mahāpraṇidhāna) of the seven past Buddhas. In view of the fact that this last chapter have independent translations both in Chinese and Tibetan, and also of the fact that quotations from this chapter only appear in Śāntideva's *Sikṣāsamuccaya*, it may be stated that this particular chapter, containing the vows of Bhaiṣ ajyaguruvaidūryaprabha-rāja, attained the greatest popularity.

About the Chinese translation of this chapter, Prof. Pelliot furnishes us with the following information: "The 12th or the last, and undoubtedly, the oldest chapter of *Fo-chouo-ta-kouan-ting-chen-tcheou-king*[2] was translated by Śrīmitra between 317 and 322 A.D.; it should, however, be observed that certain catalogues mention only nine chapters of the translation of Śrīmitra; in any case, it comprised 12 chapters at the time of the compilation of the *K'ai yuan che kiao lou*[3] in 730 A.D. Among the independent translations, it appears that

1. I should thank Dr. P.C. Bagchi for drawing my attention to this article. In my translation of the portions of this French article, I have retained the method adopted by the French writers in transliterating Chinese words.

2. Nanjio (167) remarks under this book that it is in 12 fasciculi, "each fasc. contains a *sūtra* with its own title, so that this is a collection of 12 *sūtras*."

3. "Catalogue of books on the teaching of Śākyamuni."

the first is that of Houei-kien entitled *Yao-clue-lieou-li-koung-king* and dated 457 A.D. It was mentioned in 597 in the (catalogue) *Li-tai-san-pao-ki*[1] and about 664 in the *Ta-t'ang-nei-tien-lou*[2] but it disappeared at the time of the compilation of *K'ai yuan che kiao lou* (730). The translation of Dharmagupta executed in 615 still exists (Nanjio, 170); it is called *Fo chouo yao che jou lai pen yuan king* (Bhaiṣajyaguru-tathāgata-pūrva-praṇidhāna). It is to this that reference has been made in the preface entitled *Yao che jou lai pen yuan kong tö king siu*, which preface in the Japanese Tripiṭaka has been placed by mistake at the beginning of the translation of the sūtra of Bhaiṣ ajyaguru made later on by Yi-tsing. The author of this preface was one of the collaborators of Dharmagupta. It is curious that he does not mention *Fo-chouo-kouan-ting-king* (Nanjio, 167) or the translation of Śrīmitra. He speaks only about the many inaccuracies in the translation of Kien-houei.˙ The text adopted by Dharmagupta, on the contrary, was based on three mss. and the translation was accepted after three revisions. But this translation of Dharmagupta, although it is still exant, has been eclipsed by that of Hiuan-tsang, entitled *Yao-che-lieou-li-kouang-jou-lai-pen-yuan-kong-tö-king* (Nanjio 171=*Bhaiṣajyaguru-vaidūrya-prabhāsa-pūrva-praṇidhāna-guṇa-sūtra*), and is dated 650. It is this translation that was entirely copied by the emperor K'ang-hi by his own hand in 1695 and it is this that has been partially reproduced in the *T'ou-chou-tsi-tch'eng*. This is assuredly the most popular in China. The three translations of Śrīmita, of Dharmagupta and of Hiuan-tsang, however, follow one another quite closely."

Its Tibetan Translations

In the tenth (tha) volume of the Rgyud (Tantra) of the bkaḥ-ḥgyur, leaves 433-470 contain *De. bshin-gśegs-pa bdun. gyi sṅon. gyi smon. lam. gyi khyad. par rgyas. pa* (=*Sapta-Tathāgata-pūrvapraṇidhāna-viśeṣa-sūtra*).[3] To this probably corresponds the Chinese text translated by Yi-tsing (Nanjio 172), the title of which text as restored by Nanjio is *Bhaiṣajyaguru vaidūryaprabhās* (*ādi*) *sapta-buddha pūrvapraṇidhānaguṇa sūtra*. By examining the Tibetan xylographs, I find that the first tathāgata mentioned in it is called *mtshan. legs. par. yoṅs. bsgrigs. dpal. gyi rgyal-bo*. It may be restored as *Su-yaśa-pari-granthita-śrī-rāja*. Prof. Pelliot gives the Chinese

1. "Records concerning the *Triratna*, under successive dynasties."
2. "Ctalogue of Buddhist books collected under the great Than dynasty."
3. *Asiatic Researches*, XX, p. 508-9.

name of the first Tathāgata as Chan-ming-tch'eng-ki-siang-wang-jou-lai, which may be restored as *Su-yaśaśrīrāja-tathāgata.*

In Tibetan there is also an independent translation of this work on leaves 470-484. On comparison I notice that this Tibetan version closely follows the present Sanskrit text. From the summary supplied by Prof. Pelliot from the Chinese version of Śrīmitra, Dharmagupta and Hiuan-tsang, it will be apparent that the first portions (see p. 346 para 1) agrees with the present Sanskrit text but not the rest, excepting the last few lines. In this connection, I should also point out that the quotation, which is a fairly long one, in Śāntideva's *Śikṣ āsamuccaya* (p. 175) has been taken from the text under consideration.

Popularity of Bhaiṣajyaguru in China and Japan

About the popularity of this Tathāgata in China and Japan, Prof. Pelliot writes:

"The Bhaiṣajyaguru is the Buddha of the 7th of these worlds, all of which are situated in the east, and of which Tsing-lieou-li is the furthest. It seems that the necessity of symmetry has caused the location of this happy eastern world opposite to the western Paradise. In a Chinese inscription of 776 A.D., Bhaiṣajyaguru's world of the east and the Sukhāvatī of the West are mentioned side by side, and a few lines further there is a reference to the twelve vows that he had taken when he was a bodhisattva for the welfare of beings.

From China, the Bhaiṣajyaguru passed to Japan at an early date. He is represented at Horiuji in a group in bronze; the most ancient representation is perhaps attributed to Tori Busshi; an inscription enables us to date it exactly in the year 607; it was in his honour that in the year 681 on the occasion of an illness of the Queen, the Emperor Temmei founded at Yamato the great Yakushiji, the temple of Bhaiṣajyaguru. This temple perserves even now the wonders of ancient Japanese art."

The Contents of the Sūtra

For the purpose of comparison I am reproducing in English the substance given by Prof. Pelliot from the Chinese texts as also that of the Sanskrit text:

1. "The Buddha arrives at Vaiśāli; he is surrounded by all the beings of the worlds. Mañjuśrīkumāra stands up and requests the Tathāgata to give an exposition of the vows made formerly by the past Buddhas for extricating the living beings from the miseries of

existence. Bhagavā grants the request and explains the twelve vows taken formerly, when he was a bodhisattva, by a Buddha whose world is separated from ours by Buddhakṣetras, the number of which is ten times the number of the sands of the Ganges; that Buddha iss Yao-che-lieou-li-kouang-jou-lai (Bhaiṣajyaguruvaidūryaprabha); he lives in the world Tsing-lieou-li. He wished that he himself might attain bodhi, pure and resplendaen as the vaidūrya (maṇi), and illuminate the world immersed in darkness; he wished that his name if uttered might cure maladies, release the prisoners, change into men those women who are sick of their miserable condition, procure food for the famished, or clothes for the destitute. Inshort, in that world, for innumerable kalpas there would be neither suffering nor poverty; there would be no more feminine beings, nor beings in inferior states of existence; the soil would be of vaidūrya, ropes of gold would line the routes;[1] the walls and the houses would be made of seven jewels and one would believe it to be the western Sukhāvatī.[2] In the country there would be two bodhisattvas, viz., Je-kousang-pien-tchao and Yue-kouang-pien-tchao,[3] the chief among the innumerable bodhisattvas and second to the Buddha alone; they protect the precious treasure of the law of their Tathāgata. Also all believers male and female must take the vow to be reborn in the world of this Buddha.

2. It will suffice only to think of his name for deliverance from all evils, and if one dreams of him at the time of death, Mañjuśrī-bodhisattva, Avalokiteśvara b., Mahāsthāmaprāpta b., Akṣayamati b., Pao-t'an-houa b., Bhaiṣajyarāja b., Bhaiṣajyasamudgata b.,[4] Maitreya b. will act as attendants of the deceased and conduct him to the place of delight.

3. If one makes an image of this Buddha, or if one recites the text of the sūtra, he will escape from the nine ways of death (neuf

---

1. Neither in Tibetan (vide leaf 474, 11. 4-5) nor in Sanskrit I find any passage corresponding to this.

2. Cf. कामदोषापगतापायदुःखशव्दमपगतमातृग्रामं वैदूर्य्यमयी च सा (ms. श) महापृथिवी कुड्यप्राकारप्रासादतोरणगवाक्षजालनिर्य्यूहं सप्तरत्नमयं यादृशं सुखावतीलोकधातुस्तादृशं तत्र वैदूर्य्यनिभासायां लोकधातौ तौ बोधिसत्त्वौ etc. ।

Cf. Tib. xylograph, leaf 474a, 11, 4-5.

3. The Chinese terms used by Śrīmitra or Dharmagupta or Hiuantsang are really different translations of the Sanskrit names: Sūryavairocana and Candra vairocana which are found in the present Sanskrit ms. as also in the inscription of Say-fong.

4. All these names occur in the list of bodhisattvas in the *Saddharma-puṇḍarīka* (see ante p. 342); but these names are not found in the Sanskrit Ms.

fins violentes): this is what the Bodhisattva Kieou-t'o[1] explained to Ānanda. In conclusion, having heard this instruction of Bhagavā, 12 great rākṣasa-chiefs, each having a following of 7000 rākṣasas, were converted; and they consecrated themselves to better the lot of living beings."

The Sanskrit text (in translation) begins as follows:

"Salutations to all the Buddhas and Bodhisattvas. Thus have I heard. Once Bhagavā in course of his tour came to the great city of Vaiśālī. There he stopped under a tree, giving out musical sounds, with a large number of bhikṣus, bodhisattvas, householders, gods, nāgas, yakṣas, gandharvas, etc., in short, many human and non-human beings. Then the dharmarājaputra Mañjuśrī, being inspired by Buddha, put the robe on one shoulder, knelt down and said with folded hands: O Bhagavā, tell us the names of the Tathāgatas and their former resolutions in detail for the good of all beings."

The Sanskrit text follows the first para of Prof. Pelliot's translation quite closely, as has been shown by quotations of some of the corresponding Sanskrit passages. After this, it gives the following conversation of Bhagavān with Mañjuśrī:

"There are, O Mañjuśrī, men who are unwise and avaricious and so when they give gifts, they feel pain in teir mind; they seek food for themselves and not even for their parents. These will be reborn in the animal world, but in that state if they just remember the name of Bhaiṣajyaguru, they will be born in future among men, and be able to remember their former existences and sufferings, and so will lead a pious life.

There are some who transgress the (Buddhist) precepts, or become conceited on account of their learning and look down upon others. They will be reborn in hell where, however, if they remember the name of Bhaiṣajyaguru, they will be born in future among men and become devoted followers of the Buddhist religion.

There are again some who speak ill (*avarṇaṃ bhāsati*) of others. They will be reborn as asses, horses, cows, etc. or as low-class labourers. If they remember the name of Bhaiṣajyaguru, they will be reborn as men and will become wise and obtain good friends.

There are also some who slander others (*paiśūnyābhirata*) and instigate people to quarrel among themselves, or kill animals, or

1. Its Sanskrit restoration is Trāṇamukta.

practise dreadful (Tāntric) practises (*ghoravidyām*) and so forth; they also, if they hear the name of Bhaiṣajyaguru will love their enemies or victims.

Those of the monks and nuns, male or female lay-devotees, who observe the 8 śīlas or follows the code of discipline for three months or one year will be reborn in the Sukhāvatī world of the west. Should they hear the name of Bhaiṣajyaguru, eight Bodhisattvas[1] will appear at the time of their death and conduct them to the world of gods. They may be reborn also as sovereigns of the four dvīpas, or as rich householders, and if they are females, they will lose their femininity and become males.

After this, commences the account of the merits acquired by one who makes others hear the name of Bhaiṣajyaguru, or preaches and propagates this Sūtra.

This is followed by an account of the method of worshipping the Tathāgata through an image (tasya tathāgatasya pūjā kartukāmenaśca tena tathāgatasya pratimāṃ kārapayitavyaṃ).

The worshipper is to observe the 8 śīlas, avoid impure food, choose a clean spot, burn incense, decorate4 the place with various kinds of cloths, flags and festoons. Then he is to bathe, and with a pure mind try to be friendly to all beings. After this he is to circumambulate the image with music, and read out the present Sūtra, remembering all the while the vows of the Tathāgata.

Such worship brings the worshipper wealth, sons etc. and on the other hand rids him of all worldly evils.

Those, who will hear the name of the Tathāgata as well as take the three śaraṇas, observe the five Śikṣāpadas and the Bodhisattvasaṃvaras (rules of discipline for Bodhisattvas), or become monks observing the 250 Śikṣāpadas, or become nuns observing 500 Śikṣāpadas, will always be protected by the Tathāgata from evil destiny.

The women with child will by uttering his name feel no pain at the time of giving birth to the child, and the baby will be healthy, good-looking and intelligent."

This is followed by a conversation of Buddha with Ānanda about the credibility of the results enumerated above brought about by merely hearing or uttering the name of Bhaiṣajyaguru. As usual Ānanda dares not say anything against it and expresses his deep

1. See ante, p. 347.

conviction in the same, pitying the evil lot of those who would not believe it.

After Ānanda, there appears one Trāṇamukta bodhisattva who enquires whether in future beings lying senseless on their death-bed when Yamarāja is taking stock of his merits and demerits can be revived by his relatives by making him hear the name of Bhaiṣ ajyaguru and performing the worship of the Tathāgata. He is given an answer in the affirmative, and an account of the method of worship. The worship is to be performed more elaborately by setting up seven images and so forth.

Ānanda now raises the question about the troubles of the ruling kings and the possibility of their removal by uttering the name of Bhaiṣajyaguru.

This is followed by a conversation between Ānanda and Trāṇamukta bodhisattva about the various causes of death.[1]

At last, appear the rākṣasas, whose chiefs were Kiṃca, Vajra, Sanila, Indraloka, Pāyila, Vidala, etc. who promised to utter the name of Bhaiṣajyaguru, take the three śaraṇas and the vow to preach the *Sūtra* everywhere.

The *Sūtra* ends with a discussion about the suitability of its title. Thus ends the *Bhaiṣajyaguru-nāma-mahāyāna-sūtra.*[*]

---

1. See ante, p. 347, para 3.

* I hope to publish an edition of the Sanskrit text with its Tibetan version within a short time.

Chapter - 6
Bodhicitta-vivaraṇa of Nāgārjuna

P C Bagchi

Dr. Nalinaksha Dutt has published in the *Indian Historical Quarterly*, (VII, p. 259ff.) the 'Bodhisattva-Prātimokṣasūtra' with an interesting study on it. His edition of the text is based on a manuscript preserved in the Cambridge University Library. Dr. Dutt has rightly pointed out that the last leaf of the text has not bearing on the Prātimokṣ a-sūtra and seems to contain the beginning of a new text.

The opening line bears testimony to such a hypothesis-*Namo Buddhāya Bodhicittavivaraṇaṃ vakṣye*. The title of the text was evidently Bodhichittavivaraṇa. It is preserved in the Bstan hgyur in two Tibetan translations. There is besides the Tibetan translation of a commentary attributed to Smṛtijñānamitra. The work is attributed to Ārya Nāgārjuna (klu sgrub).

(i) Byaṅ chub sems kyi hgrel pa zes bya ba —*Bodhicittavivaraṇa-nāma*, composed by Ārya Nāgārjuna and translated by Guṇākara of India. Cordier ṭCatalogue II, p. 135; Rgyud hgrel, 142, 5.

(ii) Byaṅ chub sems kyi hgrel pa, *Bodhicittavivaraṇa*, composed by Nāgārjuna, and translated by Jayānanda of Kāśmīr. Rgyud hgrel, 142, 6; *Ibid*, p. 135.

(iii) Byaṅ chub sems kyi hgrel pa'i nam par bśad paṭ *Bodhicittavivaraṇa-ṭīkā*, commentary on the work of Nāgārjuna composed and translated by Smṛtijñānakīrti, Rgyud hgrel, 142, 34, *Ibid*, p. 141.

The first translation, that of Guṇākara, is not a literal one and is often times only explanatory while the second, that of Jayānanda closely follows the text. As regards the date of the text it is for the present impossible to say whether the author is the same as the great founder of the Mādhyamika philosophy or a later personage of that name. The style and the quality of the Sanskrit in which the text is written would not go against its attribution to the authorship of the famous Nāgārjuna. But the absence of any reference to it, in the works of Śāntideva, particularly in his chapters on *Bodhicitta*, may go against such an antiquity of the text.

The commencement of Jayānanda's translation is as follows:

Da nas byaṅ chub kyi sems sgom pa'i 'grel pa bśad par bya'o l bcom ldan 'das kyis chos thams cad sems kyis rnam par brtags pa'o zes l gsuṅs pas ri zig sems ni de ñid kyi raṅ bñin ci zig zes ṅes par rtog pa rcan l dṅos pa thams cad daṅ bral ba phuṅ po khams daṅ skye mched daṅ gzuṅ daṅ 'jan ba rnam par spaṅs l. ches bdag med par mñam ñid pas l. raṅ sems gdoṅ nas ma skyes pa l. stoṅ pa ñid kyi raṅ bzin no l. zes gsuṅs so l. smras pa 'di yi don ci yin ze na l. brjod pa dṅos po daṅ bral zes te l.

वोधिचित्त-विवरणं वक्ष्ये। चित्तविटपिता सर्वधर्मा दूत्युक्तं भगवता। देवतावच्चित्तं निरुध्यते (?)। किं स्वभावमिति आह-सर्वभावविगतं स्कन्धधात्वायतन-ग्राह्यग्राहकवजितं धर्मनैरात्मासमतया [स्व] चित्तमाद्यनुत्पन्नं शूत्यता स्वभावमिति। कोऽस्य वचनस्वार्थः— सर्वभावविगतमिति।

This is sufficient to point out to the close agreement of the text and the translation of Jayānanda. The text deals with one of the most important Mahāyāna doctrines. The discovery of the complete manuscript of the text will, therefore, be eagerly looked for.

Chapter - 7
Bodhicittavivaraṇa
Prabhubhai Patel

While proceeding with my *Studies on the Bodhichitta-texts, Tibetan and Chinese*, I read with much interest the notes on the *Bodhicittavivaraṇa* by Drs. Nalinaksha Dutt and P.C.Bagchi in the *Indian Historical Quarterly*, vol. VII.pp. 285ff. and 74off. The *Bodhicittavivaraṇa* No.I (Tib. *byañ, chub, sems. kyi. 'grel. pa, zes. bya. ba*, Cordier II, p. 135, No. 5; Tanjur, Rgyud, Gi, fol. 46 b. 2-49 a. 5), which Dr. Bagchi in his note referred to above identifies with the text mentioned in the last leaf of the MS. of the *Bodhisattvaprātimokṣasūtra* published by Dr. Dutt in the same journal, pp. 259-286, mentioned above, is not identical with the other two Tibetan texts of the same title. viz. *Bodhicittavivaraṇa* No. 2 (Tib. *byañ, chub, sems. kyi. 'grel. ba*, Cordier II, p. 135, No. 6; Tanjur, Rgyud, Gi, fol. 41 b. 5-45 b. 2) and *Bodhicittavivaraṇa* No. 3 (Tib. *byañ, chub, kyi. sems. kyi. rnam. par. bśad. pa*, Cordier III, p. 358, No. 93; Tanjur, Mdo, Gi, fol. 210 b. 4-216 a. 7).

Now the first text among the three is a prose commentary on a prose passage, which defines the true nature of *bodhicitta* and is, in fact, identical with a prose passage in the *Guhyasamājatantra* (GOS, vol.LIII,p.12).[1] Besides the Tibetan translations, it has also a chinese translation named *phu-thi-sin-kuân-shih* (Nanjio, p. 199), in Skt. as Nanjio would render, *Bodhihṛdayadhyānavyākhyā*. But the same Chinese title may be translated into Skt. as *Bodhicittabhāvanāvivaraṇam*.[2]

The other two texts are two Tibetan translations of one and the same Skt. work. The original work, like the prose commentary mentioned

---

1. सर्वभावविगतं स्कन्धधात्वायतनग्राह्यग्राहकवर्जितं धर्मनैरात्म्यसमतया स्वचित्तमा-अनुत्पन्नं शून्यताभावम्।
2. See the *Alphabetical Index of the Buddhist Tripiṭaka*, ed. D. Tokiwa and thers, Tokyo, 1930, p. 125.

above, is also a commentary in verse on the same prose passage referred to above. It does not comment on the original passage verbatim, but gives an elaborate explanation of it. Both the translations agree as regards the number of verses, which is one hundred and ten. The work begins with a prose passage wherein the author states the purpose of his undertaking to write this commentary. At the end of this passage the original title of the work is found to be amplified as *Bodhicittabhāvanāvivaraṇam* which is supposed by the Chinese version of *Bodhicittavivaraṇam* No. I, referred to above.

The *Bodhicittavivaraṇa-ṭīkā* (Tib. *braṅ. chub. sems. kyi. 'grel. pa'i. rnam. par. bśad. pa.* Cordier, II, p. 141, No. 34 ; Tanjur, Rgyud, Gi, fol. 449 b. 4ff.), referred to by Dr. Bagchi in his note, is a sub-commentary of *Bodhicittavivaraṇa*, No. 2. It definitely mentions *Guhyasamājatantra*[1] as the source of the prose passage defining the true nature of the *Bodhicitta*.

All the five texts mentioned above, except the Chinese one, (which is silent on the point), attribute the authorship of the original two commentaries to *Ārya Nāgārjuna*. The *Subhhāṣitasaṃgraha* (ed. Bendall, p. 20), wherein verse No. 29 of the *Bodhicittavivaraṇa* No. 2, is cited, supports this attribution. The author of the *Bodhicittavivaraṇaṭīkā* further informs us that this *Ārya Nāgārjuna* was the resident of *Śrīparvata* and the sacrificator of the *Nāgas*.[2] It is not certain whether this *Ārya Nāgārjuna* is identical with the *Nāgārjuna* of the Mādhyamika or the Vajrayāna school. The fact that the texts of the Tibetan versions of these works happen to be included in a volume which contains many works[5] written by the later *Nāgārjuna* and not a single work written by the former one, indicates that the author of the two *Bodhicittavivaraṇas* may be *Ārya Nāgārjuna* of the Vajrayāna school.

Some verses of the *Bodhicittavivaraṇa*, No.2 are cited in different Skt. works of the Mahāyānists. These verses, so far as I have been able to identify, are given below:

Ṣaḍdarśanasamuccaya of Haribhadra, Bibl. Indica, 1905, p. 46:

वेदनारूपसंस्कारसंज्ञाविज्ञानमेव च ॥ 11[4] a—b ||

---

1. See Tanjur, Rgyud, Gi, fols. 449*b.7* and 479*a.5*.
2. *Ibid*.
3. See Cordier, II pp. 134 ff.
4. This and similar figures at the end of the verses refer to their numbers in the work mentioned.

Madhyamakavṛtti, Bibliotheca Buddhica, 1903, p. 41:

फेनपिण्डोपमं रूपं वेदना बुद्बुदोपमा।

मरीचिसदृशी संज्ञा संस्काराः कदलीनिभाः ॥12 ॥

मायोपमं च विज्ञानम्......... ॥13a ॥

Sarvadarśanasaṃagraha, Government Oriental Hindu Series, Poona, p. 30.

परिव्राट्कामुकशुनामेकस्यां प्रमदातनौ।

कुणपः कामिनी भक्ष्य इति तिस्रो विकल्पनाः ॥19 ॥[1]

Subhāṣitasaṃgraha, ed. Bendall. p. 20:

चित्तमात्रमिदं सर्वमिति या देशना मुनेः।

उत्रासपरिहारार्थं बालानां सा न तत्त्वतः ॥26 ॥

Bodhicaryāvatārapañjikā, Bibl. Indica, 1903, pp. 406, 421:

न बोध्यबोधकाकारं चित्तं दृष्टं तथागतैः।

यत्र बोध्या च बोध्यं च तत्र बोधिर्न विद्यते ॥44 ॥

अलक्षणमनुत्पादमसंस्कृतमवाङ्मयम्।

आकाशं बोधिचित्तं च बोधिरद्वयलक्षणा ॥45 ॥

Bauddhagān O Dohā ed. Haraprasada Śāstrī, p. 68:

शून्यतासिंहनादेन त्रासिताः सर्वशत्रवः ॥51 a-b ॥

Advayavajrasaṃgraha, GOS., vol. XL, 42:

गुडे मधुरता चाग्नेरुष्णत्वं प्रकृतिर्यथा।

शून्यता सर्वधर्माणां तथा प्रकृतिरिष्यते ॥56 ॥

Sarvadarśanasaṃagraha, p. 44.

देशना लोकनाथानां सत्त्वाशयवशानुगाः।

भिद्यन्ते बहुधा लोक उपायैर्बहुभिः पुनः ॥97 ॥

गम्भीरोत्तानभेदेन क्वचिद्वोभयलक्षणा।

भिन्ना हि देशनाभिन्ना शून्यताद्वयलक्षणा ॥98 ॥

---

1. This Kārikā is quoted in many works, such as *Savasiddhānta-sangraha*, Madras, 1909, p.12.

In conclusion it may be pointed out that according to the Tibetan passage (either wrongly printed or wrongly copied) cited by Dr. Bagchi (IHQ., vol. VII, p. 741), one may read in Sanskrit passage published by Dr. Dutt (op. cit. p. 285) **cittabhāvanā** (*sems. sgom. pa*) for **citta*, * *vikalpitaḥ* (*rnam. par. brtags. pa*) for **viṭhapitaḥ*, *tadeva* (*de ñid*) for '*deva**, *nirūpyate* (*ṅes. par. rtog(s). pa*) for *niruthyate* and *svacittam* (*raṅ sems*) for *cittam*.

P. S. When the above was going through the Press it was found that the *Lakṣaṇavimukta*(?)-*bodhihṛdayaśāstra* (Nanjio 1304). '*The treatise* (or *discourse*) *on the transcendentality of the Bodhicitta*' (vide the *Outlines of the Mahāyāna Buddhism* by Suzuki, pp. 292, 297.), attributed to Nāgārjuna is nothing but a prose version of the *Bodhicittavivaraṇa*. No.2.

Chapter - 8
Bodhisattva Prātimokṣa Sūtra
Nalinaksha Dutt

Prātimokṣasūtra of the Hīnayānists

The *Prātimokṣasūtra* forms the keystone of the disciplinary literature of the Buddhists. It is fortunate that not only the *Pātimokkhasutta* of the Theravādins in Pali but also the *Prātimokṣa-sūtra* of the Sarvāstivādins in Sanskrit are available for study. The later has been discovered by the Pelliot mission in the ruins of Douldour-áquor at Koutcha, and edited and published by Monsieur Ē. Huber in the *Journal Asiatique* (1913) along with a French translation of Kumārajīva's Chinese version of the work. This has been supplemented by Prof. La Vallée Poussin and Herr E. Waldschmidt. Prof. Poussin has published a fragment of the *Prātimokṣa* manuscript and the Sanskrit "*Kammavācā*"[1] belonging to the Stein Collection, as also a fragment of the Sanskrit *Bhikṣuṇī Karmavacana* (Oxford Sanskrit Ms. 1442) in collaboration with Miss C.M. Ridding, while Mr. Waldschmidt has brought out with ample philological and comparative notes the *Bhikṣuṇī-Prātimokṣa* and *Bhikṣuṇī-Vibhaṅga* of the Sarvāstivādins from the fragmentary manuscripts discovered and collected by the Prussian Turfan-expedition. The manuscripts of the *Bhikṣuṇī-Prātimokṣa* were found in Qyzil and Sangim, while those of the *Bhikṣuṇī-Vibhaṅga* were traced in the collection of paper manuscripts at Murtuq. The Chinese and Tibetan sources have also furnished us with ample materials for an exhaustive study of the *Prātimkoṣa-sūtra*, and therefore, of the *Vinaya* of the various Hīnayānic schools. Waldschmidt has fully utilised the Chinese and Tibetan versions of *Bhikṣuṇī-Prātimokṣa* and *Bhikṣuṇī-Vibhaṅga* in his work mentioned above. The editions of the *Prātimokṣa-sūtras* have greatly advanced our knowledge in as much as they have thrown light on the question of the probable form and language of the original *Prātimokṣ*

1. *JRAS.*, 1913, p. 843 ff: Nouveaux fragments de la collection Stein.

a-sūtras of the 4th or 3rd century B.C., and have thus served to suggest a solution of the knotty problem as to the language of the original Tripiṭaka.[1]

Prātimokṣasūtra of the Mahāyānists

Though our knowledge of the Hīnayānic *Prātimokṣasūtras* has made a fair progress, we are yet in the dark about the *Prātimokṣ asūtra* of the Mahāyānists. It is only through the citations made by Śāntideva in his *Śikṣāsamuccaya* and *Bodhicaryāvatāra* that we are aware of the existence of a *Bodhisattva-Prātimokṣa-sūtra*. Very likely it is this Sūtra that corresponds to the Chinese Sūtra no. 1500 (Pu-sa-chieh-pen) of the Taisho edition of the Chinese Tripiṭaka (vol.xxiv) which treats of Pārājikā and such other offences falling within the scope of a Prātimokṣa-sūtra. The only other Mahāyānic book that can be treated as a Prātimokṣa-sūtra is the Chinese *Brahma-jāla Sūtra*, of which we have a French translation (*Le code du Mahāyāna en Chine*) by De Groot.[2]

At the Library of the Cambridge University, there is a manuscript entitled *Bodhisattva Prātimokṣa Sūtra* in the collection made by Bendall from Nepal. Through the courtesy of Dr. E.J.Thomas I have been able to take a rotograph of the manuscript. It contains only ten leaves withsix lines in each page. The size of the leaf is 10 inches by 2 inches. The right-hand end of almost every leaf is so much damaged that the last word of almost each line is either lost or illegible. In the appended edition I have supplied the words as far as possible in the light of their Chinese translations where available as also of their context, and the manner of wording usual in the Buddhist Sanskrit texts.

In line 1 of the last leaf (obverse side) of the ms., we find "*Iti Bodhisattva-Prātimokṣaḥ*" (see the attached plate) showing that the writer wanted to call the work a *Bodhisattva Prātimokṣa Sūtra*. Whatever may be the writer's intention, it is evident from the contents that the present manuscript has very little to do with the *Bodhisattva Prātimokṣa Sūtra* cited in the works of Śāntideva.

The Present Manuscript

This manuscript is divided into two parts, of which the first is intended to serve as a manual for the initiation of devotees, lay or recluse, into the Mahāyānic rules of discipline, and the second is a

1. See Sylvain Lévi, JA., 1912: Hoernle, *Manuscript Remains of Buddhist Literature in Eastern Trukestan*, pp. 173-5
2. For further particulars, see my *Aspects of Mahāyāna Buddhism etc.*, pp. 293-5.

dissertation on the *āpattis* (offences) and *anāpattis* (non-offences) of a Bodhisattva. The whole manuscript is really a compilation of extracts from different works, two of which evidently are the *Bodhisattvabhūmi* and the *Upālipariprcchāsūtra*. The citations from the *Bodhisattvabhūmi* appear in the first part and have been marked in the appended text. The *Upālipariprcchāsūtra* commences from leaf 5 (reverse side-see the attached plate). Judging by the contents, the first part should be called a *Karmavākya*, corresponding to the *Kammavācam* of the Burmese and Ceylonese Buddhists, and not a Prātimokṣa-sūtra, the second part being a supplement to it. The first part corresponds roughly to the first chapter (Ordination service) of the *Kammavācam*, detailing the formalities through which a candidate is to pass to undertake the discipline of a Bodhisattva. In the *Bodhicaryāvatāra* we have an account of the ceremony of initiation of a Bodhisattva but it is written not in the characteristic form and style of a manual of initiation-the form and style in which the present ms. is written. It is in this manuscript that we for the first time come across the formal requests and announcements necessary for the initiation of a devotee into Mahāyānic rules of discipline, and I think, this is the earliest book of its kind so far discovered.

Probable age of the Ms.

The ms. is written, as will be seen from the attached plates, in Rañjā character, a very old script prevalent in Nepal about the 11th or 12th century A.D. Prof. Bendall has rendered easy our task of fixing the dates of Nepalese manuscripts by furnishing us with the tables of letters and numerals from dated mss. of various times from the 9th to 18th century A.D.[1] If the present manuscript be placed by the side of this table, it will be apparent that its letters and numerals are similar to those of the Cambridge University Library Mss. Nos. Add. 1693 and 1686, both of which have been dated by Bendall to be 1165 A.D. Of the letters, the following may be particularly mentioned as bearing the closest resemblance to those to Ms. No. 1686:-*e, ja, tha, dha, śa, ṣa* and *sa*. Of the numerals 2, 3, 4, 8 and 9 are exactly similar to those of Ms. No. Add. 1693, and 5 and 6 to those of Ms. No. Add. 1644. The date of the former ms., according to Bendall, is 1165 A.D. and that of the latter is 1139 A.D. Hence, we shall not be wide of the mark if we put the date of the present manuscript as the 12th century A.D. and its composition, say, about a century or two earlier, i.e., about the 10th or 11th century A.D.

---

1. Bendall, *Catalogue of the Buddhist Sanskrit Manuscripts*

The Ceremony of Initiation in Some of the Late Works

The ceremony of initiation is described incidentally not only in the *Bodhicaryāvatāra* but also in two other late works, viz., the *Advayavajrasaṅgraha* and the *Kriyāsaṅgrahapañjikā*.

In the *Kudṛṣṭinirghātana*, a section of the *Advayavajrasaṅgraha* recently edited by Mm. H.P. Śāstri, there is a reference to the ceremony of *Poṣadha* (Uposatha) performed by a lay-devotee. It is exactly similar to the practice still current among the Hīnayāna Buddhists in Chittagong, Burma and Ceylon. On some Uposatha days, a lay-devotee, after taking *Triśaraṇa*, takes the vow of observing eight of the ten *śīlas* for one day or more.[1] Usually a lay-devotee of the Hīnayāna school is required to observe only five *śīlas*. The *Advayavajrasaṅgraha*[2] also prescribes the same[3] for *Gṛhapati Bodhisattvas*. To this it, however adds the mantric rituals which included among other things not only a reference to the practice of *Maitrī* (Love), *Karuṇā* (Compassion), *Muditā* (Joy), and *Upekṣā* (Indifference), but also to *Pāpadeśanā*, *Anumodanā* and *Bodhicitta*.[4] It is this additional ritual that gives a Mahāyānic or Mahāyāna-Tāntric garb to the Hīnayānic ceremony.

In the *Kriyāsaṅgrahapañjikā* (A. S. B. ms.) there are not only directions for the selection of building sites for the monasteries, etc., but also an account of the duties of the Ācārya and the *Upādhyāya* towards their disciple and *vice versa*, and of the formalities for receiving a candidate into the clerical order. Mm. H. P. Śāstrī has facilitated our work by reproducing in full in his *Catalogues of Buddhist Manuscripts* (pp. 123-6) the passage containing the rules of ordination. The passage may be summarised as follows:-

Pravrajyā and *Upasampadā* ordinations are to be given be an *Ācārya* and an *Upādhyāya*. The bhikṣus did not know how to confer an ordination, so they enquired of Buddha, who gave the following directions:-

(i) The candidate should be first questioned as to whether he had any of the disqualification debarring him from reception into the Buddhist Order.

(ii) If he is found fit, he is to be imparted the *Upāsakasaṃvaras* (disciplines meant for lay-devotees), viz., *Triśaraṇagamana* and five *Śikṣāpadas*.

---

1. *Advayavajrasaṅgraha*, p.4.
2. *Ibid.*
3. *Ibid* - गृहपतिबोधिसत्त्वस्तु रत्नत्रयशरणपुरःसरं प्राणातिपातात् अदत्तादानाह् काममिथ्याचारात् मृवावादात् प्रकृतिसावद्यात् मद्यपानात् च पञ्चभ्यो विरतः।
4. *Ibid.*

(iii) He is then to choose his Ācārya and Upādhyāya.

(iv) Next he is shaved (leaving a tuft of hair) and asked whether he is still resolute to retire from household life.

(v) He is then given a new name after the school (*nikāya*) to which he belongs and made to take again the *Triśaraṇas* in his new name.

(vi) He is now to take the vow of observing the ten *Śikṣāpadas*.

(vii) He then takes the robe, bowl and the student's waterpot by uttering suitable mantras. And

(viii) Lastly he promises to observe the Uposathas and attain the five groups of acquirements, viz., *śīla*, *samādhi*, *prajñā*, *vimukti*, and *vimuktijñānadarśana*.[1]

Mm.H.P. Śāstrī is of opinion that his was the form of ordination followed by the Mahāyānists,[2] his supposition being based on the fact that the manuscript belongs to one of the last developed schools of Mahāyāna. The ceremony summarised above is, in fact, Hīnayānic without any indication which would give it a Mahāyānic tinge except that a Mahāyānic school has adopted it as its own. The absence of mention of 'Sarvabuddhas' and 'Bodhisattvas', not to speak of the high sounding promises and aspirations of a Bodhisattva, leads us to the belief that the work may have belonged to the later Mahāyānic period, but the rules of initiation given in it are taken *in toto* from some Hīnayānic book of rituals, probably a Sanskrit *Karmavākya*.[3]

In the manuscript of the *Kriyāsaṅgraha*[4] (leaf 36b = *Pañjikāsaṅgraha*, leaf 198b) preserved in the Bibliotheque Nationale, there is a passage containing a description of *Saṃvaragrahaṇa* written in the same style as that in the present manuscript. It turns as follows:

एवं विंशतिप्रकारपूजाभिः सर्वतथागतान् संपूज्य आत्मानं निर्यातयेत्। आत्मानं सर्वबुद्धबोधिसत्त्वेभ्यो निर्यातयामि। सर्वदा सर्वकालं प्रतिगृहन्तु मां महाकारुणिका नाथा महासमयसिद्धिभ्य मे प्रयच्छन्तु।

तश्च कुशलमूर्ल सर्वसत्त्वसाधारणं कर्तव्यम्। अनेन कुशलमूलेन सव4सत्त्वाः सर्वलौकिकलोकोत्तरविपत्तिविगता भवन्तु। सर्वलौकिकलोकोत्तरसम्पत्तिसमन्विताश्च सहैव सुखेन सहैव सौमनस्येन बुद्धा भगवन्तो भवन्तु नरोत्तमाः।

---

1. For the meaning of these terms, see *Visuddhimagga*, p. 234; *Milinda*, p. 98; *Mādhyamikavṛtti*, p. 433.
2. H.P. Śāstrī, op. cit., p. 126.
3. Cf. *Bhikṣuṇījarnavacana*, a fragment of which has been published by Miss M. Ridding and L. de la Vallēe Poussin; for the Pali *Kammavācam*, see JTAS., vol. VII (Ns.), pp. 1f.
4. It is a part of the *Pañjikāsaṅgraha*, commencing at leaf 163.

अनेन चाहं कुशलेन कर्मणा भवेयं बुद्धो, न चिरेण लोके देशयेयं धर्म्मं जगतो हिताय, मोचयेयं सत्त्वान् बहुदुःखपीड़ितान्। नित्यानुत्तरायां सम्यक्सम्बोदौ परिणामयेत्॥ इति बोधिचित्तोत्पादः॥ उत्पादयामि परमं बोधिचित्तमनुत्तरम्॥ इति संवरग्रहणम्॥

(Translation: After worshipping all Tathāgatas in twenty different ways, one should offer himself up, saying "I dedicate myself to all Buddhas and Bodhisattvas. Accept me always and for all times, O Merciful Lords, and give me the Mahāsamayasiddhi (lit. perfection in the great doctrine).[1]

He should wish that the merits thus acquired be shared by all beings, and thereby may all beings be free from their calamities, worldly or transcendental, and be possessed of prosperity, worldly or transcendental, and may they, easily and happily, become Buddhas, the Blessed Ones, the best of men.

By this good action may I become a Buddha, and soon preach the doctrine for the benefit of the world, and rescue beings from their many suffering. Thus he should always direct his merits to the incomparable highest knowledge. This is called the 'Development of Bodhicitta'. This is acquiring 'Bodhisattva-discipline'

This passage is preceded by a formulary ending with the remark इति पापदेशना and is followed by a description of the ceremony with the ending इति आचार्य्याभिषेकः.

In this description, the rituals for *Saṃvaragrahaṇa* occur in the following order:-

(1) Pāpadeśanā,

(2) Pūjana and Vandanā,

(3) Pariṇāmanā,

(4) Bodhicittotpāda and

(5) Ācāryābhiṣeka.

In the *Bodhicaryāvatāra* also, Śāntideva treats of the formalities to be undergone by a Bodhisattva for initiation. As they have been dealt with at length in my book, *Aspects of Mahāyāna Buddhism* (pp. 302-5), I shall mention here only the rites composing the ceremony:

(1) Vandanā and Pūjana (worshipping Buddhas and Caityas);

(2) Śaraṇagamana (taking refuge in Buddha, Dharma and Saṅgha)

(3) Anumodanā or Puṇyānumodanā (expressions of sincere approval of others' good deeds),

---

1. There is a Tibetan text called *Mahāsamayasūtra*, for details of which see Wassiljew, *Der Buddhismus*, p. 176.

(4) Adhyeṣaṇā or Yācanā (entreating Buddha to be the guide of all beings ignorant as they are),

(5) Pariṇāmanā (offering up one's merits to all beings for the sake of bodhi)[1] and then

(6) Bodhicittotpāda (development of Bodhicitta).

First Part of the Ms.

The contents of the first part, in short, are as follows:- An adept approaches a qualified Bodhisattva, and entreats him in set words for initiation into the disciplinary rules of a Bodhisattva. Then he confesses his sins (pratideśanā) formally and takes refuge in the Triratna by uttering the Triśaraṇa formulae. He now develops Bodhicitta, and transfers (pariṇāmanā) the merits so far acquired by the above rites to all beings as of the world and takes the vow of looking upon all beings as his very near kith and kin. He then formally chooses *(ācāryābhiṣ -eka)* his Ācārya who presents him to all the Buddhas and the Bodhisattvas and announces before them that so and so has been ordained by him called so and so.

It adds that if an adept cannot find a qualified Bodhisattva to give him the initiation, he should present himself before the image of a Tathāgata and declare his intention. He should then proceed with the ceremonies described above.

From this account it is apparent that the present manuscript served only as a manual of ordination, containing as it does, the formulae for the rites mentioned in the Mahāyāna works noticed before. The rites mentioned above are arranged thus:-

(1) Yācanā (entreating a Boddhisattva for initiation),

(2) Pāpadeśanā,

(3) Śaraṇgamana,

(4) Pariṇāmanā

(5) Bodhicittotpāda,

(6) Ācāryābhiṣeka, and

(7) Vijñapti (=Pāli: Ñatti=Announcement).

The Second Part of the Ms.

The second part, as stated above, is made up of extracts from the *Upālipariprcchāsūtra*, from which citations are found in the *Mādhyamikavṛtti*, *Śikṣāsamuccaya* and *Bodhicaryāvatāra*.

---

1. Cf. *Sūtrālaṅkāra*, p. 147: क्षिप्राभिसंबोधे सर्व पापं प्रतिदेशयामि यावत् भवतु मे ज्ञानं संबोधायेति प्रतिदेशनाऽनुमोदनाध्येषणा परिणामना।

In leaf 5b, line 5, it is stated that Upāli had some doubts in his mind regarding the Vinaya of the Mahāyānists and wanted to have them removed by the Teacher. His request to Buddha "*vyākarotutathāgato vinayaviniścayaṃ*" leads us to identify the work with the Chinese translation *Yiu-po-li-hwui* or *Fo-shwo-chüe-tiṅ-phi-ni-kiṅ* restored by Nanjio as *Vinayaviniścaya Upāli Paripṛcchā* [Nanjio, nos. 23 (24) & 36].[1] These two Chinese translations correspond to the Sūtra no. 325 [no.310 (24)] of the Taisho edition of the Chinese Tripiṭ aka, vol. XII, pp. 37-42-*Fo-shui-chüeh-ting-phi-ni-king*. On a comparison of the Sanskrit text as given in the present manuscript with the Chinese translation (Taisho ed., XII, no. 325), we notice that it corresponds to the Chinese translation not from the beginning but from page 39, sec. iii, line 15 upto page 40, sec, iii, line 16, including the inquiry of Mañjuśrīkumābhūta. This comparison reveals that the present ms. gives only extract from the *Upālipariprcchāsūtra* and not the whole of it. The original was larger and contained a versified portion, from which quotations are found in the *Mādhyamikavṛtti* (pp. 53, 121, 155, 191, 234, 256, 408). The last portion (Taisho ed., vol. XII, p. 41, sec. 2 to p. 42, sec. 3) of the Chinese version clearly shows that there were many verses in the original *Sūtra* towards its end. The quotations given in the *Mādhyamikavṛtti* from the *Sūtra* are authentic because the Sanskrit verses agree with those of the Chinese, e.g., in page 155, the verse: Iha śāsani suramaṇīye etc. agrees literally with its Chinese version (p. 42, sec. i, last line & fol.).

Now, if we take into consideration the quotations found in the *Śikṣāsamuccaya* and the *Bodhicaryāvatāra*, we cannot have any room for doubt as to our manuscript presenting us only with extracts from the original *Upālipariprcchāsūtra*. In three places, the *Śikṣāsamuccaya* has quoted the *Sūtra*. Two (pp. 164,* 178) of the three passages appear in the present manuscript. On comparison it becomes evident that in the *Śikṣāsamuccaya* there is an attempt to put the quotations in an abridged form. The passage cited on pp. 168-9 of the *Śikṣāsamuccaya*[2] when compared with its Chinese version (p. 38, sec. iii, II. 4 ff.) shows also that the quotation is given in a very concise form; so also is the citation[3] at p. 178.

The main object of the second part of the manuscript is to point out the two standpoints, from which the disciplinary rules were viewed by the Hīnayānists and the Mahāyānists.[4] In short, the path of

1. Cf. Tib. *Vinayaviniścaya Upālipariprcchānāma* (f. 220-243) of the Narthang edition of Kañjur (Ratnakūṭa section), vol. XXIV.
* Cf. *Bodhicaryāvatāra*, p. 139.
2. Cf. *Bodhicaryāvatāra*, pp. 153-4.
3. See text, leaf 7a, 1. 5 f.n.
4. For further elucidation, see my *Aspects of Mahāyāna Buddhism, etc.*, ch. V.

the disciplinary rules of the Mahāyānists lay in service to all beings, while that of the Hīnayānists was self-purification. This has been clearly brought out in the second portion of the manuscript, where we find the following comparisons:

1. That which is meritorious for a Bodhisattva is demeritorious for a Śrāvaka, and *vice versa*: To wit, a Bodhisattva desires for repeated births in order to be able to render service to all beings while a Śrāvaka cannot even for a moment cherish thoughts for rebirths.

2. The aim of a Bodhisattva is to work for the good of other beings (सानुरक्षा शिक्षा) but this is not necessary for a Śrāvaka (निरनुरक्षा शिक्षा).

3. If a Bodhisattva, after committing an offence, strives for a while to develop and maintain the Bodhicitta (=sarvajñatācitta), he can absolve himself from the offence (सपरिहारा शिक्षा) but this is not possible for a Śrāvaka (निःपरिहारा शिक्षा), for the latter should always be on the alert to get rid of *kleśas* (afflictions) like a man whose headdress is burning.

4. A Bodhisattva may partake of worldly enjoyments but he should at the same time maintain the *Bodhicitta*, and try to get rid of his *kleśas* (afflictions) by undergoing many births and not one (दुरानुभविष्टा शिक्षा). A Śrāvaka, however, should acquire all the *kuśalamūlas* (merit-roots) and be always vigilant like the man with a burning headdress (सावदाना शिक्षा).

5. If a Bodhisattva be guilty of actions done through *rāga* (attachment) and *dveṣa* (hatred), he is exonerated from sin in regard to those done through *rāga* but not in regard to those done through *dveṣa*, because *rāga* makes him attached to his fellow beings (सत्त्वसंग्रहाय वर्त्तते) while *dveṣa* makes him dissociated (सत्त्वपरित्यागाय वत्तते) from them, for a Śrāvaka, however, offences committed either through *rāga* or through *dveṣa* and equally blamable.

The Third Part of the Ms.

We are at present unable to give any particulars about the third part of the manuscript as there are only a few lines of it on the last leaf. From these few lines, it is however clear that the writer wanted to explain here the *Bodhicitta, Dharmanairātmya*, etc. by commenting upon some texts. It is rather striking that in the manuscript of the *Kriyāsaṅgraha* belonging to the Bibliotheque Nationale, there appears also a dissertation on Śūnya as similar to Ākāśa and so forth just after the ceremony of *Saṃavaragrahaṇa*. Other scholars will, I hope, take up this clue in future and complete the work by tracing the missing pages atleast its contents.[1]

1. A photoprint of the leaf where the comment is found is attached hereto.

TEXT

बोधिसत्त्व-प्रातिमोक्ष-सूत्रम्

Leaf 1b ॐ नमः सर्व्वबुद्धबोधिसत्त्वेभ्यः । ये च ते बोधिसत्त्वानां त्रयः शीलस्कन्धा उक्ताः ।
* a[2]
संवरशी[लं कुशलधर्म्मसंग्राहकशीलं सत्त्वार्थक्रियाशीलं[1] च ते]षु

---

* The passages within brackets [ ] have been supplied by me as the ms. is either broken or illegible at these places.

1. The passage, marked *a-d* (see leaf 2b), occurs almost *verbatim* in the *Bodhisattvabhūmi* (edition of Wogihara-Tokya 1930), pp. 152-3, where it is preceded by a detailed explanation of the three *Śīlaskandhas*, which, in short, are as follows:-

(i) संवरशीला: are all those disciplinary (Prātimokṣa) rules given in the seven (?) *nikāyas* and meant for the Bodhisattvas; they are to be practised by monks and nuns, male and female novices and lay-devotees.

(ii) कुशलधर्म्मसंग्राहकशीला: are all those good deeds performed by a Bodhisattva, physically or verbally, for attaining the highest wisdom (mahābodhi) after taking the śīlasaṃvaras (disciplines). To wit: a Bodhisattva after being well-established in śīlas, applies himself to study and contemplation, meditation (शमथ: चित्तैकाग्रतालक्षण: समाधि: -*Bodhic.*, p.287) and insight (विपश्यना—यथाभूततत्त्वपरिज्ञानस्वभावा प्रज्ञा - *Ibid.*) and finds pleasure in loneliness; shows respects to his guru in time and so forth.

(iii) सत्त्वानुग्राहकशीला: These śīlas or good deeds are of eleven kinds, as follows:-

(1) rendering friendly help (sahāyībhāvaḥ) to beings in their useful works;

(2) rendering friendly help to beings suffering from disease and so forth;

(3) giving just admonition to persons through religious discourse, or discourses on ways and means in their mundane or supremundane objects;

(4) not only remaining grateful to a benefactor but also giving him a suitable return;

(5) protecting persons from various causes of fear, e.g., lions, tigers, kings, thieves, fire, etc.

(6) consoling persons suffering on account of loss of property or relatives;

(7) offering justly (न्यायपतित:) all the necessary means of livelihood to persons who have been deprived of them;

(8) correcting a body of persons by means of proper gifts and religious discourses (सम्यक्निश्रयदानतो धर्म्मेण गणपरिकर्षणा);

(9) pleasing others by conversations, exchange of greetings, timely visits, acceptance of others' invitations to food and drink, joining, if invited, the people's worldly celebrations, in short, to avoid all actions which might displease others and to gladden them by one's own qualities;

(10) subduing, fatiguing, punishing and exiling people in order to turn them from evil to good actions by making patent to them things manifest or unmanifest and by good and tender inner will;

(11) frightening people from evils and establishing them in Buddha's doctrine by showing them hells through supernatural power and thereby causing astonishment.

बोधिसत्त्व-प्रातिमोक्ष-सूत्रम्

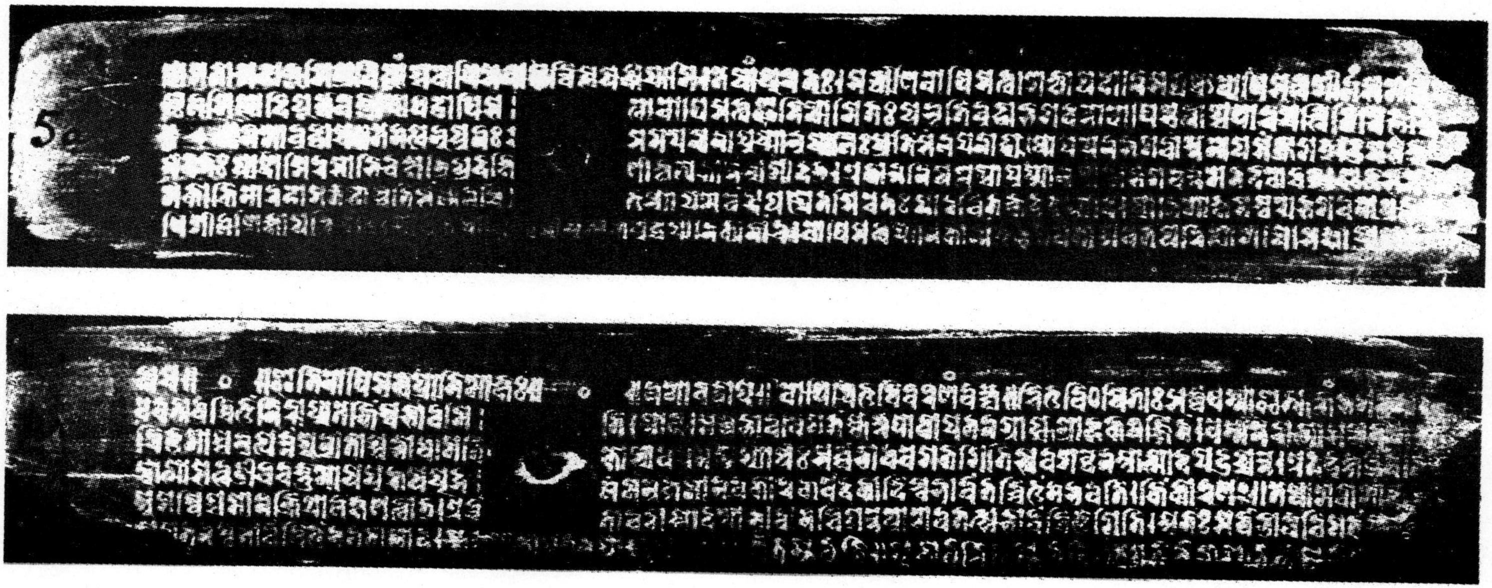

शिक्षितुकामेन गृहिणा वा प्रव्रजितेन वाऽनुत्तरायां सम्यक्सम्बोधौ कृतप्रणिधानेन सहधार्म्मिकस्य

[3]

बोधिसत्त्वश्च[स्य[1] महापुण्यनिधा]नस्य[2] वाग्विज्ञप्त्यर्थग्रहणावबोध-समर्थस्य[3] पादयोर्न्निप-

त्याध्येषणा कार्य्या। तवाहं कुलपुत्रायुष्मन् भदन्तेति वाऽन्तिकात्[4] बोधिसत्त्व [शीलसं]

[4]

वरसमादानमाकाङ्क्षाम्यादातुम्। तदर्हस्यनुपरोधेन मुहूर्त्तं[5] मदनुकम्पया दातुं श्रोतुञ्चेति॥

[5]

त्रिरेवमध्येष्य[6] एकांस-मुत्तरासङ्गं कृत्वा [द]शसु दिक्ष्वतीतानागतप्रत्युत्पन्नानां बुद्धानां भगवतां

[6]

महाभूमिप्रविष्टानां[7] च[8] बोधिसत्त्वानां सामीचीं कृत्वा तेषां गुणानामुखीकृत्य [धन]रसं

चेतःप्रसादं संजनय्य[9] नीचैर्जानुमण्डलेनोत्कुटुकेन वा स्थित्वा तथागतप्रतिमां पुरतः संस्थाप्य

संपूज्य पुरस्कृत्यैवं स्याद्वचनीयः।

[1]

Leaf 2a अनु प्रयच्छ मे कुलपुत्रायुष्मन् भदन्तेति वा बोधिसत्त्वशीलसंवरसमादानमिति।

[2]

तत[10] एकामां स्मृतिमुपस्थाप्य चित्तप्रसादमेवानुवृंहयत। न चिरस्येदानीं मेऽक्षयस्याप्रमेयस्य

निरुत्तरस्य महापुण्यनिधानस्य प्राप्तिर्भविष्यतीति। [11]एव-मेवार्थमनु[वि]चिन्तयता तूष्णीं

[3]

भवितव्यम्। तेन पुनर्व्विज्ञेन बोधिसत्त्वेन स तथा प्रतिपन्नो बोधिसत्त्वोऽविक्षिप्तेन चेतसा स्थितेन

[4]

वा निषण्णेन वा एवं स्याद्वचनीयः। शृणु त्वमेवन्ना[मन् कुलपुत्रायुष्मन[12] भदन्तेति वा[13]

---

1. *B. Bh.*, p. 152 reads: – सत्त्वस्य कृतप्रणिधानतया विज्ञस्य प्रतिबलस्य वाग्-।
2. Cf. *Bodhic.*, p. 72: – देशयामीति वाग्विज्ञप्तिमुत्थापयति। कृताञ्जलिरिति कायविज्ञप्तिः।
3. *B. Bh.*, p. 153:– बोधाय इत्येवंरूपस्य बोधिसत्त्वस्य पूर्व पादयोः-।
4. *B. Bh.*, p. 153:–अध्येषणां कृत्वा यथा तवाहं कुलपुत्रान्तिकात्।
5. *Ibid.* अस्माकं।
6. *Ibid* श्रोतुञ्चेत्येवं सम्यगध्येप्य।
7. महाभूमि evidently refers to the last of the ten bhūmis. Other names of this *bhūmi* are: –परमविहार, निष्ठागमन, तथागतभूमि, बुद्धभूमि, अभिषेकभूमि।
8. *B. Bh.*, p. 153 adds here महाज्ञानप्रभावप्राप्तानां।
9. *Ibid.* adds परीत्तं वा यस्य वा याचति शक्तिर्हेतुवलं च स विज्ञो वोधिसत्तो नीचे।
10. *B. Bh.*, p. 153 : इत्युक्ता।
11. *Ibid.* एतमेवार्थं।
12. Ms. आयुष्मंत।
13. *B. Bh.*, p. 153 : एवं नाम कुलपुत्र धर्म्मभ्रातरिति वा।

बोधिसत्त्वोऽसि बोधौ च कृतप्रणिधानः । तेन ओमिति प्रतिज्ञातव्यं । स पुनरुत्तरि एवं
[5] *b*
स्याद्व[चनीयः ।] प्रतीच्छसि त्वमेवन्नामन् कुलपुन्नायुष्मन् भदन्तेति वा बोधिसत्त्वोऽसि बोधौ
c [6]
कृतप्रणिधानो[1] ममान्तिकात् सर्व्वाणि बोधि-सत्त्वशिक्षा[पदानि] सर्व्वभ्य बोधिसत्त्वशीलं

संवरशीलं कुशलधर्म्मसंग्राहकशीलं सत्त्वार्थक्रियाशीलं च यच्छीलमतीतानां बोधिसत्त्वा[नामभूत्

यानि च

[1]
Leaf 2b शिक्षापदानि ।] यच्छीलमनागतानां बोधिसत्त्वानां भविष्यति यानि च

शिक्षापदानि । यच्छीलमेतर्हि दशसु दिक्षु प्रत्युत्पन्ननां बोधिसत्त्वानां [भवति यानि च शि/ापदानि ।
[2]
येषु] च शिक्षापदेषु येषु शीलेष्वतीताः सर्व्वबोधिसत्त्वाः शिक्षितवन्तः । अनागताः
[3]
सर्व्वबोधिसत्त्वाः शिक्षिष्यन्ते । प्रत्यु[त्पन्नाः सर्व्वबोधि-स]त्त्वाःशिक्षन्ते । तेन प्रतिगृह्नामीति
d
प्रतिज्ञातव्यं[2] ॥ त्रिरेवम् ॥

समन्वाहरन्तु[3] मां दशदिग्लोकधातुसन्निपतिता बुद्धा भगवन्तो बोधि-[सत्त्वाः ।
[4]
स]मन्वाहरत्वाचार्य्योऽहमेवन्नामा यत्किञ्चितकायवाङ्मनोलिर्बुद्ध-बोधिसत्त्वान् मातापितरौ
[5]
तदन्यान् वा सत्त्वान् समागम्येह[ज]न्मन्यन्येषु वा [जन्मां]तरेषु मयापायं कृतं कारितमनुमोदितं

वा तत् सर्व्वमैकध्यमभिसंक्षिप्य पिण्डयित्वा तुलयित्वा

---

1. *B. Bh.*, p. 153 omit *b-c*.
2. *B. Bh.*, p. 154 here has the following few lines : एवं द्विरपि त्रिरपि तेन च विज्ञेन बोधिसत्त्वेन वक्तव्यम् । तेन च समादापकेन बोधिसत्त्वेन यावत त्रिरपि प्रतिज्ञातव्यं पृष्टेन । एवं हि तेन विज्ञेन बोधिसत्त्वेन तस्य परिग्राहकस्य बोधिसत्त्वस्य यावत त्रिरपि बोधिसत्त्व-शीलसंवरसमादानं दत्त्वा प्रतिज्ञां च प्रतिगृह्य व्युत्थिता एव तस्मि (*sic.*) प्रतिग्राहके बोधिसत्त्वे तस्या एव तथागतप्रतिमायाः and then as given in this text leaf 4a, lin 4 up to बोधिसत्त्वशीलसंवरसमादानं समात्तमिति in leaf 4 b, line 3.
3. For almost a *verbatim* corrspondence of certain portions of this passage, see *Śikṣ āsamuccaya*, p. 170.

[6]
सर्व्वबुद्धबोधिसत्त्वानामाचार्य्य[स्यचा]न्तिकेऽग्रया प्रवरया प्रतिदेशनया प्रतिदेशयामि जानन्

स्मरन् न प्रतिच्छादयामि[1] ॥ त्रिरेवम् ॥[2]

[1]
Leaf 3a सोहमेवंनामा एवंदेशितात्यय इमं दिवसमुपा[दा]य आबोधिमण्डनिषदनात्

बुद्धं भगवन्तं महाकारुणिकं सर्व्वज्ञं सर्व्वदर्शिनं सर्व्ववेरभयातीतं महापुरुषम-भेद्यकायमनुत्तरकायं
[2]
धर्म्मकायं शरणं गच्छामि द्विपदानामग्यम् ॥ सोऽह-मेवंनामा एवंदेशितात्यय इमं दिवसमुपादाय
[3]
आबोधिमण्डनिषदनाद्धर्मं[3] शरणं गच्छामि शान्तं विरागाणां प्रवरम्। सोऽहमेवंनामा
[4]
एवंदेशितात्यय इमं दिवंसमुपादाय आबोधिमण्डनिषदनादवैवर्त्तिकबोधिसत्त्वसंघं शरणं गच्छामि

गणाणां श्रेष्ठम्[4] ॥ त्रिरेवम् ॥[5]

सोहमेवंनामा एवंदेशितात्ययस्त्रिशरणगतोऽनन्तसत्त्वधातूत्तारणायाभ्युद्धर-[णाय]
[5]
संसारदुःखात् परित्राणाय सर्व्वज्ञज्ञाने अनुत्तरे प्रतिष्ठापनाय। यथा ते अतीतानागतप्रत्युत्पन्ना
[6]
बोधिसत्त्वा बोधिचित्त [मुत्पाद्य बुद्ध]त्वमधिगतवन्तोऽधिगमिष्यन्ति अधिगच्छन्ति च। यथा

सर्व्वबुद्धाऽनावरणेन बुद्धज्ञानेन बुद्ध-चक्षुषा

[1]
Leaf 3b जानन्ति पश्यन्ति यथा धर्म्माणां [निःस्वभावताम (?)] नुजानन्ति।[6]

---

1. Ms. प्रतिच्छादहयामि।
2. These few lines, omitted in the *B. Bh.*, speak of the mode of confession (pāpadeśanā) adopted by the Bodhisattvas. See my *Aspects of Mahāyāna Buddhism etc.*, pp. 304-5; *Bodhic.*, p. 154; *Śikṣā.*, pp. 100ff.; 168-9; *Svayambhū P.*, pp. 116-8.
3. Ms. निषदाना।
4. For a parallel passage, see *Kriyāsaṅgraha-Pañjikā*, an extract from which is given in Mm. H.P.Sastri's *Catalogue of Buddhist Manuscripts*, p. 123.
5. Here we find the formula for *Triśaraṇagamana* of the Bodhisattvas. Cf. *Bodhicaryāvatāra*, p. 58:
   बुद्धं गच्छामि शरणं यावदाबोधिमण्डतः।
   धर्मं गच्छामि शरणं बोधिसत्त्वगणं तथा॥
6. I am indebted to Mr. D.A. Dharmacarya for helping me in the decipherment of the first three leaves, before I received Mr. Wogihara's edition of the *Bodhisattvabhūmi*.

तेन विधिना अहमेवंनामा एवंनाम्न आचार्य्यस्यान्तिकात् सर्व्वबुद्धबोधि-सत्त्वानां च

[2]

पुरतोऽनुत्तरायां सम्यक्सम्बोधौ चित्तमुत्पाद[यामि ॥ त्रिरे]वम् ॥[1]

इदं चाहमत्ययदेशनात्रिशरणगमनबोधिचित्तोत्पादजनितं कुशलमूल-मनुत्तरायां

[3]

सम्यक्संबोधौ परिणामया[मि[2] यदहं] लोके अशरणे अलयने अपरायणेऽद्वीपे त्राणं शरणं

[4]

लयनं परायणं द्वीपो भवेयम्। सर्व्वसत्त्वांश्च भवार्णवादतीर्णांस्तारयेयम्। [अप]रिनिर्वृताननावरणेन

धर्म्मधातुपरिनिर्व्वाणेन परिनिर्व्वापयेयम्। अनाश्वस्तानाश्वासयेयम् ॥ त्रिरपि ॥

[5]

सोहमेवंनामा ए[वमु]त्पादितबोधिचित्तोऽनन्तसत्त्वधातुं[3] यथा माता-

[6]

पितृभगिनीभ्रातृपुत्रदुहित्रन्यतमान्यतमज्ञातिसालोहितस्थानीयांस्तथा प्रतिगृह्णामि ।[4] प्रतिगृह्य च

यथाशक्ति यथाबलं यथाज्ञानं[5] कुशलमूलं समारोपयामि। इतः प्रभृति यत्किञ्चित् दानं दास्यामि

शीलं रक्षिष्यामि क्षां[तिं]

---

1. After Triśaraṇagamana, a Bodhisattva utters this formula for developing *Bodhicitta*. The commentator of the *Bodhic.* (p. 4) remarks that the बोधिसत्त्वशिक्षासमादानम् precedes बोधिचित्तग्रहणम्।
The *Bodhicitta* consists in the candidate's taking the vow that he will attain *bodhi* not so much to save himself as to save the wordly beings from their wordly miseries and lead them ultimately to Buddhahood. See *Bodhic.*, ch. 1; *Śikṣā.*, pp. 5ff. Cf. *Bodhic.*, p. 14:
भवदुःखशतानि तर्त्तुकामैरपि सत्त्वव्यसनानि हर्तुकामैः।
बहुसौख्यशतानि भोक्तु कामैर्न विमोच्यं हि सदैव बोधिचित्तम् ॥
2. By *Pariṇāmanā* a Bodhisattva transfers the merits acquired by him to all living beings; he should wish it from his inmost heart and not by words alone. See *Bodhic.*, p. 79, quoting *Vajradhvajasūtra* and *Śikṣā.*, pp. 29f. तच्चाध्याशयतः परिणमयति न वचनमात्रेण। तच्चोदग्रचित्तः परिणमयति। हृष्टचित्तः प०। प्रसन्नचित्तः प०। etc.
3. Ms. अनन्त।
4. Cf. *Bodhic.* p. 72: i.e. जानामि पश्यामि (op. cit.).
One of the essential conditiosn for becoming a Bodhisattva is that he must not distinguish himself or his relatives from the other wordly beings, i.e. he must think himself as one with all the beings of the world. Just as one takes care of the various limbs of his body and do not distinguish the limbs from the body, so also a Bodhisattva must look upon all the beings as parts and parcels of his body and hence any of their sufferings is his suffering. See *Bodhic.*, pp. 326 ff.; *Śikṣā.*, p. 19. : तेन तथा तता चित्तमुत्पादयितव्यं यथा यथास्य सर्व्वसत्त्वेषु पुत्रप्रेमानुगता मैत्र्युत्पद्यते।
5. Ms. यथाजामानं।

[1]

Leaf 4a संपादयिष्यामि वीर्यमारभ्य ध्यानं समापत्स्ये प्रज्ञया व्यवचार्य्य[1] उपाय-

कौशल्यं वा शिक्षिष्ये तत् सर्व्वसत्त्वानामर्थाय हिताय सुखाय[2] ॥

[2]

[उत्त]रां च सम्यक्संबोधिमारभ्य तेषां महाभूमिप्रविष्टानां बोधिसत्त्वानां

[3]

महाकारुणिकाणां महायानं सामिचीमनुप्रव्रजामि। अनु[प्रव्रज्य] बोधिसत्त्वोऽहं बोधिसत्त्व

इति मामितः प्रभृत्याचार्य्यो धारयतु[3] ॥ त्रिरेवम् ॥

[4]

ततस्तंनाचार्य्येण तस्याः प्रतिमायाः[4] पुरतो दशसु दिक्षु [बु]द्धबोधि-सत्त्वानां तिष्ठतां

ध्रियनां यापयतां; पादयोर्भिपत्य सामिचीं कृत्वा एवमागे-चयितव्यम्। गृहीतमनेनैवंनाम्रा

[5]

बोधिसत्त्वे[न म]मैदंनाम्रो बोधिसत्त्व-स्यान्तिकात् यावत् त्रिरपि

बोधिसत्त्वशीलसंवरसमादानम्। सोहमेवंनामा बोधिसत्त्व[5] आत्मानं साक्षिभूतं प्रजा[नन्][6]

[6]

[7]अस्यंवंनाम्रो बोधिसत्त्वस्य परमार्य्याणां विपरोक्षाणामपि सर्वत्र सर्व्वसत्त्वानां विपरोक्षबुद्धीनां

दश [1]

Leaf 4b दिक्ष्वनन्तापर्य्यन्तेषु लोकधातुष्वा[रोचयामि। अ]स्मिन

बोधिसत्त्वशीलसंवर-समादानम् ॥ त्रिरेवम् ॥

एवं पुनः शीलसंवरसमादानकर्म्मसमास्यनन्तरं धर्म्मता खल्वेषा यदू दशसु

[2]

दिक्ष्नन्ता[पर्य्यन्तेषु लोक]धातुपु तथागतानां तिष्ठतां ध्रियतां यापयतां महाभूमिप्रविष्टानां च

1. Ms. व्यवचारयिय्य।
2. The formula of *Pariṇāmanā* ends here. In the *Kriyāsaṅgraha* (see Intro.) it will be observed that this is one of the many declarations necessary for developing Bodhicitta.
3. Here we find the formula for आचार्य्याभिषेकः। Cf. *Kriyāsaṅgraha* (Bibl. Nat. ms.), leaf 44.
4. From here, the *B. Bh.*, (pp. 154-5) again corresponds up to समादानं समात्तमिति in the next page.
5. Omitted in *B. Bh.*, p. 154.
6. Omitted in *B. Bh.*, p. 154.
7. *B. Bh.*, p. 154, अस्यैतन्।

[3]*a*
बोधिसत्त्वानां तद्रूपं निमित्तं प्रादुर्भवति येन तेषामे[वं भवति। एवंनाम्ना बोधिसत्तेवेन एवंनाम्रो
b
बोदिसत्त्वस्यान्तिकात्[1] बोधिसत्त्वशीलसंवरसमादानं समात्तमिति ॥[2] एवं तावत् परतः
[4]
समादान[विधिरु]क्तः ॥[3]

यदि तैर्गुणैर्युक्तः पुद्गलो न सन्निहितः स्यात् ततो बोधिसत्त्वेन तथागतप्रतिमायाः पुरतः
[5]
स्वयमपि बोधिसत्त्वशी[लसंवर]समादाने वचनीयम्। एवं च करणीयम्। एकांसमुत्तरासङ्गं
[6]
कृत्वा दशसु दिक्ष्वतीतानागतप्रत्युत्पन्नानां बुद्धानां भगवतां महा[भूमि]प्रविष्टानां च बोधिसत्त्वानां

सामीचीं कृत्वा दक्षिणं जानुमण्डलं पृथिव्यां प्रतिष्ठाप्य उत्कुटुकेन वा इदं स्याद्वचनीयम्।

अहमेवंनामा

[1]
Leaf 5a दशसु दिक्षु [सर्व्वत]थागतान् महाभूमिप्रविष्टांश्च बोधिसत्त्वान् विज्ञापयामि।

तेषां पुरतः सर्व्वाणि बोधिसत्त्वशिक्षापदानि सर्व्वं च बोधिसत्त्वशीलं समाद[दे]।
[2]
यच्छीलमित्यादि पूर्व्ववत्[4] यावत् बोधिसत्त्वो बोधिसत्त्व इति। मामितः प्रभृति बुद्धा भगवन्तो

बोधिसत्त्वाश्च धारयन्त्विति विज्ञप्तिः ॥ ० ॥

[विनयविनिश्चय उपालिपरिपृच्छा*]

[3]
नमो बुद्धाय ॥ तेन खलु पुनः समयेनायुष्मानुपालिः प्रतिसंलयनान व्युत्थाय येन
[4]
भगवांस्तेनोपसंक्रामत्। उपसंक्र[म्य भ]गवतः पादौ शिरसाभिवन्द्य [5]त्रिः प्रदक्षिणीकृत्यैकान्तं

---

1. *B. Bh.*, p. 155 drops this line *a-b*.
2. Correspondence with the *B. Bh.*, p. 155 ends here.
3. The directions given in the following few lines are intended for one who cannot find a suitable Bodhisattva preceptor to give him formal initiation into the disciplinary conduct of a Bodhisattva.
4. See before leaf 2b line 1 up to मामितः प्रभृतिः in leaf 4a l. 3.

* This heading has been supplied by me; it is not given in the ms. See the attached plate.

5. Ms. त्रि for त्रिः

[5]
न्यासीदत्। एकान्तनिषण्णश्चायुष्मानुपालिः भगवन्तमेतदवोचत्। इह भगव[न्म] मैकाकिनो

रहोगतस्य प्रतिसंलीन-चित्तस्यायमेवंरूपश्चेतसि चेतःपरिवितक उदपादि। प्रातिमोक्षसंवरो भगवता
[6]
प्रज्ञ[प्तश्चा]धिशीलशिक्षापरिशुद्धिः श्रावकयानिकानां प्रत्येकबुद्धयानिकानां च।

बोधिसत्त्वयानिकानां तु भगवता [1]जीवितपरित्यागेऽपि [2]शिक्षा[प्यत्र परिदे]
[1]
Leaf 5b शिता निर्दिष्टा। तत् कथं भगवतः परिनिर्वृतस्य तिष्ठतो वा श्रावकयानिकानां
[2]
प्रातिमोक्षसंवरो वक्तव्यः। कथं प्रत्येकबुद्धयानिकानाम्। क[थं महाया]न-संप्रस्थितानां

बोधिसत्त्वानां प्रातिमोक्षसंवरो वक्तव्यः। अहं भगवता विनय-पराणामग्रो निर्दिष्टः। तस्य मे
[3]
भगवन् वि[ज्ञापयतूपा]यकौशल्यं सम्प्रकाशयतु भगवन् यथा भगवतः सकाशात् सम्मुखं श्रुत्वा
[4]
सम्मुखं प्रतिगृह्य वैशारद्य-प्राप्तः पर्षत्सु विस्तरेण संप्रकाशयेयम्। अयं मे भगवन्नेकाकिनो

रहोगतस्य प्रतिसंलीनस्यैवंरुपश्चेतसि चेतःपरिवितर्क उदपादि यत्त्वहं भगवन्तमुपसंक्र[म्य]
[5]
विनयविनिश्चयं परिपॉच्छेयमिति। तत् साधु भगवन् व्याकरोतु तथागतो विनयविनिश्चयं विस्तरेण
[6]
महती भिक्षुपर्षत् सन्निपति[ता] बोधिसत्त्वपर्षञ्च।

एवमुवते भगवानायुष्मन्तमुपालिमेतदवोचत्। तस्मात्तर्हि त्वमुपाले अन्येन
[1]
Leaf 6a प्रयोगेणान्येनाध्याशयेन श्रावकयानिकानां [शिक्षा]परिशुद्धिं वद। अन्येन

प्रयोगेणान्येनाध्याशयेन महायानसंप्रस्थितानां शिक्षापरिशुद्धिं वद। तत् कस्माद्धेतोः। अन्यो
[2]
ह्युपाले श्रावक[या]निकानां प्रयोगोऽन्योऽध्याशयः। [3]अन्यो महायानसंप्रस्थितानां बोधिसत्त्वानां

---

1. Ms जीवत
2. Ms. शिक्षा
3. Ms. अध्यासयः

[3]
प्रयोगोऽन्योऽध्याशयः। तत्रोपाले या श्रावक-यानिकस्य परिशुद्धशीलता सा महायानिकस्य

बोधिसत्त्वस्यापरिशुद्धशीलता परमदौःशील्यञ्च। या महायानसंप्रस्थितस्य बोधि [सत्त्वस्य]
[4]
परिशुद्धशीलता सा श्रावकयानिकस्यापरिशुद्धशीलता परमदौःशील्यञ्च। तत् कम्माद्धेतोः।
[5]
इहोपाले श्रावकयानिकस्तत्क्षणि[कचित्तेऽ]पि भवोपपत्ति[1] न परिगृह्णाति। इयं श्रावक-यानिकस्य
[6]
परिशुद्धशीलता सा महायानिकस्य बोधिसत्त्वस्यापरिशुद्धशीलता परम[दौः]शील्यञ्च।

कतमोपाले महायानसंप्रस्थितस्य बोधिसत्त्वस्य परिशुद्धशीलता
[1]
Leaf 6b या श्रावकयानिकस्यापरिशुद्धशीलता परमदौःशील्यञ्च। इहोपाले महायाने

संप्रस्थितो बोधिसत्त्वो महासत्त्वोऽप्रमेयासंख्येयान् कल्पान् भवोपपत्तिं परिगृह्णाति
[2]
अपरिखिन्नचित्तोऽपरिखिन्नमानसः। [इ]यं महायानसंप्रस्थितस्य बोधिसत्त्वस्य परिशुद्धशीलता

सा श्रावकयानिकस्यापरिशुद्धशीलता परम-दौःशील्यञ्च।
[3]
तस्मात्तर्हि [त्वमुपा]ले सानुरक्षां शिक्षां महायानसंप्रस्थितानां बोधिसत्त्वानां वद।
[4]
निरनुरक्षां शिक्षां श्रावकयानिकानां वद। सपरिहारां शिक्षां महा[यानसं]प्रस्थितानां बोधिसत्त्वानां

वद। निःपरिहारां शिक्षां श्रावकयानिकानां वद। दूरानुप्रविष्टां शिक्षां महायानसंप्रस्थितानां
[5]
बोधिसत्त्वानां वद। सावदानां शिक्षां श्रावकयानिकानां वद।
[6]
कथं चोपाले सानुरक्षा शिक्षा महायानसंप्रस्थितानां बोधिसत्त्वानां [निरनुरक्षा शि]क्षा

श्रावकयानिकानाम्। इहोपाले महायानसंप्रस्थितेन बोधिसत्त्वेन परसत्त्वानां परपुद्गलानां

हितमनुवर्त्तितव्यं न पुनः श्रावक[यानिकेन]।

---

1. MS भावात्पत्ति

[1]
Leaf 7a अनेनोपाले पर्य्यायेण सानुरक्षा[1] शिक्षा महायानिकानां बोधिसत्त्वानां निरनुरक्षा
शिक्षा श्रावकयानिकानाम्।
[2]
कथं चोपाले सपिहा[रा शिक्षा महा]यानसंप्रस्थितानां बोधिसत्त्वानां निः- परिहारा
[3]
शिक्षा[2] श्रावकयानिकानाम्। [3]इहोपाले महायानसंप्रस्थितो बोधिस[त्त्वोऽपि सचेत् पूर्व्वा]ह्णसमये
आपत्तिमापद्यते मध्याह्नकाले[4] सर्व्वज्ञताचित्तेनाविरहितो विहरेदपर्य्यन्तः। एवं महायानसंप्रस्थितस्य
[4]
बोधिसत्त्वस्य शीलस्कन्धः। सचेन्म-ध्याह्नसमये आपत्तिमापद्येत सायाह्न काले
[5]
सर्व्वज्ञताचित्तेनाविरहितो विहरेद-पर्य्यन्तः। एवं महायानसं[प्रस्थि]तस्य बोधिसत्त्वस्य
शीलस्कन्धः[5]। सचेत् सायाह्नसमये आपत्तिमापद्येत रात्याः पुरिमयामे सर्व्वज्ञताचित्तेनाविरहितो
[6]
[विहरे]दपर्य्यन्तः। एवं महायानसंप्रस्थितस्य बोधिसत्त्वस्य शीलस्कन्धः। सचेत्
[1]
Leaf 7b रात्याः पुरिमयामे आपत्तिमापद्येत रात्याश्च मध्यमयामे सर्व्वज्ञता[चि]त्तेना-
विरहितो विहरेदपर्य्यन्तः। एवं महायानसंप्रस्थितस्य बोधिसत्त्वस्य शीलस्कन्धः। सचेत् रात्या
[2]
मध्यमयामे आपत्तिमा[प]द्येत रात्याश्च [पश्चिम]यामे सर्व्वज्ञता-चित्तेनाविरहितो
विहरेदपर्य्यन्तः। एवं महायानसंप्रस्थितस्य बोधिसत्त्वस्य शील-स्कन्धो वेदितव्यः। एवं ह्युपाले
[3]
[सप]रिहारा शिक्षा महायानसंप्रस्थितानां बोधिसत्त्वानाम्। तत्र बोधिसत्त्वेन [6]नात्र
[4]
कौकृत्यपर्य्युत्थानमुत्पाद्यं नातिविप्रति-सारिणा भवितव्यम्। तत्रोपाले[7] [8]सचेच्छावकयानिकः

---

1. Cf. *Sūtrālaṅkāra*, p. 130: सानुरक्षं परिजनस्याविघातं कृत्वा अन्यस्मै दानात्।
2. Ms. omits it.
3. The passage marked *a-b* is cited in the *Śikṣāsamuccaya*, p. 178.
4. *Śikṣā.*, p. 178: कालसमये throughout.
5. *Śikṣā.*, p. 178 abridges the remaining few lines by saying एवं यामे यामे विधिरुक्तः।
6. *Śikṣā.*, p. 178 : नाति
7. Omitted in *Śikṣā.*, p. 178.
8. *Śikṣā.*, p. 178 : सचेत्पुनः श्रावकयानीयः पुद्गलः

b

पुनः पुनरापत्तिमापद्येत नष्टः श्रावकयानिकस्य[1] शीलस्कन्धो वेदितव्यः ।[2] तत् कस्माद्धेतोः ।

[5]

आदीप्त-शिरश्चैलोपमेन[3] हि श्रावकयानिकेन भवितव्यं सर्व्वक्लेशप्रहाणाय । एवं निः-परिहारा

[6]

शिक्षा श्रावकयानिकस्य [ह्युपाले [4]प]रिनिर्व्वाणकामस्य । कथं चोपाले दूरानुप्रविष्टा शिक्षा

महायानसंप्रस्थितानां बोधिसत्त्वानां

[1]

Leaf 8a सावदाना शिक्षा श्रावकयानिकानाम् । इहोपाले महायानसंप्रस्थितो बोधिसत्त्वो

गङ्गानदीवालिकासमान् कल्पान् पञ्चभिः कामगुणैः क्रीड़ित्वा रमित्वा परिचारयित्वा[5] बोधिचित्तं

[2]

नोत्सृजति । [अयमुपाले म]हायानसंप्रस्थितस्य बोधिसत्त्वस्य शिक्षा वेदितव्या । तत् कस्माद्धेतोः ।

[3]

भविष्यत्युपाले स कालः स समयो यन्महायान[संप्रस्थितो बोधिस]त्त्वस्तेनैव बोधिचित्तेन

सुपरिगृहीतेन स्वप्नान्तरगतोऽपि सर्व्वक्लेशैर्न्न संहरिष्यते । अपि च महायानसंप्रस्थितेन बोधिसत्त्वेन

[4]

[नैकस्मि]न्नेव भवे सर्व्वदोशाः क्षपयितव्याः । अनुपूर्व्वेण बोधिसत्त्वानां क्लेशाः क्षयं गच्छन्ति ।

[5]

परिपक्वकुशलमूलेन च श्रावकयानिकेनादी[प्त-शि]रश्चैलोपमेन हि [6]तत्क्षणिकोऽपि

भवोपपत्तिर्न्नोत्पादितव्या[7] । एवमुपाले दूरानुप्रविष्टा शिक्षा महायानसंप्रस्थितानां बोधिसत्त्वा[नां

[6]

साव]दाना शिक्षा श्रावकयानिकानाम् ।

तस्मात्तर्हि त्वमुपाले सानुरक्षां सपरिहारां दूरानुप्रविष्टां शिक्षां

[1]

Leaf 8b महायानसंप्रस्थितानां बोधिसत्त्वानां [वद । निरनु]रक्षां निःपरिहारां सावदानां

---

1. *Śikṣā*., p. 178 : श्रावकस्य पुद्गलस्य
2. Here ends the citation of the *Śikṣā*., p. 178.
3. Ms. चिलो
4. Ms. परिनिव्वान्त
5. Ms. परिचायित्वा
6. Ms. तत क्षणिको
7. Ms. नोपादितव्या

शिक्षां श्रावकयानिकानां वद। तत् कस्माद्धेतोः। महासंभारा ह्युपालेऽनुत्तरा सम्यक्सम्बोधिर्न
[2]
सुकरा एकान्तनि[विष्टेन] महायानसंप्रस्थितेन बोधिसत्त्वेनाप्रमेयासंख्येयान् कल्पान् संधारयितुं
[3]
संसरितुम्। इदं चोपालेऽर्थ-वशं[1] सम्पश्यन्[2] तथा[गतः सम्य]क्सम्बुद्धो महायानसंप्रस्थितानां

बोधिसत्त्वाना नैकान्तनिर्व्वेदकथां कथयति नैकान्तविरागकथां कथयति नैकान्तसंवेग-कथां
[4]
[कथ]यति। अपि तु खलु पुनः प्रीतिकथां प्रामोद्यकथां प्रतीत्यसमुत्पाद-सम्प्रयुक्तकथां
[5]
कथयति।[3] गम्भीरामसंक्लिष्टां सूक्ष्मां निः[कौकृत्यकथां] कथयति। निःपर्य्युत्थानकथां कथयति।
[6]
असङ्गामनावरणां शून्यताकथां कथयति। त इमां कथां श्रुत्वाऽभि[रताः संप्राप्ता न प]रिखिद्यन्ते

बोधिसम्भारञ्च परिपूरयन्ति।

अथ ह्यायुष्मानुपालिः भगवन्तमेतदवोचत्। या इमा भगवन्नापत्तयः
[1]
Leaf 9a काश्चिद्राग[संयुक्ताः काश्चित्] द्वेष[सं]युक्ताः काश्चिन्मोहसंयुक्ताः। तत्र कतमा

भगवन् महायानसंप्रस्थितस्य बोधिसत्त्वस्य गुरुतरा आपत्तयः[4]। किं रागसंप्रयुक्ता उताहो
[2] *a*
द्वेषसंप्रयुक्ताः उताहो मोहसंप्रयुक्ताः। एवमुक्ते भगवानायुष्मन्तमुपालिमेतदवोचत्। सचेदुपाले[5]
[3]
महायानसंप्रस्थितो बोधिसत्त्वो [गङ्गान]दीवालिकासमा रागसंप्रयुक्ता[6] आपत्तीरापद्येत याध्र्यकां
[4]
द्वेषसंप्रयुक्तामापत्तिमापद्यते बोधिसत्त्वयानं प्रमाणीकृत्येयं[7] ता[भ्यो गुरु]तरा आपत्तिर्येयं

---

1. Ms. वसं
2. Ms. सपश्यन्
3. Cf. the corresponding Hīnayānic expression in *Vinaya*, I, p. 15; *Dīgha Nikāya*, I, p. 141; दानकथं सीलकथं सग्गकथं कामानामादीनवमोकारं संकिलेसं नेक्खम्मे आनिसंसम्पकासेसि। अथ या बुद्धानां सामुक्कंसिका धम्मेदेसना तं पकासेसि, दुक्खं समुदयं निरोधं मग्गम्।
4. *Śikṣā*, p. 164 : का पुनर्गुर्वी मूलापत्तिः ॥ सामान्यतस्तु तत्रोक्तं। सचेदुपाले etc.
5. The portion marked *a-b* appears in the *Śikṣā*., p. 164 with the undernoted variant readings.
6. *Śikṣā*., p. 164–वालिकोपमा रागप्रतिसंयुक्ता।
7. *Ibid*. कृत्य ॥ पे ॥ इयं।

द्वेषप्रयुक्ता। तत् कस्माद्धेतोर्द्वेष उपाले[1] सत्त्वपरित्यागाय संवर्त्तते रागः सत्त्वसंग्रहाय संवर्त्तते

[5] *b*

इति। तत्रोपाले [यः] क्लेशः सत्त्वसंग्रहाय संवर्त्तते तत्र बोधिसत्त्वस्य न छलं न भयम्। यः

[6]

क्लेशः सत्त्वपरित्यागाय संवर्त्तते तत्र बोधिसत्त्वस्य छलञ्च भय[ञ्च]। अपि तूपाले उक्तं पूर्व्वमेव

रागो [2]बन्धविरागोऽल्पसावद्यो द्वेषः क्षिप्रविरागो महासावद्यः। तत्रोपाले यो बन्धविरागोऽल्पसावद्यः

संक्लेशः [[3].........]

[1]

Leaf 9b बोधिसत्त्वस्य। यः क्षिप्रविरागो[4] महासावद्यः क्लेशः स[5] बोधिसत्त्वस्य

[2]

स्वप्रान्तरगतस्यापि नैव युक्तः। तस्मात्तर्हि त्वमुपाले बोधिसत्त्वानां[6] याः का[श्चिद् रा]गसंप्रयुक्ता

आपत्तयः सर्व्वास्ता अनापत्तय इति धारय। तत्रोपाले येऽनुपायकुशला बोधिसत्त्वास्ते

[3]

रागसंप्रयुक्ताभ्य आप[त्तिभ्यो वि]भ्यति न द्वेष-संप्रयुक्ताभ्यः। ये पुनरुपायकुशला बोधिसत्त्वास्ते

[4]

द्वेषसंप्रयुक्ताभ्य आपत्तिभ्यो विभ्यति न रागसंप्रयुक्ताभ्यः। अथ [खलु त]स्यामेव पर्षदि

मञ्जुश्रीकुमारभूतः सन्निपतितोऽभूत्। स निषण्णः भगवन्तमेतदवोचत्। अत्यन्तविनीतानां भगवन्

[5]

सर्व्वधर्म्माणां [बोधाय] विनयः। एवमुक्ते भगवान् मञ्जुश्रियं कुमारभूतमेतद-वोचत्।

[6]

सचेन्मञ्जुश्रीर्ब्बालपृथग्जनाऽत्यन्तविनीतान् सर्व्वधर्म्मान् जानीयु-[स्तदपि] न भूयस्तथागतो

विनयः प्रज्ञप्येत। सत्त्वा न प्रीणन्ति[7] तस्मात् तथागतोऽत्यन्तविनीतानां सर्व्वधर्म्माणां बोधाय

विनयं प्रज्ञपयत्यनुपूर्वेणेति योनिशमु-

---

1. *Ibid*. संयुक्ता। तत् कस्य हेतोः। योऽयं द्वेष उपाले।
2. I was feeling tempted to read it as *dandha* as opposed to *kṣipra*, but as the Chinese translation supports the reading *bandha*, I have retained it.
3. नायुक्तःस may supply the sene here.
4. Ms. प्रतिरागो।
5. Ms. श।
6. *Śikṣā*., p. 164 omits the portion market *b-c* by putting पे।
7. Ms. प्रोनन्ति

[1]

Leaf 10a पादाय ॥ ० ॥ इति बोधिसत्त्वप्रातिमोक्ष ॥ ० ॥

Here ends this book, and another commences. The scribe wrote only on one side of this leaf and then probably found out that it was a different book altogether. A photoprint of the leaf is attached hereto. I am giving below the reading as far as it has been possible for me to read, hoping that it will give clue to some other manuscript.

नमो बुद्धाय ॥ बोधिचित्तविवरणं वक्ष्ये ॥ चित्तविठपिताः सर्व्वधर्म्मा इत्युक्तं भगवता ।

[2]

देवतावञ्चित्तं निरुध्यते । किं स्वभावमिति । आह । सर्व्वभावविगतं

[3]

स्कन्धधात्वायतनग्राह्यग्राहकवर्ज्जितं धर्म्मनैरात्म्यसमतया [...] चित्तमाद्यनुत्पन्नं

शून्यतास्वभावमिति । कोऽस्य वचनस्यार्थः सर्व्वभावविगतमिति । भावशब्देन आत्मादय उच्यन्ते ।

[4]

एतदुक्ते ब्रुवति[...]आत्मासत्त्वजीव-जन्तुपोषपुरुषपुद्गलमनुजमानवकारकवेदकादिस्वभावं

[5]

तञ्चित्तं न भवति । किं कारणम् । तेषामेवमादी[...]असंविद्यमानक्रियालक्षणत्वात् । एवं

[6]

तावदात्मादयो भावा न विद्यन्ते प्रागेव तत्स्वभावं चित्तमिति । अतः सर्व्वभावविगतं [...]तेन

स्वभावं चित्तं भवतीत्याह । स्कन्धधात्वायतनग्राह्यग्राहकवर्ज्जितं भवति ॥ स्वभावचित्तं

भवति ॥[.........]

Chapter - 9
An Appendix to the New Edition of the Bodhicaryāvatāra

Sujitkumar Mukhopadhyaya

It is a matter of gratification that a new edition of the *Bodhicaryāvatāra* has been published by the Asiatic Society, Calcutta.

Sixty years ago, in 1903, Asiatic Society published the *Bodhicaryāvatāra* with the *Pañjikā* of Prajñākaramati. Prof. Louis de la Vallée Poussin edited it. It has been out of print for a long time. The present edition is made by Prof. Vidhushekhara Bhattacharya, a scholar as eminent as the former editor.

It is a complete edition of the text. It contains all the *ślokas* of the *Bodhicaryāvatāra* in ten chapters.

The first edition was very rich and useful, because it contained the *Pañjikā* which is no less important than the text.

The present edition is devoid of the *Pañjikā* but rich with the addition of one hundred ninety-three *ślokas* which were not available in the first edition. The present edition contains also the Tibetan translation (in Tibetan script) of the text. It will be a valuable text book for students devoted to Indo-Tibetan Studies.

The late lamented Vidhushekhara Bhattacharya had barely completed his edition when death snatched him away from us. He had no time to revise it. His students well-versed in both Sanskrit and Tibetan were not near him; and so they could not help him in this difficult task. In such circumstances, as is natural, some mistakes have crept in.

It is a sacred duty for his past students to check and correct those mistakes. The present writer is one of his humble students who had the good fortune to be intimately associated with him for more than twenty years. In this paper an attempt is made to check mistakes and improve some of the readings of the additional *ślokas* with the help of the Tibetan translation. Printing mistakes are also checked and corrected:

Chapter III

Improvement upon the Additional ślokas

Page *Śloka* *Line*

37 29 2 Read: *bhavādhva-bhramaṇa-śrānta-jagad-viś-rāma-pādapaḥ for °śrānto jagad.°* Tib. *srid. lam. 'khyams. śiṅ. dub. pa. yi. 'gro. ba' i. ṅal. bso'i. ljon. śiṅ. yin.* The copy that I have with me reads: *°śrānta.°*

Chapter IV

42 11 2 Read: *dolāyamānaḥ saṁsāre bhūmi-prāptau cirāyate* for *°bhūmi-prāptas° cirāyate.* Tib. *sa. thob. pa. la. yun. riṅ. thogs.* My copy reads: *°prāptau.*

43 15 1 Read: *kadā tathāgatotpādaṁ śraddhāṁ mānuṣyam eva ca, for °ṣyam eva vā.* Tib reads: *°daṅ.* My copy reads: *ca.*

44 21 1 Read: *eka-kṣaṇa-kṛtāt pāpāt* (my copy and Tib. support this) for *°kṣaṇāt kṛtāt.° avicau kalpam āsyate* for *°āpsyate*; my copy *āsyate.* Tib. *gnas. 'gyur. na.*

45 25 2 My copy reads: *ciraṁ dhakṣyaty aśikṣitam.* But *dhakṣyati niścitaṁ* is supported by Tib. *gdon. mi. za.*

46 28 2 Read: *na śūrā na ca te prājñāḥ* for *na surā°*. Tib. *dpa'a. mdzaṅs. min.* My copy reads: *śūrā.*

50 43 1 Read: *atra grahī bhaviṣyāmi baddha-vairaś ca vigrahī* for *atra gṛhī°*. Tib.: *bdag. gis. zen. bya ziṅ.* According to my copy: *grahī.*

Printing Mistakes

Page	*Śloka*	*line*		
40	4	1	Read:	*yadi caiva* (separately).
40	6	1	Read:	*udghuṣya.*
48	35	4	Read:	*tiṣṭhanti.*
48	37	2	Read:	*prasabhaṁ.* Tib. *nan. gyis.*
49	39	3	Read:	*mahārtha°.* Tib.: *don. chen°.*

Chapter VIII

165 111 1 Read: *abhyāsād anyadīyeṣu śukra-śoṇita-binduṣu* for *asāreṣv anya°*. My copy reads: *abhyāsād°*. Tib.: *goms. pa. yis. ni. gzan. dag. gi. khu. ba...* Cf. *Pañjikā* under *śloka* 91: *yathā 'bhyāsād ekatvā' dhyavasāyo'smin kāye ekatvam antareṇā'pi. tathā' nekaprakāre jagaty api°*. See also *ślokas*: 115, 117, 119.

167 118 1 According to my copy: *adhy atiṣṭ had ato nāthaḥ svanāmāpy avalokitaḥ* which is better than °*tiṣṭhad atho*°. Tib.: °*de. bas*°.

172 137 1 According to my copy: *niścayaṁ kuru he manaḥ* Tib.: *yid. khyod*°.

177 157 2 Read: *bauddha-sampat-sukhān-muktā nā' bhaviṣyad iyaṁ daśā* for *bauddhaṁ sampat-sukhaṁ*°.

Printing Mistakes

168 122 1 Read: *yo māndya-kṣut*° for *yo mandya kṣ ut.*°

174 146 1 Read: °*vaktrasthe naivā'sya.*

174 148 1 Read: omit *visarga*(:) in *prakaṭā.*

175 152 2 Read: *paribhokṣye* for °*mokṣye*. Tib.: *yoṅs. su. spyod.*

178 161 1 *cyāvaya* is the better reading; so reads my copy.

179 168 2 Read: °*doṣās-tvad*° (so in my copy). Tib.: *khyod* (*tvad*).

Chapter X

229 3 2 Read: *bodhisattva-sukha-prāptaṁ bhavatv aviratam jagat for* °*sukhaṁ prāptuṁ bhavaty*° (°*tāṁ,*° my copy). Tib.: lit.: *Jagad aviratam bodhisattva-sukhadhārāṁ prāpnotu* (°*dpa'a. yi. bde. ba. rgyun. mi. 'chad. thob. śog*).

230 7 1 Read: *kādamba-kāraṇḍava-cakravāka*° for *dātyūha-kāraṇḍava*°. There is no *dātyūha* in Tib. My copy reads: *kādamba*°. Tib.: *mthiṅ.* ril. = *kādamba*; *ṅur. pa.* = *cakravāka*; *ṅaṅ. pa.* = *kāraṇḍava, haṁsa*; *bzad.* = *haṁsa, sārasa.*

231 9 1 Read: *aṅgāra-taptotpala-śastra*° (so in my copy). Tib.: *mtshon. gyi. char* (*śastra*°). So there is no need of keeping *śa* within third brackets; and query is unnecessary.

232 12 3 Read: *kim idam iti sukhenā'hlāditānām akasmād* for °*lhāditaṁ nāma kasmād.* Tib.: *glo. bur. bde. bas. tshim. pa. 'di. ci. bsam.* Cf. *śloka* 11, *1st pāda*: *trastāḥ paśyantv akasmād.*

234 18 1 Delete no. 1, on *preta* and also delete footnote no. 1, as the word *preta* is threre. Cf. Tib.: 3rd line (*yi, dvags. rnams. ni. tshim. byas. śiṅ*).

237 28 2 Read: *nirdvandā nirupāyāsāḥ* (my copy) *santu svādhīna-vṛttayaḥ* for °*niru-pāyās tāḥ*. Tib.: '*tshe. med. par.* Cf. Pali: *upāyāsa* = trouble, unrest, disturbance. *anupāyāsa*—peacefulness, serenity.

237 30 2 Read: *prāpnuvantūccatām nīcā hatamānā bhavantu ca,* for *prāpnuvantu ca tām nīcā hata*°. Tib.: *ma. rabs. rnams. ni. mtho. thob. ciṅ. ṅa. rgyal. dag. kyaṅ. bcom. par śog.* "May the depressed be uplifted and freed from pride."

242 51 2 Read: *yāvat-pramuditā* (my copy)-*bhūmiṁ* for °*pramuditāṁ bhū*°. Tib.: *sa. rab. dga'. ba. thob. bar. du.* (*pramuditābhūmer ā prāpteḥ*).

243 54 2 *yathā carati mañjuśrīḥ* is the reading of my copy which is supported by Tib.: ji. *ltar. 'jam. dhyaṅs. spyod. mdzad. pa.*

Printing Mistakes

229 1 2 Read: *tena sarve janāḥ santu bodhi-caryā-vibhūṣaṇāḥ for* tena sarvaṁ° *bodhi-caryā vibhūṣaṇāḥ* (separated).

230 4 1-2 Read: *narakāḥ* for *nārakāḥ* and read *sukhā-vatī-sukhāmodair.*

230 7 2 Read: *hṛdyā.*

Here I have pointed out some mistakes and suggested some improvements as well as corrected the printing mistakes, only of the additional *ślokas*. There are defects and printing mistakes also in other parts of the work:

(i) Variant readings of different MSS. and the Tibetan translation are not exhaustively recorded;

(ii) variant readings found in the text of Minaev or in the JBS. are very rarely quoted, unlike the edition of Poussin. For example:

Page 1, *śl.* 2, *l.* 4; here Minaev and Text-MSS. read: *bhāvayituṁ* which is not recorded.

Page 8, *śl.* 23, *l.* 2; here Minaev and Text-MSS. rad: *devānāṁ vā ṛṣīṇāṁ vā,* this is not recorded.

Page 103, *śl.* 92, *l,* 2; *kim akṣarāṇi bhakṣyāṇi*; Tib reading is different: *kim akṣaraiḥ kartavyaṁ* (*tshig. 'bru. rnams, kyis. ci. zig. bya.*). But it is not mentioned in the notes.

As for printing mistakes see p. 4, *śl* 9. *l.* 2, last word; *l.* 3, first word, p. 9, *śl.* 29, *l.* 2, second word; p. 17, *śl.* 16, *l.* 3, second word, etc.

Chapter - 10

Mahāyāna and Hīnayāna Works Known to Nāgārjuna

R. Kimura

Nāgārjuna, if not the founder, was the chief exponent of Mahāyāna Buddhism and may well claim the credit as a great systematiser of Mahāyāna Buddhism. This will be evident if we critically look to his mighty works like *Prajñāpāramitā-Śāstra*[1] and *Daśabhūmivibhāṣā-Śāstras.*[2] The former is the commentary on *Mahāprajñāpāramitā-Sūtra* and the latter on the first two of the ten Bhūmis of the *Daśabhūmi-Sūtra* of the Avataṃsaka class.

In these two Śāstras the author incidently mentions both Mahāyānic and Hīnayānic Sūtras.

(1) Those mentioned in the *Mahāprajñāpāramitā-śāstra* are as follows:

	Names of the Sūtras and Śāstras	Nos. of the Fasciculi in which they are mentioned.
1	Saddharmapuṇḍarīka-Sūtra (Nanjio cat. No. 137)	7, 9, 10, 26, 30, 32, 33, 38, 46, 50, 57, 79, 84, 88, 93, 100
*2	Māyājāla-Sūtra	6
3	Vimalakīrtti-Sūtra (Nanjio cat. No. 146)	9, 15, 17, 28, 30, 65, 85, 88, 92, 95

1. This is a commentary compiled by Nāgārjuna on the *Pañca-viṃśātisāhasrikā-prajñāpāramitā*. It was translated into Chinese by Kumārajīva during the period A.D. 402-405, of the Later Tsin Dynasty (A.D. 384-417). The original work has not yet been discovered. It consists of 100 fasciculi. This work is so important and deals with so many subjects that it may be regarded as an encyclopædia of Mahāyāna Buddhism.
2. This commentary also was translated into Chinese by Kumārajīva about A.D. 405 of Later Tsin Dynasty (A.D. 384-417). It consists of 15 fasciculi divided into 35 chapters. The original work has not yet been discovered.

4	Buddhasaṅgīti-Sūtra (Nanjio cat. No. 401)	9
5	Sūraṅgamasamādhi-Sūtra (Nanjio cat. No. 399)	10, 26, 29, 33, 34, 40, 75
6	Amitāyur-vyūha-Sūtra (Nanjio cat. Nos. 26 & 27)	9, 22
*7	Acintyamukti-Sūtra (one of the Avataṃsaka-Sūtras)	33, 50, 73, 100
8	Bhadrakalpika Sūtra (Nanjio cat. No. 403)	29, 46
9	Pratyutpanna-Buddhasammuknavāsthita-Samādhisūtra (Nanjio cat. No. 72)	29
*10	Saṅgīty-artha-Sūtra	1
11	Puṣpahasta-Sūtra (Nanjio cat. No. 425?)	33, 46, 101
12	Megha-Sūtra (Nanjio cat. No. 187 & 188)	33, 46, 100
*13	Jñānaprasthāna-Sūtra	2
14	Sūtra on making gradually complete all wisdom and virtue or Daśabhūmika-Sūtra (Nanjio cat. No. 110)	29
*15	Dharmamegha-Sūtra	33 46
16	Brahmajāla-Sūtra (Nanjio cat. No. 1087)	5, 18
17	Mahāmegha-Sūtra (Nanjio cat. 244)	33, 46, 100
18	Ṣatpāramitā-Sūtra (Nanjio cat. No. 1004?)	33, 46
19	Śrīmatīstrīparipṛcchā-Sūtra (Nanjio cat. No. 343?)	5, 18
20	Maitreyaparipṛcchā-Sūtra (Nanjio cat. No. 42?)	46
*21	Nagaraupamya-Sūtra	80
22	Kālākāla-Sūtra (Nanjio cat. No. 750)	1

23	Madhyamāgama-Sūtra (Nanjio cat. No. 542)	1, 33, 50
24	Guhyapadavajra-Sūtra [Nanjio cat. No. 23 (3)]	1, 9, 10, 26, 57, 88
25	Saṃyuktapiṭaka-Sūtra (Nanjio cat. No. 676)	5
26	Dīrghāgama-Sūtra (Nanjio cat. No. 545)	9
27	Saṃyuktāgama-Sūtra (Nanjio cat. No. 547)	7, 9, 10, 32, 54
*28	Bahugotra-Sūtra	24
29	Dhammapada (Nanjio cat. No. 1321, 1353, 1365, 1439)	1
30	Sūtra on the well-coming king Binsā (Bimbīsāra) (Nanjio cat. No. 900?)	1, 18
*31	Viśuddha-Sūtra	24
*32	Buddhadverātrī-Sūtra	1
*33	Vaśīkṛtabahumithyā-Sūtra	1
*34	Sārīputrajātaka-Nidāna	1
*35	Kalāvadāna Sūtra	1, 31, 55
36	Devaparipṛcchā-Sūtra (Nanjio cat. No. 753)	1, 26
*37	Śakradevānām-Indramukta-Sūtra	2
*38	Sīlamukta-Sūtra	2
*39	Nadhakātyāyana-Sūtra	2
*40	Avadāna-Sūtra or Sūtra on 'Leking caws go' (Nanjio cat. No. 627?)	2
*41	Nandavaradanāgarājavaśīkṛta-Sūtra	3
42	Pūrṇa-Sūtra (Nanjio cat. No. 23 (17)?]	3
*43	Śubhadaparivrājaka-Sūtra	3
*44	Pārayāṇa-Sūtra	3, 4, 31
*45	Karaṇḍaka-Sūtra	3
46	Candanāvadāna-Sūtra (Nanjio cat. 778?)	3
47	Avadāna-Sūtra (Nanjio cat. No. 735?)	11

*74	Sarvabahujanasamdeha-Sūtra	46
*75	Bodhisattvanidāna-Sūtra	38
*76	Satadvepañcadaśavinaya-Sūtra (or Sūtra on two hundred fifty vinaya)	33
77	Buddhabhāṣitajātaka-nidāna-Sūtra (Nanjio cat. No. 669?)	49
78	Akṣaramatinirdeśa-Sūtra (Nanjio cat. No. 74 & 77)	53
79	Dharmacakrapravartana-Sūtra (Nanjio cat. No. 92 & 657)	2, 33
*80	Vāṣpa-Sūtra	93
81	Jñānamudrā-Sūtra (Nanjio cat. No. 255? & 1014?)	98
82	Mahākaruṇāpuṇḍarīka-Sūtra (Nanjio cat. No. 117)	100
*83	Upāyakauśalya-Sūtra	100
84	Nāgarājaparipṛcchā-Sūtra (Nanjio cat. No. 456)	100
*85	Asuraparipṛcchā-Sūtra	100
86	Avadāna-Sūtra (Nanjio cat. No. 735?)	97
*87	Pratyekabuddhaparipṛcchā-Sūtra	20, 81
*88	Sarvadevaparipṛcchā-Sūtra	5, 90
*89	Vinavana(?)rāja-Sūtra	5
*90	Bahūdhara-Sūtra	9
*91	Jātakāvadāna-Sūtra	11
92	Ekottarāgama-Sūtra (Nanjio cat. No. 543)	20
93	Romakūpajāta-Sūtra (Nanjio cat. No. 954?)	24
94	Akṣaramatinirdeśa-Sūtra (Nanjio cat. No. 77?)	27
*95	Ratnoṣṇīṣa-Sūtra	28
*96	Daśabalā-Sūtra	31
97	Pātragamayat-Sūtra (Nanjio cat. No. 183)	38
*98	Nāgarāja-Sūtra	51
*99	Sarvabahujanahita-Sūtra	28

*100	Sāṅkhya-Sūtra	70
*101	Sarvabuddhanidāna-Sūtra	100
102	Mahāprajñāpāramitā-Sūtra (Nanjio cat. No. 1)	100
103	Mādhyamika-Śāstra (Nanjio cat. No. 1179)	1, 19, 25, 38
104	Daśabhūmika-Śāstra (Nanjio cat. No. 1194)	49
*105	Ṣatpadābhidharma-Śāstra	68, 49, 100
*106	Abhidarma-Sūtra	73
*107	Abhidharmavibhāṣā Śāstra (Nanjio cat. No. 1264)	4, 6, 29, 39

Those Hīnayānic and Mahāyānic Sūtras which have been mentioned in the *Daśabhūmivibhāṣā-Śāstra* are as follows:—

	Names of the Sūtras	Nos. of Fasciculi in which they occur.
*1	Suddhavinaya-Sūtra	2, 15
2	Daśabhūmi-Sūtra (Nanjio cat. No. 103)	1, 16
*3	Raurava-naraka Sūtra	2
4	Ārydharmamudrā-Sūtra (Nanjio cat. No. 652)	1, 2
*5	Mahottamabuddhadharma-Sūtra	2
*6	Sahāyamārga-Sūtra	1, 5, 13
7	Mahāyānaratnacandrakumāraparipṛcchā-dharma-Sūtra (Nanjio cat. No. 826)	5
8	Mahāprajñāpāramitā-Sūtra (Nanjio cat. No. 4)	5, 6, 7
*9	Praparimāṇa-Sūtra	10
*10	Trayāṅga-Sūtra	6
*11	Maharddhi-Sūtra	10
*12	Mahāyānaniścitarāja-Sūtra	7, 8, 16
13	Mahāyānamahāparinirvāṇa-Sūtra (Nanjio cat. No. 113)	1, 11
14	Sarvadharmapravṛttinirdeśa-Sūtra (Nanjio cat. No. 164)	8
*15	Mahāyāna-Sūtra	8

*16	Ekottarāgamakālī-Sūtra (Kālī-upāsikā-Sūtra of A.N., Vol. V, xxvi pp. 46?)	11
*17	Ekottarāgamabāla-Sūtra (Bālavagga of A.N. Vol. I, pp. 59?)	11
*18	Abhayarājakumāra-Sūtra	11
*19	Sarvatathāgatagatiṃgatanyāya-Sūtra	11
*20	Bhodyuttora-Sūtra	11
*21	Mahāprajñā-Sūtra	15
*22	Kāśyapa-Sūtra	10
*23	Viśuddhaguṇa-Sūtra	17
*24	Saptopāyakauśalya-Sūtra	10
*25	Karma-Sūtra	6
*26	Kūpajataromaparidhāna-Sūtra	24
*27	Lokāyata-Sūtra	9
*28	Buddhabhāṣitavibhaktābhaya-Sūtra	16
29	Tathāgatajñānamudrā-Sūtra (Nanjio cat. No. 1014)	6
30	Karmavibhāga-Sūtra (Nanjio cat. No. 697)	11
*31	Kolāupamana-Sūtra	11
32	Pratyutpannabuddhasanmukhāvasthita-samādhi-Sūtra (Nanjio cat. No. 73)	11
*33	Sarvadevanirdeśa-Sūtra	11
34	Dharmapada (See Nanjio cat No. 1304)	13

The above facts sufficiently convince us that long before the time of Nāgārjuna many Mahāyānic Sūtras were in exsistence. So it may be definitely asserted that both Mādhyamika and Yogācāra schools are based upon these Mahāyāna Sūtras and that Nāgārjuna, Maitreyanāth, Asaṅga, and Vasubandhu established there respective schools in order to systematize these doctrines.

---

* Those marked with asterisk are author's own restoration from Chinese while all others are Nanjio's.

Chapter - 11
Derivation of Pāli

S.V. Viswanatha

Though the texts of the Buddhist Canon known as "Pāli" have been fully studied and utilised for purposes of history, it is some what worthy of note that the meaning of the word 'Pāli' is not yet clear and its derivation is obscure. Recently Dr. Thomas makes the observation in regard to the subject, "let us have some evidence one way or the other, and we shall be all the better able to do justice to the other matters in this important essay," commenting on a theory of interpretation proposed by Dr. Walleser.[1]

The term as it is ordinarily understood is "Pāli," and means a 'series,' 'row' or 'line'.[2] Based on this general meaning Childers gives in his *Dictionary* the rendering of the word as a "series of text". Where "Pāli-bhāṣā" is mentioned, it is taken by him to mean "the language of the (Buddhist) sacred text" and not as "Pāli". Thus a language of known as "Pāli" is not so far recognised.

Dr. Walleser going against accepted authority points out that there was a language known as "Pāli" which he says belonged to Magdha from where it was taken to Ceylon. He derives the word in an indirect way from Pāṭali or Pāṭaligrāma where "the bhikkhus assembled soon after the death of Buddha."[3] "Pāli" is, according to him, the language of Pāṭaliputra. He finds further that the meaning of the word "Pāli" as given by Childers has to be rejected as "there is a spelling in Ceylon Mss. with cerebral ḷ, which makes the derivation highly improbable."[4]

---

1. *Indian Historical Quarterly*, Dec., 1928, pp. 773 ff.
2. It has also the meaning "dyke" (ditch, pit or cave). Vide Prof. Macdonell's *Dictionary* under "Pāli".
3. This along with a few other points raised by Dr. Walleser has been questioned by Dr. Thomas.
4. The sense of "line" or "row" is not precluded however merely by the fact of the word being "Pāḷi" instead of "Pāli", for "Pāḷi" persisted in the Malayāḷam language in the sense of "line" or "row", e.g., *kiḍakkayil pāḷi (pāḷi*=rows or compartments of a *kiḍakka*—bed).

The question to answered is, what is the original word—"Pāli or Pāḷi". The current view is that "Pāli" is more closely allied to the "Prākṛt" of Ceylon but the discovery by Dr. Walleser of "Pāli" in; some Ceylon Mss. raises the presumption that this may be the original term. It is worthy of note that the cerebral ḷ is commonly met with only in the Dravidian languages of South India; and it is therefore not very surprising to find the form "Pāḷi" as a variant of "Pāli" only in Ceylon. It appears in Tamil in another form "Pāḷi", which in the old Tamil lexcon, the Piṅgalandi *Nighaṇṭu* is rendered as "munivar vāsam" (dwelling place of *munis*).[1] It may be also equated with the word "paḷḷi" one of the synonyms given in the *Nighaṇṭu* itself, which is met with in expressions like "paḷḷi-aṛai" (bed-chamber), "paḷḷi-koṇḍa Perumāj" (the deity in the recumbent posture) and in the "paḷḷi" (mosque) of the Mussalmans (particularly the Moplahs of Malabar) in South India.[2]

It is interesting to find that the word "Pāḷi" occurs in the early Brāhmī inscriptions of South India,[3] written in characters similar to those found in the Brāhmī inscriptions of Ceylon, assigned by Bühler to at least the 3rd century B.C. These inscriptions are met with either

---

1. Instances are quite common where ḷ is used in Dravidian languages for ḻ which is found only in Tamil. A few examples may here be given:—

Tamil-Malayāḷam	*Kannaḍa*
Puḻa (river)	huḷe.
paḻaya (old)	haḷaya.
ēḻu (seven)	ēḷu.
maḻai (rain)	maḷe.
pāḻu (waste)	hāḷu.

The interchange of ḷ and ḻ in Tamil may be found in examples like:

Coḻa—Coḷa	Īḻam or Īḷam—Ceylon.
Tamiḻ—Tamiḷ.	paḻam or paḷam—fruit.
pugaḻ or pugaḷ—fame.	kēḻ or kēḷ—hear.
pavaḻam or pavaḷam—coral.	uḻundu or uḷundu—pulse,

Instances where cerebral ḷ appears in South Indian vernaculars for l in Sanskrit may be noted in the following, among others:

kāla becomes kāḷa—dark.
phala becomes paḻa or paḷa—fruit.
kalabha becomes kaḷapa (old Tamil)—young elephant.
dhavala becomes tavaḷa (do.)—white.
valaya becomes vaḷai—bangle or ring.
pravāla becomes pavaḷa or pavaḻa—coral.
sthala becomes taḷa or daḷa—peace.
khila becomes kiḷai—branch.

2. In these cases "paḷḷi" either means "bed for lying on" or a "place for prayers".
3. The word "pāḷi" occurs thrice in these inscriptions and has perhaps to be distinguished from "kāvi" and "lena" which are other words met with in them to denote a "cavern". One point of difference between the caves in Ceylon and those in South India is that in the latter are found beds, while the former do not contain any. Perhaps this fact may lead to the conclusion that "pāḷi" meant "a cave with a bed in it."

on the natural walls of caves or on the rocky beds found in them. No other meaning of the world "Pāḷi"seems possible in these cases than "residence of munis" (monks) or "beds for them to rest on." "Pāḷi" would therefore mean a cave, and this interpretation does not militate against the meaning "dyke" given to the term "Pāli" by Macdonell. The conclusion seems warranted that the name "Pāli" may gave been derived from the South and originally used to denote the language met with in these caves or the beds in them. "Pāli"is probably only a variant of the South Indian forms "Pāḷi," "Pāḷi" or "Pāḷi".[1]

It is hoped that this short note may answer the query raised by Dr. E.J. Thomas, "what does the spelling with cerebral ḷ prove?" It will also indicate that the spelling "Pāḷi" may have been the original one, as found in the early Prākṛt of South India and Ceylon. The meaning here given might set at rest also any necessity for a theory of a possible confusion of the word "Pāḷi" with "Pāli" meaning line, as conceived by Dr. Thomas in his note.

1. The original and better form of the word would appear to be "Pāḷi".

Chapter - 12
Marriage in Buddhist Literature

Bimala Churn Law

Marriageable age of girls

In the Buddhist period of Indian history we do not find any hard and fast rule about the age at which girls are to be married, nor do we come across instances of early marriage. Girls are sometimes seen to have been married at the age of sixteen. In the Asilakkhaṇa (no. 126) and the Mudu-Pāṇi (no. 262) Jātakas, we read that a princess was given in marriage when she was sixteen years old. The Dhammapada Commentary (II, 217) says that Kuṇḍalakesī, a beautiful daughter of a banker of Rājagaha, remained unmarried till the age of sixteen. It further says that at this age woman long for men— (tasmin ca vaye ṭ hitā nāriyo purisajjhāsayā honti purisalolā).

Sister-marriage

Limitations on marriage imposed by Brāhmaṇic usage are conspicuous by their absence in Buddhist literature and even sister-marriage is referred to. The mythical origin of the Licchavis as recorded in the Parmatthadīpanī on the Khuddakapāṭha (ed. by H. Smith, pp. 158-160) illustrates the point.

The Sumaṅgalavilāsinī (pt. I, pp. 258-260) presents us with another instance of marriage not allowed by Brāhmaṇic scriptures. It says that king Okkāka had five queens. By the chief queen, he had four sons and five daughters. After the death of the chief queen, the king married another young lady who extorted from him the promise to place her son upon the throne. The king thereupon requested his sons to leave the kingdom. The princes accordingly left the kingdom accompanied by their sisters, and going to a forest near the Himālayas, they began to search for a site for building a city. In course of their search, they met the sage Kapila who said that they should build a town in the place where he (the sage) lived. The princes built the town and named in Kapilavatthu (Kapilavastu). In course of time, the four brothers married the four sisters, excepting the eldest one and they came to be known as the Śākyas. The Mahāvaṃsa also refers to sister-marriage. It says that Sīhabāhu, ruler of the kingdom of Lāḷha, made his sister Sihasīvalī his queen.[1]

It is, however, difficult to say how far the Buddhist stories about the origin of some famous political communities by sister-marriage can be regarded as historical. Sister-marriage was not in vogue in ancient India even in the earliest times of which we have any record, as the story of Yama and Yamī in the Ṛg-Veda amply demonstrates. The idea was revolting to the Indians from the time of the Ṛg-Veda downwards.

Marriage of a woman with her cousin.

The marriage of cousins, on the other hand, seems to have been by no means unusual. The marriage of Princess Vajirā with king Ajātasatru the son of her father's sister, is an illustration of this kind of marriage. Magha, a householder of Magadha, married his maternal uncle's daughter named Sujātā (Dhammapada Commentary, 265). Ānanda was enamoured of the beauty of his father's sister's daughter named Uppalavannā and wanted to marry her (ibid., p. 48). This shows that cousins could marry. This is also borne out by the following Jātaka story (no. 262; cf. no. 126):

A king had a daughter and a nephew who were in love with each other. The king intended to marry his nephew with a princess of some other country and his daughter with a prince of some other kingdom. The king guarded his daughter very closely. One night he watched his daughter and let her rest upon a little bed in his presence. She lay down without going to sleep. A little while after she said, "Father, I want to bathe." "Come along, my daughter," said the king. Holding her hands the king led her to the window; he lifted her and placed her on a lotus ornament outside it, holding her by one hand. As she bathed herself, she held out a hand to the prince, the nephew of the king and lover of the daughter. The prince loosed off the bangles from her arm, and fastened them on the arm of his soft-handed page boy; then he lifted the lad and placed him upon the lotus beside the princess. She took his hand, and placed it in her father's and went away with the prince. The king considered the lad to be his own daughter; and when the bathing was over, he put him to sleep in the royal bed chamber, shut the door and set his seal on it; then setting a

1. Lāḷharaṭṭhe pure tasmin sīhabāhu narādhipo rajjam kāresi katvāna maheshiṃ Sīhasīvaliṃ (Mahāvaṃsa, Geiger's ed., p. 60; cf. *ibid.*, ch. VII., verses 67-68).

guard he returned to his own chamber and lay down to rest. The next morning he opened the door and saw the lad. The lad being questioned told the king how his daughter had fled with the prince. The king was cast down and thought, "Not even if one goes along and holds hands can one guard a woman?" Then he gave his daughter in marriage to the prince, his nephew who, on his maternal uncle's death, ascended the throne.

In the Mahāvaṃsa also we find references to cousin-marriage.[1] Cittā, daughter of king Paṇḍuvāsudeva of Laṅkā, was so very beautiful that anybody seeing her would run mad. Hence Cittā was called Ummādacittā. Afraid of a prophecy that Cittā's son would kill Cittā's brothers for the throne, the princes kept their only sister in a chamber having but one pillar and the entry to the chamber lay through the king's sleeping apartment. Cittā had only one serving woman. One day she saw her maternal uncle's son named Dighagāmani and fell in love with him at first sight. With the help of the maid Gāmani used to get into the princess's chamber stealthily every night. Matters went on in this way for sometime till Cittā was discovered to be with child. The serving woman informed the queen who, having questioned her daughter, brought the matter to the notice of the king. The king in consultation with his sons gave Cittā in marriage with her lover who was her maternal uncle's son.[2]

Suvannapālī was married and made queen by her father's sister's son named Paṇḍukābhaya.[3]

Different forms of Marriage

Marriage was usually of three forms: (1) Marriage arranged by guardians of both parties, (2) Svayaṃvara, and (3) Gandharva marriage.

The common form of marriage was that arranged by guardians of both the parties and established between two families of the same caste and equal rank. This was akin to the Prājāpatya form of marriage current amongst the Hindus. Equality of birth and not of wealth was a matter of primary consideration before the settlement of a marriage. The Sāvatthian treasurer, Migāra, for instance, considered the equality of birth before he agreed to the proposal sent by Treasurer Dhanañjaya of Sāketa for the marriage of his daughter, Visākhā with Migāra's son (Buddhist Parables, p. 161; cf. Dhammapada Commentary, vol.I p. 390). In the Babbu Jātaka (no.137) we read that a Sāvatthian girl

1. Pitucchādhītaraṃ taṃ so ādāya dhajinīpati, gantvāna Vaṅganagaraṃ saṃvāsaṃ tāya kappayi (Geiger's ed., p. 58).
2. Mahāvaṃsa, Geiger's ed., ch. IX.
3. *Ibid.*, ch. X, 78.

named Kāṇā was married to a husband of the same caste in another village. The Nakkhatta Jātaka (no.49) tells us that a gentleman of the country near Sāvatthī asked in marriage for his son a young Sāvatthian lady of equal rank. We learn from the Therīgāthā Commentary (p.260) that Isidāsī, daughter of a virtuous and wealthy merchant, was married to a merchant's son of equal position. Uttarā, daughter of Nandaka, commander-in-chief of Piṅgala, king of Suraṭṭha, was married to one of a family of equal position (Petavatthu Cy., pp. 244-257).

The Vimānavatthu informs us that a daughter of an upāsaka at Sāvatthī was married to a member of another family of equal status. (Vimānavatthu Commentary, p. 128). The Manorathapūraṇī (p. 227) tells us the Sigālakamātā who came of the Treasurer's family at Rājagaha was married to a family of equal rank.

The usual practice in the form of marriage mentioned above was that the bridegroom used to come to the bride's house for marriage. The bridegroom and his party were received with great honour and were provided with both lodging and requisites—garlands, perfumes, garments and the rest.

Exceptions regarding caste and rank are sometimes met with in several works such as the Viruḍhakāvadāna in the Avadānakalpalatā, the Therīgāthā, the Mahāvaṃsa and the Jātakas. Pasenadi, king of Kosala, married a slave-girl of the Sākya Mahānāman and took her with him in great pomp to Sāvatthī. This girl was called Mallikā, well-known for her wonderful touch. Pasenadi while intending to establish a connection with the Buddha's family by marriage, was deceived by the Sākyas who gave him in marriage, a girl named Vāsavakhattiyā, a daughter by a slave-woman of one of their leading chiefs, Mahānāman. This deception was avenged by Viḍūḍabha, son of Pasenadi by Vāsavakhattiyā (cf. Introduction to Kaṭṭhahāri Jātaka, no. 7; Dhammapada Commentary, vol. I pp. 345 ff.). Ashoka made a merchant's daughter named Devī his wife who bore him, in course of time, a son named Mahinda and a daughter named Saṅghamittā (Mahāvaṃsa, p. 88). The marriage of Kisāgotamī, daughter of a poverty-stricken house, with the son of a rich merchant was not preceded by any consideration of caste or rank (Dhammapada Commentary, II, p. 270). Similarly the equality of birth, family and wealth had to be sacrificed by the parents of Kuṇḍalakesī in marrying her with a thief with whom she fell in love at first sight from the top of her house (ibid., p. 217). Cāpā, daughter of the chief of the hunters of Vaṅkahāra country, was given to an ascetic named Upaka as his wife. Upaka lived near the hunter's house where he used to go for alms. Once the hunter had to go out for seven days on a hunting excursion. Cāpā was asked to wait upon the ascetic. The first day the ascetic came to the hunter's house for alms, Cāpā came out and gave him alms. Upaka was captivated by her beauty. He returned home and lay fasting for seven days being fired by lust. The hunter came back and learnt everything. Thereupon he gave his daughter Cāpā to the ascetic Upaka as his bride (Therīgāthā Commentary, pp. 220 ff.). The circumstances which brought about the union of the hunter's daughter with an ascetic go to show that the consideration of caste or rank was sometimes sacrificed in exceptional circumstances. Cāpā, it might be said without fear of contradiction, was given by her father to an ascetic out of respect towards the latter. The story of Triśaṇku, the Caṇḍāla chieftain, narrated in the Divyāvadāna, is the only instance indicating the marriage of a Brahmin daughter with the Caṇḍāla's learned son Śārdulakarṇa (pp. 620 *et seq*).

Svayaṃvara

The second form of marriage was Svayaṃvara or a girl's publicly choosing a husband for herself from a number of suitors assembled for the purpose. The Kuṇāla Jātaka (no. 536) refers to the Svayaṃvara marriage of princess Kaṇhā who, on seeing the five sons of the king Paṇḍu, viz., Ajjuna, Nakula, Bhīmasena, Yudhiṭṭhila and Sahadeva in Svayaṃvara assembly, fell in love with all five, threw a wreathed coil of flowers on their heads while they were standing before her, and said, "Dear mother, I choose these five men." She was allowed to have these five men as her husbands. This is evidently a reminiscence of the celebrated Svayaṃvara marriage of Draupatī recorded in the Mahābhārtha. In the Nacca Jātaka (no. 32) also we read that a princess prayed to her father for a boon that she might be allowed to choose a husband for herself. With a view to grant her prayer, the king invited all princes to a Svayaṃvara sabhā convened for the purpose. Princes from all countries assembled there. The king sent for his daughter and bade her go and choose a husband after her own heart. The girl appeared before the assembly and selected one as her life-mate. The selected husband was then found to be wanting in modesty and was therefore disapproved by the king.

Generally do we find in the Hindu literature that a person chosen by a maid in Svayaṃvara assembly becomes the husband of the maid despite his demerits. Of course in such an assembly kings and princes are suitors. But this appears to be an exceptional instance in which the final verdict rests with the bride's father.

The Dhammapada Commentary furnishes us with another reference to a Svayaṃvara marriage. It tells us that Vepacitti, king of the Asuras, refused to give his daughter in marriage to any of the Asura princes. So he said, "My daughter shall choose for herself such a husband as she sees fit." He then assembled the host of Asuras, made over a garland of flowers to his daughter and said to her, "choose for yourself a husband who suits you." The girl selected one as her husband and threw the wreath over his head: (Dhammapada Commentary, vol. I, pp. 278-279).

Gandharva Marriage

The third form of marriage is what may be called the Gandharva form of marriage in which the bride and the bridegroom make their own choice without the knowledge of their guardians, and are married without rites or ceremonies.

The Kaṭṭhahāri Jātaka (no. 7) gives us an instance of this Gandharva form of marriage. Once a king having gone in great state to his pleasure-garden was wandering hither and thither for fruits and flowers. He saw a woman who was merrily singing away as she picked up sticks in the grove. The king fell in love with her at first sight and became intimate with her. The woman knew and told the king that she would become a mother. The king gave her the signet-ring from his finger and said, "If it be a girl, spend this ring on her nurture; but if it be a boy, bring the ring and the child to me." In course of time a child was born. When the child could run about and play, he was taken by his mother to the king with the signet ring. After great difficulty the boy was proved to be the son of the king who made him viceroy and his mother queen-consort. This story reminds us of the well-known union of Śakuntalā with king Duṣyanta in the Abhijñāna-Śakuntalaṃ of Kālidāsa.

Elopement

Women were sometimes seduced and abducted. These eloped women subsequently married in some cases and in others they used to pass off as wives without going through any matrimonial rite. In the Dhammapada Commentary (vol. I, pp. 191 ff.), we read that Vāsuladattā, daughter of Caṇḍapajjota of Ujjain, was given by her father to Udena to teach her the mantra for capturing elephants. Udena fell in love with Vāsuladattā and eloped with her. Afterwards Udena married her and made her his queen. The same work (vol. II, p. 260 f.) informs us that Paṭācāra was the daughter of a rich banker of Sāvatthī. When sixteen she was kept on the topmost floor of a seven storied palace and was guarded with excessive care, but she fell in love with her own page. On the day fixed for her marriage with another youth, equal in birth and rank, she eloped with her lover, took shelter in a distant village and dwelt in a hamlet. Nowhere in this account do we find that Paṭācāra was married by the parmour subsequent to elopement. But they passed off as husband and wife and in course of time Paṭācāra gave birth to a child (cf. Therīgāthā Commentary, p. 108). The Assaka Jātaka (No. 100) also says that the king of Kosala came up with a great force against the king of Benares, slew the king and bore off his queen to be his own wife. A similar instance of the abduction of a woman is met within the Takka Jātaka (No. 63) which says that a village girl was kidnapped and kept as wife by a robber chieftain.

Seclusion of Women

To guard against elopement, abduction and unions not sanctioned by custom, women were often kept inside the purdah. We learn from the Dhammapada Commentary that a rich man's daughter, when she attained marriageable age, was lodged by her parents in an apartment of royal splendour on the topmost floor of a seven storied palace, with a female slave to guard her (vol. III, p. 24). No male servant was kept in that house (ibid., vol. II, p. 217). Daughters of noble families did not ordinarily come out of their houses but they travelled in chariots and the like, while others entered an ordinary carriage or raised a parasol or a palmyraleaf over their heads; but if this was not available, they took the shirt of their undergarment and threw it over their shoulder (Dhammapada Commentary, vol. I, p. 391).

From the instances cited above it is reasonable to hold that elopement and the preservation of chastity *inter alia* contributed largely to the observance of purdah by the tender sex before or after marriage. But there are exceptions, Visākhā, for example, while going to her father-in-law's house just after her marriage entered the city to Sāvatthi not under the purdah but standing up in a chariot uncovered showing herself to all the city (D.C., I, pp. 384 ff.). Daughters of respectable families who did not ordinarily stir out used to go on foot, during a festival, with their own retinue and bathe in the river (Dhammapada Commentary, vol. I, pp. 190, 191 and 388). These instances indeed show a relaxation of the purdah system.

Lucky days were arranged for marriage in which the bride or bridegroom was brought home or sent forth (Dīgha Nikāya, vol.I, p.11).

Auspicious days observed for the celebration of marriage

Marriage ceremonies were held during auspicious hours which were strictly observed by some. We learn from the Nakkhatta Jātaka that a naked ascetic was consulted as to whether stars were favourable for holding marriage ceremonies. The fixed day was found to be inauspicious and the bridegroom did not come to the bride's house for marriage (Jātaka, no. 49).

Dowry

The Buddhist literature hardly mentions the prevalence of dowry system in connection with marriage ceremonies. But instances of dowry being given by the bride's father are referred to in the Visākhāya-vatthu of the Dhammapada Commentary (vol. I).

The Sāvatthian treasurer, Migāra, on the occasion of the marriage of his daughter, Visākhā, well-known in the Buddhist literature, gave her as dowry five hundred carts filled with money, five hundred filled with vessels of gold, five hundred filled with vessels of silver, five hundred filled with copper vessels, five hundred filled with garments made of various kinds of silk, five hundred filled with ghee, five hundred filled with rice husked and winnowed, and five hundred filled with ploughs, plough-shares and other farm implements. Sixty thousand powerful bulls and sixty thousand milch-cows, and some powerful bull-calves were also given to her.

Bath and Perfume Money

The Dhammapada Commentary and the Jātakas tell us that marriage of girls was celebrated with bath-money given by the father to his daughter. Mahā-Kosala, father of Pasenadi, king of Kosala, married his daughter Kośala-devi to king Bimbisāra of Magadha and gave her a village in Kāsi for her bath and perfume money (Jātakas, nos. 239 and 283). Princess Vajirā was the daughter of Pasenadi of Kosala. She was given in marriage to Ajātasattu of Magadha. Kāsigāma was given to her by her father for her bath and perfume money (Dhammapada Comy., vol. III, p. 266). The Sāvatthian treasurer, Migāra, gave his daughter, on her marriage, fifty-four crores of treasure to buy aromatic powders for the bath (ibid., vol. I, p. 398).

Levy on the Occasion of a Marriage Ceremony

The custom of collecting presents (paṇṇākāran) on the occasion of a marriage ceremony is met with in the Dhammapada Commentary (vol. I, p. 182), where we read that on the occasion of the marriage ceremony of Visākhā, daughter of Dhanañjaya Seṭṭhi with the son of Migāra Seṭṭhi, presents including a hundred each of all kinds of gifts were collected from hundred villages.

Admonitions to a Married Girl

After marriage the girl was sent to her father-in-law's house with the following admonitions:[1]

1. Do not bring outside the indoor fire.
2. Do not bring inside the outdoor fire.
3. Give only to him that gives.
4. Do not give him that does not give.
5. Give both to him that gives and him that does not give.
6. Sit happily.
7. Eat happily.
8. Sleep happily.
9. Tend the fire.
10. Honour the household divinity.

These ten admonitions were interpreted as follows:-

1. If the mother-in-law or other female members of the household engage in a private conversation within the house, their conversation is not to be communicated to slaves, whether female or male, for such conversation is tattled about and causes quarrels.

2. The conversation of slaves and servants is not to be communicated to persons within the household; as such conversation is talked about and causes quarrels.

3. This means that one should give only to those that return borrowed articles.

4. This means that one should not give to those who do not return borrowed articles.

5. This means that one should help poor kinsfolk and friends who look for succour, without considering their capability of repaying.

6. This means that a wife seeing her mother-in-law or her father-in-law, should stand and not remain sitting.

7. This means that a wife should not eat before her mother-in-law, father-in-law and husband have taken their meals. She should serve them first, and when she is sure that they have had all they care for, then and not till then may she herself eat.

---

1. Anto aggi bahi na nīharitabbo, bahi aggi anto na pavesitabbo, dadantass' eva dātabbam, adadantassa na dātabbaṃ, dadantassāpi adadantassāpi dātabbaṃ, sukhaṃ nisīditabbaṃ, sukhaṃ bhuñjitabbaṃ, sukhaṃ nipajjitabbaṃ, aggi paricaritabbo, antodevatāpi namssitabbā' ti idaṃ dasavidhaṃ ovādam. Dhammapada Comy., I, pp. 397-398.

8. This means that a wife should not go to bed before her mother-in-law, father-in-law and husband. She should first perform all the duties which she owes them and then she may herself lie down to sleep.

9. This means that a wife should regard her mother-in-law, father-in-law or husband as a flame of fire or a serpent-king.

10. When a monk, after keeping residence in a remote lodging, comes to the door of a house and the housewife sees him, she must first give to such a monk whatever food there is in the house, both hard and soft; and then she may eat. (Dhammapada Comy., I, pp. 403-404).

Polygamy and Polyandry

Buddhist literature contains but one reference to polyandry. The only exception indicating the existence of polyandry occurs in the Kuṇāla Jātaka[1] in which we read that princess Kaṇhā was allowed to have at a time five husbands selected by her in a Svayaṃvara assembly. A woman could not marry more than one man at a time nor could a woman as a general rule marry twice in her life though there were exceptions.[2] We learn from the Nakkhatta Jātaka (no. 49) that on the failure of the selected bridegroom's coming to the bride's house on the appointed day the bride was given in marriage to another bridegroom. When the first bridegroom came he was told that the girl could not be married twice over. It was not the custom for a wedded wife to take another mate even if she was not loved by her husband.[3] But there are instances in which married women who were either kidnapped or seduced were kept as wives. While a woman does not generally appear to have taken more than one husband, a man appears to have married more than one woman. In the Vimānavatthu Commentary (pp. 149-156) we read that Bhaddā being barren told her husband to marry her sister Subhaddā. The husband did so. The Babbu Jātaka (no. 137) tells us that a wife delayed in coming back to her husband's house from her father's house and the husband took a second wife. The Ruhaka Jātaka (no. 191) informs us that a husband sent her naughty and deceitful wife away and took a second wife. The Assaka Jātaka (no. 207) gives us another instance of a husband's taking a

1. Jātaka, no. 536.
2. Infra.
3. "Ārā dūre na idha kadāci atthi.
paramaparā nāma kule imasmiṃ,
taṃ kullavattaṃ anuvattamānā
'māham kule antimagandhinī ahuṃ'
etassa vādassa jigucchamānā
akāmikā baddha carāmi tuyhan ti."
(Kaṇhadīpāyana Jātaka, Fausboll, Jātaka, vol, IV, p. 35).

second wife. In it we read that king Assaka of Potali, a city in the kingdom of Kāśī, took a second queen on the death of his first queen Ubbarī. In some of the Jātakas[1] we find that certain kings had as many as sixteen thousand wives. A Magadhan householder named Magha had four wives at a time, viz., Nandā, Cittā, Sudhammā, and Sujātā (D.C.,I, 265). King Bimbisāra had 500 wives (Mahāvagga, viii, I, 15). King Okkāka had five queens (Sumaṅgalavilāsinī, p. 258). The Mahāvaṃsa records that Māyā and Mahāmāyā, two uterine sisters, were given in marriage to Suddhodana (Geiger's text, p. 14). This is borne out by the fact related in the Tibetan Buddhist books as translated by Rockhill (Life of the Buddha, p.15) that Suddhodana, inspite of the rigorous provision of the law of the land prohibiting every citizen from marrying more than one woman was allowed to have two wives as a mark of gratitude for his subduing the hillmen of the Pāṇḍava tribe while a prince. Thus we see that husbands used to take more than one wife in the lifetime of the first wife or after her death. While the man had the privilege of marrying more than one woman at a time, the woman had the misfortune of enduring cruel treatment at the hands of her co-wife.

Co-wives

The worst misery for a women is to have a co-wife. In almost all cases fellow-wives quarrel with one another and make home a place to fly away from rather than to fly to for peace and comfort. A woman cannot tolerate that her husband should ignore her very existence and take pleasure with other women (Jātaka, no. 519). Sometimes barren women used to bring to second wife for their husbands for the continuance of their husband's line; but the inherent jealousy of women against their co-wives exhibits itself when their co-wives bear children and become husband's favourites. The Dhammapada Commentary (I, 45 ff.) tells us that the first wife of a householder of Sāvatthī being barren, brought another wife for her husband. When her co-wife became pregnant, she was jealous and effected abortion by administering medicine. Thrice did the woman commit this heinous crime with the result that her co-wife succumbed at last to the effect of the abortive medicine. But the cruel woman did not escape the penalty for doing this sinful deed. She was beaten to death by her husband who declared her to be the cause of the death of his pregnant wife and destroyer of his line.

The Petavatthu gives us another illustration. Mattā the wife of a householder of Sāvatthī was childless. Hence her husband took another

---

1. Jātakas, nos. 514, 538.

wife named Tissā. Being jealous of the rival wife, Mattā, one day, heaped together the sweepings and threw them on the head of her co-wife. Tissā endured humiliation and bad behaviour of her co-wife. On her death Mattā was born as a petī who suffered various miseries. One day she appeared before Tissā and requested her to offer on her account, food etc. to eight bhikkhus. Tissā bore no grudge against her co-wife despite her ill-behaviour. She did as requested, and Mattā was released from the petoloka (Paramatthadīpanī on the Petavatthu, pp. 82-89).

Divorce

Divorce was allowed but without any formal decree. Isidāsī, for instance, had to return twice to her father's house having been turned out of the house by successive husbands because she did not prove desirable for one husband after another (Therī-gāthā Comy., p. 260). No instance is recorded of similar action taken against the husband.

Remarriage of Women

Certain passages indicate that remarriage of women was not unknown in the Buddhist period. The introduction to the Ucchaṅga Jātaka (no. 67) which tells us that a woman's husband, brother and son were once imprisoned. Her loud lamentations caused the king to show her favour. The king said to her "I give you one of the three, which will you take?" "Sire," was her answer. "if I live, I can get another husband and another son; but as my parents are dead, I can never get another brother. So give me my brother, Sir." This reply of the woman indicates that a woman could probably marry more than once. The instance of Isidāsī, cited above, also illustrates the point.

Widow Remarriage

The Ceylonese Chronicle, the Mahāvaṃsa, furnishes us with an instance of widow- remarriage. In it we read that king Khallāṭanāga was overpowered by the Commander of his troops named Kammahārattaka. The Commander was killed by the king's younger brother named Vaṭṭagāmaṇi. The latter began to rule the kingdom, took his nephew, Mahācūḷika as his son and made his elder brother's wife, Anulādevī, his queen (Geiger, text, pp. 269-270).

Gift of Wife

The Avadānakalpalatā of Kṣemendra mentions that woman was man's absolute property. Man could dispose of woman in any way he liked. It tells us that Śrīsena, a charitable king of the Ariṣtā country, had a queen named Jayaprabhā. To fulfill the desire of his preceptor, a disciple came to the king and prayed for queen Jayaprabhā to be given as a preceptor's fee. Śrīsena with a smiling face gave away his queen

Jayaprabhā. But the preceptor, on receiving the desired fee, changed his mind. He sent back the queen with due respect to the king (Śrīsenāvadāna). In complying with the request of Vāhīka-muni, a disciple of Marīci, Manicūḍa, king of Sāketa, gave away his queen Padmāvatī along with her son to wait upon the old sage (Manicūḍāvadāna). Viśvantara, prince of Viśvapuri, being requested by Indra in a brāhmaṇa's guise, gave away his own wife Mādrī (Viśvantarāvadāna).

Chapter - 13
Slavery as known from the Buddhist Pāli Sources

Madan Mohan Singh

From the Buddhist Pāli sources we get a detailed account of the slaves as they lived in the society. It is supported by the contemporary Brahmanical literature. The *Vinaya* texts,[1] the *Nikāyas*[2] and the Jātakas frequently refer to both male and female slaves found in the royal harem,[3] or in the households of rich persons in capital cities, like Rājagṛiha,[4] or in the houses of villagers.[5]

That slaves were being bought and sold is mentioned both in the Buddhist texts and the Dharmaśāstras. The *Jātakas* give definite statements on this point and they also mention the price of a slave. In *Jātaka* no. 39, a Saddhivihārika (novice or disciple) is compared to a slave bought for a hundred pieces of silver punch-marked coins.[6] This suggests that a slave could be ordinarily bought for one hundred Kārshāpaṇas. *Jātaka* No. 402 states that a Brāhmaṇa, after collection of seven hundred Karshāpaṇas, thought that the amount was sufficient for buying some female and male slaves.[7] But here unfortunately the number of slaves is not given. Most probably the price of a slave was generally one hundred Karshāpaṇas, but it might have varied in a few cases. The physical fitness of a male slave and the features of a female might have been responsible for a higher price. In some cases the needy purchaser might have offered a higher price for a slave. Kauṭ

---

1. *S.B.E.* XIII. 315; *C.V.* IV. 4. 6-7.
2. *D.N.* I. 64; *M.N.* I. 452; चयो नेकानं दासगणानं चयो नेकानं दासीगणानं चयो; II. 187; *G.S.* I.128; *A.N.* II. 209.
3. *Jā,* No. 92.
4. *C.V.* VI. 4. 2.
5. *Jā,* No. 330.
6. *Jā,* I, 224. मह्यं एको सद्धिविहारिको एकस्मिं ठाने सतेन कीतदासो विय होति।
7. *Jā,* III, 343.

ilya says that the Mlecchas are not punishable, if they sell or pledge their children, but an Ārya cannot be reduced to slavery.[1] Manu also mentions the Śūtras were often bought and sold.[2]

In the *Mahābhārata* it is said that Yudhiṣṭhira gave to each of the 88000 *snātakas* engaged in the sacrifice, thirty female slaves.[3] The *Digha* and the *Aṅguttara Nikāyas* state that the Buddha had prohibited the Bhikṣus from accepting the gifts of slaves, either male or female.[4] According to a *Jātaka* story a Brāhmaṇa demanded a hundred slave girls from a king along with other requisites as his gift, and his demands were fulfilled.[5]

Categories of Slaves

The number of the categories of slaves is different with different writes. The *Vinaya-Piṭaka* mentions three categories;[6] the*Vidhurapaṇḍita Jātaka*, four,[7] other *Jātakas* refer the three additional categories;[8] the *Arthaśāstra* gives five,[9] and Manu mentions seven.[10]

The first category is of the war-captives, who were forced to accept the serfdom of the conqueror. This appear to be the earliest category. Later on, out of the unfortunate enslaves war-captives, some may have been either sold or given in gifts to others by their masters. Our authorities accept the categories of those who were either sold or given in gifts. The fourth category is of those who sold themselves as slaves. Manu makes a difference between this category and the category of those who were bought, probably because in one case it was the slave, who sold himself out of his own accord; while in the other he may have been sold by his former master. The fifth category is of the those who became slaves during the scarcity days for want of food. This category is very similar to the category of those who sold themselves of their own will. The sixth category is of those who became slaves for paying off their debts. This sixth category is of those who became slaves for paying of their debts. This category also is similar

---

1. *Kau*, III, 13.
2. *Manu*. VIII. 413.
3. *Mbh.Sabhā*. 52, 45-46.
4. *D.N.* I. 64; *A.N.* II. 209.
5. *Jā*. IV. 99.
6. *Bhikhuṇī Vibhaṅga Saṅghādusesa*, I. 2. 1. दासो नाम श्रन्तोजातो धनक्कीतो करमरानितो; quoted by Fick in *Social Organisation*, p. 307.
7. *Jā*. VI. 285 श्रामायदासापि भवन्ति एके, धनेन कीतापि भवन्ति दासा, सयमपि ह' भवन्ति एके उपयन्ति दासा भया पणुन्नापि दासा।
8. *Jā*. I. 200; IV 22, 99; Vi. 545-48.
9. *Kau*. III. 13.
10. *Manu*. VIII. 415.

to the above two; because indebtedness is generally caused by family poverty, and the debtors finding themselves unable to pay off their debts, either accepted the slavery of the creditor in order to pay of their debts in the form of labour, or they pledged themselves to others, for the amount which they owed to their creditors. The seventh and the eighth categories are of those who were born from female slaves and of those who were inherited as ancestral property. Both of these seem to be similar; but the difference was that while the former consisted exclusively of those who were born of their slave mothers, the latter could have been either bought, or received in gift, or acquired by any other means by the predecessor of one who inherited them. The ninth category was of those who were condemned to slavery as a punishment for their crimes.

The Buddhist sources do not mention the categories of those who sold themselves as slaves and those who were inherited as the ancestral property, as mentioned by Kauṭilya and Manu. It seems that the former was not differentiated from the category of those who accepted slavery of their own will; while the latter was not distinguished from the category of the slaves born in the house of the master. Thus we find that all the categories referred to in the Brahmanical sources are mentioned in the Buddhist texts. There is one category of the *Jātakas* which is not mentioned, either by Kauṭilya or Manu. This category is called slaves driven by fear in the *Vidhurapaṇḍita Jātaka*. But this category can be put under the category of the war-captives. Now, if we put together the categories mentioned by the *Vinaya-piṭaka* and the *Jātakas* on one side and the categories of Kauṭilya and Manu on the other, we find the following picture:—

Vinaya-Pīṭaka and Jātaka Stories	Kauṭilya and Manu
Slaves	Slaves
1. born of slave mothers	1. born of slave mothers.
2. bought by money.	2. bought by money.
3. captured in war.	3. captured in war.
4. driven by fear.	4. of their own accord for want of food.
5. as a punishment for their crimes.	5. as a result of judicial decrees.
6. received as gifts.	6. received as gifts.
7. for paying off debts.	7. for paying off debts.
8. of their own will.	8. who sold themselves.
	9. inherited as the ancestral property.

The number of the categories increased further in later times, and we find Nārada mentioning fifteen categories of slaves.[1]

Treatment of Slaves

As regards the treatment of slaves, we get conflicting statements. It depended on the temperament of the master that a slave received good or bad treatment. As in other countries, in India also harsh slave-owners were not unknown. There are cases in record of such slave-owners who harassed their slaves. Sometimes they were punished for their faults and mistakes. A slave who was elevated to the position of the store-keeper of his master reflected within himself, "Not always, will one care to let me have the office of a store-keeper; one good day some defect will be noticed in me and the people will thrash me, lock me up, brand me, and give me the food of a slave to eat"[2] A slave girl who had not brought home her wages of the day, was thrown down at the door of the house and beaten by her master and mistress with rope ends.[3] Beating with a rope as a consequence of the slave's fault is also enjoined by Manu.[4] But sometimes slaves were ill treated merely out of the whimsical nature of their owners. Thus, for instance, the *Aṅguttara-Nikāya* says that the slaves worked with tearful faces for fear of the rod.[5] *Jātaka* No. 63 says that the fierce daughter of a high treasurer used to revile and beat her slaves and servants.[6] The *Vessantara Jātaka* tells us that a Brāhmaṇa, who had received the son and the daughter of a king, bound them with creepers and drove away beating them with the creeper-ends. He dragged them on with a staff in his hand, holding the creeper tight.[7] As he had to go a long distance, at night he used to tie up the children with osiers and leave them lying upon the ground, but himself, in fear of wild beasts, would climb up a tree and sit in the fork of the bough.[8] This account of the treatment of the children is exaggerated, and is aimed at depicting the Brāhamaṇa as cruel and selfish to show the contrast between him and the king (Bodhisatta), who gave his children in gift.

---

1. *Nārada*, V. 25-28.
2. *Jā*. I. 451, किंचिद् एव दोसं दिस्वा तालेत्वा बंधित्वालक्खणेन अंकेत्वा दासपरिभोगेन पि परिभुञ्जिस्सन्ति।
3. *Jā*. I. 402, अथ एकं दासीं भतिं अददमानं सामिका द्वारे निसिदापेत्वा रज्जुया पहारन्ति।
4. *Manu*. VIII. 209.
5. *K.S*. I. 102; *A.N*. II. 207-8....दण्डतज्जिता भयतज्जिता अस्सुमुखा परिकम्मानि करोन्ति।
6. *Jā*. II. 295.
7. *Jā*. VI. 548.
8. *Jā*. Vi. 573.

It is true that a few slave received ill treatment from their masters; but it can bear no comparison to the treatment of Helots of Sparta, Council of Rome, and the slaves of the planters of the eighteenth and nineteenth century in America. In the western countries, slaves, used to work in chains under cruel overseers, taking a fiendish delight in exacting a pound of flesh; they used to be made over to the beasts of prey for the delectation and amusement of the rich orders of the society, as in Italy; a master could kill not more than two slaves daily to refresh his tired nerves in the warm blood and bowels of the victim.[1]

It was most probably the absence of such atrocities and beastly cruelties of the masters practised on the slaves that the foreign observers, who visited India the 4th century B.C., missed to notice the wide prevalence of this system. Megasthenes, who lived for years at Pāṭaliputra, makes no mention of the employment of slaves in Magadha. Our sources reveal that very often slaves received good treatment from their masters. In pious households they were supplied with rice, meat, and milk-rice for their food.[2] Some of them were treated as members of the family to which they belonged and were elevated to responsible posts, as was the case of Kaṭāhaka, who grew up in the company of his master's son, got his education along with him, learnt two or three handicrafts and was appointed as the store-keeper of his master.[3] A Brāhmaṇa, the *purohita* of a king, when favoured with a boon by his lord, went home and asked the desires of his family members including the female slave Puṇṇā, who expressed her desire for a mortar, a pestle, and a sieve.[4] When the son of a Brāhmaṇa died and was burnt without tear, the female slave of the family was asked, "No doubt you must have been abused, beaten, and oppressed by him, therefore you are glad at his death and weep not"; she replied, 'My lord, speak not so; this does not suit his case. My young master was full of long sufferings, love, and pity for me and was to me as a foster child, reared on the breast'.[5] Such instances of good treatment of slaves show that their relations to the members of the master's family were often of amity and harmony and that in a good number of cases they enjoyed good treatment.

---

1. Carlyle: *History of French Revolution*, p. 19.
2. *G.S.* I. 128.
3. *Jā*. I. 451.
4. *Jā*. II. 428, सो गन्त्वा ब्राह्मणिञ्च पुत्तञ्च सुणिसञ्च दासिञ्च पक्कोसित्वा 'राजा मे वरं देति, किं गणहामीति पुच्छि।...पुणणा नाम दासी मह्यं उदुक्खल-मुसलञ्च' एव सुपञ्चा 'इति।
5. *Ja*. III. 167.

From the *Arthaśāstra* of Kauṭilya, we know that in case a few masters treated their slaves badly, the state was not to be a silent spectator. On the other hand, the state interfered and such masters were punished for their unfair dealings. If a master beat a slave, or employed him in mean work, he forfeited the purchase value of the slave.[1] If a master raped a slave girl, pledged to him, he not only forfeited the purchase value, but also had to pay a certain amount of money (*śulka*) to her and a fine of twice the amount to the government.[2] Such rules prescribed by Kauṭilya indicate that during the days of the Mauryas, the position of the slaves was not very unsatisfactory. Such conditions would have existed even before this period.

In a few cases, slaves enjoyed fullest confidence of their masters. The *Nanda Jātaka* (No. 39) tells us that there was an old squire, who had a young wife, a young son, and a slave, Nanda. One day he thought that after his death, his wife being so young would marry somebody and spend all the money he had, leaving nothing for his son. So one day he went to the forest and buried the money safely under the ground. This matter was known only to the slave Nanda, who had accompanied his master at the time of burying the hoard and who was told by him to show the treasure to the young master, when he would grow up.[3] This shows how a slave could enjoy the confidence of his master more than the latter's wife in some cases.

There was every possibility of young masters falling in love with their young slave girls. What would have been the ultimate result of such unions? Kauṭilya says that if a son was born as a consequence of a master's union with a slave girl, she was no longer a slave.[4] This suggests the probability of such a slave girl being elevated to the position of a wife. It is said in a *Jātaka* story that Tissa-Kumāra, the scion of a wealthy seṭṭhi family of Rājagṛiha, gained his parents' consent to enter the monastery by resorting to go on hunger-strike. His parents were very much grieved at their son's entry to the monastery. A slave girl, who saw them weeping for their son, consoled them and took up the task of bringing him back to his house again. She was beautiful and by her feminine charm won the heart of her young master, who left the monastery and reverted to the worldly life.[5] The young master abandoned the Order for the sake of a slave girl; what would have been the relation between the two in the future is not known. The

---

1. *Kau.* III. 13.
2. *Ibid.*
3. *Jā.* I. 225.
4. *Kau.* III. 13.
5. *Jā.* I. 156-57.

incident suggests that the ultimate end of their love might have been a lifelong union in the form of marriage. In the *Uddālaka Jātaka* it is stated that the Chaplain of a king fell in love with a slave girl. A son was born from their union. He was named Uddālaka and having grown up became a great ascetic, well versed in the sacred books. When he met his father, the latter recognising him as his own son said, "Without doubt you are a Brāhmaṇa". This shows that some recognised sons from slave mothers as belonging to the caste of the father. It may be argued here that Viḍudābha, who was the son of Prasenajit and was born of Vāsabhakhattiyā, daughter of a slave girl from Mahānāma-khattiya of the Śākya clan, was reduced from his princely status to the position of a slave by his father, due to the servile origin of his mother on her mother's side.[1] But in this case the Kośala king's action was a result of his wrath on the Śākyas for deceiving him by giving the hands of a girl born from a slave mother in place of one of their own blood, which fell on his son and wife. Later, the king excused them, and Viḍuḍābha succeeded his father as the heir-apparent. It may be further argued that Viḍudābha was not respected highly by the Śākyas, when he had been at his maternal grand-father's house, and some contemptuous terms were used for him. But this also was due to the Śākyan pride of lineage, for which they were well-known. Customs and practices were different from place to place, and the opinion which was held by the Śākyas cannot be taken as a universal one.

There were also a few cases of higher caste ladies falling in love with slaves. It is said in the *Culla-Seṭṭhi Jātaka* (No. 4) that a rich merchant's daughter in Rājagṛiha actually stooped to intimacy with a slave. Getting alarmed at the idea of her misconduct being revealed to her parents, she eloped with her lover, the slave. She gave birth to two sons. When the elder son reached the age of understanding, he enquired from his mother about his relatives and asked, whether he had got any like other boys. His mother told him that he was the grandson of a wealthy merchant. At the insistence of the boy to see his grandfather's place, his mother and father started for Rājagṛiha and reached there. But she did not dare to face her father; nor the father liked to see her. However, the father did not disappoint her daughter. She was sent back with wealth and her sons were accepted by their grandfather.[2]

This shows that unions of high born ladies with low born slaves were not encouraged. It was the attitude of the society to discourage all unions of low caste males and high caste females. But, if a high born lady cultivated intimacy with a slave, such a union was tolerated,

1. *Kaṭṭhahāri Ja.* (No. 7); *Bhaddasāla Ja.* (No. 465).
2. *Jā.* I. 114-15.

though reluctantly. If the mother's father accepted a son born of it, he belonged to his family and caste. It seems that the slave girls enjoyed a better and more favourable position than the male slaves in this respect. Very often they came into close contacts with their masters and were elevated to the position of wives, losing their servile status as we have observed earlier.

Nature of their work

There were only a few slaves, like Kaṭāhaka, who were employed on high and responsible posts of storekeepers, treasurers, and private secretaries to their masters. Most of them were employed on ordinary duties of the household, and their work was manifold, which differed with the social and financial status of the master and the ability of the slaves. Slaves, living in the royal palaces and in the household of the rich Seṭṭhis, had not to do the same type of work, as the slaves in ordinary families of the villages had to perform. Generally, they seem to have been performing two types of works; viz. the household duties, and attendance on the master and the mistress. The Buddhist literature represents them as performing household duties like cooking and serving food,[1] fetching water,[2] handling plates and dishes,[3] taking charge of the granary, spreading rice in the sun and watching it,[4] and so on. Slaves of the farmer's families brought food for their masters at the field,[5] and those of ordinary families had to go out for earning wages.[6] Among the duties of attendance of the master and the mistress, we find them helping them during their bath, as accompanying them to the bathing tank and looking after their clothes and ornaments, when they entered into the tank;[7] attending on them at the time of their taking meals,[8] and so on. The nature of all these works is by no means low, and there is no indication which may lead to the conclusion that the slaves were generally employed in mean works. On the otherhand, as already referred to, we know from the *Arthaśāstra* of

---

1. *C.V.* IV. 7. 'A slave-gitl is represented as serving food to the Bhikṣus'.
   C.V. VI. 4.1. A Seṭṭhi of Rājagṛha is described as telling his slaves and workmen "Get up early in the morning and prepare congery, rice and delicacies". *Jā*. V. 293. (*Kusa*—Jā).
2. *Jā*. V. 284, Eight slave girls are represented as going to bring water, each carrying a water-pot.
   Jā. V. 413, साकिया-कोलियानं दासीसु उदकत्काय नदिं गन्त्वा... ।
3. *Jā*. I. 453.
4. *Jā*. I. 484, तस्मिं काले एका भतिया बीहिकोट्टिकदासी बीहिं गेहद्वारे आतपे पत्थरित्वा रक्खन्ति।
5. *Jā*. III. 163.
6. *Jā*. I. 402. A *dāsī* was beaten for not bringing the day's wages.
7. *Jā*. I. 383.
8. *Jā*. I. 453.

Kauṭilya that if the masters employed their slaves for works of low grade, they forfeited the purchase value.[1] The works on which the slaves could not be employed, according to Kauṭilyas were carrying the dead, sweeping ordure, urine, or the leavings of food and attendance by the female slaves while the masters bathed naked.[2] This reflects the general attitude of the society that the slaves were not to be employed for such works which were looked upon as low and impure. To go against this rule was to be a victim of the social censor, which was the forfeiture of the purchase value of a slave.

Liberation of the slaves

The earliest category of the slaves seems to be of the war captives. It can be well presumed that slaves of this category could get emancipation, if their defeated side regained its strength and conquered the enemy who had enslaved them. But such liberation was not a happening of the society in its normal course. When slavery had developed into a regular social institution, the liberation of slaves seems to be an interesting phenomenon, peculiar to the society of this country. The Buddhist sources inform us that slaves could be liberated either by accepting Sanyāsa, or by the will of the master, or by paying the latter a ransom for their emancipation. The *Dīgha-Nikāya* says that if a slave embraced the life of an ascetic, he was to be greeted with reverence and all the requisites of a recluse were to be provided for him.[3] This shows that acceptance of Sanyāsa led to the termination of one's servile status. According to the *Raṭṭhapāla-sutta* bringing happy tiding for the master would result in the emancipation of the slave.[4] In the *Sonananda Jātaka* we find a Brāhmaṇa disposing off his wealth and liberating his slaves. The *Vessantara Jātaka* represents a king as uttering after giving his son and daughter as slaves to a Brāhamaṇa, "Son Jāli, if you wish to become free, you must pay the Brāhmaṇa a hundred gold pieces; if your sister would be free, let her pay the Brāhmaṇa a hundred male and a hundred female slaves with elephants, horses, bulls, gold pieces, all a hundred each."[5] Definite information on the liberation of slaves is given by Kauṭilya. According to Kauṭilya the slaves, either bought, enslaved for court decrees, or captured in

---

1. *Kau.* III. 13.
2. *Ibid.*
3. *D.N.*, I 60-61. The Buddhist Order did not accept slaves in order to avoid interference with the right of a third party, but in the beginning they were entitled to enter the monastic fold, and the above statement refers to an earlier period.
4. *M.N.* II. 62. The mistress of the house promises to liberate her female slaves, if the news conveyed to her by the latter regarding the arrival of the former's son, who had become a Bhikṣu were true.
5. *Jā.* VI. 546-47.

war could get their emancipation by paying a certain amount as ransom to their masters. In the case of one who was bought, the amount would be his purchase value. One enslaved for fines would pay the amount of fine for which he was enslaved. If the master did not liberate his slave, after receiving the required amount of ransom, he was liable to a fine of 12 Paṇas.[1] In case a child was begotten on a female slave by her master, both the child and the mother were free.[2]

1. *Kau*. III. 13.
2. *Ibid*., III. 13.

Chapter - 14
An Early Buddha Statue from Yünnan

Walter Liebenthal

The statue reproduced on plates 1-3 hails from Yünnan province. In another paper[1] it is described as follows:

Bronze-statue of Kuan-yin P'u-sa. Originally gilded. Height about seven inches including pedestal. This is considerably damaged, the lower and some of the upper part having broken away. The remainder of the halo and three pegs which fixed it to the body are still visible on plate 3. The Bodhisattva whose Chinese name corresponds to Sanskrit Avalokiteśvara, is standing upright, the left hand carrying an alms-bowl, the right hand a willow-wisp.

The following storywent with the statue. Originally it had been in the *garbha* of the great pagoda of Ch'ung-sheng Ssunear Tali city[2] but had dropped down during an earthquake. The military, stationed in the monastery, found it and sold it. Thus it got into the market. As Chinese curio-dealers usually collect all possible knowledge with regard to the origin of their curios in the interest of their foreign customers this legend might be true though it is unverifiable. The heavy damage which the precious piece has suffered is otherwise unexplainable.

The Chinese origin of the statue cannot be doubted. But it is not impossible that it was cast by Chinese artisans in Yünnan. As much as we know now, the first bronze figures were cast there in the year 810 A.D. The style of the statue suggests rather an earlier date. During the period of the T'ang Dynasty (618-907) the folds of garments began to come off from the body and float freely while on our sample they drop stiffly and perpendicularly. Early Chinese Buddhist bronzes were copies from stone-Buddhas and follow the rules valid for stone sculpture. Besides, the halo seems to have been pointed.

---

1. *Sino-Indian Studies*, vol. V. 1 (1955) p. 67 n. 4.
2. *Monumenta Serica*, XII (1947) pp. 6-16.

If the statue was not cast in Yünnan, it might have got there with an embassy. Embassies plied between Ch'ang-an, the Chinese capital, and Tali, the capital of the Tali Kingdom, since the middle of the seventh century, but the intercourse was interrupted between 751 and 788. A the pagoda was begun in A.D. 833, the statue might have been brought to Tali between 788 and 833 A.D.

Whatever that may be, it is one of the most charming Chinese Buddhas I know of and deserves well to be published for the first time in this volume in honour of Lord Buddha.

Plate 2

An early Buddha Statue from Yünnan

Chapter - 15

Observations on the Buddhist remains at Jaggayyapeta

Debala Mitra

During my visit to the ruined *stūpa* at Jaggayyapeta, I observed a few facts, which are given below.

Burgess gives the diameter of the mound (by which he evidently means the main *stūpa*) as 31 ½ft.[1], and this has been repeated by others. Actually, the diameter is 63 ft.; Burgess evidently confused the radius with the diameter.

Burgess observes: 'the rail around this (*scil.* the procession-path) had evidently disappeared: not a fragment of it could be found'.[2] He is no doubt right in his assumption that there was originally a railing around the *stūpa*, but the latter part of his statement needs revision, for I found the upper fragment (pl. 1) of a loose limestone upright of a railing, near the edge of the procession-path, with the topmost pair of sockets complete and less than halves of the next lower pair present. With a total extant height of 2 ft. 4 in., the breadth and thickness of the fragment are respectively 1 ft. ½ in. and 5 ¼ in. The upright is chamfered towards the top, so as to produce a plano-convex section. Its top surface has the remnants of a tenon to fit into a mortise of the detachable coping. Separated from the top by a gap of 5 in. is the topmost pair of sockets, to receive the cross-bars, lenticular in shape but truncated at the ends; they are 1 ft. 3 in. long. 1 in deep, 2 in. broad in the middle and 1 in. broad at the ends. The gap between the bottom of the upper sockets and the top of the lower ones measures 3 ½ in. Thus, if the railing was a three-barred one, the total height of the upright was 5 ft. 2 in.

---

1. Jas Burgess, *The Buddhist Stūpas of Amaravati and Jaggayyapeta* Arch. Surv. Southern India, I (London, 1887), p. 107.
2. *Ibid.*, p. 107.

Burgess further says that 'the base of the *stūpa* could hardly have stopped here (*scil.* above the drum-slab): a frieze almost certainly surmounted this, but was all carried off.'[1] That there was a frieze above the drum-slab seems to be certain, for I noticed among the pieces dumped on the top of the stūpas a sculptured fragment (pl. 2), which no doubt formed the entablature of the drum-slab. Its height and thickness are respectively 11 in. and 2 in., the latter not incompatible with that of the drum-slab (the roughly-dressed top of the drum-slab has patches of lime-mortar suggesting thereby the existence of an entablature over it). The top of the fragment is finished and rounded. Its front face is relieved with figures of Buddha alternating with the representation of a *stūpa*, each within a separate compartment as in a particular group of drum-friezes from Amaravati.[2] Buddha is seen in the piece with his shoulders covered by an *uttarīya*; he holds in his left hand the hem of his upper cloth, his right hand (broken) being raised, as in the *abhaya* pose. Of the representations of the *stūpas*, only one exists; from its *harmikā* flow two sets of *chattrāvalis*, each with a garland (?) again as in an Amaravati drum-frieze.[3]

The existence of a *caitya-gṛha* at Jaggayyapeta is suggested by two circular stone pieces (pl. 3), their edges relieved with lotus petals in three tiers. That the *caitya-gṛha* enshrined a votive *stūpa* and not a Buddha image is shown by the facts that the size of the pieces is not compatible with that of the pedestal of an image and that similar decorated pieces form the base of stone-faced votive *stūpas* inside the apsidal *caitya*-halls at Nāgarjunakonda.

Nearby lies a small tapering and octagonal limestone yaṣṭi (pl. 3), 3 ft. 7 in. high, and a tiny fragment of an internally ribbed *chattra*, also of limestone; probably they formed part of the crowning element of the votive *stūpa*.[4]

---

1. *Ibid.*, p. 108.
2. *Ibid.*, pl., XLIII, 3.
3. *Ibid.*, pl., XLIII, 9.
4. The photographs published here are the copyright of the Department of Archaeology.

Plate 3

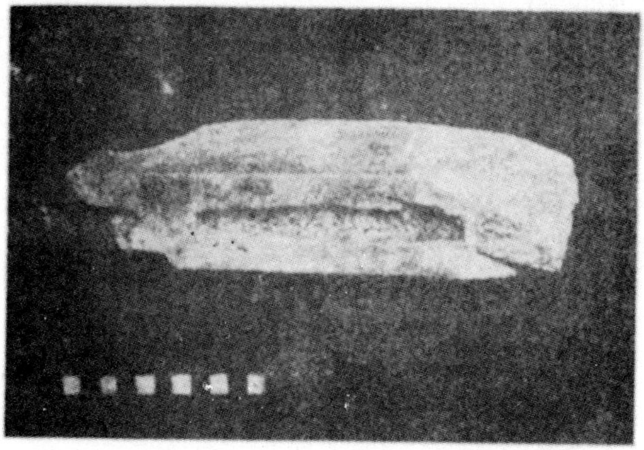

(i) Upright piece of a railing, Yaggayyapeta,

(ii) Drum-frieze,

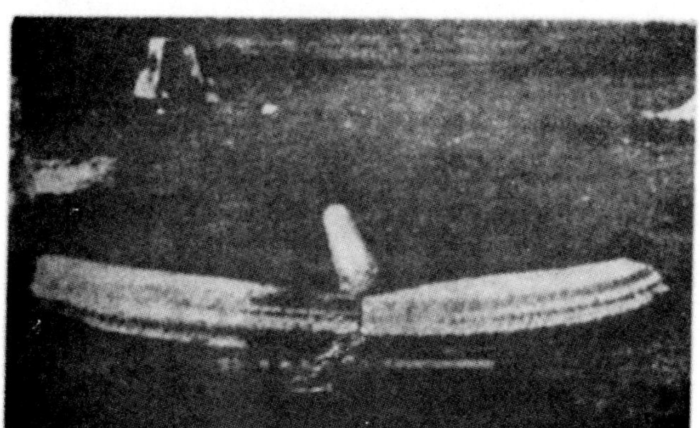

(iii) a limestone yaṣṭi and carved pieces of the base of a votive stūpa

Chapter - 16
Iconographic Notes on some Buddhist Sculptures at Ellora

R. Sen Gupta

A careful look into the sculptures and a study of the plans of the caves will prove, contrary to the belief of some scholars, that the Buddhists and the Hindus started their excavations at Ellora almost simultaneously. While working side by side they vied with each other in embellishing their excavations with sculptures and paintings. In carving out the sculptures, such features belonging to one group which appealed to the other group were readily borrowed and in this they followed no taboo.

Āyudhapuruṣa

Sometimes, the results of such borrowals have been very interesting. For examples, the imgae of Vajrapāṇi, as the right *dvārapāla* in Cave VI, is one of them where the thunderbolt, which otherwise is to be found in one of his hands, has been personified (*Āyudhapuruṣa*) as seen in the contemporaneous Śaiva excavations like Caves XXI and XXVI at Ellora, thereby making the image very interesting and a unique one, for, such an arrangement is rarely seen in the Buddhist sculptures. Vajrapāṇi, standing gracefully under a decorated foliage is holding what looks like a fly-whisk in his right hand and the left hand rests on his waist band. To his right is a female attendant with a female dwarf by her side. The thunderbolt personified (*Vajrapuruṣa*) is a striding male figure with its hands crossed looking up with the thunderbolt tucked in the head-dress. In this, it compares favourably with the descriptions of *Cakrapuruṣa* in the *Viṣṇudharmottara*. It states, "It is also to be carved in such a manner as to indicate that it is showing a desire to gaze upon Viṣṇu" (Book III, Ch. 85, vv. 13-14).

Representation of weapons in anthropomorphic forms 'came to be designated generally as the Āyudhapuruṣas, and it is worthy of note that this feature was mostly associated with the icons of Viṣṇu', although instances of their association with the Śaivite images can also be cited from Badami, Ellora and Pattadkal. Besides these sites in the Deccan, at other places like Rajgir, Deogarh etc., in the Gupta sculptures of Viṣṇu, *Āyudhapuruṣas* occur and the tradition lingers quite for some time. Mention of such *āyudhas* could also be traced in the Sanskrit drama '*Uttara Rāma Carita*' by Bhavabhūti, where Lakṣmaṇa explains to Sītā a painting depicting Rāma surrounded by the weapons, sent by the gods, as animated beings.[1]

Prof. Banerjee tracing the earliest representations of *Āyudhapuruṣa* writes, 'The earliest representations of an Āyudhapuruṣa, however, seems to go back to the Indo-Scythic period. *Vajra* appears on some copper coins of Maues as a man behind whom is carved a double-pronged thunderbolt, just in front of Zeus-Indra whose right hand is placed over his head'. But his contention that 'it is a fact that such a personification of *vajra* has not been found in later reliefs[2] is not agreeable for obvious reasons.

When compared with other extant images of the Bodhisattva Vajrapāṇi, such a representation with the *Vajra* shown as an *Āyudhapuruṣa* appears to be rather unconventional. For Vajrapāṇi, the usual way of holding the *vajra* is either to hold it in one of the hands (horizontally, or vertically) or vertically with the first and middle fingers (the latter style, apparently indicates a South Indian influence). One, therefore, wonders what might be the reason for them to choose this device. Perhaps like the other contemporaneous Buddhist as well as Brahmanical excavations where the *dvārapālas* are shown either with a *chauri* or with a lotus in one of the hands, the excavators of this cave also wanted to represent the *dvārapālas* in the like manner and while dealing with Vajrapāṇi the example of the Hindus came handy to have the desired pleasing effect.

Though not from the same site, another interesting example of *Vajrapuruṣa* may be cited. This sculputre appears, on the left wall of the hall of Cave XC at Kanheri, in an elaborate panel with Indra. Other representations of Indra in the Buddhist sculptural panels are either as one of the acolytes of the Buddha or shown as visiting the Buddha in the Indraśilā cave. This panel shows no such arrangement. Indra is seen seated to the right on a lotus below the central image of the Buddha. Behind him is seen the *Āyudhapuruṣa* seated in the same way as Indra is, with his arms crossed and the *vajra* tucked in his head.

---

1. E.B. Havell, *Indian Sculptures and Painting*, p. 157.
2. J.N. Banerjee, *Development of Hindu Iconography* (1356), p. 527.

The efficacy of *Cakra* or *Sudarśana;* an *ayudha* and the exhalted position in which it is placed has been described elaborately in the *Ahirbudhnya-Saṁhitā,* a well-known text of *Pāñcarātra-āgama* which Dr. Agrawala feels 'should be assigned to the Gupta period on the basis of its internal evidence bearing on the religious conditions portrayed in it.[1] In fact *Cakra* is glorified to such an extend as to hold it to be equal in its divine nature to Viṣṇu himself who manifests himself in the form of *Sudarśana.* A couple of instances have been cited where after worshipping the deity (*Cakrapuruṣa)* the respective kings were able to worst their enemies.

The interesting sculpture on the outer wall of the southern gallery of the first floor of Viśvakarmā caitya hall (Cave X) with four arms which carries in the front left hand a *vajra* and yet another one tucked in the head, described by Burgess.[2] and Grunwedel[3] as Vajrapāṇi requires to be reconsidered. Unfortunately the other hands are broken and save a broken handle which is in the back right hand, nothing remains. The Vajra on the head betrays its nature as an *Āyudhapuruṣa* whereas the other one in the hand suggests its being the Bodhisattva Vajrapāṇi. But then Vajrapāṇi with four arms is not known. Could it be the *Āyudhapuruṣa,* in whom Vajrapāṇi has manifested himself, an idea which might have been borrowed from the text of the Hindus as described above?

Kubera

The Buddhist god of riches is known as Jambhala and his cognizances are the *mātuluṅga* fruit in his right hand and a mongoose vomitting jewels in his left hand. In the Buddhist excavations one would naturally expect the god of riches to be sculptured so. But some of the sculptures of this god found in the Buddhist cave shrines at Ellora, however, betray the traits of Jambhala and show some interesting features.

Of these, most interesting is the sculpture[4] to be seen on the right wall of the shrine of Cave VI (7th cent. A.D.). The god there is represented in a panel at the centre, with two other Bodhisattvas flanking him. He is shown as seated in *Sukhāsana* holding a citron in his right hand and in his left hand is what looks like a book. As usual he is shown as having a protruded belly, wearing a *yajñopavīta*, ear-

---

1. V.S. Agrawala, *An Explanation of the Cakravikrama Type coin of Candragupta,* II, *JNSI.* volume XVI (1954) Part I, p. 97.
2. J. Burgess, *Elura Cave Temples in Ar. Sur. W' India,* vol. V, p. 11. Pl. XIX, 4.
3. Grunwedel, *Buddhist Art,* p. 95.
4. J. Burgess, *Archaeological Survey of Western India*, vol. V.

rings, necklace, armlets and interestingly enough, his head is adorned with a *Śikhaṇḍaka* coiffure—which is a characteristic of Kumāra.

The association of Kubera, the god of wealth, with the book[1] is very interesting. Generally, the Buddhist deities like Saraswatī, Mạñjuśrī and Prajñāpāramitā and the Hindu deities like Brahmā and Saraswati who are connected with learning and wisdom are represented with the book. Exception to these perhaps is the image of Śiva as Dakṣiṇā-murti, holding a book in his right hand shown as the teacher of the highest truth, in the Pallava temple at Kaveripakkam. But none of the iconographic text appears to have mentioned Kubera with a book. The idea of associating the book or *Vidyā* with the god of wealth, would appear to have been borrowed from the *Mārkaṇḍeya Purāṇa* where the goddess of wealth, Śrī (Lakṣmī), is stated to be the presiding deity of 'Science', described as *Padminī Vidyā*. Vāc, the goddess of learning, has also been described as the giver of wealth made to say *ahaṁ rāṣṭrī saṁgamaṇī vasūnāṁ cikituṣī Prathamā yajñiyānāṃ* etc. (Ṛgveda, X, 125). So it will be seen that from the early period the goddess of wealth is connected with wisdom, the same way as the goddess of wisdom is said to be the giver of wealth. Some such idea, as described above, might have been responsible in conceiving Viṣṇu with Śrī and Vāc as Puruṣottama, at once the abode of wealth and wisdom, thus bringing the two qualities in one which is rarely found. And it was not at all then difficult to develop the idea in making the god of wealth also of wisdom such as depicted in this image of Kubera. The idea of combining wealth with wisdom appears to have been continued in the later period also, as will be found from the descriptions of the goddess Dhanada-Tārā appearing in the *Sādhana-mālā*, where she is required to hold the book in one of her hands.[2] Her name as Dhanad-Tārā is quite significant, as one of the appellations of Kubera is known as Dhanada.

The figure of Kubera[3] on the western wall of the cell behind the landing between the ground floor and the first floor of cave XII (8th cent. A.D.) in a panel with Padmapāṇi and Tārā is also of some iconographic interest. As usual he is portrayed with a protruded belly and is sitting in *mahārājalīlā* pose. His left hand is placed on the left

---

1. R. Sen Gupta, *Journal of Indian Museums,* vol. XII, p. 37. A similar figure appears on the outer right wall of Aurangabad Cave II.
2. B. Bhattacharayya, *Buddhist Iconography,* p. 109.
3. J. Burgress, *op.cit., p. 18.*
   J. Furgusson & J. Burgess, *The Cave Temples of India,* p. 282.
   R. Sen Gupta, *op. cit.,* p. 38
   —Bhavan's Journal, vol, IV No. 15, pp. 39-41.

thigh holding the treasure bags issuing from the *nidhis* while the right hand which is placed on the right knee (in *utkutika*) is broken from the elbow. He is wearing a necklace, *karṇakunṇḍalas,* a *yajñopavīta* and his head is adorned with a *kirīṭa-mukuṭa.* On his right side is a *śaṅkha* and to his left is a *padma,* the two *nidhis,* as enjoined in the Brahmanical iconographic texts like *Viṣṇudharmottara, Amśumadbhedāgama, Pūrva Kāraṇāgama, Mayasaṃgraha* etc. In this sculputre also the traits of Jambhala are not to be found, instead the Hindu god Kubera looms large.

The sculptures described above were carved when there was no *Sādhanamālā* to determine the *Sādhanās* of the Buddhist images. That is why the images of the same Buddhist gods appear in the same site, varying from one another. At Ellora, where the Buddhists and the Hindus worked side by side, instances could be cited to show that the Buddhists drew inspirations to carve their images from the Hindus and *vice versa.*[1]

---

1. The *dvārapālas* in the pre-Rāṣṭrakuṭa excavations of the Hindus have definitely been modelled on the Bodhisattvas as *dvārapālas* in the contemporaneous excavations of the Buddhists.

Chapter - 17
Some Buddhist Antiquities and Monuments of Rajasthan

Ratna Chandra Agrawala

Archaeological excavations and explorations in different parts of Rajasthan have brought to light sufficient material pertaining to the penetration and expansion of Buddhism in this part of the country. The Buddhist antiquities and monuments of this region are of course very few in number; but they are of great importance for a student of ancient Indian History and Archaeology. It is now proposed to describe them in brief here.

1. *Bhābrū Rock Edict*:—

It was in the year 1840 A.D. that Captain Burt discovered the well-known Bhābrū[1] Rock Edict of Aśoka. The same was later on transferred to the Museum of the Asiatic Society of Bengal at Calcutta. This edict is of great interest because of its having been inscribed on a stone-slab[2] (*śilā-phalaka*) as distinguished from a stone-pillar (*śilā-stambha*). The excavations of the ancient site of Bairat have now proved that this stone-slab inscription must have originally hailed from Bairat itself. Another pillar (of Aśoka), from Bairat, was brought to light by the archaeological remains on the site popularly known as the *Bījaka-kī-Phārī*.[3] One of the fragment of such a pillar, having the usual Mauryan polish, even bears the *Brāhmī* letter *na* in the script of the third century B.C. D.R. Sahni (*ibid,* p. 28) is of the opinion that the Buddhist monument at Bairat were perhaps destroyed by the White Hun leader Mihirakula towards the beginning of the sixth century A.D.

---

1. Bhābrū is about 12 miles in a direct line to the north of Bairat, the latter being ancient *Virāṭapura* and distant about 52 miles from Jaipur City. Virāṭapura was the capital of the *Matsya* country. For details consult B.C. Law's paper in *the Age of Imperial Unity,* Bombay, pp. 2, 11, 12 etc.
2. "This stone is an irregularly shaped block of grey granite, of the kind so abundant at Bariat and measusring about 2 feet in length, the same in width and a foot and a half in thicknes" (D.R. Sahni, *Archaeological Remains and Excavations at Bairat,* Jaipur State, p. 18 and plate II for it photograph.
3. *Ibid.*, pp. 26 ff. and plate VI. a.

The Bairat Edict of Aśoka of course bears testimony to Aśoka's ardent faith in the Buddhist lore and his royal injunctions to the Buddhist friars and laymen to pay rapt attention to Buddhist ideology and to devote themselves to the study of the particular passage (seven in number) from the Buddhist scriptures.[1] The next of the Bairāṭa epigraph runs thus:—

(1) *Rpi (pri) yadasi lājā Māgadhe saṃghaṃ abhivāde (tū)-naṃ āhā apābādhataṃ ca phāsubihālataṃ ca*

(2) *vidite ve bhaṃte āvatake hamā Budhasi dhaṃmasi saṃghasī ti gālave caṃ rpa (pra)sade ca e keci bhaṃte*

(3) *bhagawatā Budhe(na) bhāsite save se subhāsite vā e cu khu bhaṃte hamiyāye diseyā hevaṃ sadhaṃmme*

(4) *cila (ṭhi) tīke hosatī ti alahāmi hakaṃ taṃ vātave, imāni bhaṃte (dh)aṃmma paliyāyāni Vinaya-samukase*

(5) *Aliya-vasāṇi Anāgata-bhayāni Munigāthā Moneya-sūte Upatisa rpa (pra)sine e cā Lāghulo.*

(6) *vāde muṣā-vādaṃ adhigicya bhagavatā Budhena bhāsite etāni bhaṁte dhaṃmma-paliyāyāni ichāmi*

(7) *kiṃti bahuke bhikhu (pā)ye cā bhikhuniye cā abhikhinaṃ Su(ne) yu cā upadhalayeyu cā*

(8) *hevaṃmevā upāsakā cā upāsikā cā eteni bhaṃte imaṃ likhā (pa)yāmi abhipetaṃ me jānaṃtu ti.*

II. *The Circular Brick-Temple at Bairat:—*

D.R. Sahni's excavations at Bairat also brought to light the remains of a Buddhist Brick-Temple which was circular in shape.[2] In his own words (*ibid.*, pp. 30-31), "this is the oldest structural temple and one of those which furnished models for the numerous rock-cut cave-temples of Western and Eastern India. The nearest approach, both in plan and design, is the *caitya* cave of about the first century B.C. in the Tulja Lena group at Junnar...... On the outside, the walls of the temples were inscribed with the Buddhist texts in the *Brāhmī* charaters of the Aśokan period. Several bricks inscribed with one or two *akṣaras* (plate V, e, o and q) were found built, in the rectangular enclosure-wall around the temple. A few of them read *pāsaṃ, visa, vi, kama* etc."

1. For detail consult Sahni, *op. cit.*, p. 18; B.C. Law, *Journal of the Pali Text Society,* 1946, pp. 93-8; D.C. Sircar, *Select Inscriptions,* I, 1942. Calcutta, pp. 77-8; D.R. Bhandarkar, *Aśoka,* 1955, Calcutta, pp. 335-6; Senart, *Ind. Ant.*, XX, p. 165 ff.; E. Hultzsch, *Corp. Insc. Ind.*, I, pp. 172 ff.
2. Cf. Sahni, *op. cit.,* plates, VII, VIII; *ibid,* pp. 28 ff., for details and description.

The existing Buddhist structure (with a *stūpa* in the interior) at Bairat has got an important bearing on the early temple-architecture in India.[1]

Referring to Hwen Tsang's notice of Bairat in the seventh century A.D. (Julien's *Hwen Tsang,* II, 206), General Cunningham (*Arch. Surv. Report,* Simla, 1871, Vol. II, p. 246) remarks that according to the Chinese pilgrim, "the capital was 14 or 15 *li* or just 2½ miles in circuit, which corresponds almost exactly with the ancient mound on which the present town is built. The people were brave and bold and their king, who was of the race of *Fei-she,* or a Bais Rajput, was famous for his courage and skill in war. *The place still posssessed 8 Buddhist monasteries but they were much reined and the number of monks was small.* The Brahmans of different sects, about 1000 in number, possessed 12 temples, but their followers were numerous, as the bulk of the population is described as heretical. Judging from the size of the town, as noted by Hwen Tsang, *the population could not have been less than four times the present number, or about* 30,000, *of whom the followers of Buddha may have amounted to one fourth.* I have deduced this number from the fact that the Buddhist monasteries would appear to have held about 100 monks each, and as those of Bairat are said to have been ruined, *the number of monks in Hwen Tsang's time could not have exceeded 50 per monastery, or 400 altogether.* As each Buddhist monk begged his bread, *the number of Buddhist families could not have been less than* 1200, allowing 3 families for the support of each monk, or altogether about 6000 lay Buddhists in addition to the 400 monks" (cf. also G.H. Ojha, *History of the Western World,* London, 1884, Vol. I, p. 179).

III. *Northern Black Polish Ware from Bairat:—*

The ancient site of Bairat also yielded the well known *Northern Black Polish* (*N.B.P.*) *Ware* which is so characteristic of the Mauryan period[2] in India. It is now extremely essential to explore the region for the distribution of the *N.B.P*[3] ware in Rajasthan.

---

1. Cf. Percy Brown, *Indian Architecture (Buddhist & Hindu Periods)*, Second Edition, Bombay, p. 15.
2. For a comprehensive list of *N.B.P.* sites in India, consult B.B. Lal's paper in *Ancient India, Bull. of the Arch. Survey of India,* New Delhi, Vols. X-XI, pp. 50 ff. and pp. 143 ff.
3. It is equally interesting to note the discovery of the *Painted Grey Ware* at Bairat (*Indian Archaeology* 1954-5—*a Review,* New Delhi, 1955, p. 61). This is much earlier in date as compared to the N.B.P. The Grey ware occurs in the regions of Bikaner and Alwar too.

IV. *Remains at Nagarī*:—

A fragmentary stone inscription, in the *Brāhmī* script on the third or second century B.C., was excavated at Nagārī (ancient Madhyamikā, near Chittaur, Udaipur region) and is now preserved in the archaeological section of the Udaipur Museum. It refers to a feeling of compassion for all beings in the following words[1]:—

(i) *Śa(vā) bhutānaṃ dayātham*

(ii) *(kār) (i) tā.*

It is just possible that this inscription was drafted and engraved under the influence of Buddhistm. The explorations at Nagarī also revealed the existence of *stūpas*[2] on the site. This bears testimony to the prevalence of Buddhism there (at Nagarī) inspite of its having been an important stronghold of the *Vaiṣṇava*[3] pantheon. Describing the remains at Nagarī, Dr. Bhandarkar (*Memoris..., op. cit.*, p. 119) writes that "it is a structure built in horizontal tiers and must be a *stūpa* as indicated by the heavy suasage-shaped garlands" (cf. *Journal of U.P. Historical Society,* Lucknow, VI (2), 1933, p. 3). Henry Cousens (*Prog. Report of Arch. Survey, Western Circle,* Poona, 1905, p. 59) also noticed an ancient lion-capital of the Aśoka period (according to his own version) lying near the image of Kaṅkālī Mātā at Nagarī. Besides this, another sculputred stone from the same size was identified as an 'architrave of some Buddhist gateway' both by Carlleyle and Cousens.

V. *Stūpas on the Fort of Chittaur*:—

Henry Cousens (*Progress Report of Archaeological Survey of India, Western Circle,* Poona, 1904, p. 45) also refers to the existence of a scattered group of some ten *stūpas* (carved in a stone) about 4 or 5 hundred yards to the north-west of Kālikā Mātā's temple at Chittaur. According to Cousens, "the larger ones stand about 3'3," high and 1'8" square at the base. They are all of one patttern. The upper portion is cylindrical, with a domed top..............Around the base of the cylindrical part is a string-course of 16 little seated Buddhas, each in a little niche. Beneath this is a constricted circular neck with lotus leaves springing from it, an upward row and a downward row. Beneath

---

1. Cf. D.R. Bhandarkar's *Archaeological Remains & Excavations at Nagarī, MASI.*, No.4, pp. 112-120; G.H. Ojha, *History of Rajputana,* Hindi, I, 1927, p. 358.
2. Cf. Satya Prakasha, *Rajasthan and its Traditions,* 1951, Jaipur, p. 25; G.H. Ojha, *op. cit.*, pp. 359-60; *Arch. Surv. Reports* by Carlleyle, VI, pp. 196 ff. and plates.
3. As is evident from the well-known Ghosuṇḍī inscription. For details consult., *MASI, 4, op. cit.*, pp. 119-20; V.S. Agrawala's paper in the Śodhapatrikā, Udaipur, IV (3), pp. 40 ff; *Ep. Indica,I XXII, pp. 203* ff.....etc.

this, again, the *stūpa* is square with projecting niches, one on each face, in each of which is a seated Buddha. There are 3 distinct positions i.e., the meditative, the witnessing and the teaching attitudes. Beneath each of these is a symbol incised. The *stūpas* are all a good deal weather worn, so that the finer detail of the carving is lost. The hair is apparently not curly but long and is done up into a considerable knot on the top of the head." These pieces have now been preserved and exhibited in an order on an open platform in front of the Śriṅgāra Chaurī at Chittaur itself.

VI. *Absence of Buddhist Remains in Western Rajasthan:—*

The ancient sites of the former states of Jodhpur, Jaisalmera, Sirohī and Bikaner[1] do not appear to have yielded anything tangible which may have some bearing on the expansion of Buddhism in Western Rajputana. But no conclusion can be hazarded till extensive exploration and excavation work is conducted in this direction. Hwen Tsang refers to the declining condition of Buddhism at *Pi-lo-mo-lo,*[1a] identified with modern Bhīnmāla or ancient Śrīmāla, distant about 120 miles from Jodhpur. According to his information, there was only one *saṅghārāma* (monastery) at Bhīnmāl and that too belonged to the *Hīnayāna* sect. It was inhabited by 100 monks who were followers of the *Sarvāstivāda* Sect (cf. Samuel Beal's *Buddhist Records of the Western World*, Vol. II, London, p. 270; G.H. Ojha, *Hist. of Raj., op. cit.*, I, 1927, p. 10).

It is equally interesting to note the dearth of Buddhist finds both from Nagar or Karkoṭanagar and Sāmbhar situated in the Jaipur unit of Rajasthan. As regards the ancient site of Rairh[2] (Jaipur unit), Dr. K.N. Puri (*Excavations at Rairh*, Jaipur State, p. 57) remarked that "Buddhism had no influence, whatsoever, although traces of contact with the Buddhist world have been established by the discovery of a fragment of Chunar sand-stone bowl, a few pieces of highly polished Buddhist pottery and steatite caskets similar to relic-caskets found on Buddhist site for the enshrinement of the body relics".

VII. *Remains at Lalsot:—*

"The town of Lalsot, 50 miles from the city of Jaipur, once possessed an ancient Buddhist *stūpa* of a considerable antiquity. Six

---

1. Dr. L.P. Tessitory is said to have discovered traces of the foundations of, what he thought, might have been Buddhist *stūpas* at Muṇḍā and Pīra Sultāna in the Bikaner region (H. Goetz, *The Art and Architecture of Bikaner State,* 1950, Oxford, p. 58).

1a. Some of the scholars even hesitate in accepting this identification.

2. Nagar and Rairh were important seats of the Mālava republic: cf. *Arch. Surv. Report,* Simla, VI for the finds from Nagar.

red stone pillars, belonging to the railings of this monument, have in modern times been utilised in the construction of the *chatrīs* or cenotaphs. These pillars are 5 feet high, square at the base and at the top and octagonal in the middle portion."[1]

VIII. *Kota Buddhist Inscription*:—

It is interesting to analyse the opening verses of the Kota Buddhist inscription engraved on a stone, built into a recess under a flight of stairs on the right hand as one enters the Barkhārī gate of the inner wall of the town of Shergarh (Kota Division). It records the construction of a Buddhist temple and a monastery to the east of mount Kośavardhana by the feudal chief Devadatta.[2] It specifically refers to firm belief in trinity,[3] greatness of Buddha, law of Sugata, the Buddhist Church etc., in the following words:—

ओं नमो रत्नत्रयाय । जयंति वादाः सुगतस्य निर्म्मलाः समस्तसंदेहनिरासभासुराः । कुतर्क्क–सम्पातनिपातहेतवो युगान्तवाता इव विश्वसन्त्तेः ।।१।। यो रुपवानपि विभर्ति सदैव रुपमेकोप्यनेक इवभाति च यो निकामं । आरादगात्परधियः प्रतिमर्त्त्यवेद्यो यां निर्ज्जितारि रजितश्च जिनः स वो व्यात् ।।२।। भिनत्ति यो नृणाम्मोहं तमो वेश्मनि दीपवत् । सो व्यादः सौगतो धर्मो भक्तमुक्तिफलप्रदः ।।३।। आर्यसंघस्य विमलाः शरच्छसि जिताश्रियः । जयन्ति जयिनः पादाः सुरासुरशिरोर्च्चिताः ।।४।।

This testifies to State-patronage accorded to Buddhism in this area as late as the end of the 8th or the beginning of the 9th centruy A.D. It is of course regretted that we have absolutely no information about the Buddhist antiquities of an early period from Kota region.

IX. *Buddhist Caves in the Jhalawar Region*:

Dr. Impey[4] is said to have visited the Buddhist cave at Kholvī[5] (situated in district Jhālāwar of the Kota Division) first of all. Later on, General A. Cunningham visisted the place and presented a vivid account of the caves and the topes at Kholvī in his *Arch. Survey Report, op. cit.*, pp. 280-88 and plate lxxiv. He infers (*ibid*, p. 286) that "the

---

1. Satya Prakash, *Rajasthan and its Traditions*, Jaipur, 1951, p. 25.
2. For the Sanskrit text of this epigraph, consult E. Hultzsch, *Ind. Antiquary*. XIV, pp. 45-6 and M.L. Sharma's, *Kotā Rāja kā Itihasa*, Hindī, Vol. I. Appendix III and p. 27; cf. also *Bhandarkar's List of Brāhmī Inscriptions of N. India*, serial no. 21.
3. i.e., *Buddha, Dharma* and *Saṅgha*.
4. Consult his paper in the *Journal of the Asiatic Society of Bengal*, Calcutta, V, p. 336.
5. About 30 miles from Augar and also 30 miles from the Dhamnār caves.

Kholvī excavations are most probably of a later date then the caves of Dhammār[1] and Bāgh in Mālwā and of Kārlī, Ellora and other places in Southern India." He (*ibid*, p. 288) even assigns them a date ranging from 700 to 900 A.D. The Buddhist caves at Kholvī thus have to play a great role in the realm of Buddhist iconography and architecture of Rajasthan during the post-Gupta period. In this connection, mention may also be made of a colossal standing figure of Buddha at Kholvī. It measures about 12 feet in height and depicts the Buddha in the mode of teaching with his left hand raised to the breast (cf. *ibid,* p. 285 for details; also consult J. Fergusson, *History of Indian and Eastern Architecture,* London, 1899, Book I, pp. 162-3 for the later date of the Kholvī caves).

It is equally interesting to study the cave architecture as presented by the Buddhist caves at Vināyakā (or Vināyagā or Binnāyagā) situated about 8 miles from Kholvī. Śrī M.M. Śāstrī (Custodian of the Kota Museum) has recently informed me that some Buddhist caves exist at Haṭhiagor (situated in the Jhālāwār region) too. It now appears that the region round about Kholvī[2] and Vināyakā was once an important stronghold of Buddhism. Śrī G.L. Vyas (Custodian of the Jhālawār Museum) has also stated that there exist about 16 Buddhist caves at Bināyakā and that some Buddhist *stūpas* can be seen in front of these caves. Besides this, some images of seated Buddha have also been carved out nearby.

A passing reference may also be made to the discovery of the Mandsor Inscription of the *Mālava* year 524. It opens with the auspicious phrase *siddhaṃ* whereas the first verse is a *maṅgalācaraṇa* expressing adoration to *Sugata* (the Buddha; *Epigraphia Indica,* XXVII, no. 1, pp. 12 ff.):—*Siddhaṃ. Ye(ne)dasamudbhavanirodha-paraṃparāyā magnaṃ jagadvidhaduhkhanirantarāyām. Tittrāsunā tripadironiradeśi dharmmastasmai namostu Sugatāya ga(tā)ya śāntim* i.e., "Obeisance to *Sugata,* wishing to save the world (which is) plunged in the uninterrupted series of births and deaths closely associated with misery in various forms, enjoined a religion consisting of 3 steps (stages) and who attained peace" (*ibid*, p. 16). It refers to the consctruction of a "stūpa accompanied by a well [in commemoration] of the *Buddha,* who having overcome the evil influences of all elements (*dhātu*) preached the accomplishment of all actions, the stūpa, the

1. Dhamnār caves are situated in the State of Madhya Bharat. For Dhamnār caves, consult Percy Brown, *Indian Architecture (Hindu and Survey Buddhist),* Second edition, p. 143; Cunningham's *Archaelogical Survey of India Report,* Simla, 1871, Vol. II, pp. 270 ff. and plates.
2. One has to pass through Dug (the headquarters of a *tahsil* of the Jhālāwār Distt.) on way to the Kholvī caves.

structure of which was as white as the *kunda* flower and the moon and the pinnacle of which touched the clouds" (*yo dhātumātre hatadhātu-doṣaḥ sarvvakṛyā siddhim uvāca tasya. Kundenduśubhrobbhravighṛi-ṣṭayaṣṭiriyaṃ kṛto dhātudharaḥ sakūpaḥ*). This *stūpa* was situated within the limits of the *Lokottara Vihāra* (verse 18) and this led M.B. Gadre (*ibid.*, p. 13) to suggest that the latter "was possibly the proper name of some local Buddhist monastery, probably named after the *Lokottaravāda* sect of the *Hīnayāna* form of Buddhism."

The phrase "*Syādvādagrahanigrahāgadavidhirvvi-dhvastavaitaṇḍikachadmā Saugatagarvvaparvvatabhidāvajrapratā-podhanaḥ......ryabhaṅgakṣamaḥ Śrī Vedāṅgamuniḥ prasiddhamahimā yasya prasādaṃ vyadhāta*" occurring in the Inscription of V.S. 1028 from Ekaliṅgajī (14 miles from Udaiur; *JBBRAS*., Bombay, XXII, old series, verse 17, lines 15-16, pp. 166-7) of course refers to the existence of unhappy relations between the adherents of the Buddhist and the *Śaiva* pantheons. Vedāṅgamuni, of this record, was a follower of the *Lakulīśa-Pāśupata* sect and has been described, here, as a great opponent of the Jainas (belivers in the *Syādvāda* philosophy) and the Buddhsits (cf. *saugata; sugata*=Buddha) alike. It is regretted that this inscription fails to throw any light on the causes of this revolt against Jainism and Buddhism in this particular case.

This is a brief account of some Buddhist remains from Rājasthāna. The material, in this direction, is of course very scanty but the existing Buddhist monuments and remains of the region are very important for the reconstruction of the religious history of the area during the early historic and the pre-mediaeval periods.

Chapter - 18
The Absence of the Buddha Image in the Prekushan Period

D. K. Sinha

During the course of the famous controvery regarding the origin of the Buddha image Dr. A.K. Coomaraswamy[1] and Shri O.C. Gangoly[2] had contended that sculptors of the pre-Kushan age were quite capable of representing Buddha in anthropomorphic form but they did not do so only because of the religious interdiction of the Pali Canon. Of course of the problem has been discussed from the archaeological point of view but little effort has been made to verify the Pali Canon with regard to this so-called interdiction problem. This paper is an attempt in this direction.

The most important sources to rely upon are the sayings of Buddha (*Buddha-vacana*) embodied in the Nikāyas. The authenticity of the Pali literature, which was reduced to writing in the Ist century B.C.in Ceylon, is itself a subject of controversy between the scholars. However, it will not be out of place to mention that Buddha followed the literary convention of his period by embodying the preachings in a *sūtra* style of set phrases and compressed logic. These were to be memorized thoroughly. The same episodes are, therefore, repeated in several Nikāyas. This very principle is the guiding factor over the entire arrangement and spirit of the Pali canon. This technique is very significant because this *sūtra* style leaves enough scope for the monks to make commentaries of the saying of Buddha and make it more intelligable with detailed arguments and conversation.

The Theravād philosophy is of rationalistic morality and ethical in nature. Buddha lays stress on his preaching more than anything else including his personal adoration. The *Mahāvastu* instructs for

---

1. Coomaraswamy, A.K., "The origin of the Buddha image," Boston Museum Bulletin, Vol. IX, No. IV.
2. Gangoly, O.C., "The antiquity of the Buddha image." The cult of the Buddha, ospsiatische Zeitschrift, New Folge, XIV.

the worshippers of Tathāgata "O bhikkhus, whoever renders ritualistic adoration (*Satkāram*) to the Tathāgata, thus purified by means of flowers, fragrance, festoons, flags and music and by applying fragrant paste, one can not measure the limit of his spiritual merit." "In *Vajrachedika-sūtta* also the Master says whoever says you that he has seen me and yet has transgressed the Dhamma, are not seen by me. Whereas the man who keeps the Dhamma dwells even in my sight hough he may be at the distance of the ten thousand miles." Here the following of the preachings has been given preference over the personal adoration of Buddha. But here only order of preference is prescribed and the idea of adoration also does not necessarily imply image worship though it may be one of the prominent factors for the same.

Conception of Buddha's personality

"The usual expression, in which Gautama Buddha is referred to, in the Pali texts, is "*Tathāgato araham sammāsambuddho*" (Tathāgata the perfect the fully enlightened). The description found in the Nikāyas is generally as follows. The Tathāgata is fully aware of the nature of the five constituents (*khandhas*) of a being, their origin and decay, he is completely free from all thought—constructions and mental aberrations, including the notions of one-ness, Mine-ness, Egoism and other mental proclivities, he is endowed with ten supernormal powers (*bala*) and four kinds of infallibility (*vesārajja*) heis the embodiment of clear vision, perfect knowledge, immaculate *dharmas*, absolute purity, he is the propounder of the truth, guide for the welfare of all beings, bestower of immortality and lord of *dharmas*."[1] A legend refers a discourse between Brahman and Buddha. The Brahman wants to know whether the Buddha is a man, a God, a Deva, a yaksha or a Gandharva. Buddha replies that he is none of these. He says "I have conquered all *āsavas* through the nonabandonment of which I might have become a god, have been abandoned and cut off at the root like a cut off palm tree with complete cessation of becoming and without liability to arise in future; and likewise those *āsavas* through which I might have become a Gandharva or a yaksha or a man. Just as a blue white or red lotus born and growing in the water and having over come the world, do I dwell unstained by the world. Remember Brahman that I am a Buddha."[2] According to the above Buddha was a being who could

1. Nalinaksha Dutta, Early Monastic Buddhism, p. 295.
2. Anguttara Nikāya, p. 38-39.

be compared with himself only. But this reported event also does not serve the purpose. It does not describe the personality of Buddha in explicit terms and from a layman's point of view but lays stress on a meta-physical and doctrinal stand point though it is clear that Buddha does not include himself within the category of man at least.

Legends occur in many places in Nikāyas. No doubt much credence can not be attached to the historicity of such legends but their conception give an insight into the popular belief of the period and into the truth of the sentiments if not of facts. As such the sayings leave enough scope for drawing inferences about the subtle intentions of Buddha. Even otherwise also oral tradition is the basis of the entire Pali Canon and the discourses start with the world "So I heard" (*evaṁme sutam*).

The *Brahmajāla-sutta* of the *Digha-Nikāya* states "the outer form, O brothern, of him who has won the truth stands before you but that which binds it to rebirth is cut to twain. So long as his body shall last, so long the gods and men behold him. On the dissolution of the body neither gods not men shall see him."[1] Shri O.C Ganguly[2] is of the opinion that the above passage can be interpreted as an interdiction of the Buddha image. But there is nothing to interpret it that way. The passage only explains the state of *nibbāṇa* and cessation of cycle of birth and death. No doubt, after the dissolution of the body neither gods nor men can see him but the image worship also does not require the physical presence of the Master and for representing him through the medium of stone, wood or clay.

Buddha used to say—"whoever sees me sees the Dhamma and whoever sees the Dhamma sees me." This idea may be the starting point of the *Trikāya* conception of Buddha. But at the same time there is no taboo in 'seeing' the Master. According to the above Buddha's personality is identified with Dhamma and can hardly be interpreted as an interdiction about the image worship. Moreover notwithstanding what Buddha said his personality was given the highest place of honour by the lay people because as early as in Pali literature we start getting the reference of the 'Three jewels' (*triratna*) and the people used to mention first Buddha then Dhamma and then *samgha.*

---

1. Uchhinnabhava nettlko bhikkhave tathāgattassa kāyo titthati. Yāvassa kāyo tthassatittāvȧ na dakkhanti eva manussā. Kāyassa bheda jivita pariyādāna na nam dakkhanti deva manussā.
2. Shri O.C. Ganguly, Antiquity of the Buddha image.

This formula was in vogue during the life time of Buddha. But utterance of taking refuge in the Buddha even after his death clearly suggests an attempt to establish relationship between the worshipper and Tathāgata who had attained *parinirvāṇa*. Dr. Coomaraswamy (Buddha and the Gospel of Buddhism, p. 225) rightly remarks that 'the growth of this very conviction deter-mined the development of the Buddhist iconolatory and all the mystical theology of the Mahāyāna.' Moreover in the early Buddhist monuments it is Buddha and none else who is being worshipped by the lay people through the medium and variety of symbols.

Of course Buddha always appealed to the reason of the people and never asked any boby to follow his words blindly but did the laitly also believe like that? Had it been so, his super-human qualities would not have been established as early as in the Pali Canon. Buddha himself gives details of his super human qualities[1] and even describes the virtuous acts done by him in previous births as a result whose merits he was bestowed with the super human qualities (*Mahāpuruṣ a-lakṣaṇa*). He very often narrates his previous births (*pubbenivāsa*) and always used to satisfy the queries of the monks whether a particular person, after death, had attained *nirvāṇa* or not. Naturally he must have been regarded as a being much different from the ordinary man. Attribution of superhuman qualities must have created awe and reverence in midst of the masses and later on served as ready source of iconographic elements for the sculptors of the Kushān period when Buddha assumes the full status of God and when the idea of devotion is perfected according to the Mahāyāna conception.

All these can definitely be regarded as the hazy appearance of the idea of deification of Buddha. As deification progresses the man completely merges in the abstract and Buddha becomes a personification of Dhamma. The *Majjhima Nikāya* describes Buddha's birth as a wonderful miracle (*āścārya abhūta dhamma*).

Buddha's personality has been viewed by another very significant angle. In many of his discourses he discusses some questions which he calls "not fit for explanation" or "inexplain-able" (*Avyākṛita*).[2] Whether Buddha exists after death or not is also one of the *avyākṛita* questions. Manluṅkya-putta even asks the reason for

---

1. Digha Nikāya-Lakkhaṇa sutta, Mahāpadāna sutta; Majjhima Nikāya, Brahmāyu suttanta, Sela suttanta.
2. Digha Nikāya, potthapāda sutta; Majjhima Nikāya, Chulamāñlukya suttanta, Aggivachhagotta suttanta, Samyutta Nikāya, 21/5.

these questions being called *avyākṛita*. Buddha says that he does not explain these questions because they are neither useful for *nirveda* nor for *nirodha* nor for *abhijñā*, nor for *Sambodha* nor for *nirvāṇa*. The question about the Buddha's existence after death is very specific in nature and Buddha's evasīon in replying it must have created a void which could be interpreted in many ways later on.

The denunciation of Rūpa

The five *skandhas* include *Rūpa* also. This *Rūpa* is not only the form of the Master but denotes every thing in the universe which is tangible to the sense-organs and is transitory. That is why it has been defined as the "form seen by the eyes" (*Cakṣu vijñeya rūpa*). Buddha always preaches[1] that all the five *skandhas* are transitory and whatever is transitory (*Anitya*) is a source of misery. No Bhikkhu should have any attachment to the elements which are sources of misery because this "*Rūpa*" as seen by the eyes" (*Cakṣu Vijñeya Rūpa*) invites all sorts of attachments to ones mind.

Firstly the denunciation is very general and philosophical in nature. Secondly it does not imply any binding in beholding Buddha for hearing his words either during his life time or beholding him through other mediums after death. However it reflects Buddha's intention of being detached with the idea of 'form' in any manner.

The idea of worship

The rationalistic outlook of Buddha in asking the people to believe only which appeals to their reason unmistabably shows the preference given to wisdom over respect. The last words of Buddha are very important. He asks Ananda not to be worried about having a teacher after death. He asks him to take refuge unto himself and *Dhamma* will be his teacher. He says "It may be that in some of you the thought may arise that the word of the master is ended and you have no teacher any more. But it is not thus that you should regard it. The *Dhamma* which I have given to you, let that be your teacher." It is evident here that he gave highest prominance to *Dhamma*. But his worship in the form of image may be unimportant for him but at least not mentioned here. The *Brahmajāla sutta* of *Digha Nikāya* lists

1. Samyutta Nikāya, XXII,
Digha Nikāya, Mahāsatipatthānā sutta;
Majjhima Nikāya, Mahārāhulovāda suttanta;
Lakutikopam Suttanta, Satipatthāna Suttanta, Mahāssapur Suttanta;
Sutta Nipāta, Sāriputta Suttanta;
Vinayapitaka, Mahāvagga, Anattalakkhaṇa suttanta.

several low acts done by some Brahmans and monks. These include *Adichyupatthānaṃ* and *Mahātupatthānaṃ*. The former can be interpreted as "worship of the great ones" or "worship of Mahabrahmā." Unless we interpret *Mahatupatthānaṃ* as "worship of the great ones" the reference is not relevant here.

It is very significant that at the time of *Mahāparinirvāṇa* Ananda puts a very specific question. He asks Buddha what should be done of Buddha's body after *Mahāparinirvāṇa*. Buddha replies "Ananda; be always indifferent towards the body worship of Tathāgata."[1] Of course Buddha intended to leave his disciples in the charge of Dhamma (Dhammadayada)[2] but this injunction should be taken with caution because immediately after saying the above Buddha continues that his body should get the same treatment as given to an emperor (*chakravarti*). He prescribes four classes of persons worthy of stupas (*stūpārha*) i.e. Tathāgata, paccheka-Buddha).

Tathāgata sāvaka (a true hearer of Buddha's words or the direct disciple), and an emperor. How to reconcile with both the statements if we believe that they are authentic and without any distortion or interpolation? But actually it is not contradictory. The difference is very subtle here. He is against the conviction of attaching any idea of worship to the mere body but is not against the sanctification of the sacred memory of the great ones by erecting stupas. But what are this stupas for? Apparantly for paying homage and doing worship. It can further be explained by another reference. The Vakajataka records following conversation between the Buddha and emperor Bimbisara. The emperor says "when you are gone, O blessed one, I shall be unable to do you honour, to make you the customary offerings, and it will grieve me. Give me a lock of your hair. Give me the pairings of your finger nail. I shall place them in shrine in midst of my palace. Thus shall I retain something that is part of you and each day shall I decorate the shrine with fresh garlands and I shall burn rare incense. The Master responded "Take my hair, take this pairings and keep them in a shrine but in your mind keep what I have taught you." Here Buddha is still careful in laying emphasis on his preachings but he, at least allows the erection of chaityas enshring relics in memory, reverence or worship of his personality. "Buddha is said to have directed his disciples to bury his remains

1. Digha Nikāya Mahāparinibbāṇa sutta—"Abyāvatā mā tumhe Ānanda hoth Tathāgatassa sariyapujāya.
2. Majjhima Nikāya, Dhammadāyāda Sutta.

under a tumulous, a so-called stupa, traditional sepulchre of worldly monarchs. And he further ordered that after his death the faithful should visit especially those four places which were linked with the chief events of his life[1] Nāgasena[2] also clarifies this point to king Menander (probably 2nd Century B.C.) and says that the real seeker of truth should undertake self discipline and contemplation rather than the worship of the relics of the Buddha. He further informs the king that had Buddha not said so then the Bhikhus would have taken his bowl and his robe and would have occupied themselves with paying reverence to the Buddha through them. It is interesting to note here that later on actually the worship of *uśṇiśa* (jewelled turban) and hair relic (*keśadhātu*) became in vogue and are represented in the Early Buddhist Monuments.

Accounts of the Chinese travellers

Last but not the least is the following tradition with regard to the image worship narrated by Fahian who says "when Buddha went to Traystrimsa and preached the law for the benefit of his mother for ninety days, Prasenjit, longing to see him caused an image tobe carved in *gośirśa* sandalwood and put in the place where he usually sat. When Buddha on his return entered the *Vihāra*, this image left its place and came forthto meet him. Buddha then said to it. "Return to your seat. After I have attained *Parinirvāṇa* you shall serve as a pattern to the four classes of my disciples." Thereupon the image returned to its seat. This was the very first of the image of Buddha and that which men subsequently copied."[3]

It is interesting to note that Hieun Tsiang also noticed this sandalwood image at Śrāvasti.[4] He also states that the king Prasenjit, having heard that the king Udayan had caused a sandalwood figure of Buddha to be carved, also caused this image to be made. It shows that two sandalwood images were carved-one at Kosala and the other at Kauśāmbi during the reigns of Prasenjit and Udayana respectively. About the Kauśāmbi image Hieun-Tsiang states the following "In the city within an old palace, there is a large *vihāra* about 60 feet high, in it is a figure of Buddha carved out of sandalwood, above which is a stone canopy.

---

1. Vogel, The Buddhist Art (Introduction).
2. Milinda Panha, translated by Rhys Davids.
3. Legge, pp. 55-56, Samuel Beal, Chinese accounts of India, Vol. I, p. 26.
4. Samuel Beal, Chinese Accounts of India, Vol. III, p. 261.

It is the work of the King U-to-Yen-na (udayana). By its spiritual qualities (or between its spiritual marks) it produces a divine light, which from time to time shines forth. The princes of various countries have used their power to carry off this statue, but although many men have tried none of the members could move it, and they pretend that the likeness is a true one; and this is original of all such figures. When Tathāgata first arrived at complete enlightenment, he ascended upon the heaven to preach the law for the benefit of his mother and three months remained absent. This King (i.e. Udayana) thinking of him with affection, desired to have an image of his person, therefore, he asked Mudgalyayanputra, by his spiritual power, to transport an artist to the heavenly mansions to observe the excellent marks of Buddha's body, and carve a sandalwood statue. When Tathāgata returned from the heavenly palace, the carved figure of sandalwood rose and saluted the Lord of the world. The Lord then graciously addressed it and said, "the work expected from you is to toil in the conversion of heretics and to lead in the way of religion of future ages."[1] Fahian also visited Kausambi but he does not mention this image later on seen by Hiuen-Tsiang. It does not appear probable that Fa-hian would have afforded to miss the sight of this sandalwood image of Buddha here and this omission is really surprising.

Out of the above tradition a presumption may arise that wooden images might have preceeded the stone sculptures as in the case of rock cut architecture which was definitely preceeded by wooden structures. But there are more points against the authenticity of these traditions than in their favour. Firstly these traditions have been referred by Chinese travellers who came to India in the 5th & 7th Century A.D. when Buddhist images were being carved in plenty and in that situation it would have been quite possible for the masses to coin legends for justifying the anthropomophic representation of Buddha. Secondly the archaeological corroboration in this respect is nil. Thirdly, for carving the earliest Buddhisattava figures of the Kushan age sculptors would not have depended uon the early Yaksha figures for deriving iconographic elements and these figures would have sufficiently been evolved stylistically if we suppose that images of Buddha were carved right from his life time.

---

1. Samuel Beal, Chinese Accounts of India, pp. 254-255.

Fourthly the Chinese travellers depended upon the traditions about the antiquity of these sandalwood images. During their visits to Sravasti and Kausambi, they hardly had any means to verify the antiquityof these sandalwood images seen by them, Fifthly they mention many traditions and legends about the minor events of Buddha's life and miracles performed by him which are not found in the Pali Canon. Not only this, Fa-hian has made responsible even the emperor Asoka of placing a standing figure of Buddha of sixteen feet hight ina Vihara built by him at Sankissa.[1] It is not known whether this image was of sandalwood or of stone but no suchimage of the time of Ashoka has so far come to light. Last but not the least it will be impossible to justify the deliberate ommission of Buddha's figure in his life scenes depicted profusely in the Sunga and Andhara period, at Bodhgayā, Sānchi, Bhārhut and other places if we suppose that Buddha's images were carved right from his lifetime.

We have already observed that such late traditions can hardly be regarded as authentic.

From the above it can be concluded that Buddha was not against the age old tradition of sanctification of holy spots and erection of chaityas and stupas. Regarding body worship also he simply wants his disciples to remain indifferent. He gave supreme position to Dhamma and lavelled the question abut his existance after death, as *avyākrita*. As such the interdiction about the image worship is only tacit and indirect and only inference can be drawn that Buddha was against the formulation of his image. At the same time had the interdiction been unequivocal or categorical it could not have been broken easily in the beginning of the Kushan period. It is also noteworthy that irrespective of what Buddha said his personality was never considered second to *Dhamma* and the organisation by the masses.

1. Samuel Beal, Chinese Accounts of India, Vol. V, p. 23.

Chapter - 19
A Bodh-Gayā Image Inscription
B.M. Barua

The inscription, dealt with here for the first time, is incised on the pedestal of a figure of the Buddha representing the stage of effort prior to his attainment of Buddhahood. The inscription consists of four lines, the first of which is nearly intact and the last has almost completely disappeared with the peeling off of stone from the inscribed surface. The two intermediate lines, too, have been materially damaged in parts apparently for the same reason. The possibility of restoration of the missing letters and words is far remote until a counterpart of the inscription is somehow discovered on the pedestal of another figure of the same description. The figure is evidently carved in the red sand-stone of Mathurā, and the inscription is written in that form of Brāhmī characters that goes to connect it with the large number of Jaina and Buddhist image inscriptions that are incised during the reign of the Kuṣāna rulers, Kaṇiṣka, Huviṣka, Vāsiṣka and Vāsudeva, and it may be that chronologically it is somewhat posterior to them.

Its language, like that of the Mathurā inscriptions of the Kuṣ āna age, is not quite Sanskrit in the sense that it does not entirely keep clear of Prākṛt elements, such as those which linger in the words *bodhisatvapaṭimā sīharathā, upāsikāye, sahāyetīye* and *pūjāye*.

It is dated in Saṃvat 64 of a then current era, the identity of which is still a matter of dispute. If its reference is to the Śaka era, its date must be set down as A.D. 142 (78+64); if to the Gupta, the date is A.D. 384. So long as the contemplated era remains uncertain,[1] the main guide to chronology is bound to be an argument from the general development of Indian iconography, palæography and official language. Such an argument may enable the historian to assign safely

1. Some of the local scholars suggest the Kalachuri as the probable era. This era commenced in A.D. 249.

the inscribed figure to the 2nd or the 3rd century A.D. The lower limit of its date may be fixed with the help of Fahien's account of Bodh-Gayā. This Chinese pilgrim visited Bodh-Gayā in the beginning of the 5th century A.D. He noticed a novel feature in the development of the artistic life of Bodh-Gayā, in that he could see a few figures of the Buddha installed in the then existing sanctuaries,—the earlier sanctuaries that were chiefly the erections of Kuraṅgī, the elderly queen of King Kauśīkiputra Indrāgnimitra. The figure of the Buddha was out of the question at about the close of the 1st century B.C., when Kuraṅgī set up the old stone-railing around the original Bo-tree, the little Diamond-throne temple, the old Jewel-walk shrine, etc. at Bodh-Gayā. The inscribed image under notice must be one of the figures seen by Fahien on the sacred site of Bodh-Gayā at the time of his visit. The epigraph also attests that two such images were installed, both of which were *sīharathā*, each resting, probably as it did, on the back of a pair of lions, as is the case with some of the Bodhisattva figures in the sculptures of Amarāvatī.

The incompleteness of the text of the inscription will always be regretted for the simple reason that it refers to some other works of merit, the nature of which can no longer be ascertained. It is interesting, however, to observe that the shrine in which the two Bodhisattva figures were installed is described in the inscription as *amātyadhura-vihāra*. *Dhura* is a Buddhist technical term and means 'way'. There are two kinds of *dhuras* : *gantha-dhura* (way of study) and *vipassanādhura* (way of meditation) open to the followers of the Buddha. It may be that the shrine containing the two figures was a sort of chamber for study or meditation which was erected by a royal minister. The figures are described as *śailikā-bodhisatva-paṭimā*, the stone images of the Bodhisattva. The text given here is based partly on the remnant of the lingering inscription on the pedestal of the image in the Indian Museum and largely on the photograph published by Cunningham of the colossal figure and of the inscribed pedestal in his *Mahābodhi*, pl. XXV.

Text

L. 1 Mahārājasya Tr(i)kamalasya[1] sa[ṃ] 60 4 (gri) (3) (di) 5 ?? sya pū(r)vvaya[2] bh(i)kṣu - vinaya(dharas)ya vihārasya sadhevihārī vitā[3].........kṣu.........

1. Cunningham reads *Tukamāla* or Lüders, *Trīkamata*.
2. The intended spelling may be *pūrvvāyāṃ*.
3. The intended spelling may be *sārdhavihārī vinā*.

Plate 4

An image from Bodh Gayā

L. 2 Amātya-dhura-vihāre svakena samartho ś?????(ś)ailikā bodhi-satva-paṭimā sīharathā pratisthāpayati 2 [.] Upāsikāye arthadha(r)ma-sahāyetīye dhat?...... ? kṣu......ye sarvvā......

L. 3 ....(s)ahāyatā dharma-kathikena ??tā [-] Imenā kuśalamūlena mātāpitṛṇā[ṃ] pūjāye bhavatu upādh?.........jāye.........

L. 4 ....ye ? vva.........[.]

Translation

L. 1 Just prior to Saṃvat 64, the third month of the hot season and the fifth day of (the reign of) the great ruler Trikamala, the fellow-monk.........residing in the monastery of a Vinayadhara Bhikṣu (a monk conversant with the Vinaya discipline).........

L. 2 set up by his own means two lion-supported stone-images of the Bodhisattva (the Buddha still inthe stage of effort) in the monastic chamber (for study or meditation) erected by (a royal) minister. By a Buddhist female lay worshipper who was the helper of the cause to the advantage of the efficacious doctrine (*arthadharmasahāyetrī*).........

L. 3 a work of merit has been done by a preacher of Buddhism with the help......... Let (the merit) arising from this root of good serve for the honour of mother and father (and for the benefit of the preceptor.........and progeny).........

L. 4 ....

Chapter - 20
The Earth Goddess in Buddhist Art
O. C. Gangoly

In the great drama of the Great Enlightenment (mahāsaṃbodhi) in the Life of the Buddha—the Contest with the Victory over Māra (Māra dharṣaṇa), Māra-Vijaya, cp. the epithet "Mārābhibhu") is a major incident in the story. Though the contest with Māra is alluded to in the early texts (*Dīgha-nikāya,* ii, 261; iii, 260), we do not come across any details and particulars of the Asssault of Māra and his defeats until we come to the Pāli commentaries and the later texts, which seems to suggest that although legends relating to the details of the contest may have grown up quite early, in the shape of poetical embellishments, the actual mythological development, with significant iconographic details, belongs to later times.[1] The account given in the *Mahāvastu* (ii. 281, here cited in Thomas' abridged version) is earlier than the verion of the Pāli commentaries and of the *Lalita-vistara*, and is probably derived from earlier sources: "Then the Bodhisattva..........removed from his robe his golden arms with netted hand and copper-hued nails..........and with his right hand smote the earth.[2] Then the great earth roared and sounded forth a deep and terrible sound, Māra's army so mighty, so well arranged, alarmed, terrified, agitated, distracted and horrified, dispersed and melted away." This text notwithstanding its tiring verbosity does not offer any new embellishment or details of the incident. The commotion of the Earth is reffered to in the *Dīgha Nikāyas,* (*Mahāparinibbāna-sutta,* iii, 13-19) where it is stated that the Earth shakes, trembles and agitates (*paṭ havi kampati, samkampati, sampakampati, sampavedhati*) on the advent of various significant incidents in the Birth and Life of the Buddha e.g. the Conception, the Birth, the Enlightenment etc. The *Mahāvastu* account is perhaps the earliest authority for the "Earth-touching gesture" (***bhūmi-sparśa-mudrā***) plastically rendered in the iconography

---

1. See B.C. Law's paper: 'Buddhist Conception of Māra, in *Buddhiṣtic Studies*, Ch. X.
2. The corresponding passage in the *Lalita-vistara* [Lefmann 318] runs as follows: "*dakṣiṇena pāṇinā sarva-kāyaṃ parimārjya saliḍhaṃ mahiṃ parāhamati sma.*"

of the image, of which the earliest sculptural rendering occurs in the images of the Amarāvatî and the Gāndhāra School. Yet the legend of the Earth being called to witness, though implied, is not explicitly indicated in the *Mahāvastu* version. In the Pāli commentaries the incident is developed (it is impossible to say if this is an independent development, or a loan from earlier floating legends) in the form of a spirited dialogue between the Bodhisattva and Māra: "Verily I fear not, Māra." "Why dost thou not fear?" "Through having perfomed the perfections of the merits of alms-giving and others." "Who knowest that thou hast given alms?" "Is there need of a witness here, evil one? When in one birth I became Vessantara and gave alms, through the power thereof this great earth quaked seven times in six ways, and gave witness. Thereupon the great earth as far as the ocean quaked, uttering a terrible sound." "And Māra terrified at hearing it like a dropped stone lowered his flag, and fled with his host." In the *Nidānakathā* there is a slightly developed version" "And withdrawing his right-hand from beneath his robe, he stretched it forth towards the "earth," and said: "Art thou, or art thou not witness of the seven hundred-fold great gift I gave in my birth as Vessantara?" And the great Earth uttered a voice, saying: " I am witness to thee of that!" overwhelming as it were the hosts of Māra as with the shout of hundreds of thousands of foe." (Rhys Davids, *Buddhist Birth-Stories,* Broadway Translations, pp. 195-196). The significant development in this version is in the fact that while in the two earlier texts the earth testifies by a 'trembling', here, the Earth speaks out in a voice. In the next version (that of the *Lalitavistara)* the voice assumes a visible form: "The Great Earth as soon as touched by the Bodhisattva, shook and trembled (in six forms of agitation). Like unto the brass vessels used by the citizens of Magadha, when struck by a piece of wood, the Great Earth, when struck by the hand of the Bodhisattva, rang out in a metallic twnag which vibrated and resounded. And then the Spirit of the Great Earth known as the lmmovable (*Sthāvāra nāma mahā-prithivîdevatā*) splitting the ground with tremor, very near the Bodhisattva and showing half the body (*ardha-kāya*) decked with all manner of jewels, and bending the same with joint palms thus addressed the Bodhisattva: "That is so, "O! Super-man, that is so. I am eye-witness to what Thou hast uttered.........With these words, Sthāvarā, the Spirit of the Great Earth, after having administered all manner of chastisements to the sinful Māra, and having displayed her glory, disappeared then and there with he cortêge." (Free translation of Lefmann's text of the *Lalita Vistara*, II, pp. 318-19). In this version, the chastisement of the Earth Goddess does not put to flight Māra and his army. He does not give up his attack but changes his tactics and sends his two daughters to

Plate 5

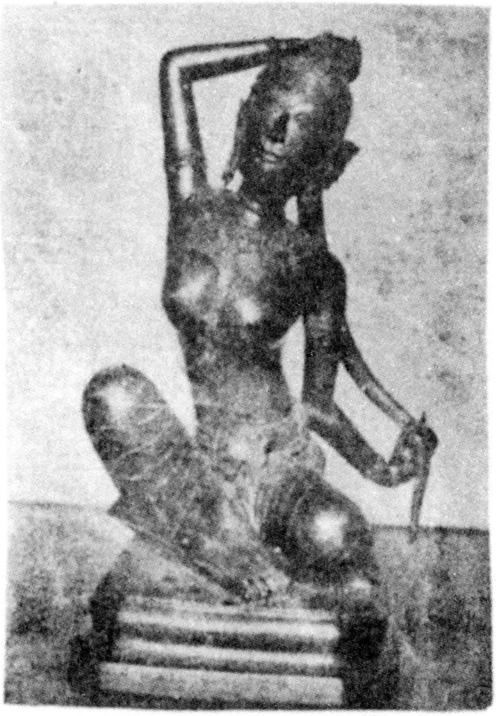

Earth-Goddess, Bronze, Bangkok Museum

Plate 6

Fig. 1: Effigy on pedestal of a Gandhāra Image,
No. 777, Lahore Museum,

Fig. 2: Effigy on pedestal of a stone Image of Bhūmi-sparśa Buddha,
No. B (c) 2, Gupta Period, Sarnāth Museum

tempt the Bodhisattva. An effigy of the Goddess, seen up to the waist, and emerging out of lotus petals—appear to be represented on one of the fragments of the Gāndhāra School (Lahore Museum, No. 777). (Fig. 1).

In one of the images, in 'earth-touching gesture', of the Gupta period (?) dug up at Sarnāth, on the pedestal, half the figure of the Earth Goddess is depicted as emerging from the surface of the earth carrying a vessel (*kalasa*) of sacred water. In this connection the *Vessantara Jātaka*, and its various plastic illustrations come to our aid. According to the old Vedic practice,[1] every gift has to be ratified and consecrated by the rite of sprinkling of holy water (*abhiṣeka*). In the Bharhut relief illustrating the gift of the Jetavana grove by Anāthapiṇḍika and in Gāndhāra reliefs illustrating the *Vessantara Jātaka*, King Vessantara carries a water-vessel (*bhṛṅgāra*) from which he pours the lustral water in ratifying the gift of the Elephant which is followed by other gifts of all his possessions including his children and wife. It is the accumulated merit of the great gifts, the great sacrifices of the Buddha (or, in words of Māra's elephant Giri-mekhalā. "the uttermost gift given by thee, Siddhārtha") collected in the bosom of the Earth in the shape of the waters of the donative rituals, poured from the ritual vessel (*abiṣeka-kumbha*). And it is this piece of concrete evidence that the Earth-Goddess carries up in a vessel as represented in a tiny figure on the pedestal of more than one relief, at Sarnāth, one of which is cited, here, in Fig. 2.

In a later development of this legend we are treated to a more poetic version. According to this developed and more imaginative version, the waters from the ritual vessel consecrating the various gifts of the Buddha in his former life percolated through the soil, and drenched and soaked the heavy tresses of the long hair of the Earth Goddess (*Vasundharā*. And when summoned by the Bodhisattva to testify to his donative merits, accumulated through the ages, the Goddess, who was carrying the ritual waters (*dakkhiṇodaka*) hidden in her hair, wrung her long tresses with her hand, and streams of water, like unto the ganges, flowed out of her hair in mighty torrents and swept away Māra and his formidable army. This is the version which has been unearthed by that astute scholar Dr. Coedés, from a late Pāli text known as *Paṭhamasaṃbodhi*, very well-known in Mss. current in Siam and Cambodia. I quote the relevant passage "Bho Avanitala! mayhaṃ samatiṃsa pāramiyo pūrentassa Vessantarattabhāve

1. "In Ancient India there existed the custom of the donors pouring water upon the ground when they made donations of land or endowed temples and the like (*Salila-dhārā-pūrvvakaṃ*)" (S.C. Mitra: 'On an Ancient Indian Custom'. *Hindusthan Review,* April, 1918, p. 332).

ṭhatvā puttadāra-pariccāgaṃ katvā sattva-satakamahādānaṃ datvā samaṇā vā brāhmaṇā vā sakkhikatā n'atthi. Bho Avanitala! idāni kasmā na sakkhîti. Tadā Vasundharā-vanitā Bodhisatttssa sambhātānubhāvena attānam sandhāretuṃ asakkontî Paṭhavîtalato uṭṭhahitvā itthisāmaññatāya Bodhisattassa pūrato ṭhatvā: "Tāta Mahāpurisa! ahaṃ tava sambhāraṃ jānāmi, tava dakkhiṇodakena mama kenā allīyanti, idānti parivattaryissāmî"—ti vadantā viya tāvad eva attano kesa parivattitvā visajjesi. Tassā kesato udakaṃ pati taṃ yathā Gaṅgodakasotaṃ pavattati—Atha te Mārasenā......palāyiṃsu. Girimekhalapādā pana pakkhalitvā yāva sāgarantam pavisanti."

Rendered in a free translation, the passage reads as follows.

"O! Earth! I have achieved the thirty Perfections and in my existence as Vessantara, I made the sacrifice of my wife and of my children and I have distributed gifts by several hundreds at a time but I have no monk nor Brāhmaṇa to bear testimony (to my assertion). O! Earth, why are you not (coming forth) as my witness now? Then Lady Vasundharā, being unable to hold herself by the sense of appreciation of the weight of spiritual treasures of the Bodhisattva, came forth from beneath the Earth, and assuming the common form of women placed herself in front of the Bodhi sattva, said: 'Respected Super-Man! I know of the magnitude of thy (spiritual) riches, the tresses of my hair are saturated with the ritual-water of your gifts, let me wring out the water now'. With these words she immediately began to wring her tresses of hair and discharge the water. From her hair water oozed out like the flow of the water of the river Ganges... ... ... At this, the army of Māra being unable to keep its footing, fled away. The feet of elephant Giri-mekhalā slipped and it was washed away into the sea'.[1] This developed version of the story with picturesque embellishments has not been traced in any text earlier than the *Paṭhamasaṃbodhi*, which cannot be precisely dated. The earliest plastic representation of this version has been traced by Dr. Coedés in a sculpured stéle

1. H. Alabaster (*The Wheel of the Law*, London, 1871, pp. 154-155) who gives an English version of a life of the Buddha', derived from Siamese sources has rendered the story in the following words:

"And the angel of the earth, unable to resist his invocation, sprang from the earth in the shape of a lovely woman with long flowing hair, and standing before him answered: O Being more excellent than angels or men! It is true that when you performed your great works you ever poured water on my hair. And with these words she wrung her long hair, and a stream, a flood of waters gushed forth from it. Onward against the host of Māra the mighty torrent rushed. His generals were over-turned, his elephant swept away by the waters, his royal insignia destroyed, and his whole army fled in utter confusion, amid the roarings of a terrific earthquake, and peals of thunder crashing through the skies." If Alabaster's version is an accurate translation, then the Siamese text used by him must have been a different text.

from Ankor Vat, datable about the 11th century. On this relief (Fig. 5) which represents the Assault of Māra, the image of the Earth-Goddess is indicated (unlike the situation on Gupta reliefs) on the left side of the seated Buddha, standing on a lotus and holding the tresses of hair in her hands. Māra on his elephant Giri-mekhalā is shown in two positions, one at the beginning of the assault on the left corner, and second time on the right side—at the moment when the feet of the elephant squids in the inundation as suggested by the text cited by Coedés. This version of the legend must, therefore, be earlier than the 11th century, and has to be distinguished, in fundamental details, from earlier version of the legend followed in the relief of the Gupta School (6th to 7th century) cited from Sarnāth. The fundamental innovation is the elimination of the jar, containing the donative water of lustration (*dakkhiṇodaka*), and the replaçing of it by tresses saturated with them. This version has no parallel in any Buddhist reliefs hitherto discovered in India. Though no lithic representation has been forthcoming, Coedés believed that the version probably developed on Indian soil. In some of the Tibetan illustrations of the story, as for instance, on a Tibetan banner (Bacot Collection, Musée Guimet, Paris) here cited in a drawing (Fig. 4), the Earth-Goddess at the centre, carries no jar. Curiously, though no Indian illustration of the version has been found in India, illustration have been traced in Burma, Cambodia and Siam. Another curious development of the form of the Earth-Goddess in Greater India consists in the fact that while in India, in the examples so far traced,—it occurs as a subordinate figure, introduced in the scenes depicting the Assault of Māra, as *one* of the *dramatis personae* in the story,—in Burma and Siam, the figure is represented independently, as we shall presently see.

In Burma, the figure of the Earth-Goddess known under the name of Vasundharā (vulgarized in Burma as 'Wasundhāye') occurs in almost all the pagodas, represented in the form of a gracious lady, either seated or standing, with the tresses of her hair brought over her left shoulder, across her bust, and represented in the act of squeezing out water from her hair. A majority of the examples, at least, belongs to fairly early times. A fragment of a sculpture in stone representing Vasundharā has been found at Wethali (Vesali) in Arakan in 1920, which (according to the Superintendent, Archaeological Survey, Burma), "may be safely assigned to the 9th or 10th century." Another, example in wood (now in the Pagan Museum) has been dug up from a ruined temple near Pagan and have been assigned to the 14th or 15th century (Fig.7). It is markedly Chinese in style, and it has been suggested that it may have come from China. If this suggested *provenance* is correct—the version of the legened must have been also current in Chinese Buddhism. There is some doubt in orthodox Buddhist circles in Burma if the Earth-Divinity is a male or female. In all known examples it is a goddess, and should be so, as she must have long tresses of hair from which she has to squeeze out water. The doubt may have been suggested by the word "mahāpṛthivî-devatā" in the *Lalitavistara*, but other words in the same text leave no doubt that it is a goddess. The only other Burmese example which remains to be cited is the representation of the goddess in a very late fresco on the walls of the Arakan Pagoda at Mandalay.

The most important example from Cambodia has been cited above. The only other example so far known occurs on one of the façades of the sanctuary at Vat Nokor near Kompong-Cham (Fournereau, *Ruines Khmerés*, pl. 71) (Fig. 6). But, the finest examples, all of them independent figures, have come from Siam. A fine bronze figure of the Divinity (now in the Bangkok Museum) was cited by Fourcreau many years ago and is here reproduced in the Frontispiece. It is a seated form and in its graceful pose undoubtedly represents one of the finest example of Siamese sculpture, unhappily not noticed by May in his excellent monograph. An equally fine example in standing pose has been cited by Salmony in his study of *Sculpture in Siam* from which it is borrowed here (Fig.8). Two other representations in stone reliefs (said to have come from Ayuthia) have been cited by Salmony (Plate 69, A & B) which appear to be related to the images of Vasundharā. They are differently posed, one wringing her hair by stretching the left arm while the other twists her hair across her right arm. The first one is depicted in a dynamic movement almost imitating the poses of flying Apsaras, while the other one is represented in a seated pose. They appear to have been decorative slabs on the façade of some temple. In the absence of particulars of their provenance it is impossible to speacualte about their function. At any rate, in the pose of twisting their hair these figures (Salmony, Pl. 69) are closely related to the images of Vasundharā, if they do not actually represent the Earth-Goddess. A painted pottery relief from Svargaloka, (Siam) cited by Coedés (Pl. XI, *Ars Asiatica*, vol. XII) may be a representative of the Goddess and recalls, in its floral base from which the adorning figure emerges, a similar motif in the Gāndhāra piece cited above (Fig. 1). The representation of the Earth-Goddess in independent figures met with in Siam and Burma, unrelated to the story of Māra's Assault, calls for an explantation. For, in the Indian representations, the goddess is never represented as an independent icon. It s very significant that in Siam this Angel of the Earth (Vasundharā) has a Siamese popular name "Pra Torani" (Torani=*dharaṇi*, earth, and she is a very popular goddess worshipped as the great mother of all mankind (Thomson, *Lotus Land*, p. 93). And the use of the image as an independent icon may be explained by the fact that Vasundharā is generally placed in Ordination Halls, in Siam as well as in Burma, and performs the function

Plate 7

Fig. 3: Effigy on pedestal on a Stone Image of the Buddha, Pāla School, Indian Museum, Calcutta.

Fig. 4: Portion of a Tibetan Tangka, Musée Guimet, Paris.

Plate 8

Fig. 5:
Stone Relief from Angkor-Vat, *c.* 11th century.

Fig. 6:
Relief from the façade of a Buddhist Temple, Vat Nokor, near Kompong-Cham,

Fig.7:
Seated Earth-Goddess, Bangkok Museum, Siam.

of a witness to any donation of gifts or offering, or to any other acts of merits on the part of a lay-worshipper. This function appears to have given to the Earth Goddess an independent status in Burmese and Siamese Buddhism calling for a separate icon of the goddess unrelated to the story of Māra's Assault. In these independent representations she is the ever-present divinity of the Earth an eye-witness to all the acts of merits or demerits of all human beings.

This is borne out by the Formula of Dedication in Pāli still used in Burma by donors in consecrating any gift the Earth-Goddess Vasundharā being invoked by them as a witness to the meritorious act. That this Formula is modelled on the legend of Vasundharā and the ancient practice of pouring 'libation water' (*dakkhiṇodakaṃ*) in Formula (*Kammavācā*) here given in translation, the text being quoted in the footnote:

"Reverend Sir: We pin our faith in the doctrine of Karma and its fruition. We take upon ourselves the observance of the five precepts. Having done so we also give in charity all these charitable commodities to your, venerable sirs, by the pouring of libation water.

May we, venerable sir, by virtue of this good deed quickly attain nirvāṇa where rebirth, old age, disease and death are unknown. As long as we have not attained nirvāṇa so long and for that period of time, in the course of our repeated rebirths, may we experience and enjoy the bliss of the best form of human and heavenly happiness better than the happiness enjoyed by others.

Reverend Sir! We share this merit of ours with our parents of excellent virtue, with our teachers, with all our kinsmen and friends etc., with our kings and deities.

May the aforesaid living beings get equal share of merit with us and may they rejoice over our act of merit.

Should we forget about our this act of merit, may the Earth-god or goddess Vasundharā stand as our witness."[1]

---

1. "Mayaṃ bhante kammañca kammaphalañca saddhahitvā tisaraṇena sahā pañcasîlaṃ samādiyāma. Samādiyitvā imāni nānā dātabbavatthūni āyasmantānaṃ dakkhiṇodakaṃ pātetvā dema.

Mayaṃ bhante iminā puñña-kammena ajātiṃ ajaraṃ avyādhim amataṃ nibbanaṃ sighaṃ pāpuṇissāma. Yāva nibbānaṃ na pāpuṇissāma tāva saṃsāre saṃsarantā atiukkaṭṭhaṃ parchi adhikataraṃ manussasaṃpattiṃ ca dibbasaṃpattiṃ ca anubhaveyyāma.

Mayaṃ bhante idaṃ puññabhāgaṃ guṇavisiṭṭhatarānaṃ mātāpitūnnañca ācariyanañ ca ñātimittasamūhādînaṃ ca devānañ ca dema yathā vuttā sabbasattā amhehi samaṃ puññabhāgaṃ labhitvā anumodantu. Amhesu pamattesu pi ayaṃ Vasundharā amhākaṃ sakkhiṭṭhāe tiṭṭhatu."

[The writer is indebeted, for the above citation, to the kind courtesy of the Superintendent, Archaeological Survey, Burma Circle].

The group of representations of the Buddhist Earth-Goddess cited, here, offer a very interesting phase of myth-making in Buddhist religion and help us to relaize how the tiny effigy on the seats of the images of a type of the Buddha of the Gupta period develops into an independent icon with almost a cult of its own. Incidentally, the developed legend offers to the artists of Siam an opportunity to present the Earth-Goddess in remarkably conceived sculptural forms of exquisite movement and grace. Though the earliest representation of the goddes appear to have been formulated in Cambodia,—the Siamese sculptors render the icon in an original and a characteristically local style of their own.

Since the above was set in type several new data have cropped up which, while they complicate the problem of the iconography of Pṛthvî Devî, and its evolutional forms, help to study the forms of this goddess from the Hindu Brahmanical point of view.

Several representations of the goddess have been recently traced on some mediaeval Hindu monuments of the South, of which the earliest example is the one on a pillar of the maṇḍapa in front of the Bṛhan-nāyiki shrine, at the Bṛhadîśvara temple (an early eleventh century Cola temple) at Tanjore. It is impossible to say if this is the earliest representation of the goddess on a Brahmanical monument, as we have not been able to trace any earlier example. (Photo No. 1498 of 1936-37, Office of the Superintendent for Epigraphy). Of later examples, the mosty significant are those appearing as bas-reliefs on some Vijaynagara monuments. One occurs on a pillar in the Kalyāṇa-maṇḍapa of the Viṭṭhala-swāmin temple at Hampi, Bellary (Photo No. 1456 of 1936-37, *Ibid*). Another occurs on a pillar in a subsidiary maṇḍapa at the Acyutarāya temple at Hampi (Photo No. 1385 for 1935-36, *Ibid*). Yet another occurs on the basement of the Gopura of the Hazara Rāma temple at Hampi (Photo No. 1388 for 1935-36, *Ibid*) As will appear from the drawings (Figs. 9, 10 & 11) cited, here, from these examples, all of them represent a female figure wringing out here hair, very much in the fashion of the figure as it occurs in Burmese Art. In the earlier Buddhist representation on the Gupta Images in the Sarnāth Museum, the goddess is not represented in the act of wringing out her hair. Otherwise, it would have been easier to claim that the Brahmanical sculptors of the Cola and Vijaynagara temples, cited above, must have derived the iconology of the Earth Goddess, depicted by them, from Buddhist models. None of the Siamese and Buddhist examples appears to be as early as the 10th or 11th century, and, possibly, could not have provided precedents for the Brahmanical reliefs referred to above. The Earth Goddess has an independent tradition in

Plate 9

Fig.8: Standing Earth-Goddess, Bangkok, Siam.

Hindu Brahmanical pantheon. Bhūmi Devî or Bhauma Devî the Earth-Spirit of Vedic times, receives offerings according to the prescriptions of the Gṛhya Sūtras.[1] In early Vedic conception the goddess Pṛthivî is closely associated with Dyaus (the Heaven spirit) and is invoked jointly with Dyaus. In the *Ṛgveda* (V. 84) she has but one short hymn of her own, while a long and interesting hymn is ascribed to her in the *Atharvaveda* (xii. 1). "She is great, shining and firm, and quickness the earth, by *scattering rain from a cloud"*, in which act she appears to borrow an attribute of Dyaus himself. As a matter of fact, Parjanya (son of Dyaus) the Spirit of the rain-cloud quickens the earth with rain, and the Pṛthvî Devî as the wife of Parjanya absorbs all the showers of rain that descend on her. From the Vedic point of view, it may be suggested that the Earth Goddess will carry in her tresses all the water that descend from the Rain-clouds, and she could easily wring out any amount of water from her flowing tresses. In a physical sense, any amount of water could be dug out of the earth (the tresses of the goddess), and, the Earth is the perennial source of water for wells, tanks, or reservoirs.

The imagery of the Earth and her tresses of hair saturated with water can thus be independently derived from the Vedic sources without reference to the Buddhistic tradition—which itself may have borrowed the imagery from the original Vedic source.

In later Puranic conception Bhūmā Devî (the Vedic Earth-spirit) is one of the consorts of Viṣṇu. And in South Indian metal images, Viṣ-ṇu is frequently represented as standing in the centre with Lakṣmī Devī on one side, and Bhūmā Devî, on the other. Krishna Sastri (*South Indian Images of Gods and Goddess,* 1916, Madras, Fig. 33, p. 53) cites the drawing of Vaikuṇṭha-nārāyaṇa, with a female figure depicted on the serpent couch, which may represent a donor, but which one is tempted to identify as Bhūma Devî (Pṛthvî Devî) as it is represented very much in the same manner as the effigy of the Earth Goddess on the pedestal of some of the Gupta Buddhas at Sarnāth cited above.

But could we trace the iconography of the Buddhist formulation of the Earth-Goddess to Vedic sources? As Dr. Coomaraswamy has pointed out the nearest and probably the direct equivalent is Vasupatnī (*ṚV.* I, 164, 27). The *Ṛgveda* offers a few hymns to the Earth, but as yet offers no definite material for visual conception. The *Atharvaveda Saṃhitā* (Book XII) devotes a string of 63 hymns,

1. *Gobbila Gṛhya Sūtra* iii, 7. 3; *Āśvtalāyana Gṛhya Sūtra,* ii, 1. 15; *Śāṅkhāyana Gṛhya Sūtra,* iv. 15; *Pāraskara Gṛhya Sūtra,* ii. 14, 9; *Āpastamba Gṛhya Sūtra,* xviii, 5; xix, 22.

addressed to the Earth and describes her many virtues and characteristics. Four of these hymns are relevant for our purpose—as they emphasize on the Goddess raining down her bounties, and 'sprinkling us with her splendour.' Some of these hymns use the figures of speech of raining down "milk" or "streams" of prosperity. One hymn (XII, 52) describes the "broad Earth as wrapped and covered with rain"— suggesting perhaps the imagery of the Goddess having her tresses soaked with water. The relevant hymns are cited below in Whitney's translation (Harvard Oriental Series, vol. II, 1905, pp. 662, 670, 671).

"7. She the earth (*Bhūmi pṛthvī*), whom, the Angels sleepless, defendall the time without failure—let her yield (*duh*) to us honey, what is dear; then let her sprinkle us with splendour."

"9. On whom the circulating waters flow the same night and day, without failure—let that earth (*bhūmi*) of many streams (*dhārā*) yield us milk; then let her sprinkle (us) with splendour."

"10. * * * Let that earth (*bhūmi*) to us, a mother to a son, pour out (*vi-srij*) milk (to me)."

"42. * * * To the Earth, whose spouse is Parjanya, fattened (soaked) by the rain, be homage."

"45. Let the Earth * * * yield me a thousand streams of property, like a steady un-resisting milch-cow."

"36. * * * let thine arranged seasons, years, let day-and-night, O Earth, yield milk to us."

"4. Ye who bears the streams (*srotaya*) IV. 26, 4."

Though the Vedic texts do not provide directly ready-made materials for an iconic conception—for the Earth Goddess in the Buddhist formulation—in the image of a woman wringing out water from her hair,—there are enough seed-ideals in the figures of speech used in the texts quoted above, which may have offered materials for the later iconography.

Plate 10

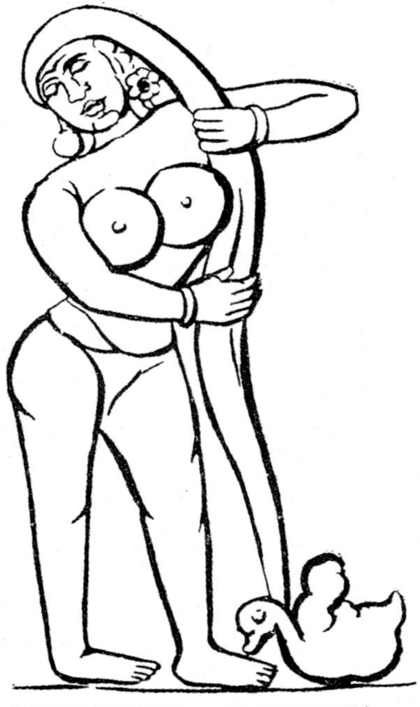

Fig. 9:
Gopuram, Acyutarāya Temple,
Hampi.

Fig. 10:
Kalāṇa-maṇḍapa,
Vitthala-Swâmin Temple,
Hampi.

Fig. 11:
Gopuram, Hāzra Rāma Temple.
Hampi.

Chapter - 21
The Harmikā and the Origin of Buddhist Stupas

J. Przyluski

The *harmikā* is a square block of masonry placed on the top of the stūpa cupola, and is sometimes decorated in the manner of a pavilion. Fergusson took it for an imitationof a relic-casket. E. Senart criticized this suggestion, saying,: "By all that we know of buddhic relic caskets, nothing is more unlike one of them than this small pavilion behind its railing." But E. Senart's own interpretation does not seem more satisfactory. According to him, the stūpa is a stone reproduction of the round hut of the early fire-worshippers, and the *ḥarmikā* imitates the altar of the fire. Unfortunately, supposing the dome of the stūpa derived from the round hut, one fails to see why the altar should have been placed on the roof instead of beneath it.

M.G. Combaz thinks that the *harmikā* is a reproduction of the pavilion erected in front of the Bodhi tree or around it. The tree beneath which Śākyamuni became Buddha was an object of particular reverence. In the early days it must have been surrounded by pales, and a pavilion crowned by the parasol of sovereignty had probably been built around, or in front of it.[1] M. Combaz thinks that an assimilation took place between the *yūpa* of the stūpa and the Bodhi tree and that, when the *yūpa* bearing the parasol was identified with the sacred tree, the shrine which surrounded, or was placed before it, became the *harmikā*.[2]

---

1. For a representation of this pavilion, see A.K. Coomaraswamy, *Early Indian Architecture, Bodhi-gharas,* Eastern Art, ii, p. 225, Philadelphia, 1930.

2. *Dévolution du stūpa en Asie,* in Mélanges chinois et bouddhiques, II, pp. 196-199. M. Combaz considers another hypothesis without, however, insisting on it. Speaking of the *harmikā*, he says: "Is it, in India, a vestige of the 'shelter,' mentioned in the Brāhmaṇic rituals as the protection given to the urn containing the ashes of the dead before they are buried for good?"

Two series of facts go against this explanation. For, one thing, we notice very often on the stūpa or sculptures on the relievos of Bārhut, Sāñchī and Amarāvatī, a *harmikā* topped with one or several parasols, but the top of a *yūpa* is not to be seen above it, and this goes against the supposition that the *yūpa* preceded and inspired the erection of the pavilion. Then, in Buddhist texts, we see that the sacred trees were originally enclosed in a fence (*vāra*), in order to retain the water of the ritual sprinklings.[1] Later on, as well shown by A.K. Coomaraswamy,[2] this fence was completed by the construction of a frame to allow the watering of the tree from its top, and this took the shape of a pavilion, but its use ws well known and the pole of a stūpa could not be mistaken for a tree which had to be watered.

In an important work on the Barabuḍur, M. Mus offers, a new explanation. In the stūpa he sees a closed microcosm containing, beneath a roof which is the vault of heaven, a miniature of the cosmic mountain—this mountain being shown under the shape of a *prāsāda*, that is to say, of a pyramid of terraces,—and the whole construction being lost in the mass of the stūpa. According to this theory, the *harmikā* would be the top of the Mount Meru piercing through the celestial vault, and towering above it.[3]

"Our hypothesis," says M. Mus, "would admit of great reinforcement if it could be proved that the square top of the stūpa was meant by the Indians themselves to picture the top of a *prāsāda*." And this is precisely what the term *harmikā* seems to confirm. We can hardly question that the word is here the technical term which describes the "look-out" which crowns a pile of terraces. Buddhaghosa himself could vouch for it if needed. Here are the terms in which his own commentary on the *Cullavagga,* VI, 1, 2, describes a *prāsāda* provided with this convenience: "The word *hammiya* means a many-storied succession of terraces, the highest of which is topped by a pavilion.[4] It is interesting to note that the pavilion on the top of the Meru forms so essential a part of it that, in the composition of some painting of Touen-houang, it has probably been considered quite to indicate figuratively the Mount itself,—which characteristics it bears in suggesting the happy life led by the gods on it lofty summit. The description of this palace is a very common-place feature

1. J. Przyluski, *La Légende de V Empereur Aśoka,* pp. 267, 433.
2. *Early Indian Architecture,* p. 225 and foll.
3. P. Mus, *Le Barabuḍur*, BEFEO, XXXII, 1932, 1, p. 381 and foll.
4. Cf. SBE., vol. XIII, p. 173, n. 1.

of the Buddhist texts, because it sums up essentially the domain of the gods. The term *harmikā*, connected with the architectural notion of the *prāsāda,* would lead us back perfectly, through this connection, to the second explanation of the top of the stūpa given above: *devatā kotuwa*, in Sinhalese "citadel of the gods."

"Considering everything, if in Central Asia the painter of the *Vimalakīrtinirdeśasūtra* believed that he indicated the cosmic pyramid very clearly when he drew the little pavilion which crowns it, how can we help concluding that a similar speculation may quite possibly have happened, *mutatis mutandis,* where the *harmikā* of the oldest Indian stūpas is concerned?"[1]

It is permitted to suppose that, after the beginning of the Christian era, when the ideas relating to the stūpa had already undergone some changes, the *harmikā* was conceived as a "look-out" imitating the pavilion of the gods on the top of the Meru. But we cannot very well admit with Mr. Mus that this conception was an original one, and that "the cosmic mountain may be found in the earliest stūpas, concealed under the envelope."[2] When thinking of old stūpas, we see of course the big monuments of Bārhut and Sāñchī. But we must not forget that many stūpas were very much smaller than these. Here is an extract from a *Parinirvāṇa-sūtra*, translated into Chinese:

"All the Bhikṣus inquired of Ānanda: "What is the rule of the funeral?" He answered: "We must go out of the town, towards the east a distance of 30 li of the town, there is a village. This village is called Wei-Teheu. At the crossing of four ways a pole shall be set up and a funeral monument shall be erected. The flat-stones to cover it shall be made of jade. These stones must be 3 ft. square. The stūpa shall be 15 ft. square. The urn of gold containing the *śarīra* shall be placed exactly in the centre of it. A stūpa shall be erected and a mast shall rise out of it, at the top of which flags and silk stuffs shall be hung. Incense shall be burnt and lamps shall be lit; it shall be cleaned, dusted and strewn with flowers, and the 12 categories (of worshippers) shall rejoice from morning till night and shall honour it" (*Tripiṭ.*, ed. Tok, XII, 10, p. 21, col. 7).

The stūpa described above is of a late model, as we see it topped by a pole and covered with hard stone. However, its dimensions are

1. P. Mus, *ibid.*, p. 382-383.
2. *Ibid.* p. 382.

moderate. Of course the value of the Chinese foot has varied with the different dynasties, also from a state to another. But if we adopt as a basis its actual average length: 0m. 35, we find 5m. 25 to be the length and width of the monument.

If a stūpa of the Buddha, built at a comparatively late period, had a diameter of only 5m., the stūpas of the disciples must have been smaller still, and it seems incredible to think that each one of these monuments could have been supposed to enclose the highest mountain of the universe—that which upholds the roof of heaven.

We believe that another explanation must be sought for for the presence of the *harmikā*.

According to the old Brāhmaṇic rituals, the shape and proportions of the *śmaśāna* varied with the different schools. It could be either circular or square. With the Mādyandhina and the Baudhāyana it could not exceed the length of a man. As to the height, it was proportioned to the height of the deceased. With the Mādyandhina, the *śmaśāna* of a Kṣatriya was as high as a man standing; for a Brahman it went up only to the mouth, for a Śūdra it stopped at the knees.[1]

As very well pointed out by Caland, the tomb was very small; it was feared, if the dead man were given too much space, he would try to carry away a companion with him.[2] The first Buddhists probablyfollowed this rule, with the reserve that the tomb of a Buddha was larger than that of a disciple.

On the supposed site of Kapilavastu, a number of Buddhist tombs were found, clustering around a larger monument: prisms of brick, with no domes and with a square foundation. When announcing their discover, Barth observed their resemblance with the Brāhmaṇic funeral monuments.[3] We believe the *harmikā* to have been originally the dead man's dwelling, and the cube of masonry which crowns the bigger stūpas is an imitation of the brick prisms with a square basement discovered at Kapilavastu.

---

1. J Przyluski, *Le Parinirvāṇo et les Funérailles du Buddha,* p. 209.
2. The legend of the Rāhula stūpa, in the Kapiśa, as recorded by Hiuan-Tsang, sounds lke an echo of similar beliefs: a minister, having built a stūpa carries the relies to it himself and remains walled up in the stūpa, which closes up magically behind him. See Beal, *Si-yu-ki,* I, p. 61 and P. Mus, *ibid.,* p. 390.
3. *Œuvres de A. Barth*, II, p. 311, n. 2 and see *Le Parinirvāṇa et* les *Funérailles,* p. 210.

With the development of the Buddha-Cakravartin's legend appeared the notion that his tomb should have the dimensions of a palace, that is to say, of a pyramid of terraces: a *prāsāda*. This plan included as a matter of course a massive basement, crowned by a pavilion: the cupola of the stūpa stands for the basement; the *harmikā* is the pavilion, it is the deceased's dwelling, as its name seems to imply, and it perpetuates the Brāhmaṇic *śmaśāna*.

We do not question that the foundation may have been gradually replaced by the image of the cosmic mountain, where the king of the gods resides. But these ideas have not been more than accessory, in all probability, to the development of the stūpa.

The stūpa was, originally, the tomb of a Tathāgata, of a Pratyeka-buddha, of a listener of the Buddha, or of a Cakravartin.[1] Where a Tathāgata or a Cakravartin, both equal in dignity, were concerned, one may have thought of Mount Meru. But for the tomb of a disciple there could be no question of a *prāsāda*, not to speak of a miniature of Mount Meru.

It can be objected that if the *harmikā* was the house of the deceased, a casket containing his remains should, logically, have been placed in it. But, against logic rose the wish to hide the relics from the greed of thieves, and the builders were obliged to bury them deep.

In the study of this arduous problem we do not see the point of using a figure that M. Foucher and, recently, M. Mus have examined at length. It is an image engraved on some coins in the North-West.

"The stūpa," says M. Mus, "is clearly drawn in section. Inside the cupola, a central pillar indicated by a straight line rises up from the bottom and is crowned by what M. Foucher declares to be a parasol: his supposition is grounded on similarities which lend some veracity to it. This image, he adds, has probably lost its signification as time went, and the error may have led to think that it showed a bow and arrow.

"Error, or deliberate interpretation? The question deserves to be studied again. It is difficult to admit that the Buddhists could have so deeply misread the holiest symbol in their religious art, especially when the bow and arrow are given a place of such minor importance

1. *Mahāparinibbāna,* V. 12; *Dīrghāgama* in Chinese, *Tripiṭ*, ed. Tok., XII, 9, p. 17a col. 15.

in the catalogue of their sacred images. If they have chosen at all this far-fetched interpretation, it can be owing to an allegorical sense, only. The cosmic axle is often identified in the Indian belief with the ray of sunlight piercing the spaces when the sun reaches its zenith. Though we cannot insist on this point, which is worthy of a special study, we may remind the reader that the celestial arrow is another illustration of the same cosmological conception.

"If the stūpa is entirely built around the cosmic axle, does it not present an unexpected similarity with a bow an its arrow?

"And this is our explanation of this symbolical figure."[1]

We are not convinced that this symbol has anything in common with the stūpa. The Annamites, before the feast of the New-Year, draw with lime on the earth the picture of a bow and arrow, in order to frighten away the evil spirits. The image printed on the North-Western coins may possess the same prophylactic value. The resemblance with a stūpa is doubtful and far-fetched. We consider it wiser not to bring in this drawing in a discussion on the origin of the stūpas.

From a passage in the *Śatapatha Brāhmaṇa* we learn that in ancient times square tombs were made by the people who were 'godly,' that is probably by the Aryans, whilst the round tombs were made by 'asuric' people, that is probably by the Non-Aryans.

"Now the Gods and the Asuras, both of them sprung from Prajāpati, were contending in the (four) regions (quarters). The Gods drove out the Asuras, their rivals and enemies, from the regions, and being regionless, they were overcome. Wherefore the people who are godly make their burial-places four-cornered; whilst those who are of the Asura nature, the Easterners and others, (make them) round (*yā āsuryaḥ prācyās tvad ye tvat parimaṇḍalāni*), for they (the gods) drove them out from the regions."[2]

Mr. A.C. Banerji, who has recently quoted this passage, adds: "It is quite possible that the round form of Asura burial mound ultimately gave birth to round stūpas found all over India, because Buddhism, after all, is a religion of Eastern India."[3]

Besides, attempts have been made to trace the origin of the South-Indian temples to a primitive architecture that existed in the

---

1. P. Mus, *Le Barabuḍur*, p. 386.
2. *Sat. Brāh*, SBE, vol. xliv, pp. 423-24.
3. *JBORS.*, vol. XX, part II, 1934, p. 182.

South prior to the advent of Brahmanism, Buddhism or Jainism.[1] As observed recently by M.V. Krishna Rao,[2] "the practice of constructing megalithic tombs and sepulchral memorials that was prevalent among certain tribes and castes of South India in the early centuries of the Christian era, and the testimony of epigraphical evidences showing the erection of Śiva temples as memorials on tombs of important personages seem strongly to justify the latter point of view. The crude megalithic structures, dolmens, cromlechs and hero-shrines essentially tumular and external, spread all over Mysore and the South, might have been the nucleus on the basis of which the early Buddhist architecture of the South developed."

But not in South-India only, the early Buddhist architecture was preceded by megalithic tumuli. "Pre-buddhic sepulchral mounds, some of which nearly 40 ft. high, and whose antiquity may be traced back five or six centuries B.C., exist near the villages of Lauriya and Pakhri; they are made of several layers of earth piled around a thick wooden pillar which bores through them all and the fragments of which have been found inside the tumulus; human remains, calcinated, have been discovered in it, and a small leaf of gold bearing the print of a naked goddess."[5]

So every element of the stūpa existed already in Pre-Buddhist India. The *harmikā* perpetuates the Brāhmaṇic square tomb; as to the cupola and the railing of the stūpa, they have many points in common with the sepulchral mounds and the cromlechs of the megalithic period. However, it does not seem likely that the early Buddhists should have erected stūpas to honour the relics of the Buddha and of the saints.

In the society where primitive Buddhism developed, nothing prepared the minds for the celebration of a cult of the relics. The corpse was a thing unclean, dangerous, which must be kept away from human habitation. Some remains of this custom appear in the more ancient ceremonial of the Buddha's funeral.[4] It was indeed long before the time when the people regarded possession of his relics as leading to prosperity.

Many changes in the ideas must be supposed to have taken place in the interval: first,the ashes of Buddha lost their ill-omened

1. *Annual Report of the Archæol. Depart.,* Southern Circle, 1914, p. 34.
2. *Quarterly Journ. of the Mythic Society,* July-October 1934, Jan. 1935, p. 163.
3. *Annual Rep. of the Arch. Surv. of India,* 1906-1907, pl. XXXIX, XL.
4. *Le Parinirvāṇa et les Funérailles,* pp. 179, 194, 213.

character and became the objects of a recognized cult. It was admitted that one could acquire merit by paying reverence to the ashes of the Bhagavat, and they were looked upon as a source of blessings for the community which possessed them.

I have pointed out elsewhere[1] that in the times of Hiuan-tsang, there were three kinds of funerals: the corpse was either burnt, thrown into a river, or carried away into the jungle. It is probable that after the Buddha died, his corpse was immersed in the Ganges, or buried alongside the river. This may be the reason why, according to an ancient tradition, his corpse was first of all placed in a trough of oil (*teladonī*), to the purpose of preserving it from corruption until it could reach the river.

Some worshippers asserted that the corpse of the Buddha had been carried by the flood as far as the ocean[2] and, notwithstanding the traditions which record the division of the relics, the people remained convinced that the remains of the Buddha had been first trusted to the guard of the *nāga.*[3]

The Brāhmaṇic custom ordered that the corpse of a holy hermit be buried on the banks of a river flowing out to the sea. It was not burnt, but was buried in the sand with the staff of the deceased and his water-jug.[4] This practice was probably followed for the funeral of the early Buddhist ascetics, but for the newly converted laics tombs of masonry were built, square or round according to the custom of the countries, and similar by their shape and dimension to the tombs of the Śākya discovered at Kapilavastu.

We are now faced with the following problem: when, and under the exertion of what influences, were the earlier stūpas erected, that is to say, constructions devoted to the cult of the relics were made. When the big stūpas like those of Bārhut and Sāñchī were built, the Buddha was not a human holy man any more, he was a Cakravartin king; he had become both a *rājādhirāja* and a *devātideva.* The transformation of the tomb into a stūpa derives necessarily from these changes in the ideas. In other words, we are to find out at what time and in what country the notion of a kingly and godly big funeral shrine, combining the square Brāhmaṇic tomb with the heavy megalithic tumulus, had taken birth.

---

1. *Le partage des reliques du Buddha*, in *Shogo Kenkyu*, I.
2. *Mahūraṃsa*, chap. 31, v. 17 and foll.
3. *Le partage des reliques*, p. 39 and foll.
4. Caland, *Bestattungsgebräuche*, p. 94. See also Finot, *RHR*, 1897, p. 216.

Plutarch records that after king Menander's death his ashes were divided between the cities, and that over each one of the shares memorials (*mnêmeia*) had been constructed. Before Menander, Alexander had been deified. And the Indo-Greek kings, having inherited part of his glory and of his empire, were probably given the rank of deities as well. The indication given by Plutarch's testimony must by no means be neglected. We will show that in the times of the Indo-Greek kings, the ancient sepulchral mound and the Brāhmaṇic tomb may have welded together under the combined influences of Scythian, Parthian and Greek elements. In this mixed society the Scythians were constructors of sepulchral mounds, the Greeks contributed a new technic, and the Parthians perpetuated the cult of the king of kings. This is where the notion of the huge stūpa, essentially a regal mausoleum and religious building, must have been born.

From the north of the Black Sea to the Caspian stretches a country of steppes, which extends into Asia as far as the Altaï. On these immense spaces several pastoral races have lived who have played a prominent part in the history of Asia in general, and more particularly, of India: Turks, Mongols, Scythians, Aryans, Ougrians, etc.... The best known at the prehistorical period are the Seythians. Let us examine briefly the tombs which have been discovered in the northern part of Caucasus and of the Black Sea.

The mounds found in the Kuban (North-East of the Caucasus), belong to two different types: common on princely; the social rank of the dead ruled the dimension of his tomb.

In the big kurgan of Maikop, the tomb was divided into three rooms and it is supposed to have sheltered a high personage and his wives.[1] North of Pont, the tombs are always covered by a tumulus and these kurgans have a circular basis. Their size is not always the same: generally they do not exceed 3m. in height, and 30 to 50m. in diameter. Some of the mounds, however, are 15m. high with a diameter of 80m. Sometimes the kurgan covers several tombs instead of one.[2]

It appears then that the kurgans are just as diverse in kind as the Buddhist stūpas. The latter are either individual or collective tombs, the tombs of kings, of Buddhas, on of disciples. When the

1. Menghin, *Weltgeschichte der Steinzeit*, Wien, 1931, p. 455.
2. *Ibid.*, p. 460.

Buddhist stūpa is compared to the *zikkurat* or to Mount Meru, the more developed type only thought of. But the actual one is infinitely more complex.

Besides, the big stūpas do not appear before the second century B.C. Their construction in India seems to have coincided with the invasions. This fact raises the question whether some pastoral tribes—constructors of kurgans—may not have played a part in the creation of the Buddhist stūpa. We hear it often said that the latter has a hemi-spherical roof. But the dome of the big Sāñchī stūpa is not in reality an exact hemisphere: its diameter at the base is decidedly more than double its height, as observed on the pastoral kurgans.

True enough, the first Scythian invasions seem posterior to the first big stūpas. And although it is impossible to give with any certitude a date to the Bārhut stūpa, it was probably built prior to the establishment of the Śaka dynasties in India. But we must not forget that there was the influence of the barbarians on Buddhist art before the Indian soil was actually conquered by them.

The contact between India, the West and the North was first achieved in the Greek kingdoms. Greek kings like Menander have rendered a great help to the creation of a mixed society, composed of Greek elements, Seythians, Hindus etc., where Buddhism found a ready soil for its development. Greco-Buddhist sculpture was born through this intermixture of races, and at the same time the type ofthe big stūpa was being elaborated. A certain amount of truth lies probably at the bottom of the tradition which relates the erection of memorials on the ashes of Menander. The sculptures on the railing of the Bārhut stūpa bear Kharoṣṭhi characters, which proves the collaboration of artists from the North-West.[1]

"The Besnagar pillar," says J. Ph. Vogel, "was set up by one Heliodoros who calls himself a Greek ambassador from king Antialkidas to king Bhagabhadra. It clearly shows in what manner, about the middle of the second century B.C., Greek influence could penetrate from Graeco-Bactrian kingdom to the Hindu states of Central India."[2] But when we speak of Greek influence we must by no means imagine a purely Hellenic factor, far from it. The Graeco-Bactrian kingdom was an aggregate where the Śaka and the Parthians were numerically more important than the actual Hellenes. Patañjali, whom

1. L De La Vallée Poussin, *L'Inde au temps des Mauryas*, p. 162.
2. *Arch. Surv.*, 1908-1909, p. 33 and see La Vallée Poussin, *ibid.*, p. 244.

we place about the middle of the 2nd century,[1] looks upon the Śaka-Yavana as non-impure Śūdras. It appears that as far back as Menander's time the Scythians, associated with the Greeks, already enjoyed a certain ascendency upon the Brahmans.

Rêsumé: the big stūpas built prior to the advent of the Christian era, appear to us as hybrid monuments, revealing different influences.

(1) The tomb of the early converted laics was probably similar to the pre-Buddhist tombs; its dimensions were small because the deceased was an object of dread and it was feared that he would try to drag down a companion with him; its base was round or square; it was the room of the dead man. In the later stūpas, the *harmikā*—that is to say the dead man's 'dwelling,'—perpetuates the Brāhmaṇic tomb.

(2) At the time when the northern influence began to exert itself, the stūpa developed into its real form. It took the shape of a mound, the dimension of which was proportioned to the social importance of the dead man. But the former room of the dead man does not disappear: it is placed on the top of the mound like a 'look out' on the top of a hill, whereas his ashes are hidden away under the dome as was the custom in the ancient tumuli.

---

1. On the much contested point of the date of Patañjali, see La Vallée Poussin, *ibid.*, pp. 199-202.

Chapter - 22
A temple of the Buddhist God Mahākāla

Debala Mitra

Mahākāla is one of the most fierce deities in the Vajrayāna pantheon. In the *Sādhanamālā* as many as eight *sādhanas* are devoted to his worship, four out of which describe the two-armed variety of the deity, the *dhyāna* being as follows:

Śrī Mahākāla-bhaṭṭārakaṁ dvi-bhujam=eka-mukhaṁ kṛṣṇa-varṇaṁ tri-nayanaṁ mahā-jvālaṁ karttri-kapāla-dhāri-dakṣiṇa-vāma-bhujaṁ muṇḍa-māl-ālaṅkṛit-orddhva-piṅgala-keś-opari pañ-ca-kapālaādharaṁ daṁṣṭrā-bhīma-bhayāṇakam bhujaṅg-ābharaṇa-yajñ-opavītam kharvva-rūpaṁ sravad-rudhira-mukham=ātmānaṁ jhaṭiti niṣpādya[1]....

(The worshipper) quickly transforming himself as the illustrious lord Mahākāla, who has two arms, one face, a black complexion and three eyes, who is brilliantly blazing, whose right and left hands (respectively) hold a chopper and a skull-cup, who bears five skulls on his tawny hairs which rise upwards and are adorned with a garland of heads,[2] who is fierce with his terrible fangs, whose *yajñopavīta* has the ornaments of snakes, who has a dwarfish body and from whose mouth trickles forth blood...

When four-armed, the deity carries either a sword and a *khatvāṅga* or a *daṇḍa* and a *triśūla* besides the usual *kartri* and *kapāla*. The attributes in the hands in the six-armed variety are *kartri,* rosary, *ḍamaru, kapāla, śūla* and *vajrapāśa*. When the deity is conceived as sixteen-armed, he is eight-headed and four-legged with his Śakti in his embrace, the attributes in his hands being *kartri,*

---

1. B. Bhattacharyya, *Sādhanamālā,* vol. II (Baroda, 1928), p. 585.
2. This is the literal translation, but the intended meaning will be 'who is decorated with a garland of heads and who has on his rising tawny hairs five skulls.'

vajra, elephant-hide, *mudgara, triśūla*, sword, the staff of Yama, *kapāla*, bell, goad, white chowrie, *ḍamaru* and human head.[1]

Whether one-headed with two, four or six arms or eight-headed with sixteen arms, the god is always meditated in the most terrific form conceivable—with a dwarfish body, terrible fangs, blood trickling forth from his mouth, hairs rising upwards, snake-ornaments and the *sarpa-yajñopavīta*. His functions are equally awe-inspiring. The *sādhanas* give details of the procedure of his worship in the Tantric rite of the *māraṇa* (destruction). He is invoked for tearing off the flesh and drinking the blood of an infidel who is adversely disposed to the *ācāryas*, is hostile to the Three Jewels and kills many living beings. He feasts on human flesh.

Ācāryye yaḥ sadā dveṣi kupito Ratnatraye'pi yaḥ |
Aneka-sattva-vidhvaṁsī Mahākālena khādyate ||
Chedayet aṅga-māṁsāni pived-rudhira-dhārayā |
Śirasi viniviṣṭo'sau tīla-mātraṁ tu karttayet ||

The concept of this Vajrayāna deity (he is invoked as Vajra-Mahākāla in some *sādhanas*) was no doubt based on the terrific aspect of Śiva, as attested by the name and the attributes.

Mahākāla is the tutelary god of Mongolia.[2] His images are very common in Nepal, where he is sometimes represented by his head only.[3] In India, however, his images are rarely to be met with: in fact with the solitary exception of the image descri-bed here, I have not come across any representation of this deity.

The image in question is enshrined in a badly-preserved temple on the top of the Ratnagiri hill (District Cuttack), well-known for its Buddhist relics.[4] The temple is a living shrine, the deity, known both as Mah*ākāla* and Mahākālī, being taken as a Hindu divinity. The hereditary priests living in the village worship it both with Vaiṣṇava and Śākta *mantras*. Except in the *bhoga-mantra* he is nowhere invoked as Mahākāla.

---

1. Bengal Asiatic Society's MS. No. Ga 8059, folios 335 & 36, describe eight-armed and twelve-armed varieties of this form. cf. R.D. Banerji, *Eastern Indian School of Mediaeval Sculpture* (Delhi, 1933), p. 93, fn. 4 & 5.
2. A. Getty, *The Gods of Northern Buddhism* (Oxford, 1928), p. 161.
3. B. Bhattacharyya, *The Indian Buddhist Iconography* (Oxford University Press, 1924) p. 120.
4. R.P. Chandra, *Exploration in Orissa*. Mem. Arch. Surv. Ind. No. 44 (Calcutta 1930), pp. 12-13.

The image (2'4" high) of stone,[1] fixed on the back wall of the temple facing west, is a two-armed pot-bellied dwarfish figure wearing *sarpa-aṅgadas, sarpa-yajñopavīta, valaya,* necklace and large ear-studs. His coiled hairs rise upwards like flames. His face is now covered with a thick layer of vermilion.[2] He holds in his left hand a *kapāla* and in his right a *kartri*. The image corresponds in almost all respects to the textual description of the two-armed varietyof the deity as cited above.

As only a few Buddhist temples have survived today, the description of the temple itself will not be redundant. It consists of a *deul* (sanctum) made of khondolite and sandstone, and a *jagamohana* (porch) built mostly of bricks with a sprinkling of stones, the latter limited to the floor, doorway and pillars. The upper part of the *jagamohana* with the thatched roof is a modern restoration.

The *deul* (28 ft. high up to the top of the *khapuri*), *pañca-ratha* on plan, is of the usual *rekha* type. Its vertical body below the curvilinear spire is divided into five parts. The lowest portion, the *pābhāga*, consists of three plain mouldings, *khurā, kumbha* and *vasanta*. The *jāṅgha* is divided into two (*tala* and *upar*) by a set of three mouldings clasped by a vertical band, *bandhana*, the central moulding of the latter being relieved at intervals with a roundel containing a floral motif. Both the *jāṅghas* are plain. The central projections of the south, north and east sides have each a small niche, now vacant, above which acting as a *chajja* is a *khurā*-shaped moulding. The latter is the lowermost of the three mouldings on the central projection of the upper *jāṅgha*, the central being *koni*. The *baraṇda*, from the top which the spire starts, consists of five mouldings—

khurā, pheṇi, noli, paṭā and *vasanta*, the last broader than the rest. The *noli* is relieved at intervals with a roundel containing a rosette. Immediately above the *baraṇḍa* is a row of lotus-petals, one on each segment of the spire. The latter is plain except for a rampant lion, with open mouth, resting on a plain rectangular block. The lion on the front face is at a higher level than its smaller counterparts on other three sides. Its rumps are relieved with a roundel containing a rosette. The central projection of the front side of the spire is

1. The nature of the stone which is now blackened by oil, cannot be exactly determined. It may be khondolite, which is locally available.
2. No amount of persuation could make the priests agree to its removal. According to them the face is chiselled out.

distinguished for the representation of a small *pañca-ratha* temple below the lion. The crowning members consists of a *beki*, an enormous *amlā* and a flattish bell-shaped member called *khapuri*. The pinnacle above the last is made of two parts, the upper one with a central lid-like depression inside covering the lower one is shaped like a *stūpa* and has a central perforation for the insertion of a *chatra* (umbrella) or a banner.

The lowest ceiling of the sanctum is formed of one (two?) slab supported by an iron beam at the centre and rest on seven corbels. There is a corbelled niche above the doorway. The door-jambs, lintel and the architrave are all plain, the last two supported by an iron beam at the centre. The temple was originally plastered, as patches of plaster can still be seen sticking to it. The masonry is dry, the stone being kept in position by their weight and balance aided by iron cramps and dowels.

Inside the *jagamohana*, at each of its four corners, is a round, tapering khondolite pillar, made in six segments. The base is square, while the capital is *pheṇi*-shaped with a cable-moulding below. The shaft is relieved at intervals with niches containing Buddha, seated in *varada* and *bhusparśa-mudrā,* Tārā, seated in *lalitāsana* holding the stalk of a blue lotus in her left hand, right being in *varada*, Vajrasattva seated cross-legged carrying in his right hand a *vajra* against his breast and a *ghaṇṭā* in his left, Āryasaravatī (?), seated in *vajra-paryaṅkāsana* holding in her left hand the stalk of a blue lotus on which rests a manuscript, her right hand being in *varada,* a four-armed Bodhi-sattva seated in *lalitāsana* with his right foot resting on a peacock, one of his left hands holding the stalk of a full-blown lotus, the upper right carrying a rosaryand the lower right being in *varada*, etc. The workmanship of the figures is not of high order.

On each of the north and south sides of the *jagamohana* are a corbelled niche. One of the stones of the left jamb of the passage leading to the door of the shrine is relieved wth two amorous couples.

In the absence of any inscription or other databie objects it is very difficult to date the temple with exactitude. It does not however, appear to be later than the twelfth century but may be even somewhat earlier. It is worth noting that in spite of its Buddhist affiliation it is architecturally identical with the Brahmanical temple of Orissa: in fact, but for the enshrined deity, the crowning member (which in this case seems to have been a *stūpa*) and the Buddhist figures on the pillars in the *jagamohana,* there is nothing to distinguish it from a typical Brahmanical temple of the Kaliṅga order.[1]

1. The photographs published here are the copyright of the Department of Archaeology, Government of India.

Plate 11

A temple of the Buddhist God Mahākāla

Chapter - 23

The hair and the Uṣṇīṣa on the head of the Buddhas and the Jinas

Ramaprasad Chanda

The disposition of hair and the representation of the so-called *Uṣṇīṣa*, 'turban', on the head of the image of the Buddhas and the Jinas (Tirthaṅkaras) are the most puzzling questions of Indian iconography. In an article entitled "The Buddha's *cūḍā*, hair, *uṣṇīṣa*, and Crown" Dr. Coomarswamy has dealt with the questions in detail (J.R.A.S., 1928, pp. 815-840). Without going over the whole ground covered by that essay I shall venture to suggest other solutions of the puzzles.

The literary evidence for the hair on the Buddha's head relied on by modern scholars is a passage in the introduction to the commentary on the Pāli Jātakas known as the Nidānakathā which is thus translated by Rhys Davids:—

"Then he thought, 'These locks of mine are not suited for a mendicant. Now it is right for any one else to cut the hair of a future Buddha, so I will cut them off myself with sword.' Then, taking his sword in his right hand, and holding the plaited tresses, together with the diadem on them, with his left, he cut them off. So his heir was thus reduced to two inches in length, and curling from the right, it lay close to his head. It remained that length as long as he lived, and the beard the same. There was no need at all to shave either hair or beard any more."[1]

The Bodhisattva (future Budha) Guatama then threw the hair and diadem together towards the sky. Sakka received them into a jewel casket, and enshrined them for worship in a caitya (temple) in the heaven of the Thirty-three gods.

This narrative reads like an expansion of the legend briefly tol in the *Lalitavistara* and the *Mahāvastu*, and illustrated in a bas-

1. *Buddhist Birth Stories* translated by T.W. Rhys Davids, London, 1880, p. 86.

relief on one ofthe pillars of the southern gateway (c. 50 B.C.) of the great stūpa of Sāñcī,[1] and in a panel on a corner pillar of the great rail of the stūpa of Bharhut[2] (c. 125 B.C.). The term *cūḍāmaha,* "worship of hair", not only occurs in the inscription on the Bharhut rail pillar, but also in the *Lalitavistara* and the *Mahāvastu*. But this legend is unknown to the Pāli Nikāyas and must have originated after their compilation. In the life of Vipassi in the Mahāpadāna-sutta of the Dīgha-Nikāya, the framework of which is the common factor of the biographies of all the Buddhas including Gautama, it is narrated that when the future Buddha (Bodhisattva) was driving in a chariot towards the park he saw a shaven-headed (*bhaṇḍu*) man, a *pravrajita* (wanderer) wearing yellow robe. When the Bodhisattva was told by the charioteer who the shaven-headed man was and had a talk with the latter, he said:—

"Come then, good charioteer, do you take the carriage and drive it hence back to my rooms. But I will here cut off my hair and beard (*kesamassuṃ otāretvā*), and don the yellow robe, and go forth from home to homelessness."[3]

A somewhat different story is told of the renunciation of the Bodhisattva Gautama in four of the Suttas of the Majjhima Nikāya (Nos. 16, 36, 85 and 100). The charioteer and the shaven-headed monk in yellow robe have no place in the narrative. We are simply told:—

"There came a time when I, being quite young, with a wealth of coal-black hair untouched by grey and in all the beauty of my early prime—despite the wishes of my parents, who wept and lamented—cut off my hair and beard, donned the yellow robes and went forth from home to homelessness."[4]

In the Subha-sutta (99) of the Majjhima Nikāya a Brahman Saṅgārava calls Gautama Buddha a *muṇḍaka samaṇa*, "shaven-headed monk."[5] So by the time when the sculptors of Mathurā began to carve images of Gautama Buddha there were two rival traditions relating to hair on the Buddha's head: an older one now preserved in

1. Sir John Marshall, *A Guide to Sāñcī*, Calcutta, 1918, p. 51, pl. vi b.
2. Coomaraswamy, *History of Indian and Indonesian Art,* London, 1927, pl. xii, fig. 44; Bachhofer, *Early Indian Sculpture,* Paris, 1929, pl. 24.
3. *Dīgha Nikāya* (P.T.S.), vol. II, p. 28; *Dialogues of the Buddha* translated by T.W. and C.A.f. Rhys Davids, pt. ii, London, 1910, p. 22.
4. *Majjhima-Nikāya* (Pali Text Society), Vol. I, pp. 163, 240; Vol. II, pp. 93, 212; *Further Dialogues of the Buddha* translated by Lord Chalmers, Vol. II, London, 1926, p. 115.
5. *Majjhima-Nikāya*, Vol. II, p. 210.

the Pāli Nikāyas represented Gautama as *muṇḍaka* or shaven-headed monk; and another tradition preserved in the *Mahāvastu*, the *Lalitavistara* and the *Nidānakathā* represented him as having cut his hair with his sword leaving part of it intact on the head. The shaven-headed images of the Buddha found at Mathura, Mankuar and Sarnath represent the older tradition, and the images of the Buddha with hair on the head arranged in ringlets represent the other and more popular tradition, because it is found both in Sanskrit and Pāli texts.

Gautama Buddha was not an ordinary monk. He was born with the thirty-two marks of a Mahāpuruṣa (superman). These marks distinguished the Bodhisattva Gautama from the ordinary Arhats. These marks are fully decribed in two of the Suttas of the *Dīgha Nikāya* (Mahāpadāna-suttanta and Lakkhaṇa-suttanta) and the *Lalitavistara*. Two of these marks that relate to the head are *uṣṇīṣa-śīrṣa*, "having a head like a royal turban," and *pradakṣiṇāvarta-keśaḥ*, "having hair (arranged) in ringlets turning to the right." The commentator Buddhaghosa in his *Sumaṅgala-vilāsinī* (*Mahāpadāna-sutta-vaṇṇanā*) says that the term *uṇhisasīsa* (*uṣṇīṣaśirṣa*) may be explained in two different ways either denoting the fullness of the forehead or the fullness of the head. The fullness of the forehead may be caused by a strip of muscle (*maṃsapaṭala*) rising from the root of the right ear, covering the entire forehead, and terminating in the root of the left ear. As a head with such a strip of muscle on the forehead looks like a head wearing a turban, it is therefore called a turban-like head or turban-head. The other explanation defines the turban-head as a fully round head symmetrical in shape like a water bubble.[1]

The smooth head without any mark of hair like the head of the well-known colossal Bodhisattva dedicated by the Friar Bala in the third year of Kaniṣka at Sarnath, the head of the Bodhisattva image from Katra in the Mathura Museum,[2] the head on the fragment of the Buddha-Bodhisattva image from Mathura in the Museum of Ethnology at Munich,[3] and of other images of the same type, shows slight elevation above the forehead. This elevated part reaching from the root of the right ear to that of the left appears to me to be the plastic representation of the *maṃsapaṭala*, the strip of muscle on the forehead of the turban-head, spoken of by Buddhaghosa. The thick lock of curled hair on the top of the head of the Katra and the

1. *Indian Historical Quarterly*, Vol. V, no. 4, Supplement, p. 77.
2. Vogel, *Catalogue*, plate VII; Coomarswamy, *History of Indian and Indonesian Art*, Fig. 84; Bachhofer, *Early Indian Sculpture*, plate 81.
3. Bachhofer, *Early Indian Sculpture*, plate 82.

munich images is curled like the snail shell (*kaparda*). Coomarswamy observes, "That the remainder of the head is smooth does not mean that it is shaved, but simply that all the long hair was drawn up close and tight over scalp into the single tress."[1] This single curled tress is marked by parallel lines indicating individual hairs of which it consists. If the sculptor had intended to represent hair on the rest of the head, he would certainly have adopted the same convention instead of leaving the area smooth. Smoothness therefore indicates that the rest of the head is clean-shaven. One standing image of the Buddha with smooth head in the Mathura Museum has a smooth bump.[2] The tress of hair curling like a snail shell on the top of the head of the images of the Buddha referred to above evidently represents *śikhā* or top-knot. Gautama prescribes in his *Dharmasūtra* (iii, 14, 23) that an ascetic "may either shave or wear a lock on the crown of the head."[3]

The artists of Mathura in the Kushan period produced another type of the Buddha head with short hair arranged in ringlets turning to the right and a bump or fleshy protuberance on the top covered by ahir arranged in the same way. All the Buddha images of the post-Kushan period with the exception of the Mankuar image have a head of this type. The term *uṣṇīṣa* is usually applied to this bump. Is it correct? As we have stated above, *uṣṇīṣa-śīrṣa*, turban-head, is a head which is either round in form like a turban, or has the appearance of a head wearing a turban even when bare on account of a strip of muscle covering the upper part of the forehead. Head of either type is turban-like in outline only. A very important part of the royal turban is the crest. A head, turban-like in outline, but without crest, cannot be recognised as a turban-head in the strict sense. Therefore the addition of a bump or fleshy protuberance on the top was evidently thought necessary to turn the head of a Mahāpuruṣa to a perfect turban-head. The so-called *uṣṇīṣa* on the Buddha's head is the crest of the *uṣṇīṣa* and not the *uṣṇīṣa* itself. So it should be termed crest instead of *uṣṇīṣa* to avoid misunderstanding.

The early Jaina literature, so far available, does not render us much help in solving the puzzles relating to the head of the images of the Jinas. In the *Ācārāṅga-sūtra* it is said that when the Jina Mahāvīra turned an ascetic—

"Mahāvīra then plucked out with his right and left (hands) on the right and left (sides of his head) his hair in five handfuls. But

---

1. *J.R.A.S.*, 1928, p. 827.
2. Vogel, *Catalogue*, plate XV (a).
3. *Sacred Books of the East*, Vol. II, p. 194.

Śakra, the leader and king of the gods, falling down before the feet of the Venerable ascetic Mahāvīra, caught up the hair in a cup of diamond, and requesting his permission, brought them to the milk ocean."[1]

In the *Kalpasūtra* it is said that Mahāvīra as well as his twenty-three predecessors did the same—plucked hair in five handfuls and turned shaven-headed monks. Only the image of one of the Jinas, Ṛṣ abha, the first in the series, is shown as wearing matted locks like the Brahman Jaṭila monks carved on the Śuṅga monuments. The images of the other twenty-three Jinas mostly show heads with bump covered by hair arranged in ringlets becoming the Mahāpuruṣa. But images of the Jinas with shaven head are not unknown. Coomarswamy has published a seated image of the Jina Pārśva with smooth head from Mathura[2] where the different types of the images of the Jinas were carved for the first time.

1. *Sacred Books of the East*, Vol. XXII, p. 199.
2. Coomarswamy, *The Origin of the Buddha Image*, fig. 43.

Chapter - 24
Some Images and Traces of Mahāyāna Buddhism in Chittagong

Narendra Nath Law

In 1927 I went to Chittagong. There I was very kindly invited by the Aggamahāpaṇḍita Dhāmmavaṃsa Mahāthera of the well-known Buddhist monastery of the place to pay a visit to the institution, which I did gladly. In the monastery, I was shown among other interesting articles a few Mahāyānic images collected by the Aggamahāpaṇḍita was good enough to furnish me with photographs of the images, some of which are reproduced here, along with the particulars about their find-spots. The identification of the images, well-known as they are, needs no remarks. But I feel that they should be made known to scholars interested in Buddhism, as they may throw some light on the history of Buddhism in the district of Chittagong. The following is the list of the images (which except one are all metallic) with particulars about their find-spots:

I [Plate I (a)]—Figure of (Vajrāsana) Gautama Buddha, 7-1/2" in height, seated cross-legged in *Bhūmisparśamudrā* with a *vajra* on the seat. The base contains the following inscription in characters of 11th-12th cent. A.D.

ये धर्मा हेतुप्रभवा हेतुन्तेषान्तथागतो ह्यवदत्। तेषाञ्च यो

निरोध एवम्वादी महाश्रमणः देयधर्मोयं धर्मकस्य मातापित्रो.........

Procured from Thakurpuni Temple (Paṭiyā) where it was removed from a *dargā* in South Raozan (Kāukhāli).

II [Plate I (b)]—Figure of (Vajrāsana) Gautama Budha, 7-1/4" in height, seated cross-legged in *Bhūmisparśamudrā* with a *vajra* on the seat. The base contains two lines of inscription in characters of 11th-12th cent. A.D.:

देय धर्मोयं प्रवर महायायिनः ....(the remainder not legible).

III Figure of Gautama Buddha in *Bhūmisparśamudrā*, 4-1/4" in height, seated cross-legged. Procured from Mirasarai (Chittagong).

IV [Plate (c)]—Figure of Gautama Buddha, 3-3/4" in height, seated cross-legged in *Bhūmisparśamudrā*. It has the mark of a circular seal on the back containing the Buddhist formula:

ये धर्मा हेतुप्र। भवा हे ?? न्त। यागतो ह्यवदत् ते। (यों) यो निरोध। एवं वादी महाश्रमण: ॥

(5 lines in characters of 11th-12th cent. A.D.) Procured from Satbaria, P.S. Paṭiyā, Chittagong.

V Figure of Gautama Buddha, 3-1/2" high, seated cross-legged in *Vyakhyānamudrā* (preaching posture). Procured from Satbaria, P.S. Paṭiyā, Chittagong.

VI Figure of Gautama Buddha, 9" high, seated cross-legged in *Bhūmisparśamudrā*.

VII Figure of Gautama Buddha, 8-1/4" high, seated cross-legged in *Bhūmisparśamudrā*.

VIII Standing Gautama Buddha, 6" high, the right hand in the *abhaya* pose and the left in *varada*.

IX [Plate II (a)]—Figure of Bodhisattva Avalokiteśvara (Padmapāṅi) in *Lalitāsana* (the right leg hanging down), left hand bearing a lotus with stem. It is 6" high. A Dhyānī Buddha appears on the head-dress. The base contains the following inscription:—

देय धर्मोयं। श्रीभरीत(?) क। ....

Procured from Tekota, P.S. Paṭiyā.

X [Plate II (b)]—Figure of Bodhisattva Mañjuśrī, 8-3/4" in height, seated in easy posture (अर्द्धपर्य्यङ्कासन) with a *Sanāla Utpala* in the left hand. In the head-dress is represented the Dhyānī Buddha Akṣobhya in the earth-touching attitude (भूमिस्पर्शमुद्रा). On the base occurs the following inscription:—

.... १ देयधर्मोयं तिगिरीकस्य in characters of the 11th cent. A.D. Procured from the monastery of North Joara (Paṭiyā).

XI [Plate III (a)]—Figure of the Buddhist god of riches, Jambhala, 4-1/4" in height, the right hand holding a citron and the left hand a mongoose. The god is pot-bellied. The base contains a fw purses full of coins. Procured from Bhandargaon, P.S. Paṭyā.

XII [Plate III (b)]—Figure of Tārā in *Lalitāsana,* 5" in height, left hand holding a lotus and right hand a (?) Procured from Mirasarai, Chittagong.

Plate 12: I

(a): (Vajrāsana)
Gautama Buddha,

(b): (Vajrāsana)
Gautama Buddha,

(c): (Paryaṅkāsana)
Gautama Buddha

Plate 13:II

(a): Avalokiteśvara,

(b): Mañjuśrī

Plate 14:III

(b) Tārā (Lalitāsana)

(a): Jambhala,

Plate 15: IV

a: Tārā (Lalitāsana)

Plate 16: V

(b): Inscription on the back of the image of Tārā (Plate 15:IV a)

XIII (a) [Plate IV (a)]—*Black chlorite stone* figure of Tārā seated in *Lalitāsana,* the right hand in *varada* pose and the left hand bearing a *Sanāla Utpala.* A stūpa on the right side above. The base contains 2 lions couchant on two sides and a pair of devotees in the middle. It is 7" in height.

XIII (b) [Plate IV (b)]—On the back of the above are inserted six lines of inscription:—

ये धर्मा हेतुप्र- । भा हेन्तुं तेशा ऽन्त । यागतः एवं वालि (?) जो निरोध । बुद्ध धर्म । महा (ग्र ?) थमः ॥ १ देयधर्मोयं माया । शवः ॥ काड इन्द ॥

The date indicated by a chronogram (under the कटपयादि system) appears to be 1308 *Śaka*=1386 A.D. Procured from Udayapur, Hill Tippera State.

From the palæographic point of view, the images belong to the 11th or 12th century A.D. Artistically they may be attributed to the Eastern School of Art which flourished in Bengal and Behar from the 9th to the 13th century. In physiognomical characteristics, specially the facial, they bear a close resemblance to similar images unearthed at Sārnāth and Nālandā, the frontiers of Assam, and the hills of Arakan. Though there are striking similarities between some of the images e.g. those of Tārā, Avalokiteśvara and Mañjuśrī found at Chittagong and those of Nālandā, Vikrampur (Bengal) and elsewhere, there are other images which indicate the hand of local artists, who had inherited the artistic tradition of the Eastern School of Art. The lack of liveliness in the facial and pysiognomical expressions, the static poses, the rigidity in the treatment of the curls of hair and the folds of the *saṅghāṭī*, in short, a dullness noticeable in the general treatment leaves no doubt in our minds that they are productions of local artists with poor accomplishments aiming to produce replieas of what they saw elsewhere.

Topographically the images can be divided into two classes:

(i) Those found in the Paṭiyā sub-division, viz., the images of meditating Buddhas in Bhūmisparśamudrā, Avalokiteśvara, Mañjuśrī and Jambhala, and

(ii) those found at Mirasarai (near Sitakund) and in the Hill Tippera State, viz. the images of Buddha and the goddess Tārā.

I-VII. Of the seven (vajrāsana) images of Buddha, in the sitting posture, six have one of their hands pointing to the earth as witness (Bhūmisparśamudrā) and one has two hands put together in the preaching attitude (vyākhyānamudrā). The eighth image of Buddha is in the standing posture, with the right hand in *abhaya* (protection from fear) pose and the left hand in *varada* (gift-bestowing). These images may very well belong to either Hīnayāna or Mahāyāna but it is quite clear that they form a distinct group and show wide divergence in facial features and general treatment from the stone and bronze images which began to be imported into Chittagong from Burma direct or through Arakan. Artistically, they belong to the Bengal School of Art. On the bases of two of the images (figs. I and II) and on the back of another image [Pl. IV (b)] appears, though imperfectly and in incorrect Sanskrit, the undermentioneed versified formula of the law of causation which appears at the end of almost all the important Mahāyāna works:

ये धर्मा हेतुप्रभवा हेतुन्तेषां तथागतो।

ह्यवदत्तेषां च यो निरोध एवंवादी महाश्रमण: ॥

(*Mahāvastu*, III, p. 461]

The corrupt Sanskrit of the inscriptions clearly shows that the donors wanted to have the formula reproduced in Sanskrit. Then again, the expressions *deyadharmo'yam; deyadharmo'yam pravaramahāyāyinaḥ;* and *deyadharmo'yam Tīgirikasya* show that the donors used Sanskrit and not Pāli. On the base of more than a dozen of the images found at Sārnāth appear exactly the above-mentioned expressions, e.g., *deyadharmo'yaṃ Skandavarṇasya* or *Dhanadevasya* or *Kumāraguptasya* (*Sārnāth Catalogue*, pp. 41, 44, 66); *deya-Śākyabhikṣor-Buddhapriyasya* or *Śrīvinaya*... or *Bandhuguptasya* (*Ibid*., pp. 53, 68, 69). Still more striking is the agreement of the inscription *deyadharmo'yaṃ pravaramhāyāyinaḥ* [Fig. II] with that on some of the Sārnāth images, in which the wordings are: *deyadharmo'yaṃ mahāyāyinaḥ paramopāsaka* (*Sārnāth Catalogue*, p. 135) or *deyadharmo'yam pravaramahā-yānānuyāyī paramopāsaka Māgadhīya Śrī Śāmaṅkasya* (*Ibid*., p. 123). Inscriptions of this nature are found only on the images of the Gupta period and not on those of the earlier. The similarity enables us to draw the inference that these Chittagong images represent also the ame period as that of the Sārnāth images, and the type of Buddhism that prevailed at Sārnāth. They also prove that the donors could not have belonged to the School of Buddhism prevailing at present at Chittagong; hence the seven images of Buddha are, in fact, relics of the old school of Buddhism followed by at least some families in Chittagong.

IX. The ninth image is that of Avalokiteśvara Bodhisattva who has takenthe vow that he will not have Bodhi until all beings have attained the same. He is the incarnation of compassion and is always anxious to help the people in distress. It is really the image of Khaṣarpaṇa Avalokiteśvara, the characteristics of which are described thus in the *Sādhanamālā* (translated in the *Buddhist Iconography,* p. 37):

'His person is as resplendent as the rays of a crore of moons; he wears the crown of chignon, bears the image of Amitābha on head, and sits on the moon over the double lotus in the Ardhaparyaṅka attitude; his body is decked in all ornaments; he has a smiling face, is aged about twice eight years, exhibits the Varada pose in the right hand and holds the lotus with a stem in the left.'

The image under discussion cannot be said to have been executed with all the details required by the *Sādhanamālā*, but yet it reveals an effort to produce the Khaṣarpaṇa form of Avalokiteśvara Bodhisattva. It may be compared with the image of Khaṣarpaṇa discovered by Mr. N.K. Bhattasali in the Vikrampur Pergana of East Bengal. (For its representation, see *Buddhist Iconography*, plate XXI).

As Avalokiteśvara is said to have been an emanation of the Dhyānī Buddha Amitābha, the image should bear on its crown the representation of Amitābha. In the crown of the present image also there appears a Dhyānī Buddha, which evidently should be of Amitābha.

X. The tenth image is of Mañjuśrī Bodhisattva who occupies thesame place in the Mahāyāna tradition as Ānanda in the Hīnayāna. He represents knowledge, i.e. Buddhist scriptures which dispel ignorance. In many of the faith-arousing Mahāyāna-sūtras, Mañjuśrī appears as the interlocutor. According to the tradition, it was at his instance that many Mahāyāna-sūtras were delivered by the Teacher. He is said to have been an emanation of Akṣobhya, and as such his images should bear on the crown the image of the Dhyānī Buddha Akṣobhya. The present image also bears one such figure on the crown. It may well be compared with the image in the Indian Museum reproduced by Dr. Bhattacharya in his *Buddhist Iconography* (plate The history of the evolution of the Tārā conception has been dealt with by Dr. Hirananda Sastri, Pandit Girishchandra Vedāntatīrtha and Dr. Benoytosh Bhattacharya. It will suffice here to say that Tārā is really the personification of Prajñā, more correctly *Prajñāpāramitā*, which alone can turn a Bodhisattva into Buddha. In the Mahāyāna philosophy, *Prajñā* is sometimes identified with Śūnyatā or the highest truth, and as everything issues out of, or more correctly is, if anything, an appearance of Śūnyatā, Buddhas or Bodhisattvas are nothing but the emanations of Prajñā. The literature dealing with the Śūnyatā philosophy is called *Prajñāpāramitā-śāstra.* So Prajñā represents in short the highest truth as well as the literature (dharma) which inculcates that truth. In the early days of Mahāyāna Buddhism, there were not wanting poetical compositions in which the abstract notion of knowledge was deified. The first few verses given in the *Aṣṭasāhasrikā*, and *Pañcaviṃśtisāhasrikā* reveal how this deification started:

ॐ नमो भगवत्यै आर्य्य प्रज्ञापारमितयै ॥

निर्विकल्पे नमस्तुभ्यं प्रज्ञापारमितोऽमिते ।

... ...

पोषिका जनयित्री च माता त्वमसि वत्सला ॥

यद्बुद्धा लोकगुरवः पुत्रास्तवः कृपालवः ।

तेन त्वमसि कल्याणि सर्वसत्वपितामही ॥

... ...

सुदुर्बोधासि मायेव दृश्यसे न च दृस्यसे ॥

वुद्धैः प्रत्येक वुद्धैश्च श्रावकैश्च निषेविता ॥[1]

The transition from the abstract notion of truth, as expressed in the salutatory verses, to the conception of *Prajñāpāramitā* as the Divine Mother (see *Bl.*, pp. 84-86) was an easy one. In Java there has already been found an image (Havell, *Indian Sculpture and Painting,* pl. XIV, pp. 84-86; *Buddhist Iconography*, pls. XXVII, XXXVI c) known as *Prajñāpāramitā*. The *Tārārahasyavṛttikā* and other *Tāntric* works also give the appellation of Prajñāpāramitā to the goddess Tārā.

It may be safely stated that by the time Mahāyānism reached Bengal (about the ninth century) it had already had a long career, which converted the abstract notion of *Prajñā* into the goddess Prajñāpāramitā and thence into Tārā. So when Bengal received its Buddhism, the conception of Tārā had become common and she represented and replaced the Dharma of the Buddhist Trinity. Once she was turned into a goddess, the Divine Mother, there was no end

---

1. Cf. *MahānirvāṇoTantra,* Śiva addressing Pārvatī in the verses:
त्वमाद्या सर्वविद्यानामस्माकमपि जन्मभूः ।
त्वं जानासि जगत् सर्व्वं न त्वां जानाति कश्चन ॥

of the various forms in which she began to be worshipped (for a detailed account, see *Bl.*, pp. 37ff).

All these images are undoubtedly reminiscent of a Mahāyānic religious wave that passed over Chittagong 8 or 9 centuries ago. The fact that there has not been found at Chittagong any old temple or site which may be pointed out as a permanent place of worship of the Mahāyānists constrains us to conclude that there were only stray families or teachers at Chittagong who professed the Mahāyānic faith. It is not improbable that they were mostly settlers hailing from Kāmākhyā and Orissa which had become important centres of Tantric Buddhism from the 9th or the 10th century A.D. It may also be surmised tht there were ancient Buddhist temples at Chittagong and that they were later on converted into Hindu temples or places of worship, the Buddha being made a Śiva and the goddess Tārā a Pārvatī or Kālī.[1] The Buddhists of Chittagong even now pay annual visits to Candranātha hill where a temple of Śiva has been erected by the Hindus in later times.[2]

Most of the images show a close affinity with those of Nepal in art and technique, proving thereby that they belong to that Eastern School of Art which reached Nepal from Bengal. Tāranātha suggests that this transmission took place in the 9th century, when king Devapāla was the ruler of Bengal. The time of Devapāla is usually taken to be in the 9th century A.D. and the period of his reign witnessed the highest development of Bengal-Magadhan art (*Bāṅglār Itihās*, I, p. 206). His name has come down to us as a patron of Buddhism, and of the Nālandā University. Without attempting to be definite with regard to the time of the introduction of Mahāyāna Buddhism into Chittagong, it would not be wide of the mark to conclude on the basis of the marked affinity of the images with those found at Nālandā and other Mahāyānic centres including Nepal that the form of Buddhism which the Pāla kings of Bengal supported reached Chittagong during the ascendancy of the Pāla dynasty. At the same time it cannot be stated that this later phase of Mahāyānic Buddhism did not leave any mark on the beliefs and customs of the people in the district of Chittagong. Of these marks the following are worth mentioning:

---

1. In the *Śivaśaktisaṅgamatantra* "Akṣobhya (Buddha) is put down as a synonym of Śiva, and Tārā of Śakti." Dr. Hirananda Sastri, *Origin and Culture of Tārā*, p. 13.
2. The Śiva temple stands a few feet apart from the ruins (very likely the base of an old Buddhist temple) which form the object of worship of the Chittagong Buddhists.

Even at the present day, most of the Buddhist villages within the paṭiyā sub-division in Chittagong have a small piece of land set apart for the worship of the goddess called by them *Mā Magadheśrarī*. They do not set up any image there but they have a fixed time and special mantras to perform the worship, and one of the peculiar features of this worship is that the officiating priest is invariably a Buddhist layman. This practice of worshipping a goddess unknown in Hīnayāna cannot but be a relic of the Mahāyānic worship of goddesses.

Then there is the other tradition within living memory that the Buddhists formally worshipped Sarasvatī, the goddess of learning. The Chittagong Buddhists were and still are under the impression that they were worshipping a Hindu goddess. But the fact is that Sarasvatī is as much a Buddhist goddess as a Hindu at least from after the date of the *Sādhanamālā*. In this Buddhist work, she is counted as one of the most widely worshipped goddesses of the Buddhist pantheon and is believed to "confer wisdom, learning, intelligence, memory, etc." (*BI*., p. 150). It may therefore be stated that the Chittagong Buddhist continued up to recent times the worship of the goddess Sarasvatī, a remnant of a Mahāyānic religious practice of the 11th century A.D.

Another remarkable trace of this mediæval form of Buddhism is found in the custom of the believing Buddhists of Chittagong uttering *Phra Tārā Saṅgha* when they start on a journey, go to bed or apprehend any evil. Mr. S.C. Das writes in the *Chittagong District Gazetteer* (p. 65) that *Phra Tārā* means *Ārya Tārā, Phra* being the Burmese equivalent of *Ārya. Phra* in Burmese also refers to 'Buddha'; hence, I think, *Phra Tārā Saṅgha means* Buddha, Tārā and Saṅgha. Now Tārā evidently here stands for Dharma, and we have seen before that Tārā is nothing but the personification of the *Prajñā-pāramitā* representing the Mahāyānic dharma.

It is remarkable that the Chittagong Buddhists were at one time the worshippers of Tārā of Mahāyāna (Tantric) Buddhism. In the seventeenth century, when with the decay of Buddhism in Bengal, the Buddhists of Chittagong were about to be Hinduised and actually began to worship the Hindu deities (*Chittagong District Gazetteer*, p. 68), the great Buddhist priest of Arakan, Saṅgha Rājā (derived, I think, from Saṅgharāja=the leader of the Buddhist Saṅgha Rājā (derived, I think, from Saṅgharāja=the leader of the Buddhist Saṅgha of Arakan) came to Chittagong on his way back to Arakan from Bodh-Gaya (*Chittagong District Gazetteer*, p. 67). At this time, a communication was established between Arakan and Chittagong, and there were both immigrations and emigrations. This Arakanese Saṅgha Rājā, who knew nothing but Hīnayāna Buddhism as prevailing in Burma and Arakan, was averse to the Tantric religion followed by the Chittagong Buddhists, and by his great personal influence gave a turn to the decadent Buddhism by persuading the people to follow his own sect. As a matter of course, the Arakan-Burmese Buddhism came to be super-imposed on the original Bengal Buddhism, and in course of time with the disappearance of good teachers of the Bengal School, the Arakaṇ-Burmese school prevailed upon the people of Chittagong and made them out-and-out followers of the type of Hīnayāna Buddhism prevailing in Ceylon and Burma.

Chapter - 25
Old Buddhist Shrines at Bodh-Gaya

B.M. Barua

Inscriptions

Here our task is to compile the various inscriptions which still linger on the remnants of the pillars of the Jewel-walk shrine, the edges of the upper surface of the covering stone-slab of the old Diamond-throne and the different parts of the old Stone-railing; and as regards the old Stone-railing, both those which were incised when it was first erected or repaired, and those which were incised in after ages having no bearing on the history of its construction. We are to offer our own readings and interpretations only in those cases where previous attempts have proved unsatisfactory; in the remaining cases we are to remain content with quotations from previous publications. But the gouping and arrangement of the inscriptions are to be entirely our own.

1. Pūrva-Pāṣāṇa-Lekhā: Writings on the Old Stone-Railing

The writings on the old Stone-railing consist of certain Brāhmī inscriptions found engraved on some of the rail-pillars, the rail-bars and the coping-pieces. Along with these may be considered those consisting of certain Brāhmī letters on the shafts and fixed bases of the pillars of the Jewel-walk-shrine, and a mutilated inscription on the upper edge of the outer *Vajrāsana* or Diamond-throne.

The Brāhmī letters on the shafts and fixed bases of the pillars of the Jewel-walk-shrine were nothing but some visible signs or marks to indicate (1) which of the pillar-shafts was meant for which of the fixed pillar-bases, and (2) the relative position of these pillars and their fixed bases set up in two rows on two sides of the raised platform inside the Jewel-walk-shrine. As Sir Alexander Cunningham points out, in each row there were eleven pillars, each of the pillar-shafts and fixed pillar-bases being marked with a separate Brāhmī letter and the same letter marking the fixed pillar-base as well as the corresponding pillar-shaft. Thus in each row of eleven pillars there were two rows of Brāhmī letters, the row on the south side of the platform representing two series of eleven vowels, one on the line of fixed pillar-bases and the other on that of pillar-shafts, and the row on the north side of the platform representing two series of the first eleven consonants, one on the line of fixed pillar-bases and the other on that of pillar-shafts. The eleven vowels comprised, according to Cunningham, *a, ā i, ī, u, ū, e, ai, o, au,* and *aḥ,* and the eleven consonants were *ka, kha, ga, gha, ṅa, ca, cha, ja, jha, ña, and ṭa.*[1] No one can reasonably doubt the accuracy of Cunningham's statement except with regard to the specification of *aḥ* as the eleventh vowel. If it be that Cunningham had actually found the *aḥ* mark on the eleventh fixed pillar-base, we would have no grounds for reasonable doubt. In the Indian alphabetical system *aḥ* being rather a vowel-sign than a vowel-letter, it would seem more probable that the eleven vowels were *a, ā, i, ī, u, ū, ṛ, e, ai, o,* and *au.* We have to understand from Cunningham's own statement[2] that he observed just six letters, the volwel *a* on the westerly pillar-base in the southern row, and the consonants *ka, ga, ca, ja* and *ṭa* on the five pillar-bases in the northern row.[3] The vowel *a* was traced also on a pillar-shaft, which now stands on the westerly base of the northern row.[4] The fact that this shaft is marked with the letter *a* is enough to prove that it stood originally on the westerly base of the southern row. The list published by Dr. Lüders on the strength of Sir George Grierson's paper contains the letter *a, ka, ṅa* and *ca.*[5]

Of the six letters noticed by Cunningham, the letter *a* was traced on the shaft and also on the fixed base of the first pillar of the southern row, counted from west to east; the letter *ka* was found on the first pillar-base of the northern row, opposite *a*; and the remaining four letters, *ga, ca, ja* and *ṭa*, were found on the 3rd, 7th, 8th and 11th bases of the same northern row. Irresistible is the conclusion drawn by Cunningham from these data, that the eleven pillars of the southern row were serially marked with eleven vowels and those of the northern row with the first eleven consonants, the pillars being observed and counted in each row from west to east.

---

1. Cunningham's *Mahābodhi*, p. 8.
2. Ibid., p. 16.
3. See Pl. I, No. 1.
4. Cunningham's *Mahābodhi*, Pl. IV.
5. *List of Brāhmī Inscriptions,* No. 938.

The letter *a* as was found by Cunningham on the base and the same letter as he found it on the pillar-proper represent two different forms, in each of which, however, the two left strokes meet the vertical line, leaving a small space between them. The letter *ka* is dagger-shaped, that is to say, it appears in the form of a plus sign withthe lower part of the vertical stroke longer than the upper. The letter *ga* shows a prominently rounded top, instead of being sharply angular. The letter *cha* is of a double-looped butterfly pattern. The letter *ja* appears in a form in which the two semi-circular curves meet each other vertically in a straight line instead of forming a loop in front. And the letter *ṭa* represents a vertically set segment of a circle.

All these letter-marks may go to show that the masons, craftsmen or artists, employed to fashion and set up the pillars and their fixed bases, hailed from or, at least, had to do their work in, that part of India where Brāhmī was the prevalent form of writing.

The order of eleven vowels in the southern row and that of the first eleven consonants may serve to prove either (1) that the pillars and their fixed bases were serially set up in each row from west to east, or (2) that these were maṛked with letters in this order.

The difference observed in the two forms of the same letter *a*, as it was incised on the pillar-base and on the corresponding pillar-shaft, has, perhaps, to tell its own tale. Having regard to the fact that these two forms of *a* distinguish the majority of the inscriptions on the old Stone-railing, we may be inclined to think that the pillar-bases and the pillar-shafts were marked by two different scribes or 'engraver-writers' (*lekhaka, lipikara*). In the absence, however, of the remaining pillar-shafts and their letter-marks, it is impossible to hazard any more than a surmise or conjecture about the marking of the pillar-bases and pillar-shafts by two scribes.

Cunningham has rightly observed that the arrangement of letters on the pillars of the two rows "has an important bearing on the antiquity of the Indian alphabet, as it shows that the several characters had already been arranged in their present groups as gutturals, palatals, cerebrals, dentals, labials, semi-vowels, and sibilants."

On the surviving fragments of the old Stone-railing we can trace as many as twenty-two votive labels engraved on seventeen rail-pillars, rail-posts and gate or corner pillars, three rail-bars and two coping-pieces. In al these labels we find the use of altogether twenty-one letters and seven letter-signs, as the subjoined two tables will indicate:—

1. Table of Letters

Vowels — *a, i.*

Consonants — *ka, kha, ga, gha, —, ca, —, ja, —, ña, ṭa, —, —, —, —, ta, —, da, dha, na, pa, —, ba, —, ma, ya, ra, —, va, —, —, —, sa, —, —.*

2. Table of Letter-signs

Signs for *ā, i, ū, e, o, ṃ, ra,* stop.

As regards the Brāhmī letter-forms, their importance lies -- the fact that they enable us at once to divide the votive labels broadly into two groups, the first comprising those inscriptions in which one of the two forms of the letter *a* detected on some of the pillar-bases is associated with that form of the anchor-shaped letter *ya* in which two separate curves at the base meet in the vertical line, and the second comprising those inscriptions in which the second form of the letter *a* is associated withthat form of the anchor-shaped letter *ya* in which the vertical line stands on a single semi-circular curve at the base. It will also be noticed that in all the labels the letter *ka* is dagger-shaped; the letter *ga* is still sharply angular; the letter *ta,* too, shows a sharp angular form; the letter *ja* has precisely the same form as on the pillar-bases; the letters *gha* and *pa* have each a flat base; the letters *ma* and *va* have a triangular body; the leter *ra* represents a cork-screw pattern; and the vowel-sign for *i* presents an abruptly out-stretched elongation. It is just in one example that we trace a form of the letter *ma*, in which the upper stroke stands above a circle without touching each other, precisely as in the form of the letter *ma* on the Sohgaura Copper-plate and in the Brahmagiri and two other South Indian copies of Aśoka's M.R.E. I. In this particular case the letter *a,* too, has form different from those noticed above.

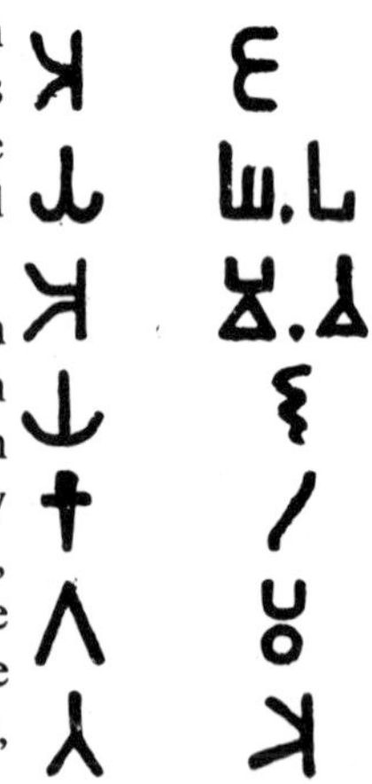

Thus comparing the Brāhmī letter-forms in these in scriptions, we can discriminate in them three kinds of hand-writing, and the conclusion which may be drawn therefrom will undoubtedly be this, that either three different groups of masons, craftsmen or artists were employed, or among the masons, craftsmen or artists employed to do the work in connection with the old Stone-railing, three, at least, had done the work of scribes.

As for the *Vajrāsana* inscription, the Brāhmī letter-forms are mostly like those of the railing inscriptions. But it will be noticed that the letter *ra*, as we find it in the *Vajrāsana* inscription, is a simple vertical line, instead of being of a cork-screw pattern.

In accordance with their position on the different component parts of the Stone-railing we may conveniently deal with the votive labels bydividing them into three separate groups, the first comprising those inscriptions which are incised on the rail-pillars, the second comprising those incised on the rail-bars, and the third comprising those on the coping-pieces.

1. Those on the Rail-pillars

A. Nos. 1-15

[Noticed by Prinsep, *JASB.*, 1836, Vol. V, p. 658, Pl. XXXIII; *JASB.*, 1837, Vol. VI, p. 468, with facsimile; Kittoe, *JASB.*, 1847, Vol., XVI, part I, p. 339, with facsimile; Cunningham, *ASR*, 1871, Vol. I, p. 10, Pls. VII, IX; *ASR,* 1873, Vol. III, p. 88, Pl. XXVI; Fergusson, *Tree and Serpent Worship*, p. 130 (facsimile only); R.L. Mitra, *Buddha Gayā,* 1878, pp. 182 foll; Indraji, *IA*, 1880, Vol. IX, p. 142; Cunningham, *Mahābodhi*, 1892, p. 15, Pl. X; Lüders, *List of Brāhmī Inscriptions* in *EI.* 1909-10, Vol. X, Nos. 939-42; Bloch, *ASI,* Annual Report, 1908-9, p. 147.]

a. Text on 14 Rail-posts[1]

Ayāye Kuraṃgiye dānaṃ [.]

"The gift of the Noble Lady Kuraṅgī."

b. Text on one Rail-post[2]

Ayāye Kuraṃgiye dinaṃ [.]

"Donated by the Matron Kuraṅgī."

[Notes:—Dr. Bloch has rightly pointed out that "not less than fifteen times (which is to say, on not less than fifteen rail-posts) was met with the following well-known inscription:—*Ayāye Kuraṃgiye dānaṃ,*" and that "in one instance, the inscription has *dinaṃ*, which, of course, is Sk. *dattam*, 'given'." The honorific epithet *Ayā*, Sk. *Āryā*, "the Noble Lady," seems to signify the benevolence and high social position of Kuraṅgī as well as her superior rank as a Buddhist nun or lay woman by reason of her age and advanced spiritual state. In other words, it is not unlikely that Kuraṅgī, as her epithet *Ayā* indicates, joined the holy order of the Buddhists and was held in

1. See Pl. I, Nos. 2-13.
2. Pl. I, No. 14.

high esteem for her noble deeds, remarkable personality, high social position as a queen, and spiritual outlook and insight. (See Barua and Sinha's *Barhut Inscriptions*, note on *Ayā*). Here *Ayā* might, perhaps, be better rendered as "Matron." Cunningham is perfectly right in suggesting that *Kuraṃgī* is a female name meaning 'fawn-eyed,' or with eyes like the *Kuraṃgī* deer. *Dinaṃ*, even if it were not due to an error on the part of the scribe, is as good a reading as *dānaṃ*, the use of *dinaṃ* (=dinnaṃ) as a substantive being not uncommon in Pāli (cf. *dinnaṃ hoti mahapphalaṃ*, where *dinnaṃ* simply means *dānaṃ*, "a gift" (literally, that which is given away as a gift).]

B. No. 16

[Noticed by Bloch, *ASI,* Annual Report, 1908-9, p. 147.]

Text on another Rail-post[1]

Rāño Iṃ(dāgimi)trā [.......] (S)irimāye [dānaṃ.]

Text as might be restored

Rāño Iṃ(dāgimi)trā[sa pāsādā-cetikā-] (S)irimāye [dāuaṃ.]

"The gift of Sirimā (Śrīmatī), a female donor from the palace of KingIndrāgnimitra."

[Notes:—Dr. Bloch is the first to observe that the name of Indrāgnimitra is met with in a "mutilated inscription on one of the railing pillars, where he appears to have had the title 'King' (*Rāño*; gen. sing.) added before his name." But, curiously enough, no attempt whatever was made since, either to decipher and restore the text of this inscription or to discuss the whole of its importance. It is quite true, as Dr. Bloch has pointed out, that Indrāgnimitra has been honoured in this inscription with the title of *Rājā*, "King." It will be seen that the inscription was damaged in the middle on account of a mortice cut through it on that portion of a face of the rail-post where the missing letters were incised. The space covered by the breadth of the mortice is large enough, as will appear from similar spaces on other rail-posts bearing inscriptions, to contain seven Brāhmī letters. As for the restoration of the letters that are now lost, there is hardly any reason for doubting that the letter coming immediately after *trā* of *Iṃdāgnimitrā* is *sa* and that the syllable *sa* is the genitive singular termination: *sa*=Pāli *ssa*=Sk. *sya*. The reasons for restoring the remaining six letters as *pāsāda-cetikā* will be set forth when we come to deal with two inscriptions on two coping-

1. Pl. I, No. 15.

pieces. For the equation of the name *Sirimā* with *Śrīmatī*, the reader is referred to Barua and Sinha's *Barhut Inscriptions*, note on *Sirimā devatā*.]

C. No. 17

[Noticed by Bloch, *ASI*, Annual Report, 1908-9, p. 147.]

Text on the N.E. Corner-pillar[1]

Rāño Brahmamitrasa pājāvātiye Nāgadevaye dānaṃ [.] "The gift of Nāgadevī, the wife of King Brahmamitra."

[Notes:—Pājāvatī is the same word as the Pāli *pajāpati* and the Sk. *prajāvatī*. Following the authority of Sanskrit lexicon and literature. Cunningham and Lüders have interpreted the word *pājāvātī* in the sense of *bhrātṛjāyā,* "brother's wife" or "sister-in-law." Bloch has explained this word as meaning "wife" and Bühler, too, has done the same in translating the votive labels on the stone-railings of the Sāñchi Stūpas (*EI,* vol. II). It would seem that as, on the one hand, the rendering of *pājāvātī* by "brother's wife" is wide of the mark, so, on theother hand, the rendering of it as "wife" may seem too wide in denotation. According to Pāli usage, which is clearly illustrated by a passage in the Vānarinda Jātaka (Fausböll, No. 57), a wife is to be called a *pajāpati* only when she is with child. *Pāli* passage:—*Tasmiṃ pana kāle eko kumbhīlo sapajāpatiko tassa nadiyā vasati. Tassa sā bhariyā Bodhisattaṃ aparapāraṃ gacchaniaṃ disvā Bodhisattassa hadaya-maṃse dohaḷaṃ uppādetvā kumbhīlaṃ āha.* (*Now there lived in those days in that river a crocodile and his mate*; and she, being with young, was led by the sight of the Bodhisatta journeying to and fro to conceive a longing for the monkey's heart to eat. So she begged her lord).

If this be the correct explanation of *pajāpati, pājāvātī* or *prajāvatī*, the text of the inscription under notice may be taken to imply that the north-eastern corner-pillar was donated by Queen Nāgadevī when she was about to be a mother. But there are certain Pāli passages in the Vinaya (Sutta-vibhaṅga) where the word *pajāpati* has been used in the general sense of "a wife." Here attention may be particularly drawn to two passages: (1) Sutta-vibhaṅga, Bhikkhu-vibhaṅga, Saṅghādisesa, II. 1, 1, in which the word *bhariyā*, meaning "a wife," occurs as a synonym of *pajāpati*; and (2) *Ibid.*, Saṅghādisesa, V. 1, 1, in which an unmarried girl (*apatikā kumārikā*) is said to have been engaged as a suitable bride for an unmarried young man (*apajāpatika Kumāraka*).]

1. Pl. I, No. 16.

II. Those on the Rail-bars

D. No. 18

[Noticed by Cunningham, *Mahābodhi*, 1892, p. 16, No. 2, Pl. X; Lüders, *List of Brāhmī Inscriptions* in *EI*, 1909-10, Vol. X, No. 945.]

Text on a Rail-bar[1]

Amoghāsa dānaṃ [.]

"The gift of Amogha."

[Notes:—The rail-bar bearing the above inscription was removed to and is now exhibited in the Bārhut Gallery hall of the Indian Museum, Calcutta, as Bg. 2.]

E. No. 19

[Noticed by Cunningham, *ASR*, 1873, Vol. III, p. 89, Pl. XXVI; R.L. Mitra, *Buddha Gayā*, p. 184, No. 3; Indraji, *IA*, 1880, Vol. IX, p. 142; Cunningham, *Mahābodhi*, 1892, p. 16, No. 3, Pl. X; Lüders, *List of Brāhmī Inscriptions* in *EI*, 1909-10, Vol. X, No. 946; Bloch. *ASI*, Annual Report, 1908-9, p. 156.]

Text on another Rail-bar[2]

Bodhirakhitasa Ta(ṃ)bapa(ṃ)nakasa dānaṃ [.]

"The gift of Bodhirakṣita, the Tāmraparṇika—a man belonging to Tāmraparṇi."

[Notes:—The rail-bar bearing the above inscription was removed to and is now exhibited in the Bārhut Gallery hall of the Indian museum, Calcutta, as Bg. 1. Here the really important word requiring explanation is the geographical patronymic *Taṃbapaṃnaka*, derived from *Taṃbapaṃni*, Pāli *Tambapaṇṇi*, and Sk. *Tāmraparṇi*. *Taṃbapaṃni*, as known to Aśoka, was the southernmost land which lay to the south of his Indian empire (R.E. XIII). Rev. A.P. Buddhadatta has collected certain interesting Pāli references in the introduction to his edition of Buddhadatta's Manuals (Pāli Text Society publication), which go to prove that the name *Tambapaṇṇi* was applicable not only to the island of Ceylon but also to that part of the Deccan which was situated to the south of the Tambapaṇṇi (Tāmraparṇi) river. The Aśokan sense, too, does not pre-clude the possibility of inclusion of this part of South India in the territorial limits of Tambapaṇṇi. The account of Prince Vijaya's conquest of

---

1. Pl. I, No. 17.
2. Pl. I, No. 18.

Ceylon in the Pāli chronicles suggests that the island of Laṇkā came to be known as Tambapaṇṇi, on account of the fact that when Prince Vijaya landed on its sea-shores, the palm of his hand was touched by the copper-coloured particles of sand. We might say that originally the name Tambapaṇṇi was restricted to the south-western part of the island of Laṅkā where the beaches were covered with copper-coloured sand. Gradually, as we may suppose, the name came to be applied and even exclusively applied to the whole cf Ceylon. As regards *Taṃbapaṃnaka* of the Bodh Gayā Inscription, Cunningham and Bloch seem to be perfectly right in identifying Tambapaṇṇi with Ceylon.]

F. No. 20

[Noticed by Cunningham, *ASR*, 1873, Vol. III, p. 89, Pl. XXVI, 2; R.L. Mitra, *Buddha Gayā*, 1878, p. 183, No. 2; Lüders, *List of Brāhmī Inscriptions* in *EI*, 1909-10, Vol. X, No. 947.]

Text on a third Rail-bar

Pāṭihāra .. Nā .... dānaṃ [.]

"The gift of the door-keeper (with
Nā as the initial of his name)."

Or,

"The gift of a man of Pratīhāra.
(the initial of whose name is *Nā*.)"

Or,

"The gift of (the city-judiciary) of Pratīhāra."

[Notes:—Cunningham who first noticed it found the inscription "to comprise thirteen letters, of which the 5th, 6th, 8th, 9th, 10th, and 15th were illegible. The inscription might, perhaps, be restored as:—

Pāṭihārā[kāsa] Nā [...sa] dānaṃ [.]

Here *Pāṭihāra* may be treated either as an official designation or a place-name, and *Nā* may be treated either as an initial of a personal name, or of an official designation, such as *Nāgarika*.]

III. Those on the Coping-pieces

G. Nos. 21-22

[Noticed by R.L. Mitra, *Catalogue and Handbook of the Archaeological Collections in the Indian Museum,* 1883, Part I, pp. 130 foll; Cunningham, *Mahābodhi*, 1892, p. 15, Nos. 8-10, Pl. X; Lüders, *List of Brāhmī Inscriptions* in *E1*, 1909-10, Vol. X, Nos. 943-4; Bloch, *ASI*, Annual Report, 1908-9, p. 147.]

a. Text on a Coping-piece[1]

(Rāño Kosi)ki-putrāsa Iṃdāgimitrāsa pājāvātiye jivāputrāye Kuraṃgiye dānaṃ [:] rājā-pāsādā-cetikā-(Siri)mā(ye) [dānaṃ.]

b. Text on another Coping-piece

[Rāño Ko] siki-putrāsa Iṃdāgimitrāsa pājāvātiye jivāputrā-ye Kuraṃgiye dānaṃ [:] rājā-pāsādā-cetikā-Si[rimāye dānaṃ.]

"The gift of Kuraṅgī, the wife of King Indrāgnimitra, the son of Kauśīki,—Kuraṅgī who is the mother of living sons: the gift (as well) of Sirimā (Śrīmatī), a female donor from the royal palace of King Indrāgnimitra."

[Notes:—Cunningham and other Indian epigraphists have agreed in reading the letter before *putrāsa* as *ka*. With regard to the first inscription, Cunningham was able to note that there were traces of two other letters before *ka*, the one immediately preceding it being no other than *sa*. He was led even to think that *saka* before *putrāsa* might be taken as the latter part of the name of Aśoka. The presumption as to the possibility of occurrence of the name of Aśoka in these inscriptions is due to a bias under which Cunningham and the rest of the old school of Indian epigraphists conducted their researches. This presumption has no sound basis for its justification, first, because *Asoka-putra* as a personal epithet of King Indrāgnimitra is meaningless; and, secondly, because the three letters before *putrāsa* may still be read as *Kosiki*, with the result that King Indrāgnimitra has been represented in these coping inscriptions as a *Kauśikī-putra*. We can go so far as to suggest that there are traces of two other letters before *Kosiki-putrāsa*, and that these may be read as *Rāño*. Even if this suggestion do not bear scrutiny, there is one inscription on one of the rail-posts to prove that *Rājā*, "King," was the title of Indrāgnimitra, we mean the Bodh-Gayā Stone-railing Inscription, No. 16 The epithet *Kosiki-putra* is a matronymic like *Gāgīputa, Gotiputa* and *Vāchhīputa* of the Bārhut E. Gateway Inscription, not to mention the hosts of other similar matronymics which are met with in both inscriptions and literary texts. As regards *Kosiki-putra* itself, it may be noted that the *List of Brāhmī Inscriptions* published by Lüders includes one inscription (No. 94), in which *Kośīki* is found as a surname of Śimitrā; a second (No. 105), in which *Kośīkiputra* occurs as a surname of Sihanādika; a third and a fourth (Nos. 159, 662) in which *Kosikiputa* is employed as a surname of a Buddhist monk; a fifth (No. 1079), in which *Kosikiputa* adorns the name of Mahāraṭhi

1. Pl. II, No. 19.

Viṇhudata; a sixth (No. 1100), in which *Kosikiputa* is an ornament of the name of Mahārathi Mitadeva; and a seventh (No. 1196) in which *Kosikiputta* appears as a surname of Nāgadatta. Finally, in the "Śuṅga Inscription of Ayodhyā," edited by Mr. K.P. Jayaswal, we find that *Kauśikīputra* has been used as a surname of a high personage. The epithet signifies that King Indrāgnimitra was a son of Kauśīkī who was a lady of Kauśika or Viśvāmitra *gotra*.

Cunningham has translated *pājāvātī* (Pāli *pajāpati,* Sk. *prajāvatī*, Bengali *poyāti*) by "brother's wife," and Lüders by "sister-in-law." But it would seem strange that in one inscription Nāgadevī should be introduced as *pājāvātī* (the "brother wife" or "sister-in-law") of King Indrāgnimitra. We cannot but welcome Bloch's rendering of it as "wife" in view of the fact that, according to the Pāli usage, the word *pajāpati* is a synonym of *bhariyā*, in some instances it denotes "a wife who has a clear prospect of becoming a mother." Here we have to make a distinction between a *pājāvātī* and a *jivāputrā pājāvātī.* As for the distinction, it may suffice to say that a *pājāvātī* is either simply "a wife" or she is "a wife who is about to be a mother," and a *jivāputrā*[1] *pājāvātī* (*jīvaputrikā* praj*āvatī,* Bengali *jeyas poyāti*) is, on the other hand, "a wife who has not only become a mother but can be proud of being a mother of living children." Bloch has rightly remarked that "Indian ladies still consider it a pride to call themselves *jīvaputrā* 'a mother of living sons,' an expression very familiar to every reader of ancient Indian inscriptions."[2]

Kuraṅgī was a *jivāputrā pājāvātī* of King Kauśikiputra Indrāgnimitra, King Indrāgnimitra's wife, who was a mother of living sons. This may help us to explain why in each of the fifteen rail-post-inscriptions Kuraṅgī has been honoured as an *Ayā* (Sk. *Āryā*), "a Noble Lady," "a Matron."

Cunningham has regretted the loss of the latter part of these important records. As regards the first coping inscription, he has found traces of eleven Brāhmī letters after *Kuraṃgiye dānaṃ*, the first nine of whic read *rāja-pāsāda-cetikā sa.* Bloch reads these nine letters as *rājā-pāsāda-cetikāsa* and translates this expression in relation to the preceding words: "(the gift of Kuraṅgī, the wife of

1. Lüders' interpretation of *jīvaputrā* in the sense of "daughter of Jīvā" does not deserve any comment.
2. Cf. Aśoka's edict on his Second Queen's donations, which contains the king's order directing the high officials at Kauśāmbī to re-label all the donations made by his second queen by inscriptions recording them as: "[Donations] of [his] second queen Kāluvākī, the mother of [Prince] Tīvala."

Indrāgnimitra and the mother of living sons), "to the *caitya* (*cetikā*) of the noble temple," taking the word *rājā* before *pāsāda* as an epithet *on ornans*, distinguishing the temple as a particularly large and stately building, similar to such expressions as *rājahastin* 'a noble elephant,' *rāja-haṃsa* 'a goose (as distinguished from *haṃsa* 'a duck'), etc." Cunningham has translated the expression by "the royal palace, the caitya," suggesting that "the mention of the *rāja-pāsāda* would seem to connect the donor with the king's family." Lüders doubtfully suggests "to the king's temple" as a rendering of *rāja-pāsāda-cetikāsa*.

Before giving countenance to the hitherto suggested reading and rendering of *rāja-pāsāda-cetikā sa* one has to consider and decide these two points: (1) is the letter, after *cetikā, sa* or *si*? and (2) what are the three letters after *cetikā*. It can hardly be doubted that the letter after °*cetikā* is not *sa* (the Dative singular termination) but *si*, and that the three letters may still be read as *Sirimā*. If so, it is not difficult to restore the missing syllables and complete the first coping-inscription as *rājā pāsādā-cetikā-*(*Siri*)*mā*(*ye*) [*dānaṃ*], and to complete the second coping-inscription as *rājā-pāsadā-cetikā-Si*[*rimāye* dānaṃ]. We have already dealt with the rail-post inscription, *Rāño Iṃdāgimitrā*[*sa*.......] *Sirimāye* [*dānaṃ*], in which the female donor has in some way been connected with King Indrāgnimitra. As to the nature of the connection, it all depends on the missing expression which filled the middle part of the mutilated inscription. Seeing that the expression *rājā-pāsādā-cetikā* precedes the name of *Sirimā* in the first coping-inscription, it may be safely surmised that the seven missing letters of the rail-post-inscription recorded the expression *pāsādā-cetikā* after *sa* of *putrāsa*. Considering the text of the first coping-inscription in relation to that of the rail-post, we find no other alternative than to regard *Rāño Kosikiputrāsa Iṃdāgimitrāsa rājā-pāsādā-cetikā* or *Rāño Iṃdāgimitrāsa pāsādā-cetikā* as an epithet of *Sirimā*, in the same way that *pājāvātī jivāputrā* is an epithet of Kuraṅgī.

Now the question is—what does the epithet *pāsādā-cetikā* or *rājā-pāsādā-cetikā* signify? Is there any reference here at all to the temple at Bodh-Gayā? The question must, in our opinion, be answered in the negative for the simple reason that the construction or existence of the Bodh-Gayā temple prior to the visit of Fa-Hian (first quarter of the 5th century A.C.) is inconceivable. Cunningham was perfectly right to suggest that the donor was somehow or other connected with the royal palace. Here the word *cetikā*, a feminine form of *cetaka* (Prakrit *ceyaga*), may be consistently interpreted in the sense of *dātri*, "a female donor." Sirimā (Śrīmatī) was a female donor from the royal palace of King Indrāgnimitra. We cannot interpret *cetikā* as "a female attendant unless it is a mistake for *ceṭ ikā*. The *rājā-pāsādā*, "royal palace," may be regarded as the name of a Buddhist monastery built at Bodh-Gayā to commemorate the name of King Indrāgnimitra, compare, *Migāra-mātupāsāda*, which was the name of the Buddhist monastery built by Viśākhā, the daughter-in-law of Migāra.

Our reading and rendering of the two coping-inscriptions will help the reader to ascertain that the two coping-stones bearing these records were joint donations of Kuraṅgī and Sirimā, the former being the elderly wife of King Indrāgnimitra and the latter a female donor from the palace of the same royal personage.

IV. That on the Diamond-throne[1]

H. No. 23

[Noticed by Cunningham, *Mahābodhi*, 1892, pp. 20, 58, Pl. X. 11; Lüders, *List of Brāhmī Inscriptions* in *EI*, 1909-10, Vol. X, No. 948.]

a. That on the west and south sides

W—? pajāya? agā?ya hitāya;

S. mātā-(pituno kā)rito [.]

b. Text on the north side ?

[Notes:—Cunningham rightly says that "all that remains of this inscription is so much injured that very little can be read consecutively." There are faint traces of a large number of letters on the western edge, about 35 letters preceding three which one may tentatively read as *pajāya*. We cannot but agree with Cunningham when he says that towards the end, on the right hand, one may read "the well-known words *māta-pita*, 'mother and father'." But we must differ from him when he tends to hold that "the letters certainly belong to the Indo-Scythian or early Gupta period, about the 2nd. century A.C.," and that the two words which distinctly precede *māta-pita* are *patimā patiṭhapat*, "statue established." It would seem that a new set of letters was incised on an earlier one at a later age, and that the forms of earlier letters are in no way very different from those of the inscriptions of Kuraṅgī and Nāgadevī on the rail-posts and coping-pieces of the Old Stone-railing. The language of the

1. Pl. II, No. 21.

earlier inscription, too, seems to bear resemblance with that of the well-known inscriptions of Kuraṅgī and Nāgadevī.]

Importance of the writings

The historical importance of the writings, considered in this section, lies, first of all in the fact that from the close similarity of the Brāhmī letter-forms, it may be inferred that the Old Stone-railing bearing the donative inscriptions of Kuraṅgī, Sirimā, Nāgadevī and others, the old Diamond-throne bearing a donative inscription on the upper edges of its covring stone-slab and the Jewel-walk-shrine bearing the Brāhmī letter-marks on the shafts and fixed bases of its two rows of pillars were erected at the same time, and, probably, under the auspices of certain common donors. The twofold impression which may be gathered from the study of the votive labels inscribed on the rail-pillars and the coping-pieces and which lingers is (1) that originally when the Stone-railing was erected, the rail-bars remained uninscribed, which is to say, that the three rail-bars recorded as donations of Amogha, Bodhirakhita of Taṃbapaṃni and another donor of Paṭihāra (?) were somewhat later additions, and (2) that the entire Old Stone-railing at Bodh-Gayā, together with the Old Diamond-throne and the Jewel-walk-shrine, was a memorable erection of devotional female piety. The first of these two impressions is strengthened as we consider that the length and letter-forms of the inscribed rail-bars, notably that donated by Amogha, differ considerably from those of the uninscribed rail-bars in that portion of the Stone-railing which appears to have been donated only by Kuraṅgī.

On as many as fifteen rail-pillars we trace inscriptions recording them in bold letters as donations of Ayā Kuraṃgī. It is only on one of the inscribed rail-pillars that we come across an inscription recording the same to be a gift from Sirimā who was connected in some way with King Indrāgnimitra. Only one of the surviving corner-pillars is recorded to have been a gift from Nāgadevī, the wife of King Brahmamitra. Two pieces of old coping-stones which now survive are labelled each by an inscription, in which Kuraṃgī and Sirimā figure as joint female donors. It is very interesting indeed to find that here Kuraṃgī has been represented not as *Ayā*, "Noble Lady" or "Matron" but as King Kosikiputra Iṃdāgimitra's wife who had the pride of having been a mother of living sons. Both here and in the rail-post inscription, Sirimā has been represented as *cetikā* or female donor from the royal palace of King Iṃdāgimitra. The south side of the quadrangular Stone-railing bears only the inscriptions of Kuraṃgī. From all these facts, the impression cannot but be this, that the Old Stone-railing, and, *à posteriori*, the two other old shrines were mainly a pious erection of Kuraṃgī.

The Old Stone-railing at Bodh Gayā must have been erected by Kuraṅgī, Sirīmā and Nāgadevī either during the reign of King Indrāgnimitra or during that of King Brahmamitra. If the inscribed corner-pillar commemorating the piety of Nāgadevī, represented as the wife of King Brahmamitra, was donated along with the donations of Kuraṅgī, it is difficult to think that this Stone-railing was erected during the reign of King Indrāgnimitra, unless it be supposed that Indrāgnimitra and Brahmamitra reigned together, which seems, however, unlikely. Both Indrāgnimitra and Brahmamitra, as their names imply, were rulers of the same Mitra family, and, what is more, in the absence of any evidence to prove the contrary, both of them must be regarded as kings of the same place, we mean, of Magadha, Bodh Gayā, nay, the whole of Gayā it being an integral part of the kingdom of Magadha throughout the historical period of its existence. The erection of the inscribed Stone-railing at Bodh Gayā by Kuraṅgī and Nāgadevī is not, however, the only reason for assuming that Indrāgnimitra and Brahmamitra to be kings of Magadha. Over and above this, we find that Bahasatimita (Bṛhaspatimitra), evidently a king of the same Mitra family, has been expressly mentioned in the Hāthigumphā Inscription of Khāravela as contemporary ruler of Magadha (*Māgadhānaṃ rājā*).[1]

If it can thus be satisfactorily proved that Indrāgnimitra, Brahmamitra and Bṛhaspatimitra were all kings of Magadha and rulers of the same Mitra dynasty, it is important to inquire if any clue maybe obtained from the inscriptions and sculptures of the Bodh Gayā Stone-railing to the chronological succession of them.

So far as the inscriptions of Kuraṅgī and Nāgadevī go, these clearly indicate that theStone-railing was erected when Nāgadevī, the wife of King Brahmamitra (*Brahmamitrasa pājāvatī*), was not yet a mother, and when Kuraṅgī, the wife of King Kauśikīputra Indrāgnimitra, wa an elderly lady, a mother of living sons (*jivāputrā pājāvatī*), honoured in fifteen rail-post inscriptions with the epithet of *Ayā*, "Noble Lady" or "Matron." The epithet *Ayā* may be taken

---

1. Barua's *Old Brāhmī Inscriptions in the Udayagiri and Khaṇḍagiri Caves*, I, 13; Jayaswal's reading in JBORS., vol. III, part IV, and vol. IV, part IV; Indraji's reading in *Actes du Sixieme International Congres des Orientalistes*, part III, sec. II, pp. 152-177.

even to suggest that Kuraṅgī undertook to erect the Stone-railing and two other shrines at Bodh Gayā after her retirement from the world, and after she had assumed the vows of a Buddhist nun and resided in a monastery built at Bodh Gayā commemorating the name of King Indrāgnimitra, her deceased husband, the monastery itself having been known by the name of "King Indrāgnimitra's Palace" (*Rāño Iṃdāgimitrā*[*sa*]*pāsāda*°) or "Indrāgnimitra's Royal Palace" (*Indāgimitrāsa rājā-pāsāda*). From this, it maybe clearly inferred that the pious donations were made by Kuraṅgī rather when she became a queen dowager to King Brahmamitra than when she remained in her full gloryas the queen of King Indrāgnimitra. In other words, the historical importance of the inscriptions of Kuraṅgī, Sirīmā and Nāgadevī lies in the fact that these, when properly studied, afford us a definite epigraphic evidence to prove that King Brahmamitra was the immediate successor of King Indrāgnimitra in the throne of Magadha.

Now as to the bearing of the sculptures of the Old Stone-railing at Bodh Gayā, it is to be noted that inseveral instances their designs are inspired by those of the Barhut bas-reliefs, which is to say, that they are posterior to the carvings of the Barhut Inner Railing. As has been shown elsewhere,[1] the Barhut Stone-railing with its quadrants, returns, gateways, carvings and purely ornamental devices is a purely Śuṅga art and architecture. The ornamental gateways which were pious donations of King Dhanabhūti were last additions that were probably made towards the close of the Śuṅga-Mitra reign. On the other hand, from a comparative study of certain common representations, notably those of the Sun-god, it becomes increasingly clear that these were handiworks of art of the same period, the Bodh Gayā reliefs appearing to have been somewhat earlier than those of some of the Orissan caves on the hills of Udayagiri and Khaṇḍagiri.[2] And fortunately enough, in the Hāthigumphā Inscription on the Udayagiri hill, Bahasatimita (Bṛhaspatimitra) finds mention as the contemporary king of Magadha who was subdued by King Khāravela in the twelfth year of his reign.[3] Thus if any idea of succession of the Mitra kings can be formed on the ground of the close similarity of the handiworks of art, it will be that King Bṛhaspatimitra, a contemporary of King Khāravela, was the immediate successor of

1. Barua's paper—"Age of the Stūpa of Barhut" in the Proceedings of the Fourth All-India Oriental Conference.
2. Barua's *Old Brāhmī Inscriptions in the Udayagiri and Khaṇḍagiri Caves*, pp. 285-6; views of Dr. Stella Kramrisch in *Ibid.*, pp. 310 foll.
3. *Ibid.*, p. 45.

King Brahmamitra during whose reign Kuraṅgī, Sirīmā and Nāgadevī completed their pious erections at Bodh Gayā.

If Bahasatimita (Bṛhaspatimitra), mentioned in the Hāthigumphā Inscription as a contemporary of King Khāravela, be taken to be the immediate successor of King Brahmamitra, it is impossible to identify him with Puṣyamitra, the Senāpati Puṣyamitra who is the traditional founder of the Śuṅga or old Mitra dynasty.[1] As a matter of fact, none of the three above-mentioned Mitra kings can be definitely identified with any king either of the Śuṅga or of the Kāṇva dynasty.[2] The same remark holds true of three other Mitra kings, (1) Bṛhāsvātimita, represented as the father of the elderly Queen Yaśamatā in Yaśamatā's Brick-tablet, found in Mathurā[3]; and (2-3) [? Dhar]mamitra, mentioned as the father of Viṣṇumitra, and Viṣṇumitra, mentioned as the father of Idrāgibhadrā (Indrāgnibhadrā) in the inscription of Gautamīmitrā.[4]

On both palæographic and linguistic grounds the Brick-tablet of Yaśamatā must be assigned to a date, whichis earlier than the inscriptions of Kuraṅgī, Sirimā and Nāga-devī. As regards its palæography, the Brāhmī letter-forms are "still Mauryan."[5] Dr. Vogel feels inclined toassign it on account of the character to "third or second century B.C."[6] And as regards its language, it will be noticed that still the spelling of *Jivaputrā* is *Jivaputā* and that of *°mitra* is *mita*, although Mathurā is its find-place. We have been inclined elsewhere to equate *Bṛhasvātimita* of this tablet with *Bṛhatsvātimitra* or *Bṛhaspatimitra*. But now we finally abandon Dr. Vogel's equation of it with *Bṛhaspatimitra* and adhere to the first alterantive, and hold that Queen Yaśamatā's father was King Bṛhatsvātimitra (cf. Pāli *Behapphala*=*Behāphala*=Sk. *Bṛhatphala*), and not *Bṛhaspatimitra*. It seems likely that Bṛhatsvātimitra was the precursor of King Indrāgnimitra.

---

1. K.P. Jayaswal identifies Bṛhaspatimitra with Puṣyamitra mainly on the ground that in the Sāṅkhyāyana Gṛhya-Sūtra (I. 26. 6), Bṛhaspati is mentioned as the presiding deity of the Puṣya constellation. See, for criticism, Barua's *Old Brāhmī Inscriptions*, pp. 277-9.
2. *Ibid.*, p. 275.
3. JRAS., 1912, p. 120, where J. Vogel reads: *Jivaputāye rājabharyāye Bṛhāsvātimitadhitu Yaśamatāye k□āritaṃ.*
4. I.H.Q., vol. II, no. 3, p. 442, where N.G. Majumdar reads: ....*mamitrasa rāño Viṣṇumitrasa dhitu Īdrāgibhadrāye dhātiye Gotamiye Mitrāye dānaṃ thaṃbho.*
5. Barua's *Old Brāhmī Inscriptions*, p. 274.
6. JRAS., 1912, p. 120.

As for King [Dhar]mamitra and his son King Viṣṇumitra, neither the palæography nor the language of Gautamīmitra's Inscription stands in the way of regarding them as successors of King Bṛhaspatimitra.

There cannot be any serious objection to identifying Khāravela's contemporary Magadhan king Bahasatimita with Bahasatimita of the coins that "have been found at Kosam, about thirty miles south-west of Allahabad, and at Ramnagar (Ahichatrā) in Rohilkhaṇḍ,"[1] and with King Bahasatimitra, mentioned in one of the two Pabhosa cave inscriptions as the nephew of King Āsāḍhasena of Adhichatrā.[2] Mr. Jayaswal identifies Bahasatimitra of this inscription outside the Pabhosa cave with Puṣyamitra on the ground that it assigns the date of excavation of the cave for the residence of the Kāāyapīya Arhats to the tenth regnal year of Udāka (Odraka, Odruka or Ārdraka) who finds mention in the Purāṇas as the fifth king of the Śuṅga-Mitra dynasty.[3] Mr. Jayaswal's theory is untenable, not to say, absurd on the face of it. For if Bahasatimitra were the same person as Puṣ yamitra, the first king of Śuṅga-Mitra dynasty, is it not inconceivable that his maternal uncle King Āsāḍhasena could be a contemporary of Udāka, the fifth king of the same dynasty? In the absence of the word *rājño* preceding *Udākasa*, it is difficult to say at once whether *Udāka* is the personal name of a king or the local name of the place where the cave was excavated. Dr. Kiel-horn, who has edited the two Pabhosa inscriptions for *EI*, vol. II, observes that all the four letters representing *Udākasa* are doubtful. There is nothing to prevent one reading them as *Ūdāka(si)*. And if the Pabhosa expression *leṇaṃ kāritaṃ Ūdākasi* be on a par with *iyaṃ kubhā... Khalati-kasi* of Asoka's Third Barābar Hill Cave inscription, the year *dasama-savachara* must be interpreted as the regnal year of King Āsāḍhasena himself.

The discovery of a purely Sanskrit inscription in Brāhmī orthography prior to the birth of Christ is still a pious hope. The evidence of the so-called "Śuṅga Inscription of Ayodhyā," published by Mr. Jayaswal, cannot surely be brought forward to prove the case.This inscription, as read by Mr. Jayaswal, yields the following text[4]:

---

1. V.A. Smith's *Catalogue of the Coins inthe Indian Museum, Calcutta,* pp. 146, 158, 185; JRAS., 1912, p. 120.
2. *EI.,* vol. II, p. 242.
3. *JBORS.*, vol. III, part IV, pp. 477-8.
4. JBORS., vol. XIII, Parts III-IV, p. 247.

Kosalādhipena dvir-aśvamedha-yājinaḥ Senāpateḥ Puṣ yamitrasya ṣaṣṭhena Kauśikīputrena Dhana... dharmarājñiḥ pituḥ Phalgudevasya ketanaṃ kāritaṃ [.].

We prefer to read *Ṣaṣṭhena* for *ṣaṣṭhena,* and *dharma-rājñaḥ*[1] for *dharmarājñīḥ,* and to imagine that the word *Dhana*...is a genitive form "*Dhana*..[*sya*]," and not an instrumental case "*Dhana*..[*na*]." The crux of the inscription lies indeed in deciding (1) whether *Ṣaṣṭ ha* is a personal name or it is an ordinal (*ṣaṣṭha*, "the sixty," "sixth son, brother or descendant of Puṣyamitra);[2] (2) whether the person who erected the *ketana* of Phalgudeva was connected by blood with Puṣyamitra or not; (3) whether Phalgudeva was the father of he king or of the queen of Kosala; and (4) whether one or two *ketanas* (perhaps meaning memorial shrines)[3] were erected. In accordance with the interpretations hitherto offered, the ruler of Kosala, named Dhana.., who was the sixth son, brother or descendant of Puṣyamitra caused to be made a *ketana* of Phalgudeva, the father of his queen. But the more plausible interpretation seems to be this, that the ruler of Kosala, named Dhana.., erected the *ketana* of Puṣyamitra, and Kauśikīputra Ṣaṣtha erected the *ketana* of Phalgudeva, who was the father of the ruler of Kosala. If this be the right interpretation, it follows that the inscription is far from being a record of the Śuṅga period.

Bṛhatsvātimitra, Indrāgnimitra, Brahmamitra. Bṛhaspatimitra, [Dhar]mamitra and Viṣṇumitra were all kings of a Mitra dynasty. Until we are in possession of a definite evidence to connect them either with the Śuṅga-Mitra or or the Śuṅgabhṛtya Kāṇva kings, it would seem far safer to think with Dr. Raychaudhuri that they belonged to a neo-Mitra dynasty that rose into power on the disruption of the rule of the Kāṇvas. The interest of Yaśamatā's brick-tablet is that it shows that the neo-Mitras were connected by a matrimonial alliance with the ruling family of Mathurā. The interest of the Pabhosa Cave Inscription is that it shows that they were connected by the same alliance with the ruling family of Ahichatrā.

The interest of the so-called "Śuṅga Inscription of Ayodhyā" is that it is probably the record of a time when the official language became Sanskrit, and Kosala was still under the sway of some kings

---

1. Ramaprasad Chanda would read °*rājñāk*, I.H.Q., vol. V, No. 4.
2. Ramaprasad Chanda has sought to establish with some apt quotations from the old strata of the *Mahābhārata* that the ordinal in such a context may be safely taken to mean "the sixth in descent." I.H.Q., vol. V, No. 4.
3. See Ramaprasad Chanda's note in I.H.Q., vol. V, No. 4.

whose boasted ancestor was Puṣyamitra, the traditional founder of the Śuṅga-Mitra dynasty. The interest of the Bodh-Gayā inscriptions of Kuraṅgī, Sirīmā and Nāgadevī is that they clearly prove that the Stone-railing was erected during the reign of King Brahmamitra and that Brahmamitra was the immediate successor of King Indrāgnimitra. The interest of the Hāthi-gumphā Inscription is that it unmistakably proves that Bṛhaspatimitra, the king of Magadha, was a contemporary and weaker rival of Khāravela. Lastly, the interest of the inscription of Gautamīmitrā is that it definitely proves that King Viṣṇumitra, the father of Indrāgnibhadrā, was the son and immediate successor of King [?Dhar]mamitra.

2. Uttara-Pāṣāṇa-Lekhā: Later Writings on the Stone-Railing

The later writings on the Bodh-Gayā stone-railing comprise three inscriptions incised at different periods of time.

The first inscription is written on the inner face of a coping-stone belonging to the south side of the Old Stone-railing. It consists of two lines, the beginning and the end of each of which are mising. "The style of writing employed in the inscription allows us," says Dr. Bloch, "to put down the date at about the 6th or 7th century A.D."

The second inscription in two lines is written on the inner face of a broken fragment of another coping-stone belonging apparently to the south side of the ancient railing. "Its characters agree in every respect," says Dr. Bloch, "with the writing of the first inscription."

And the third inscription in ten lines is written on the upper part of a rail-post. It is written int he Devanāgarī characters by Saṃgatta for Jinadāsa who has been described as a *Paṇḍita* from the Parvata country, and may be assigned to as late a date as the 15th or 16th century A.D. The author of the inscription was evidently a learned pilgrim from Nepal or a Himalayan state near about it.

A. No. 1

[Noticed by Cunningham, *ASR.*, 1873, Vol. III, p. 99, No. D. Pl. XXIX; R.L. Mitra, *Buddha Gayā*, 1878, p. 192, No. 5, Pl. II; Indraji, *IA.*, 1880, Vol. IX, pp. 142 foll.; Cunningham, *Mahābodhi*, 1892, pp. 23, 58, Pl. XXVII, Lüders, *List of Brāhmī Inscriptions* in *EI*, 1909-10, Vol. X, No. 950; Bloch, *ASI.*, Annual Report, 1908-9, p. 153.]

Text as read and rendred by Bloch

1.1 ....kārito yatra Vajrāsana-vṛhad-gandhakuṭī [.] Prāsādam=arddha-trikair=ddināra-śatais-sudhā-lepya-punar-ṇṇavīkaraṇena saṃskariṭam[.] Atr=aiva ca pratyaham=ā-candr-ārkk-ā-tārakaṃ Bhagavate Buddhāya go-śata-dānena ghṛta-pradīpa ākāritaḥ[.] Prāsāde ca khaṇḍa-sphaṭita pratisa-mārādhane tat-pratimāyāṁ ca pratyahaṃ ghṛta-pradīpo go-śaten=āpareṇa kāritaḥ[.] Vihāre=pi Bhagavato raitya-Buddha-pratimā(yāṃ go-sāten=āpareṇa ghṛta-pradīpaḥ......[.]

1.2 ....(ghṛta)-pradīpākṣayanīvini(ba)n(dha)ḥ vihār-opayo(gya) kāritas=Tatrā=pi (u)payogāya mahantam=ādhāraṃ khānitaṃ, tad-anupūrvaṃ c=utpāditam [.] Tad=etat=sarvvaṃ yan=mayā puṇy-opacita-sambhāraṃ tan=mātāpitroḥ p(ūrvaṃgamaṃ kṛtvā...) [.]

"1.1 ....has been made, where the great Gandha-kuṭi[1] of Vajrāsana[2] (*sc.* Buddha) is. The temple[3] has been adorned with a new coating of plaster and paint, at the cost of 250 *dināras*. And in the temple a lamp of *ghee* has been provided for the Lord Buddha by the gift of a hundred cows, for as long as the moon, sun, and stars shall endure. Also, by another hundred cows, in addition to the cost of small, perpetually recurring repairs to the temple, provision, has been made for another lamp of *ghee*, to be burnt daily before the image inside the temple. By another hundred cows provision has been made for having a lamp of *ghee* burnt before the brass image of the Lord Buddha in the Monastery (*vihāra*).........

1.2 ....a perpetual endowment of a lamp of *ghee* has been made for the benefit of the Monastery. There also......a large water reservoir has been dug out for the use of the noble congregation of monks, and to the east of it a new field has been laid out. Whatever merit may have been acquired by me by all this, may this be for the benefit of my parents at first........."

---

1. "The word *gandhakuṭī* means 'a chamber, where Buddha used to reside,' hence a shrine, containing an image of Buddha.' It would be useless to try and find out which of the many small shrines, the foundations of which cover the ground all around the temple at Bodh-Gayā, has been referred to in this inscription. Possibly the large temple onthe west side of the Bodhi Tree, mentioned by Hiuen Tsiang, may be meant."
2. "The word *vajrāsana* (l. 1) is occasionally met with as a name of Buddha, the meaning which it clearlyhas in this inscription."
3. "The temple (*prāsāda*) naturally must have been the same edifice which we still have at the present day, although it certainly has undergone a number of alterations."

[Notes:— Sir Alexander Cunningham was inclined to take this inscription to be a Brāhmī epigraph of so early a date as the reign of Huviṣka, and to believe that it was intended to record the construction of the Diamond-throne, the Fragrant-chamber and the Bodh-Gayā temple itself. But Dr. Bloch's reading and rendering of the inscription has served to show that it is far from recording such a fact. It is impossible to think that the epigraph is of so early a date as Huviṣka's reign. The inscription records some work of merit done near about the great Fragrant-chamber enshrining the Diamond-throne, and records also the amount spent for adorning the temple with a new coating of plaster and paint, and, what is more, it contemplates the need of a suitable provision to be made for "perpetually recurring repairs to the temple." The Diamond-throne, the great Fragrant-chamber and the temple itself were already there when the inscription was caused to be incised on the coping-stone of the ancient railing. We think it safer to interpret the expression *Vajrāsana-vṛhad-Gandhakuṭī* as signifying an architectural representation of the Diamond-throne retreat of the Buddha than to treat *Vajrāsana* as a name of the Buddha. The inscription must indeed be considered as later than the erection of the temple, and referred to a time when the temple needed to be repaired with a new plaster and paint coating.]

B. No. 2

[Noticed by Bloch, ASI, Annual Report, 1908-9, p. 156; JBORS, 1918, vol. IV, part IV, pp. 405-11].

Text as read and rendered by Panday

[1.1] Laṅkā-dvīpa-narendrāṇāṃ Śramaṇaḥ kula-jo bhavat[1] [1]

Prakhyātakīrttir=ddharmātmā sva-kula-am-bara-candramāḥ [II (1)]

Bhaktyā tu bhikṣuṇā-nena Buddhatvam-abhikāṃkṣatā [1]

Kārāratna-traye samyak kāritaḥ[2] śāntaye nṛṇām II (2)[1]

Ito[3] mayā yat=kuśalaṃ hy=upārjjitam

Tad=astu bodhāya[4] ◡ — ◡ — ◡ —

◡ — ◡ — — ◡ ◡ — ◡ — ◡ —

---

1. Bloch reads *bhavet*.
2. Bloch reads *kāritā*.
3. Bloch reads *tato*. Pandav says, "The first letter of the third verse is distinctly *i*—two dots with a vertical stroke on the right."
4. Bloch reads *tadasty upādh(yā)ya*. According to Panday, "The letter after *tadastu* is *bo*, not *pā*." This means indeed a material improvement in both reading and sense.

[1.2] Śubhena tenaiva (pha)lena yujyatām [11(3)]

"The virtuous Śramaṇa Prakhyātakīrtti having been a descendant of the rulers of the Island of Laṅkā (Ceylon) (has become) moon to the firmament of his family (*v.* 1)."

"This monk, through devotion, desirous of attaining Buddhahood, caused to be performed proper acts of worship at the Ratna-traya [the Buddhist Holy Triad] for the peace of mankind (*v.* 2)."

"Whatever merit has been acquired by me through this, let tis be for the enlightenment (of)......Let that veryauspicious reward be shared by (*v.* 3)."

[Notes:—Here the two words which need explanations are *kārā* and *ratna-traye.* In the opinion of Dr. Bloch one "can hardly imagine it (*kārā*) to mean 'a prison' as it generally does," and as to *Ratna-traya*, "it may refer to some sacred spot within the Bodhi area at Bodh Gayā, where, perhaps, a symbol of the 'three jewels'—Buddha, Dharma, and Saṅgha, may have stood." But Mr. Panday has convincingly proved by a number of apt quotations from the Divyāvadāna, pp. 133, 166, 289, 329, 420, and 583, particularly by one from p. 329 (*Buddhe Dharme Saṅghe Kārān akariṣyat*), that *Kārā* is "a fairly well known term in Buddhist literature meaning 'acts of worship,' and Dr. Bloch's conjecture as to the existence of a symbol of the three 'jewels at Bodh Gayā having the shape of three wheels placed upon a pillar is not tenable." The *Ratna-traya* is but a collective expression denoting the Budhist Holy Triad enumerated in the Divyāvadāna passage as *Buddha, Dharma* and *Saṅgha.*]

C. No. 3

Text

[1.1] //Namo Buddhāya//
[1.2] Parvatādāgata-pa-
[1.3] ṇḍita-Jinadāsa te-
[1.4] na Śrīmān Mahābodhi-
[1.5] bhaṭṭāraka-darśana-
[1.6] kṛta-yad punyaṃ ta-
[1.7] dbhavati mātā-pi-
[1.8] tṛ- purvagamaṃ kṛtvā
[1.9] ana(n)ta-punyaṃ likhā-
[1.10] pitaṃ// //Saṃgatta//

"Salutation to the Budha. The merit which is acquired by Jinadāsa, a learned man who came from Parvata, the mountainous country, by means of visiting (the place) to have a viw of the

Mahābodhi (shrine which reigns on the spot) in its glory as the supreme lord falls, first of all, to the share of the parents. Having done this infinite work of merit, it is (here) caused to be written. [Written by the scribe] Saṃgatta."

Chapter - 26
A Rare Type of Bodhisattva-Images from Sanchi

Debala Mitra

In the exterior southern niche of Temple 45 at Sanchi, dating from the tenth-eleventh century, is a two-armed male deity: the head which had a circular halo around it is broken; the damaged right hand is in *varada-mūdrā* and the left, holding the stalk of a half-blown lotus, rests on the seat. Flanked by a female attendant on either side, he is seated in *lalitāsana* on a double-petalled lotus with a peacock below it, the pendant right leg resting on another lotus. He is richly bejewelled and is clad in an undergarment held by a girdle studded with gems; a pleated scarf encircles his body. But for the broken head the sculpture (pl. I)[1] would have been one of the best specimens of medieval art. Another image (pl. II), with almost identical features, again with its head broken, is exhibited in the local museum.

Sir John Marshall, probably thinking the sculpture as the representation of the male counterpart of Mahāmāyūrī, also known as Vidyā-rājñī, tentatively identified it with Mayūravidyārāja.[2] Such a deity, however, does not find mention inthe extant texts on Buddhist iconography. Besides, there is hardly any similarity between this sculpture and the representation of Mahāmāyūrī, the personification of the Tantric text of that name. The peacock in the sculptures is the only point which might have led Marshall to associate them with the goddess of the Pañcarakṣāmaṇḍala. But the *dhyānas* of Mahāmāyūrī, as given in the *Sādhanamālā,* do not prescribe the peacock as her *vāhana* but lay down that she should hold peacock-tail or feather in one of her hands.[3] On the other hand the *varada* pose of the right

---

1. Photographs reproduced on pls. I-IV are the copyright of the Department of Archaeology, Govt. of India.
2. J. Marshall, *Monuments of Sanchi*, vol. I, p. 74.
3. B. Bhattacharyya, *Indian Buddhist Iconography* (Oxford, 1924) p. 111.

hand and the lotus held by theleft hand in the sculptures suggest their affiliation with some form of Avalokiteśvara.

Of all the deities of the later Buddhist pantheon, of whom *dhyānas* are available, that of Vajradharma Lokeśvara is the nearest approach to the sculptures under discussion. This form of Avalokiteśvara is thus described in the *Sādhanamālā*:

Taṁ sitaṁ rakta-varṇaṁ tu padmarāga-sama-dyutim
Pañca-Buddha-makuṭa-dharaṁ harṣeṇot phulla-locanam
Vāmato spardhayā nālaṁ dhṛtvā ṣoḍaśa-patrakam
Padmaṁ vikāśayantaṁ ca hṛdi dakṣiṇa-pāṇinā
Mayūropari madhyasthe niṣaṇṇaṁ candra-maṇḍale
Sattvaparyaṅkam ābhujya sa-śṛṅgāra-rasotsavam
Caityāntastha-mahākarma-kūṭāgāra-vihāriṇam
Bhāvayed Vajradharmāgryaṁ nityaṁ bodhiṁ avāpnuyāt[1]

(The worshipper) should meditate on that supreme Vajradharma, who is of reddish white complexion, who has the brilliance of the *padmarāga* gem, who holds on his crown the five Buddhas, whose eyes beam with delight, who, while proudlyholding in his left hand a lotus-stalk, causes a sixteen-petalled lotus to bloom on his chest with his right hand, who is seated in the centre of alunar orb on a peacock while enjoying his animal-seat, who is festive with amorous sentiment and who lives in the sanctum inside a *caitya,* where great performances take place. (The worshipper meditating this form) obtains the *bodhi* eternally.'

The Sanchi sculptures agree in almost all the details with the above description of Vajradharma Lokeśvara, except that the right hand is in *varada*[2] and is not placed on the breast in the attitude of causing a lotus to blossom.[3] The *dhyāna* does not specifythe *āsana* of the deity but the *lalitāsana* of the sculptures is not unbecoming a

1. *Sādhanamālā,* ed. B. Bhattacharyya, I (Gaekwad's Oriental Series, XXVI, Baroda, 1925), p. 33.
2. Of the two illustrations give by B. Bhattacharyya inhis *Indian Buddhist Iconography,* one (pl. XXIV e.), taken from the paintings of the modern Nepalese artists, has a manuscript in his right hand, while the other (pl. XLVIII), as found on the wooden panels of the Macchandar Vahal *vihāra* at Kathmandu, shows his right hand in *abhaya-mudrā*, pp. 51 and 180.
3. The half-blown lotus inthe left hand of the sculptures may possibly signify the 'causing of a lotus to bloom.' In the analogous case of Tārā as the attendant of Khasarpaṇa, the *sādhanas* say that she should cause to bloom a stalked lotus with her right hand (*sanālaṁ utpalaṁ dakṣiṇakareṇa vikāśayantī*), Bhattacharyya, *ibid*, p. 37, but often in sculptures she holds a half-blown lotus in her left hand, the empty right hand being in some *mudrā* (cf. *ibid.,* pl. XXI).

Plate 17

Bodhisattva-images from Sanchi
Vajradharma Lokeśvara (?), Temple 45,
Sanchi, ht. 2' 4"

Plate 18

Vajradharma Lokeśvara (?), Sanchi Museum,
ht. 2' 3¾"

god 'who is festive with amorous sentiment,' with which is also consistent the rich ornamentation of the sculptures. As the crown along with the head is broken in both the images we cannot be sure whether it bore the effigies of the five Dhyāni Buddhas, as enjoined in the *sādhana* of Vajradharma Lokeśvara.

It may be noted, however, that the images of Vajradharma Lokeśvara, truly answering to the description in the *Sādhanamālā*, are not unknown. In the gallery of the Indian Museum is exhibited an image (pl. III)[1] of the deity, hailing from Bihar. Richly bejewelled he is seated in *paryaṅkāsana* on a *viśvapadma* (double-petalled lotus) resting on a throne supported by a pair of peacocks; he opens against his breast petals of a lotus, the stalk of which is held by his left hand. On his *karaṇḍa-makuṭa* are shown five Dhyāni Buddhas in three rows of three, one and one each respectively. The oval halo is inscribed with the Buddhist creed and a donative record in characters of *circa* tenth century. In front of the throne is a dwarfish fierce-looking figure with bristling flame-like hair in *pratyālīḍha* attitude; with his right hand he brandishes a mace (*mudgara*), while his left hand is shown against his breast with the index finger raised and holding a noose (*tarjanīpāśa-hṛdayastha vāmakaraṁ*). This figure may stand for Kṛṣṇayamāri as described in one of the *sādhanas* quoted by B. Bhattacharyya in his *Indian Buddhist Iconography,* p. 71. The description tallies in most of the details with it except in the matter of the buffalo-mount which is absent here. A second representation of the deity (pl. IV) exists in the reserved collection of the said museum.[2] The main deity seated on a *viśvapadma* supported by a pair of peacocks is remarkably similar to the preceding, but here he is flanked by two goddesses seated in the same *āsana*, the left one of whom holds *vajraghaṇṭās* in her both hands. She may be described as the goddess Vajraghaṇṭā, one of the four 'guardians of the gates' associated with such Vajrayāna deities as Lokanātha and Vajratārā. The *sādhanas* describe her as one-faced and two-armed carrying a bell surmounted by *vajra*. The attributes in the hands of the right hand goddess are broken. Above these goddesses are the representations of a *viśvavajra* and *ratna*(?) on a stand. On the pedestal is a three-headed six-armed dwarfish deity with terrible appearance, open mouths and bare fangs in *ālīḍha* attitude; in his right hand he

1. No. 3784. The photograph has been reproduced on pl. IX (a) of R.D. Banerji's *Eastern Indian School of Mediaeval Sculpture*. There it is labelled as Vajrapāṇi.
2. No. 3798. Both these sculptures are noticed in T. Bloch's *Supplementary Catalogue of the Archaeological Collection of the Indian Museum,* pp. 61-62 where they are described as Padmapāṇi.

carries a sword, a mace and a *padma*; of his left hands, one holds a *pāśa*, the second broken and the third is in *kaṭihasta* pose. This deity may stand for another variety of Kṛṣṇayamāri as described in the *Sādhanamālā*.[1] The absence of mounts in both the forms of Kṛṣ ṇayamāri, as represented in the pedestal of the two Vajradharma Lokeśvara images, may be due to their being attendant deities. On two sides of this figure on the pedestal are two goddesses, the left one of whom standing in *ālīḍha* pose and holding a *kartṛ* and a *kapāla* is equally awe-inspiring and dwarfish, corresponding in her iconographic details to Ekajaṭā; the right one holding a rosary and a *kamaṇḍalu*(?) stands in *pratyālīḍha* attitude. The sculpture, dating from *circa* tenth century, comes from Nalanda.

1. *Indian Buddhist Iconography,* pp. 72-73.

Plate 19

Vajradharma Lokeśvara, Indian Museum
(No. 3784), ht. 1' 10"

Plate 20

Vajradharma Lokeśvara, Indian Museum
(No. 3798), ht. 1' 8"

Chapter - 27
The Jaina References in the Buddhist Literature

Kamta Prasad Jain

The Buddhist literature contains many important and useful references to Janisim, some of which are as follows:

Let us examine first the *Dīgha Nikāya (Dialogues of Buddha*— S.B.B.). In its Kassapa Sīhanāda Sutta a set of ascetic practices is given and it is said about it that the practices give are "accounted in the opinion of some Samanas and Brāhmaṇas, as Samanaship and Brāhmaṇaship." Rhys Davids ascribes them to the Ājīvika recluses. A similar list of ascetic practices is also given in the *Majjhima Nikāya* as 36 and Prof. H. Jacobi thinks them to be the usages of the Acelaka recluses whom he recognises as the followers of Makkhali Gosāla and his two predecessors (*Jaina Sūtras,* II, xxxi). But now it is a known fact that the followers of Makkhali Gosāla were stylted Ājīvikas and those of Pūraṇa Kassapa Acelakas (*ERE.,* vol. I). Most probably the word 'Acelaka' was used at that time in a general sense in the same way as the word 'Śramaṇa', because we find the Jaina recluses mentioned as 'Acelakas' in the Buddhist literature (e.g. Pāṭika Sutta, *D.N.* Acela Pāṭ-ikaputta was a Jaina). The Jaina recluses styled themselves with this epithet in the Jaina Śāstras, as we shall see below. Consequently the above-mentioned ascetic practices could not be ascribed to the Acelakas, for they were not the followers of Makkhali Gosāla or of any other teacher. We can however take them as those of the Jaina recluses, because the Jainas are known in their Śāstras by the epithet 'Acelaka' and because the above practices coincide with those given for them in their Śāstras. In this event these practices could hardly be assigned to the Ājīvikas. Obviously in doing so, there remains another difficulty as well, namely that the Ājīvikas of Buddha's time were not all strict vegetarians. (See *Jātakas,* I, p. 390 and *Jaina Sūtras*, II, p. 409); and the ascetic practices referred to above put forth vegetarianism to be practised by its adherents. Hence it seems improbable that they can be ascribed to the Ājīvikas. Probably they have been intended for the Nigganṭha samanas (Jaina monks) of Buddha's time. A comparative treatment of them along with the rules of Jaina Muṇis as given in the Jaina Śāstras will convince the reader that they are really meant for the Jaina Muṇis.

Now the very first practice given in the above mentioned list of the Buddhist Sutta is: "He goes naked." Of course today there is a dissension in the Jaina church on this point. The Diagambaras agree while the Śvetāmbaras raise their voice against it. But leaving the apparent dissension aside, we come straight to the respective Canons of both the sects. For the Digambars it is no matter of disagreement. Their earliest authority can be cited in its support. Kundakundācārya of the first century A.D. descsribes it as an esssential duty of the Jaina recluse (See *Pravacanasāra,* pt. III). Another reliable authority is that of the *Mūlācāra* of Ācārya Baṭṭakera. He, too, describes this practice as one out of the 28 root-characteristics or essential duties (Mūla Guṇas) of a Jaina Muṇi and describes it in the following way:—

"Vatthājiṇavakkṇa ya ahavā pattāiṇā asaṃvaraṇaṃ,

Ṇibbhūsaṇaṃ ṇigganṭhaṃ accelakkaṃ jagadi pūjjaṃ." 30.

"A bodily state, void of all garments of hemp and hair, of grass, bark, and leaves and clear of every ornament and covering of decency, i.e.a stark naked state and the heart free from every knot of anger, deceit, etc. is said to be the worshippable Acelaka-ship or nakedness." In the Śvetāmbara Canons, we find also the nakedness to the feature of a Jaina recluse. In the eighth chapter of their *Ācārāṅga Sūtra*, it is styled the 'highest state' of a recluse (*Jaina Sūtras,* I, p. 56).

A naked sādhu is called "Jinakalpī" in the '*Pravacanasāroddhāra Prakaraṇa-ratnākara*' (Bhimsingh Manekji's edition, p. 134). But this division of Jaina Muṇis into Jinakalpī and Sthavira-kalpī seems not to have been expressed clearly in their older and authentic books, Aṅgas, etc. So it is open to doubt whether it was raised in a later and more self-conscious period. In their *Ācārāṅga Sūtra* there is given a course of practices for attaining the status of a Jaina Muṇi, somewhat similar to that of Digambara Śāstras. The author of the *Ācārāṅga Sūtra* first describes the highest order of nakedness; then passing on to various other rules, he comes again to the attire of a Jaina Muṇi. Here he describes a gradual mode of renunciation for a would-be Jaina Muṇi. Naturally it is not at all possible that a householder would adopt the naked state of a Jaina Muṇi all on a sudden. The summit could be reached by gradual steps only. Hence the Śvetāmbara author, tooo, first allows a novice, "aspiring to freedom from bonds," to keep on three clothes only (see *Jaina Sūtra*, pt. I, p.

69). Then he exhorts him gradually to keep on two clothes and then one or none (*Ibid.*, p. 71). Now it is quite clear here that the Śvetāmbara author tries to alter a gradual course to suit his conceptions; otherwise he would have prescribed nakedness as the last compulsory rule. In their '*Uttarādhyayanasūtra*' a clear evidence of the kind is discernible, for we find in it its sixth and seventh chapters styled "khuḍḍagāniyaṇthijjaṃ" (kṣullaka-nirgraṇthīyam) and "Ailayaṃ" (Aialaṃ) respectively, though the interpretation of these is not the same there as accepted by the Digambaras. Still it is enough to infer that the writer of this Śvetāmbara Sūtra was quite aware of the older form and meaning of these two words, which are found in the Digambara Śāstras in their original form and meaning as we shall see below. Hence it is safe to assume that the attire of the Jain Muṇis originally was a naked state of nature. The Buddhist [*Divyāvadāna,* p. 165; *Jātaka Mālā* (S.B.B.), vol. I, p. 145; *Dhammapadaṭṭhakathā* (PTS.), Visākhāvatthu, vol. I, pt. II, p. 384; *Dialogues of Buddha,* iii, 14; *Mahāvagga*, 8, 1; 5, 3; 1, 38, 16; *Cullavagga,* 8, 28, 3,; *Saṃyutta Nikāya* 2, 3, 10, 7, and *Dhammapada,* p. 3] and Brāhamaṇical (*Ṛgveda,* x, 136; *Varāhaminhira-Saṃhitā*, 19-61, 45-58; *Mahābhārata* 3, 26-27, *Rāmāyaṇa,* Bālakāṇḍa, Bhūṣaṇa Ṭīkā, 14-22) evidences too support the view of the Digambara Jaina Śāstras in as much as the apparent attire of a Jaina Muṇi is being upheld by them as nakedness. The Digambara Śāstras describe the preparatory course of renunication thus: A would-be Muṇi (Udāsīna Śrāvaka) in the preliminary stages of development keeps on at first three clothes; and as he makes progress on the path he diminishes his wants and keeps only two and then one garment only, i.e. loin-cloth. The latter are called the 'śrāvakas of the highest stage' (Uttama Śrāvaka), and they are also known as Kṣullaka and Ailaka. In the Buddhist literature, we have the mention of these śrāvakas in thier similar synonyms as the Digambaras say, i.e. "Eka-vastradhārin" and "white-clothed" ones (*Ind. Ant.*, 43). A later Buddhist commentator, Buddhaghoṣa, styles them "Muṇḍa Sāvakas" (Udāsīa śrāvaka), "Niggaṇṭhas" (Uttama śrāvaka) and "Better Nigaṇṭhas" (Naked Muṇi) *(Dial. of Buddha,* S.B.B., Intro. and Fausböll's *Dhammapada*, p. 398). I should here point out that the word "?Niggaṇṭ-ha" is not used always in the Buddhist literature in the sense of a Jaina Muṇi. At times we find it used even for a vowless Jaina householder (see my book "Buddha and Mahāvīra"). It seems that it was used at the time of Buddha in the same sense as the word "Jaina" is being used nowadays and the "Arhat was used for the Jainas during mediæval times. Along with the Buddhist literature, the mention of the Jaina Muṇi in the Brāhmaṇical literature, too, is in the shape of 'vivasana,' 'dig-vāsa,' etc (see "Vīra" vol. II) which aslo supports our view that the ancient attire of the Jaina Muṇis was nakedness, as is still adhered to by the Muṇis of the Digambara sect of the Jainas.

Thus we find that in both the sects of the Jaina, nakedness, which was the ancient attire of Jaina Muṇis, is accepted as an object of worship for the laity and as an essential mark of the Samanaship, though, of course, the Śvetāmbara school has now altered it to fit its own conceptions; but in the ealiest portion of thier *Ācārāṅga Sūtra* it is highly spoken of in its old sense. In this way, we find that the first rule of the Buddhist book referred to coincides with that of the Jaina Muṇis.

In the similar way, the rest of the practices can be traced in the daily routine of a Jaina Muṇi:

Buddhist	Jaina
2. He is of loose habits (performing his bodily functions and eating in a standing posture, not crouching down as well-bred people do).	2. This constitutes the 24th (non-bathing), 26th (non-brushing of teeth) and 27th (taking meal in a standing posture) Mūlaguṇas of a Jaina muṇi. See Mūlācāra 31-33.
3. Hew licks his hands clean, etc. (after eating; and not washing them as well-bred people do).	3. It is known that a Jaina Muṇi takes food in the hollows of his hands and takes the food thus placed without taking it into morsels and turning it from jaw to jaw (see also *Jaina Sūtra*, I, 57). The Buddhist author seems to point here to this practice.
4. (When on his round for amls if politely requested to step aside etc.), he passes steadily on...	4. It is described in full in the commentary on Eṣaṇā Samiti in Mūlācāra viz. 'Bhikṣāvelāyāṃ jñātvā praśānte dhūmamuśalādi-śabde gocaraṃ praviśen muniḥ tatra gacchann atidrutam, na mandam, na vilambitaṃ gacchet. 121.
5. He rufuses to accept food brought (to him, before he has started on his daily round of alms).	5. In Eṣaṇā Samiti the recluse is allowed to take only pure food void of 46 doṣas (defilements) and in procuring it he will not have

	concern of mind, speech and body. It must not be specially prepared for him. So he accepts not food brought to him (*M. Gāthā* 13).
6. He refuses...food (if told it has been specially prepared for him).	6. In it, too, as Kārita and Anumodanā doṣas are apparent, it is Auddeśika food.
7. He refuses to accept any invitation, etc.	7. The same is the case here.
8. He will not accept (food taken) from the mouth of the pot or pan, etc.	8. It is Sthāpita or Nyasta doṣa
9. (He will) not (accept) food within the threshold, etc.	9-10. These are Prāduṣkāra doṣa.
10. He will not (accept food) placed within the sticks, etc.	
11. (He will) not (accept food) placed within the pestle, etc.	11. It is the Unmiśra Aśana doṣa.
12. When two persons are eating together he will not accept..........if offered to him by only one of the two.	12. It is Anīśvara Vyaktāvyakta Anīśārtha Doṣa.
13. He will not accept food from a woman suckling baby etc.	13-14. These are described among the 35 Dāyaka Aśana doṣas.
14. He will not accept food from a woman talking with, etc.	
15. He will not accept food collected...in drought.	15. It is Abhighāta-Udgamadoṣa.
16. He willl not accept food where a dog is standing.	16. It is Daśaka doṣa (see also Jaina-Sūtras).
17. He will not accept food where flies are swarming by.	17. Prāṇi-jantu-vadha doṣa.
18. He will not accept fish, nor meat, nor strong drink, nor intoxicants, etc.	18. It requires no corroboration" "Khīra-dahi-sappi-tela-guḍa-lavaṇāṇaṃ ca jam pariccayanam. Titta-kaṭu-kasāyaṃ vilamadhurarasāṇaṃ ca jam cayanam 155. Chattāri mahāviyaḍī ya honti navaṇīda-majja-maṃsa-madhū. Kankhāpassaṃgadappā-saṃjamakārīyo edāo. 156.

19. He is a "One-houser" etc.	19. It is the Vrataparisaṅkhyātā Practice.
20. He takes food only once a day or once every two days, etc.	20. It is the Sākāṅkṣaṇākṣana Vrata.

Thus the very first reference in the Buddhist book to the Jainas is of great importance and it gives a more reliable and accurate evidence about the very vexed question of the Jaina Church *i.e.* the attire of ancient Jaina Muṇis. It makes it clear that it was "Digambara" or "Acelaka."

The next reference noteworthy in the aforementioned Buddhist book is to the 'Cātuyāma Saṃvara' of Jaina Muṇis. It is described in the following way in the Sāmaññaphala Sutta:

"A Nigantha, O king, is restrined with a fourfold self-restraint. He lives restrained as regards all water; restrained as regards all evil; all evil has he washed away; and he lives suffused with the sense of evil held at bay. Such is the fourfold restraint. And since he is thus tied with this fourfold bond, therefore is he, the Nigantho (free from bonds), called Gatatto (whose heart has gone, that is to the summit, to the attainment of his aim), Yatatto (whose heart is kept down i.e. is under command."

Commenting on this the learned translator remarks that "the series of riddles in this difficult passage is probably intended to be an *ironical imitation of the Nigaṇṭha's way of talking*." Gogerly has caught the general sense fairly enough, but his version is very free, and wrong as to two of the words, and it gives no idea of the oracular form in which the original is couched. Burnouf's rendering is quite wide of the mark. The first of the 'Four Restraints' is a well-known rule of the Jainas, not to drink cold water on the ground that there are 'souls' in it (see the discussion in the *Milinda Pañha*, II, 85-91). Professor Jacobi (*Jaina Sūtras,* II, xxiii) thinks "the 'Four Restraints' are intended to represent the four vows kept by the followers of Pārśva. But this surely canot be so, for these vows were quite different."

So let us see, what did the Buddhist authors mean by this 'Fourfold Restraint'. We know that the advantages of the life of a Jaina Muṇi are discussed herein. Hence it has concern with the mode of their life. Knowing this we should explore, if any corresponding assertion is traceable in this connection in the Jaina śāstras. Fortunately we easily find such a passage in the *Ratnakarṇḍaka* of Śrī Samantabhadra Svāmī of the 2nd or 3rd century A.D. He defines a Jaina recluse thus:

"Viṣayāśāvaśātīto nirārambho 'parigrahaḥ,
Jñānadhyānataporatnas tapasvī sa praśasyate" 10.

Herin, too, the fourfold characteristics of a Jaina recluses are given. He should be void of all passion and desires (viṣayeṣu-sragvanitādiṣv āśā ākāṅkṣā tasyā vaśam vaśam adhīnatā, tadatīto viṣ-ayākāṅkṣārahitaḥ), should keep himself aloof from all kinds of traffic ('nirārambhaḥ' parityaktakṛṣyādivyāpāraḥ), should wipe off all 'parigrahas' ('aparigraho bāhyābhyantara-parigraharahitaḥ) and remain absorbed in knowledge and meditation of Self. ('jñānadhyānataporatanaḥ' jñānadhyānatapāṃsy eva ratnāni yasya etadguṇaviśiṣṭo yaḥ sa tapasvī guruḥ 'praśasyate ślāghyāte). Comparing this with the fourfold restraint described in the Buddhist book, of course, we find no particular difference whatsoever. The Buddhist author at the outset says that 'he lives restrained as regards all water.' Now if your take its true sense, it means that a Jaina Muṇi keeps himself quite aloof from every kind of traffic. He could not himself take even the water for his use, which is a very essential thing for the upkeep of our daily life. This could be said in other words that a Jaina Muṇi is quite 'Nirārambhī.' Here perhaps, it might be objected that the Buddhist author has not described this in clear words and as such it is doubtful to take his meaning in the above way. But I would explain this reason of writing in a riddle form, i.e., the Buddhist author meant to imitate the Tīrthaṅkara's way of talking (Divya Dhvani) in an ironical fashion; and hence he is scarcely quite clear. This points to the Jaina belief that a Tīrthaṅkara's speech is understood by all, because one 'Māgadha Deva' interprets it in such a way that every creature present at the auspicious occasion easily grasps its meaning. Besides it that the restraint of water is really intended to point the 'Nirārambha' condition of a Jaina Muṇi is apparent from the fact that taking water for use is a work of a householder, who does not observe the Ahiṃsā vow in full. Svāmī Baṭṭakera confirms this view, while describing the 'Piṇḍasuddhit' or observances in connection with food. In the gāthā "Adhakammuddesiya adhovajheya etc." the Ācārya first makes this clear that the Udagama doṣas are concerned with "Adhahakarma" i.e. activities of a layman in arranging for pulling oneself on as a true householder. Hence this 'adhahakarma' has connection with the layman only. The Muṇi will have nothing to do with his doings, because it is said that in exerting after the worldly business or in procuring water, food, etc. the six kinds of living organs are destroyed. And a Jaina Muṇi is under vow that he will never cause hurt to any living being by mind, speech and body. So the Adhahakarma i.e. acquiring and ar-ranging food, water etc. rests entirely on an Asaṃyamī (vowless) host. The Saṃyamī (Muṇi) would have no concern with it. Consequently by referring to the restraint of water, the Buddhist author did mean nothing but the 'Nirārambha' condition of the Jaina Muṇi, as is denoted in the above Jaina śloka as a characteristic of a Jaina Muṇi.

Next to it, the Buddhist author says that "He (Jaina Muṇi) lives restrained as regards all evil.' This restraint is quite in agreement with the first assertion of Śrī Samantabhadra, that the Jaina Muṇi is void of passions and desires, which are the sole causes of sin. Hence he lives restrained as regards all evil. Further on, the Buddhist author says that the Jaina Muṇi has washed away all evil. Being void of all sins, all evil he would naturally wash away. The third mark of distinction in the above Jaina śloka is of the same meaning; i.e. 'Aparigrahs.' Outer and inner, both kinds of Parigraha, has he washed away. Outer 'Parigraha' is nothing but clothes, house, money, relations, etc.; and the worldly cravings, infatuations, passions, etc. are the inner 'Parigrahas'. These both a Jaina Muṇi keeps away from him. Lastly the Buddhist author says that 'He lives suffused with the sense of evil held at bay.' Similar is the last assertion of the Jaina Ācārya with regard to the mode of life of a Jaina Muṇi. He says, the Jaina Muṇi remains absorbed in the knowledge and meditation of Self, which means, in other words, that he is self-suffused and no evil can touch him. In this wasy we find the explanation of the 'Catyyāma Saṃvara' of a Jaina Muṇi; and the meaning of this difficult passage of the Buddhist book is quite clear from it. This surely does not refer to the four vows of Pārśva.

If there remains anything in this connection then it is but the words 'Gatatto,' 'Yatatto' and 'Thitatto.' Of course the identical synonyms for them have not come to any notice so far in the Jaina Śāstras, but the meaning of them could be traced in the Jaina Śāstras.[1]

The following assertions of the *Iṣṭopadeśa* of Śrī Pūjya Pāda also denote the same fact:—

Abhavac cittavikṣepa ekānte tattvasaṃsthitiḥ.
Abhysyed abhiyogena yogī tattvaṃ nijātmanaḥ 26.

"He in whose mind no disturbances occur and who is established in the knowledge of the self such an ascetic should enagage himself diligently in the contemplation of his soul, in a lonely place."

Bruvann api hi na vrūte gacchann api na gacchati,
Sthirīkṛtātmatattvas tu paśyann api na paśyati. 41
Kim idaṃ kīdṛśaṃ kasya kasmāt kvety aviśeṣayan,
Svadeham api nāvaiti yogī yogaparāyaṇaī. 42 *Ibid*.

"He who has firmly established himself in the knowledge of the self such a one does not speak while speaking, does not move while moving and does not see while seeing. The ascetics immersed in the

1. See the *Pravancanāsāra* (5, 6, 42) of Śrī Kundākunda Ācārya of the 1st century A.D.

process of self-realisation has no awareness of even his body, being undisturbed by questions such as what is the soul? What is its nature? Who is its master? From whom is it derived? Where does it reside? and the like.—(Discourse Divine).

From these it is clear that the meaning of the words used by the Buddhist author are traceable in the Jaina Śāstras. And it is most probable that the Jaina Muṇis were known by these special epithets at that time.

The next reference in the '*Dialogues*', to which I would draw the attention of the reader is the ancient view of a soul in the form of 'Eternalists.' The Buddhist author there expresses the ancient view of the soul. He says that there are sophists who, having recollection of the previous births and dwelling places, etc. declare the etenity of the soul. These he divides into three according to the degree of recollection of previous births. The fourth group of upholders of this very view about the eternity of the soul are said to have reached to this belief by argumentations. All these four kinds of sophists are described to hold that the soul is eternal and the world is giving birth to nothing new, is steadfast as a mountain peak, as a pillar firmly fixed; and these living creatures though they transmigrate and pass away, fall from one state of existence and spring up in another, yet they are for ever and ever. Now though in connection with these beliefs the Buddhist author has not named the particular sect yet looking at the obvious similarities, I believe that they refer to the Samanas of Lord Pārśva's Tīrtha. In the Jaina Purāṇas we find this exact narration of knowing the past lives and upholding the eternity of the soul and the world. Really the Buddhisst author condemns these theories but he has not been successful in his aim, because the above assertion clearly shows that though souls transmigrate yet they remain the same all round, *i.e.* it points to the Niśçaya (Real) and Vyavahāra (Material) point of view of Jainism which the Buddhist author has failed to discriminate.

Fortunately it coincides with the Jaina narration further on and the Jaina Śāstras describe the Jaina Munis of Pārśva's Tīrtha of different capacities.[1]

Amongst them Kevalajñānī, Śrutajñānī, Avadhijñānī and Vādī should be compared with those mentioned by the Buddhist author. These Munis really confirm their conceptions of the soul and the world in the same way as described in the above mentioned Buddhist passage. A similar list of the followers of Śrī Pārśva is, also, given in the Kalpasūtra.[2] This it seems hold with much accuracy that the Samanas

1. See *Uttara Purāṇa,* 149ff.
2. *Jaina Sūtras,* pt. I.

referred to here who upheld their philosophical speculations in the above way, were Jaina Muṇis of Śrī Pārśva's Tīrtha.

It is also noteworthy that these references of the authentic Buddhist book of old prove the credibility and authenticity of the Digambara Jaina Śāstras further on than hitherto accepted. From these we, also, see that the Jaina conceptions were the same even near Lord Mahāvīra's predecessor Śrī Pārśva.

Chapter - 28
Buddhist Education in Pāli and Sanskrit Schools

E.J. Thomas

The subject of Buddhist education is bound up with several still unsolved problems, but it is possible to limit the subject by marking off some of those questions on which scholars are still much divided. One of these problems is the question of the locality or localities where those schools arose that established different forms of the writings held to be the word of Buddha. The mot accessible of the works of these schools are the Pāli Canon, and Sanskrit works wihc contain Mahāyāna works as well as works of Hīnayāna schools closely related to the Pāli tradition.

There is an article on Buddhist education Hastings' *Encyclopaedia of Religion and Ethics,* but for the earlier period it confines itself entirely to the reports of the Chinese pilgrims, that is to say, it si entirely silent about the thousand years after the death of Buddha, during which all the various forms of the Canon had become fixed, and when the education and instruction described by the Chinese pilgrims had been established for centuries. Yet there is considerable evidence both external and internal to show what the educational methods were.

We do not need to ask how much the earliest Buddhism borrowed from other schools. Windisch's article on Brahmin influence on Buddhism shows how little is really known about the actual movements in the earliest period.[1] Windisch points out that brahmins who entered the Order would bring their knowledge and literary practices with them. Our present question is what this knowledge and literary practice was after it had become assimilated and established in Buddhist institutions.

---

1. In *Aufsätse E. Kuhn gewidmet,* München, 1916.

Besides the Pāli Canon a considerable body of literature in Sanskrit of several schools is known. Most of it has been described in the catalogues of Rajendralal Mitra[1] and Bendall,[2] and the most important parts have been published. Works that survive only in Tibetan and Chinese are also now becoming more accessible. The earliest stage of literary activity may be called that of systematisation. It must be mentioned here, that current views as to its significance are too divergent to make it possible to say anything that may claim to be final.

There is a view still current in the West, which supposes that the orthodox Buddhist holds the Scriptures to exist now in the form in which they were uttered by Buddha, and as recited at the first Council. The Buddhist accounts of the Councils may not harmonise with the demands of modern historical criticism, but they contain nothing so unhistorical as that. Buddhaghosa knew as well as we do that the Canon contains much that is not the direct word of Buddha. He expressly refers to that which was recited and that which was not recited at the first Council.[3] Throughout the commentaries we find notes on passages that are said to have been added by one of the Councils. Not only have we Suttas that are said to have been given by disciples after the death of Buddha, but Buddhaghosa quotes a verse which says that out of 84,000 suttas 2,000 were uttered by bhikkhus.[4] The whole of the *Niddesa* is attributed by the commentator thereon to Sāriputta.[5]

On the other hand there has often been a less excusable uncritical attitude among Western scholars, against which Mrs. Rhys Davids has recently made a vigorous protest.

"When believers in the East and historians in the West will come up out of the traditional attitude, when we shall not hear church-editing called Buddhavacanaṃ *and thought of as Gotama-vacanaṃ*—when we shall no more read: "The Buddha laid down this and denied that,' but 'the Buddhist church did so'—then we shall at last be fit to try to pull down super-structure and seek for the man."[6]

1. *Sanskrit Buddhist Literature of Nepal,* Calcutta, 1882.
2. *Catalogue of the Buddhist Sanskrit Manuscripts in the University Library, Cambridge*. Cambridge, 1883.
3. Vin. Com., i. 18.
4. Ib., i, 29.
5. The commentator on Th. I, 527 quotes Nd. I, 143 (Bhāgī vā Bhagavā) and attributes it to Sāriputta (Dhammasenāpati).
6. Majjhima Index, p. vi.

The fact of this editing, which is recognised both by Buddhist commentators and modern crities, implies a stage of literary activity, of which we know nothing as to actual details. Not only are there the variously classified compilations of the *Aṅguttara* and *Saṃyutta*, but the *Dīghal* and *Majjhima* show much elaboration also. The former is in three vaggas, and the first vagga, although it deals with such various subjects as the sixty-two heresies, caste, sacrifice, brahmin ritual, and miraculous powers, has been given an appearance of uniformity by the insertion in each sutta of the document known as the sīlas. The *Majjhima* is classified in much more detail and with more reference to the subject-matter in fifteen vaggas. The whole of the Pāli Canon in fact shows evidence of the sam careful classification.

What this stage of Buddhist study really implied cannot be properly answered until we known more about the corresponding arrangements of those forms of the Canon belonging to contemporary schools that are extent in the Chinese. Very divergent views are at present held, as by Prof. Keith and Prof. R.O. Franke.[1] There can be little doubt that the system of arrangement is earlier than the recording of the Canon in writing, and that the chief motive was to serve as a help to the memory. We find examples of commentary already incorporated in the suttas, but the first distinct evidence of material intended for definite instruction is found in the *Niddesa*. Much of the matter of this work is also found in Abhidharma works and in the verbal commentary of the Vinaya, and it will be convenient to take the *Niddesa* first.

As is well known this work is a commentary on the fourth and fifth sections of the *Sutta-nipāta*, together with a commentary of the same nature of the *Khaggarisāṇs sutta,* which is found in the first section. The matter of which it consists can be divided into three types:

(1) Portions of doctrinal commentary on important words in a style similar to the portions of commentary occasionally found in the suttas. The matter and often the language is drawn from the suttas, and in addition illustrative passages from the suttas are frequently quoted direct, and in the case of prose quotations regularly introduced by the words, *vuttaṃ pi h'etaṃ Bhagavatā*. Verse quotations, which sometimes appear to be non-canonical, are more frequently adduced without any mention of the source. In the case of verse 844, the

1. Keith, *Buddhist Philosophy*; Franke, *Introd.* to his translationof the *Dīgha*.

Niddesa simply adopts as its commentary a whole sutta from S. iii, 9, which consists of a commentary on that verse.

(2) Concise definitions of individual words, such as, *sappo vuccati ahi, āsanaṃ vuccati yattha nisīdanti.* The matter of this portion sometimes corresponds with such definitions in the verbal commentary of the Vinaya.

(3) It is in the third type that the most characteristic feature of the *Niddesa* is seen. This consists of lists of synonyms of the word commented on. Such lists are not used to explain the meaning of a word in a particular context. They are repeated in the same form wherever the word occurs, and were evidently intended to be learnt in the same way as the more modern kośa. In the case of the verbs the synonyms often consist of all the possible compounds of he same verb, *yutto, payutto, āyutto, samāyutto, sampayutto; vedhati, pavedhati, sampavedhati.* In the case of important words all the various synonyms. evidently drawn from the scriptures, are given in long lists. The result is that some of the synonyms are often unintelligible apart from the context in the sutta from which they are taken. In a long list of synonyms of *taṇhā* (Nd. I, 8) *sibbinī* 'sewer' occurs, and the reason for this is seen from A. iii, 399; Sn. 1040, where it is an epithet of *taṇhā*, and from where it has no doubt been taken. Among the synonyms of *sadā* (Nd. I, 18) occurs *avīci*. This is evidently due to analysing it as *a-vīci* 'without a wave,' and hence 'continuous.' *Vammīko* as one of the synonyms of *kāya* comes from the parable of the ant-hill in M. i, 142.

Much of this is also found in the Abhidhamma books, but in the *Niddesa* it is used as general matter applied to passages for which it was not immediately intended. Some of the correspondences are as follows: *chando* Nd. J. 2=Dhs. 1097, Vbh. 374; *tassa* Nd. I. 2=Vbh. 393; *mano, pīti*, Nd. I, 3=Dhs. 6, 9; *taṇhā* Nd. I. 8=Dhs. 1059; *sati* Nd. I, 10=Pug. 25; *macchariya* Nd. I, 37=Dhs. 1122, Pug. 19; *paññā* Nd. I, 44, 77=Pug. 25, Dhs. 16; *māyā* Nd. I, 79=Pug. 19; *gantha* Nd. I, 98=Dhs. 1135; *kodha* Nd. I, 215=*āghāta* Dhs. 1154, cf. Pug. 18; *sāṭheyya* Nd. I, 395=Pug. 19; *ṭhiti* Nd. I, 501=Dhs. 10.

Minor differences occur, and in some cases quite different treatment, cf. *puthujjana* Nd. I, 146 and Pug. 12. There is a triple division of *pucchā* Nd. 339 with no reference to the fourfold division of D. iii, 229, Dhs. Mahāvyut. 85.

The verbal commentary on the Vinaya is les developed than either the Niddesa or the Abhidhamma works. It is occupied with explaining words concisely, in a given context without lists of synonyms.

This shows a system for learning the vocabulary of the Canon, and for explaining archaic forms, but no further grammatical teaching occurs apart from the description of certain terms as particles. *Addhā ti ekaṃsavacanaṃ* (with seven other svnonms for *ekaṃsavacanam*); *nā ti paṭikkhepo*. Even such a sandhi as *iccāyasmā* is not resolved into *iti*, but *iccā* is separated and explained like all such particles as *padasandhi, padasaṃsaggo, padapāripūrī, akkharasamavāyo, vyañjana-siliṭṭhatā*.

In the *Niddesa* we thus have direct evidence of a general system of instruction applied to a definite work, consisting of interpretation, doctrinal teaching and in the verbal expositions the beginnings of grammar. The Abhidhamma books and related works like the *Paṭ isambhidāmagga* give other traces of its existence. It appears to be this system which is expressly referred to in the *Niddesa* (I, 234) and other places as the four kinds of analysis (*paṭisambhidā*): the analysis of meanings (*attha*), of conditions (*dhamma*), of grammatical analysis (*nirutti*), and clearness of insight (*paṭibhāna*).[1]

The *Nirutti* of the *Niddesa* is of the kind that we should expect to exist when Pāli was a living language. All the grammatical analysis that was required was a knowledge of those words in the Scriptures that had become obsolete, and the explanation of unusual grammatical forms by means of the current expression. The method was not confined to the Pāli tradition, as we find the same four divisions called *pratisaṃvida* in the *Mahāvastu* (iii. 321) and *pratisaṃvit* in the *Mahāvyutpatti* (13), and this *nirutti* method has reacted on the style of the later sūtras.

The practice of learning off strings of synonyms might be expected to influence the style of those who passed through such a course of instruction. We appear to find an instance of it when Buddhaghosa[2] thus describes an earthquake: *ayaṃ mahāpaṭhavī... kampi saṃkampi sampakampi sampavedhi*. Here we have the same

---

1. They are also found in a sutta (A. ii, 160) which is attributed like the *Niddesa* itself to Sāriputta. It probably belongs to the same stratum of scholarship. The Abhidhamma statement of *paṭisambhidā* in Vbh. ch. xi is discussed by Mrs. Rhys Davids in the *Points of Controversy*, pp. 377ff.; cf. Ps. i, 88.

2. Vin. com. I, 30.

series of compounds as we find repeatedly in the *Niddesa,* and Buddhaghosa is only using an earlier phraseology. It appears not only in the later commentators but also in Sanskrit and especially Mahāyāna works. In several of these a standing description of an earthquake occurs. The synonymous verbs *kamp- vidh- cal- kṣubh-* are given, followed by *raṇ* and *garj* and each is expanded into compounds with *pra* and *sampra.*[1] If this stood alone, it might be taken merely as the verbosity of a particular author, but there are other instances, and they often correspond with series of synonyms in the *Niddesa.* The *Niddesa* has *sakkaroti garukaroti māneti pūjeti.* The *Avadāna-śataka* p. 8 exactly corresponding has *satkṛto gurukṛto mānitaḥ pūjitaḥ.* The *Mahāvastu* has the same adding *arcitaḥ.* In Mahāyāna works this is expanded, being preceded by *puraskṛtaḥ* and followed by *arcitaḥ* and *apacayitaḥ* (Saddh-puṇḍ. 5; Karuṇāpuṇḍ. 2). Similarly the latter sūtra has the series *harṣaṇīya toṣaṇīya prasādanīya avalokanīya prahlādanīya manojña.* All the synonyms that we find need not have arisen from the method that we find in the *Niddesa.* Some of them were doubtless incorporated from old texts, but the practice of compiling such lists is certain from what we find in the *Niddesa,* and the correspondences in the lists makes it probable that there was intercourse between different schools and common methods of teaching.[2]

Among Mahāyāna works there are two compendiums which have some relation to the *Niddesa.* The *Dharmasaṃgraha* is a compilation of terms, but it is mainly doctrinal. The *Mahāvyutpatti* was evidently intended for grammatical instruction as well. It gives the complete declension of *vṛkṣa* (210), epithets of Buddha and Bodhisattvas and their qualities, synonyms of the teaching and names of sections (66), epithets of Nirvāṇa (95), terms of salutation (97), synonyms of *tuṣṭa* and *raudra* (145-6), synonyms of *sattva* (207) almost corresponding with Nd. I, 12, miscellaneous adjectives (223), a long list of all the stock words and phrases that occur in a sūtra (244), and a list of diseases (284), which only partially corresponds with that in Nd. I, 17. Much of this is *nirukti* in the sense of the Pāli *nirutti.*

At present there is no general agreement as to where the Pāli language as we know it developed. It is usually agreed that the oldest works in verse show traces of having been composed in a different

1. Lal. v. 449; Karuṇāpuṇḍ. 3; Mahāvyut. 151.
2. It may be noticed that the term *nirdeśa* is frequent in Mahāyāna sūtras.

dialect. The natural conclusion is that the canonical works were preserved in a monastery or closely related group of monasteries, where a different dialect was spoken, and where the original dialect of the texts was entirely effaced, except so far as metrical facts compelled the preservation of special forms. Doubtless this Pāli language that we know was at first a living and spoken language, but in the course of centuries, say from the time of Aśoka to the end of the second century A.D., it would come to be as much a learned language as Sanskrit. The fact of the Niddesa itself seems to show that this Pāli was then a current language, but that *nirutti*, grammatical analysis, was becoming necessary for the interpretation of the texts. Nothing profitable can be said about the earliest date at which the Niddesa may be put. Any such theory would only tell us that a work of that name existed, but the occurrence of a geographical term in any particular passage would only allow us to infer the date of that passage. We can see from its different forms and readings that it underwent changes and received additions, and in the case of a work used continuously for instruction this would be inevitable. Its application of Abhidhamma material for a general purpose seems to show that it is later than the Abhidhamma books, and its reference to one of the Alexandrias (Allasanda) founded after the Greek invasion, to Bengal, Burma, and Java, would suggest that it became established and was used as a text-book during the first two centuries B.C. It has no reference to the pāramitā, and although it gives the 37 constituents of enlightenment, it does not use the term *bodhipakkhika-dhammā*.

In the case of the literature of the Sanskrit schools we can draw further information concerning the materials and methods of education. The works are much later than the *Niddesa*. They refer frequently to writing, and the mention in the *Mahāvyutpatti* of Kaniṣka and Aśvaghoṣa puts this work later than the first century A.D., but it is probably two or three centuries later than this, as it contains evidence of contact with Greek astrology. The dates usually assigned to the chief texts range from the second to the seventh century. The four methods of analysis with *nirukti* are preserved, but we may infer from the fact that the language was Sanskrit and from the production of a kāvya like the *Buddhacarita* in the first century A.D. that grammar was a fully developed study.

Wherever the texts of this literature originated, we can at least assume from the accounts of the Chinese pilgrims that down to the seventh century Magadha was the chief district of their study.[1] Mr. J.N. Samaddar in his interesting account of the monasteries of Nālandā, Vikramaśīla (east of Bhagalpur) and Odandapura (Bihar) calls them universities, and draws several remarkable parallels with these modern institutions. The proposing of hard questions by the keeper of the gate at Nālandā becomes matriculation. The teaching is said to have been both tutorial and professorial. The Master of the Law is taken to be the Vice-Chancellor, and the writing up of the names of famous scholars over the gates is compared to the granting of diplomas.

This is what is inferred from Hiuen Tsiang, but it is I-tsing who describes the actual studies.[2] From Prof. Takakusu's account it appears that grammar was based entirely on works of brahminical schools, the Sūtras of Pāṇini, the Kāśikā of Jayāditya, the Mahābhāṣ ya of Patañjali, and three works by Bhartṛhari. It is not clear from this whether the Sūtras were those of Pāṇini in their original form, but Pāṇini was certainly known to the Buddhists.[3] He is mentioned in the Laṅkāvatāra-sūtra, and Tārānātha in his history tells a wonderful story of his acquirement of grammatical science. The chief form however in which the Pāṇinean grammar was studied by these schools appears to have been Candragomin's *Cāndravyākaraṇa*, which is put at the beginning of the seventh century. This is the only grammar which is mentioned in Bendall's list along with commentaries on it, chiefly that of Ānandadatta, and in the Tanjur the grammatical works as given by Csoma are either Candragomin's work or others still later.

The *Niddesa* also shows the beginnings of lexicography, and its continuation appears in the *Dharmasaṃgraha* and *Mahāvyutpatti*. Its full development is seen in the *Amara-kośa* of Amarasiṃha, who

1. The vihāra of Vikramaśīla is mentioned in the colophon of one Ms. (Mitra, p. 229), and according to Mr. Samaddar Nālandā occurs (*Glories of Magadha*, p. 104ff.).
2. Ch. 34. ed. Takakusu.
3. Dr. B.C. Law has pointed out in Buddhaghoṣa a passage reminscent of Pāṇini, V. 2, 93. It may be asked whether this comes directly from Pāṇini or from some adaptation, but it certainly corresponds much more closely with Pāṇini than with the corresponding sūtra and vṛtti of Candragomin, IV. 2, 97. The Pāli grammar of Kaccāyana is later than Buddhaghoṣa and belongs to the literature of Ceylon. Later works, says Geiger, follow the models of Sanskrit grammar and lexicography slavishly, and apply their system mechanically to Pāli. Geiger, *Pāli Lit. und Sprache*; Franke, *Gesch. und. Krit. der einheim. Pāli-grammatik.*

was a Buddhist himself. It is not mentioned by I-tsing, and Winternitz puts it between the sixth and eight centuries. There are several copies of it in Bendall's list, and it is also in the Tanjur.

Apart from philosophy, which formed part of the doctrinal teaching, two important secular subjects are medicine and astronomy. That medicine must have been studied early we know from the Vinaya, as the sixth chapter of the Mahāvagga is devoted to medicines and surgery. I-tsing mentions cikitsā-vidyā, but there is nothing in the surviving literature to indicate that it ever became an independent study. He does not mention jyotiṣa among the vidyāṣ, and it is clear that as astrology was an integral part of astronomy and the chief motive of its study, the latter science could not be expected to flourish so long as Buddhism forbade interpretation of the stars (e.g. Sn. 927 and Nd. I, 381).[1] It came in when the practice of astrology revived. The only astronomical work mentioned in Mitra's list is a ṭīkā on the Jain work *Sūryaprajñapti*. Among the Buddhist fragments from Central Asia edited by Hoernle is an astrological work which shows that it is based on Greek astrology, and that Buddhism had come to adopt astrological practices. There is also evidence of Greek influence in the list of the nine planets in *Mahāvyut*. 164. The first seven of them beginning with Āditya are in the order of the days of the week, and this order, which depends on an elaborate assignment of a planet to each of the 24 hours of the day, came from Greece.[2]

It is certain that the monasteries of Magadha were the chief places where this Sanskrit literature was studied, and probably also the region of its origin. It represents the product of several schools and shows certain relations with Pāli works. But the views of scholars concerning the district where Pāli, as we know it, originated are so divergent that it is impossible to do more than draw attention to a problem still in need of solution. It is the question not of the original language of Buddha and his first disciples, but of the Pāli of Ceylon. The Pāli of the time of Buddhaghosa was no living language, except in so far as it may have been learnt and used within each monastery.

---

1. The knowledge of astronomy among the Buddhists has been treated in the writer's article *Sun, Moon, and Stars* (*Buddhist*) in Hastings' *Ency. of Rel. and Ethics*.
2. The Ptolemaic order of the planets is Saturn, Jupiter, Mars, Sun, Venus, Mercury, Moon. The lord of the first hour of Sunday is the Sun, of the second hour Venus, and so on. This makes the Moon the lord of the first hour of Monday, and so on throughout the week.

The commentaries of that time were translations and adaptations in Pāli of those already existing in Singhalese. The traces of an earlier dialect surviving in the Canon may be survivals of the dialect in which it existed when it was taken to Ceylon. But it is the Pāli as used by Buddhaghosa which the Singhalese tradition calls Māgadhī.[1] The view that Pāli really was the language of Magadha is generally rejected, and various attempts to fix the district in India where Pāli developed have been made on the assumption that it must have been somewhere else than Magadha.

Oldenberg sought it in SouthIndia, probably in the kingdoms of the Andhras or Kaliṅgas.[2] According to Prof. R.O. Franke its original home was in a district somewhere in the middle to the west of the Vindhya mountains. "Accordingly it is not impossible, though naturally a pure supposition, that the city of Ujjen, which evidently had become a centre of culture comparatively early, also formed the centre of the dialect-area of literary Pāli."[3] This was also the view of Westergaard and E. Kuhn, which Oldenberg expressly rejected. Sir George Grierson holds that "we have a strong reason for concluding that literary Pāli is the literary form of the Māgadhī language, the then *koine* of India, as it was spoken and as it was used as a medium of literary instruction in the Takṣaśilā University.[4] The conclusion of Rhys Davids was that "Buddhism born in Nepal, received the garb in which we now know it in Avanti, in the far West of India," and he held that this was nearer to the other view "so often put forward as convenient that Buddhism arose in Magadha and that its original tongue was Māgadhī."[5] These are the results of thirty years of research.

Geiger has taken the unpopular course of holding that the tradition of the Chronicles and commentaries is the true one, and that what they call Māgadhī is Māgadhī.[6] Oldenberg's statement that

1. Buddhaghosa was told to go and translate the Aṭṭhakathā into *Magadhānaṃ nirutti*, Mhvs. p. 251 (Turnour), quoted by Dr. B.C. Law, *The life and work of Buddhaghoṣa*, p. 75.
2. Vinaya, Introd., p. I.
3. Pāli und Sanskrit, p. 138. By literary Pāli Dr. Franke merely means the Pāli as generally understood. The reason is that he uses the general term Pāli to include the spoken Aryan languages of the whole of sub-Himalayan India and Ceylon; ib. p. vi. There is nothing to be said against the terminology except that it has not won general acceptance, and that scholars still call these languages Prakrit.
4. Commemorative Essays presented to Sir. R.G. Bhandarkar, p. 123.
5. Cambridge History of India, 1. 187.
6. Pali Litteratur und Sprache, p. 3.

"it is certain that the Pāli language is not the Māgadhī language," merely means that it is no the language of the Asokan inscriptions. There is not slightest reason why the texts of the Canon should have been adapted to the spoken language of the time of Aśoka. It is far more likely that the dialect of the texts had already begun to form a sacred language, and we know that there was a rule in the Vinaya saying that the monks were to learn the word of Buddha in its own grammar or dialect, *anujānāmi bhikkhave sakāya niruttiyā buddhavacanaṃ pariyāpuṇituṃ,* and Buddha-ghosa understands this as meaning in the Māgadhī language. It is true that this sentence has been understood against both grammar and tradition in a quite opposite sense, but this does not now need discussion.

The latest attempt to solve the question has been made by Dr. M. Walleser,[1] who also decids for Magadha, but it cannot be said that within the space of twenty-four pages he has done justice to the arguments of his predecessors. He further prejudices his own case by asserting that Pāli means not the body of sacred texts but the language in which they were composed. However, his evidence for the phrase *pāli-bhāṣā* rests merely on Childers, and ignores such decisive passages as that of the *Mahāvaṃsa* referred to above, and thus translated by Dr. B.C. Law: "The Pāli (text of the Tripiṭaka) only (*pālimattaṃ*) has been brought over here. The Ceylon commentary is current among the people of Ceylon. Please go there and study it, and then translate it into Māgadhī (*māgadhānaṃ niruttiyā parivattehi*)."[2] But Dr. Walleser has certainly made the claims of Magadha more probable, and it may be hoped that deeper investigation of the geographical question will lead to the establishing of further links in the history of Buddhist scholarship.

---

1. *Sprache und Heimat des Pāli-Kanons*. Heidelberg, 1924.
2. *Life and Work of Buddhaghoṣa*. p. 74.

Chapter - 29
Buddhist Evidence for the Early Existence of Drama

O.H. De A. Wijesekera

In his masterly survey of the evolution of the Sanskrit drama, Professor Berriedale Keith summarily disposes of the relevant Buddhist evidence with the unequivocal statement that "The extreme dubiety of the date of the Buddhist Suttas renders it impossible to come to any satisfactory decision regarding the existence of drama at an early date, while the terms employed, such as Visūkadassana, Nacca and Pekkhā, and reference to Samajjas leave us wholly without any ground for belief in an actual drama."[1] But a critical examination of the Pāli Nikāyas shows us that the evidence afforded by these collections of dialogues throws much more light on this obscure problem than may be implied in a cursory allusion to the occurrence of such terms as Visūkadassana etc., and, that the available facts establish, with an appreciable degree of certainty, for the beginnings of dramatic spectacles in Inia, if not for the Sanskrit drama in a primitive form, a date that anticipated the one assigned to it by Keith *at least by a century, if not more.*

Professor Keith bases his main argument for the conclusion that "......the Sanskrit drama came into being shortly after, if not before, the middle of the second century B.C.,"[2] on the criticism of Kātyāyana's rule regarding the use of the imperfect tense and the occurrence and import of the words Naṭa, Śobhanika (or Śaubhika) and Kathaka etc., as found in the *Mahābhāṣya* of Patañjali whom he places "with reasonable assurance" about 140 B.C.[3] For him, Indian literature before the time of Patañjali contains no positive evidence for the existence of drama even in aprimitive form. Referring to the

---

1. *Sanskrit Drama*, p. 43.
2. *Ibid.*, p. 45.
3. *Ibid.*, p. 31.

mention of 'Naṭasūtras' in Pāṇini (iv. 3. 110f.) whom he places in he fourth century B/.C., he remarks: "But we unfortunately are here as ever in no position to establish the meaning of Naṭa, which may mean no more than a pantomime."[1] It is regarded as significant that Naṭa does not occur in the *Yajurveda* list of "persons of every kind covering every possible sort of occupations." In the *Mahābhāṣya*, however, he sees more certain evidence: "We seem in fact to have in the *Mahābhāṣya* evidence of a stage in which all the elements of drama were present; we have acting in dumb show, if not with words also; we have recitations divided between two parties. Moreover, we hear of Naṭas who not only recite but also sing....We cannot absolutely prove that in Patañjali's time the drama in its full form of action allied to speech was present, but we know that all its elements existed, and we may legitimately and properly accpt its existence in a primitive form."[2]

Now, it is difficult to understand how the importand word Naṭ a which occurs a number of times in the Pāli literature has escaped the notice of Prof. Keith. In the Nikāyas there are references to Naṭ as and even Naṭagāmaṇis who were not merely mimes or dancers, but were clearly 'comedians' who *by mimicry and words* delighted audiences at fairs and shows. In the *Gāmaṇi Saṃyutta* we meet with the following:—

"Ekamantaṃ nisinno kho Tālapuṭo Naṭagāmaṇi Bhagavantam etad avoca: Sutam me taṃ bhante pubbakānaṃ ācariyapācariyānaṃ naṭānaṃ bhāsamānānaṃ: Yo so naṭo raṅgaṁajjhe samajjamajjhe saccālikena janaṃ hāseti rameti so kāyassa bhedā param maraṇā Pahāsānaṃ devānaṃ sahavyataṃ upapajjatīti. Idha Bhagavā kiṃ āhāti."[3] "Then Tālapuṭa, the chief of the village of dancers, came to the Exalted One, saluted him and sat down at one side. So seated Tālapuṭa said to the Exalted One: 'I have heard, lord, traditional teachers of old who were actors speaking (in this wise): "A player who on the stage or in the arena makes people laugh and delights them with truth and falsehood, on the dissolution of the body after death, is reborn in the company of the Laughing Devas." What does the Exalted say regarding this matter?.'

It goes without saying that the above passage is of great importance for the subject, origin of dramas, in that it contains not

---

1. *Ibid.*, p. 31.
2. *Sanskrit Drama,* pp. 36, 37.
3. *S.* IV. p. 306 § 3.

only the important word Naṭa, but also refers to a number of other facts. One important fact that emerges from a careful scrutiny of the above quotation is that the Naṭa was originally a figure of mirth (hāseti, rameti), thereby supporting the contention in favour of an at least partly secular origin for the drama. Let us take the important terms one by one. First of all, the name of the interlocutor itself is highly suggestive of he source of the main inspiration of comedy. The name Tālapuṭa (*not* Talapuṭa Tāla—being supported by two Burmese Mss. and Cy.; cp. also *Th.* 1. 1145, p. 103) alludes to the custom quite common in ancient India of using nicknames for reputed persons (cp. 'Kaṇāda,' name of the author of the Vaiśeṣika Sūtras, which literally means 'atom-eater'). Here 'tāla-' must mean 'musical rhythm' or 'beating time' as found in the ancient texts on musical theory. The second member of the compound viz. '-puṭa' means 'the hollow of the folded palm.'[1] The reference is no doubt to the practice prevalent even today among Indian musicians of beating time by clapping in either leading an orchestra or teaching pupils the rudiments of rhythm. This sense agrees perfectly well with the connotation of the word Naṭagāmaṇi or 'leader of Naṭas,' a term that later obtained vogue in dramatic theory as a designation for Sūtradhara or Nāṭyācārya.[2] This identification of Naṭagāmaṇi and Sūtradhara leaves no room for doubt as to the former's connection with drama proper. Moreover, we may dismiss the suggestion of the commentator Buddhaghosa as unwarranted, though highly amusing, when he explains Tālapuṭa as referring to the person's "bright complexion which was like the colour of a ripe palmyra nut severed from the stalk" (bandhanā-mutta-tāla-paka-vaṇṇo viya mukha-vaṇṇo vippasanno ahosi, *Sāratthappakāsinī*, III. 102). Woodward's "basket of woven palm-leaves" for 'Tālapuṭa' is clearly beside the point.[3]

Next, the phrase 'pubbakānaṃ ācariyapācariyānaṃ naṭānaṃ,' despite its stereotyped phraseology, must be taken in the context to refer to a genuine tradition regarding generations of such 'Naṭa-preceptors' of the past,—a fact that cannot be ignored in discussing the nature of the Naṭa-sūtras mentioned by Pāṇini. As for the key-word Naṭa itself, the succeeding sentence proves without a shadow of doubt that the persons referred to here were *at least comedians if not actors of comedies,* who entered the stage (raṅga) to delight and

1. Cp. *Miln.* p. 87, 'hatha-puṭa.'
2. *Vide* Keith, *ibid.*, p. 360.
3. *Book of Kindred Sayings,* p. 214, fn. 1.

make people laugh, with—and this is the most important fact—*truth and lies* (saccālikena; Buddhaghosa: 'saccena ca alikena ca,' *Sāratth.*, III. 193, which also shows that Woodward's "counterfeiting of the truth" falls far short of the actual significance). So these Naṭas were much more than mere mimes or dumb actors. Furthermore, we may suggest with some plausibility that the word 'alike' here might contain an implicit reference to 'fiction,' that is to say, fabricated anecdotes which form part of the stock-in-trade of comedians everywhere in the world. Important also is the word 'raṅga'[1] inasmuch as it must needs refer in the context either to an arena in general or to a play-house or theatre. The term is found in Pāṇini (vi. 4. 27) and the Petersburg Dictionary has (s.v.). "Theater, Schaubühne, Schauplatz, Arena;" in the technical literature raṅga is universally used for 'stage.'[2] Similarly, this passage makes it certain that the word 'samajja' denotes a concourse of people come together for amusement, a 'show' where the Naṭas took a leading rôle. In this connection we may observe that the *Rāmāyaṇa* in one of its genuine portions (ii. 67. 15) refers to 'samājas' where Naṭas and Nartakas, comedians and dancers, delight themselves.[3] According to Prof. Winternitz,[4] this part must have been composed earlier than the third century B.C., and as we shall see later the Buddhist reference is equally old, if not older, from which it may be inferred that at this time the samājas or samajjas were a recognized institution. It may be mentioned that 'naṭa-nartakāḥ' occurs in the Anuśāsana Parvan of the *Mahābhārata* (xiii. 33. 12), and that the commentator Nīlakaṇṭha takes the compound to mean 'comedians and dancers' a sense that may not seem so improbable as Kieth supposes (p. 28) when taken in the light of the Saṃyutta passage. We may suggest, *en passant,* that the older root nṛt (*vide* naṭa, Petersburg Dict.) with its derivatives nartaka, nṛtya etc. in Sanskrit, and naṭṭaka, naṭṭakī (*Th.* I. 267),nacca, naccaka etc. in Pāli referred to *dancing,* whereas its later dialectical form naṭ which gives naṭa, naṭaka, naṭī (also nāṭya in Skt.) etc. signified *gesticulation* and in course of time came to be applied to the art of the 'comedian' and thence to 'acting' proper. As for Pāli, the distinction seems to have been preserved at least in pre-Christian times,[5] though the

1. Cp. *Vinaya*, II. 10, 12.
2. *Vide* Keith, p. 359; cp. Manu, iv. 215 "raṅgāvataraka," "stage-player" according to Bühler.
3. Keith, p. 29.
4. *History of Indian Literature,* vol. 1, p. 516.
5. *Miln.*, p. 359 'naṭa-naccaka.'

commentators often confuse the two (VvA. 210 naṭati=naccati). In the face of the above facts the conclusion is irresistible that the Naṭas were originally a class of *comedians who performed on the stage or at assemblies using words to delight their audiences,* and that Pāṇini's Naṭasūtras may, therefore, legitimately be taken to refer to something more than mere rules regulating the mode of gesticulation of the pantomime.

Another important passage bearing on the subject is found in the Brahmajāla Suttanta of the *Dīgha Nikāya*, containing as it does a list of terms denoting various amusements and shows (visūkadassana):—

"Yathā vā pan'eke bhonto samaṇa-brāhmaṇā saddhā-deyyāni bhojanāni bhuñjitvā te evarūpaṃ visūkadassanaṃ anuyuttāviharanti-seyyathīdaṃ naccaṃ gītaṃ vāditaṃ pekkhaṃ akkhānaṃ pāṇissaraṃ vetālaṃ kumbha-thūnaṃ Sobha-nagarakaṃ.........iti vā iti evarūpā visūkadassanā paṭivirato Samaṇo Gotamo ti" (*D.* I., p. 6, § 13). Professor Rhys Davids rendered this passage as follows:—"Or he might say: 'Whereas some recluses and Brāhmaṇas, while living on food provided by the faithful, continue addicted to visiting shows; that is to say, nautch dances, singing of songs, instrumental music, shows at fairs, ballad recitations, hand-music, the chanting of bards, tam-tam playing, fairy scenes,........Gotama the recluse holds aloof from visiting such shows."[1]

Here 'naccaṃ gītaṃ vāditaṃ' refer to the old conception of 'samgīta' or 'triple symphony,' viz., dancing, singing and instrumental music. Such entertainments are said to have been held at public assemblies such as those already referred to, concourses or fairs, samajjas[2] and at the so-called mountain-fairs or giragga-samajjas[3] said to be frequented even by ministers and other high personages.[4] The word 'nacca' may refer to the dancing of both sexes; female dances are specifically called 'lāsa'[5] and the four are sometimes mentioned together.[6] The last no doubt refers to an old practice and it is of significance for the later division into tāṇḍava and lāsya types attributed to Śiva and Pārvatī respectively.[7]

---

1. *Dialogues* of the *Buddha*, Pt. 1, pp. 7, 8.
2. *Vide D.* III. 183.
3. *Vin.* II, 107.
4. *Vin.* II. 150.
5. Skt. lāsaḥ; cp. *Miln.* p. 331, 'lāska'=female dancer.
6. *Vin.* II, 10 "naccanti pi gāyanti pi vādenti pi lāsenti pi."
7. *Nāṭyaśāstra,* 1. 2; Keith, p. 12.

On doubtful, but not negligible, importance is the word 'pekkhaṃ' which is clearly a *collective-abstract* formation with the suffix 'a' from 'pekkhā' (Skt. prekṣā > *praikṣaṃ) as most words in the list are (cp. pāṇis-saraṃ < pāṇissaro). The Sanskrit is not found in any work earlier than *Manusmṛti*[1] and *Harivaṃśa*.[2] Rhys Davids refuses to agree with Weber, Neumann, Burnouf and others who saw in the Pali 'pekkhā' "theatrical representations," and remarks: "But it is most unlikely that the theatre was already known in the fifth century B.C."[3] It is significant though that Buddhaghosa equates the word to 'naṭa-samajjaṃ'[4] a gloss that establishes the connection, at least in tradition, between 'pekkhā' and 'samāja' as evidenced by the quotations from the Sanskrit sources, and also connects these shows with the activity of the Naṭas who, as seen from the Saṃyutta passage, performed also at samajjas.

Commenting on 'akkhānaṃ' the exegetist says that it refers to "recitations of Bhārata and Rāmāyaṇa" ('Bhārata-Rāmāyanādi, taṃ yasmiṃ thāne kathīyati...' *Sum.* I. 84); the word 'kathīyati' no doubt refers to the work of the Kathakas mentioned by Patañjali. But, if these recitations were of any "epics," it is clear on chronological grounds that the reference is not to the *Mahābhārata* and *Rāmāyaṇa* as we now have them but to the original "ballad" form of these legends. In the case of the former, Winternitz calls it "the old heroic poem" which he believes[5] is *contained* in the so-called "nucleus" of the *Mahābhārata*. The latter, according to him, "......was composed in the third century B.C. by Vālmīki on the basis of ancient ballads."[6] The word 'vetālaṃ' meaning 'the chanting of bards,'[7] also alludes to similar recitations of wandering minstrels. The occurrence of these two terms in the list is of considerable importance for the subject of the origin of drama for, as Keith himself points out, "while the epics cannot be said to know the drama, there is abundant evidence of the strong influence on the development of the drama exercised by the recitation of the epics" (p. 29). The Sigāla Sutta[8] gives 'akkhānaṃ'

1. 'Prekṣā-samājaṃ' ix. 84; ix. 264.
2. 'Prekṣāsu tu subahvīṣu' 8702, 8685.
3. *Dial.* 1. 7. fn. 4.
4. *Sum.* 1, 84; cp. III. 946.
5. *Sum*, 1. p. 459.
6. *Ibid.*, p. 517.
7. Rhys Davids; cp. "naṭavaitālika-stotra nartakāḥ sūtamāgadhāḥ" *M.Bh. i.* § 940, *Hariv.* 8575, referred to *sub* Naṭa in the Petersburg Dict.
8. *D.* III. 183.

as one of the six features of the samajjas where, as we have already seen, the Naṭas took a leading part, and, thereby establishes the contact between the 'comedians' and the 'ballad reciters.' Moreover, our passage proves that these ballad recitations, from which probably developed in the course of time the vocation of the Kathakas, were at least as old as the oldest dialogues of the Pāli Canon, if they were not already popular in the time of the Buddha. Consequently, the inspiration for the origin of drama from this source must be admitted to be much older than the middle of the second century B.C. as has been supposed by Keith (p. 45).

But the most important word in the list is undoubtedly the term 'Sobhanagarakaṃ'—a term that has intrigued both the old and the new commentators. The reading itself is far from settled. The Sinhalese MSS read 'Sobhanagarakaṃ' 'Sobhanakārakaṃ' and 'Sobhanagaranaṃ,' whereas a Burmese MS. of the text has 'Sobhaṇakaṃ.' The Sinhalese MS. of the commentary gives the reading 'Sobhanagarakaṃ,' a Burmese MS. of the same having a variant 'Sobhaṇagaṃ.' It may be observed that the Burmese MSS. of text and commentary do actually agree, for the -g- of the latter can easily be explained as phonetic variation of -k- in the former, the presence of the cerebralized -ṇ- in both (as opposed to the dental in all Sinh. MSS.) supporting the identification. These variants may point to two main traditions: 'Sobhanagarakaṃ' among the Sinhalese, and 'Sobhaṇakaṃ' among the Burmese. Now what is important is that both these forms can be satisfactorily explained, though the latter is by far the more likely historical one as we shall presently see. If the reading is taken to be 'Sobhanagarakaṃ' the allusion may be to the city of Sobha which, as Weber discovered,[1] may refer to the city of the Gandharvas by that name. He quotes from a commentary on Śatarudriya: 'Sobha iti gandharva-nagaram' referred to also by Rhys Davids.[2] So this compound viz. 'Sobha-nagarakaṃ' may mean 'a collection of Sobha-denizens,' i.e., 'a troupe of Gandharvas,' with a probable reference to the traditional connection of these celestial musicians with the drama. On the other hand Rhys Davids' translation 'fairy scenes' is only a surmise based on the gloss 'paṭibhāna-citta' of the commentary, which as we shall see below is not what Buddhaghosa considered as the more probable sense. Now to take the other reading viz. 'Sobhanakaṃ,' this is grammatically to be

1. *Indische Studien,* II. 38.
2. *D.* 1, 6 fn. 1.

explained as a *collective formation,* of the same order as 'pekkhaṃ' discussed above, from a Pāli masculine noun 'Sobhanaka.' This brings us to the most important observation that this is no other than the Pāli counterpart of Sanskrit 'Śobhanika' as found in the *Mahābhāṣ ya* of Patañjali, the suffixes -aka and -ika being syntactically interchangeable. Now, Patañjali, in justification of the use of the present tense for deeds of the remote past as found in such sentences as 'He causes the death of Kaṃsa' etc., say that the *present* is permissible "because the sense is, not that they are being actually done, but that they are being decribed."[1] He then sets out three such modes of description of which the first refers to the profession of the Śobhanikas: 'ye tāvad ete śobhanikā (v. 1. śaubhikā) nāmaite pratya-ksaṃ Kaṃsaṃ ghātayanti pratyaksaṃ Baliṃ bandhayanti' (iii. 1. 26). Here Keith argues that these were pantomimists: "The obvious view, that of Weber, that we have a reference to a pantomimic killing and binding, seems irresistible" (p. 33). The only doubt according to him is whether the Śobhanikas used words (p. 34). Anyway he leaves the question open whether the reference is to 'actors' in the proper sense. Whatever the real sense of the term may be, the fact is clear that the Pāli word 'Sobhanaka' also refers to the same, or at least a similar, cláss of performers. Once this identification is regarded as plausible the word 'Sobhanakaṃ' in the Dīgha passage must be taken to mean 'a troupe of Śobhanikas,' and, this is exactly how Buddhaghosa seems to have understood it, for he comments: 'Sobhanagarakaṃ (v. 1. Sobhaṇagaṃ) ti naṭānaṃ abbhokiraṇaṃ, Sobhanagarakaṃ (v. 1. Sobhanakaraṃ) vā paṭibhāna-cittan ti vuttaṃ hoti.'[2] The hesitancy of the editors regarding the reading and syntactical considerations incline one to the view that what probably Buddhaghosa meant to say was: 'Sobhaṇagan ti naṭānaṃ abbhokiraṇaṃ Sobhanagarakaṃ vā (*sci.* ti pi pāṭho), paṭi-bhāna-cittan ti vuttaṃ hoti,' the first word 'Sobhaṇagaṃ' occuring in the Burmese MS. of the commentary being only the phonetic variant of 'Sobhaṇakaṃ' found as Burmese variant for the text. In any case, the important fact is that Buddhaghosa was more inclined to favour the meaning naṭānaṃ abbhokiraṇaṃ' than the sense 'paṭibhāna-cittaṃ;' hence he places the former phrase at the beginning and gives the latter only as a possible alternative introduced by 'vā.' As for the exact significance of 'naṭānaṃ abbhokiraṇaṃ' it seems fairly likely

1. Keith, p. 32.
2. *Sum.* 1. p. 84.

that what is meant here is 'a troupe (*lit.* crowd, concourse) of actors.' The verbal noun 'abbhokiraṇaṃ' is formed from the root kṛ, to scatter, with the prefixes abhi- and ava-. Syntactically we may regard this as equal in sense to ā-kiraṇa (cp. ākiṇṇa, crowded), for it is observed that the use of the compound prefix 'abhi+ava' corresponds, probably with slightly more intensive sense, to that of 'ā'.[1] Hence we may conclude that the term 'Sobhanagarakaṃ' or 'Sobhaṇakaṃ' of the *Dīgha Nikāya* alludes, as is implied in the gloss of Buddhaghosa, to some class of Naṭas,—an interpretation that has the support of Indian tradition as recorded by Kaiyaṭa in his comment on the word 'Sobhanika' of the *Mahābhāṣya*[2] and, that these Naṭas were either the *same* persons as referred to by Patañjali's 'Sobhanikāḥ' or at least were *their precursors* in the art.

We have seen that Prof. Keith's reluctance to discuss the Buddhist evidence is based on two presuppositions: first, to use his own words, 6the extreme dubiety of the date of the Buddhist Suttas," and second, the supposed paucity of information contained in the Pāli literature—he refers only to Nacca, Pekkhā and Visūkadassana—concerning the question of dramatic origins (p. 42). We hope that the second point has been somewhat satisfactorily answered by the foregoing discussion. Now it remains to be seen how far the expression "extreme dubiety of the Buddhist Suttas" is historically justified. It is admitted on all sides that the Pāli Canon *en masse* is a growth of considerable duration and that the last word is yet to be said on the question of chronology. But this or any such consideration must not blind us to the important fact that, so far as the early Nikāyas and the Vinaya are concerned, there is enough evidence to prove that in substance, apart from their literary form, they go back to a period considerably anterior to the third century B.C. With certain reservations and limitations, we may say with Winternitz "that our Pāli Tipiṭaka, at least the Vinaya and Sutta Piṭaka, does, on the whole, correspond to the Māgadhī Canon of the third century B.C."[3] This is proved by the edicts of Aśoka, particularly the Bairāt or Bhābhrū Edict (249 B.C.) which shows, in the opinion of the same authority, that the Pāli Canon on the whole is pre-Aśokan (p. 25). Now this 'Māgadhī Canon' must have taken at least a century

1. Cp. Pāli abbhokāsa, open space, = ākāsa, space; Skt abhyavaskandana=āskandana, attacking; abhyavahāra=āhāra, food, etc.
2. 'Kaṃsādyanukāriṇāṃ naṭānāṃ vyākhyānopādhyāyā,' *vide* Keith, p. 33, fn. ii.
3. *History of Indian Literature,* II, p. 5; cp. p. 608.

to have evolved into the hypothetical form in which we conceive it, and the language itself must have closely resembled the canonical Pāli. Indeed we must not, as is usually done, unduly exaggerate this linguistic, properly dialectical, difference because, as Winternitz himself admits, the 'Canon of the Vibhajjavādins,' a century after the Buddha's demise, was probably in an older form of Pāli (p. 13). Furthermore, we may now accept as a historical fact that Moggaliputta Tissa, 236 years after the demise of the Master, convened an assembly of monks at Patna "with the object of compiling a Canon of texts of the true religion or the Theravāda" (p. 6), and that the *Kathā-vatthu,* ascribed to Tissa himself who presided at the Council, presupposes not only the texts of the Vinaya Piṭaka and of *all the Nikāyas* of the Sutta Piṭaka but the other books of the Abhidhamma Piṭaka as well. "It would be quite feasible," says Winternitz, "to assume that the book (*Kathāvatthu*) was not written until the time of the compilation of the Canon by Tissa himself......" (pp. 11, 12). These considerations would suffice to show that Bühler was not far wrong, when, in the last work he published, he expressed the opinion that the Nikāyas as we have them in the Pāli "are good evidence, certainly for the fifth, probably for the sixth, century B.C.," a conclusion that was endorsed by Prof. Rhys Davids who added: "......that will probably become, more and more, the accepted opinion. And it is this which gives to all, they tell us, either directly or by implication, of the social, political, and religious life of India, so great a value."[1] It is, of course, true that these statements must necessarily be modified in the light of later research, but no such consideration, we believe, can invalidate the main proposition that the early Nikāyas, at leat the *Dīgha, Majjhima* and *Saṃyutta*, do, on the whole, contain "good evidence," if not for the period of Buddha's own activity (*c.* 535-485 B.C.), at least for that of his very early disciples to whom must be ascribed the creation of the original tradition embedded in these works. As for the genuineness of the particular passages forming the subject-matter of our present investigation, we may without hesitation observe that neither the Brahmajāla Sutta nor the Gāmaṇi Saṃyutta, from which we have quoted, betrays any evidence whatsoever, whether linguistic or otherwise, of lateness or spuriousness of composition; on the other hand, the Naṭagāmaṇi dialogue shows every sign of being a record of an actual event both by the tone of naturalness running through the whole narrative and also in point of style and

1. *Dial.* 1, p. xx.

method, while the Brahmajāla Sutta, though obviously a résumé of the existing philosophical and religio-social institutions of the time, contains material that is proved to be old by the very obscurity of its terminology and the close resemblance of doctrines discussed to the ideas of the ancient Upaniṣads.[1]

Now to sum up: We hope we have succeeded in proving that the evidence afforded by the Nīkāyas is of considerable importance for the problem of the evolution of drama in India, particularly for the history of the key-word Naṭa and also of Śobhanika, and, that the available evidence would take back its origin to at least *the third or fourth century B.C.*, if they do not conclusively prove that there were dramatic spectacles of some kind, probably comedy *in nuce,* in the time of the Buddha himself. This conclusion is supported by the further consideration that if, as Prof. Keith himself admits, "the Vedic ritual contained within itself the germs of drama" (p. 23), and if, as Winternitz has shown with great plausibility, the beginning of the Vedic literature was nearer to 2500 or 2000 B.C. than to 1500 or 1200 B.C. as generally held[2] then it makes the belief well-nigh impossible that with such materials as present in the Vedic culture, the ballad recitations which seem to be pre-Buddhistic, as shown above, and other tendenciesw reflected both in Sanskrit and Pāli literature, the drama, at least in some crude form, could not have come into being all throughout the course of a whole millennium. The fact that the Naṭa of the Saṃyutta is a 'comedian' shows that in its origin the secular influence on the drama was also considerable and that it was not evoked solely "by the combination of epic recitations with the dramatic moment of the Kṛṣṇa legend,"[3] a contention that gains strength by the fact that the earliest dramas we possess, viz., those of Aśvaghoṣa, have very little in common with the epics or the Kṛṣṇa legend in point of theme and subject-matter.

---

1. Cp. Rhys Davids, *Dial.* I p. xxvi.
2. *Calcutta Review,* Nov. 1923.
3. Keith, p. 45.

Chapter - 30
The Gāmabhojaka in the Buddhist Birth-stories

Atindra Nath Bose

The Jātakas contain interesting references to the duties and powers of the *gāmabhojaka* or the *gāmika* who played an important part in India's rural economy from the earliest times. These few but weighty remarks pieced together, lead to certain broad probabilities which ill accord with the theory given currency in some quarters that he was a typical product of the free institutions and corporate life of the ancient village system.

The headman frequently appears in the rôle of an absentee landlord who dwells in a town not necessarily in close proximity and periodically visits his village zemindary. In the *paccupannavatthus* Anāthapiṇḍika often goes to supervise the affairs of his village leaving his house at Sāvatthi (I. 365, 412). Sometimes the absentee lord is preoccupied with mercantile pursuits and the village is an additional source of income possibly unearned, where he goes only to realise his dues traversing a long journey on cart (I. 413, V. 164). Sometimes he makes the journey for collecting debts accompanied by his wife (II. 341, III. 107). In one case he is seen attaching a cart of a defaulter in satisfaction for what was du to him (III. 66).

Wherefrom was the ownership derived? The earliest trace of this type of landlord villages is found in the *Taittirīya Saṃhitā* where it is told in connexion with the performance of certain sacrifices by a person hankering after a village (grāmakāma) how the gods concerned 'bestow him creatures led by the noses' (II. 1.1.2) how they 'present his relations to him and make the folk dependent on him' (ibid. 1.3.2) and how they enable him to hold the mind of his peers (ibid. 3.9.2). These cryptic expressions mean, if anything, that the village lordships acquired in the first instance by individual exertion, afterwards received the seal of royal confirmation. The

Jātakas belie throughout the tradition embodied in the *Śatapatha Brāhmaṇa* that land must not be given away by a king even on the plea of a sacrificial fee (XIII. 7, 15). The recipients of royal bounties are not always Brāhmaṇas and the donations of villages are almost invariably accompanied by the conventional phrase "yielding a hundred thousand a year" (*satasahassutthānaka* I. 420; III. 229; V. 350, 371). In the Mahāummaga Jātaka, Bodhisatta on his way from Uttarapañcāla to Videha sends men to receive the revenue of the eighty Kāsi villages which king Culani had given him (VI 463). The grantee in this and similar occasions when he is a town-dweller appears to be out of touch with village administration except so far as is necessary for collection of revenues. It is likely that he obtained not the *administration*[1] but the revenues of the village, *i.e.*, benefits without-responsibility; and as the big money-lender he asserted his furtive power still further in his rural preserves not always with happy results. Instances of pious men like Anāthapiṇḍika are fortuitous and there is little reason to believe that his charitable acts were dictated by any customary obligation implicit in ownership.

The headman is not necessarily, rather rarely, the mainspring of the gāma's corporate life and collectivist enterprise. In this respect he differs from the *jeṭṭhakas* of the industrial *gāmas* or of the trade-guilds. In the Kulāvaka Jātaka Bodhisatta is the moving spirit of the sturdy gāma life and the headman is put to the thought when these men used to get drunk and commit murder and so forth, I used to make a lot of money out of them not only in the price of their drinks but also by the fines and dues they paid (*ahaṃ pubbe etesu suraṃ pivantesu paṇātipātādīni karontesu cāṭikahāpaṇa divasena c'eva daṇḍabalivasena ca dhanaṃ labhāmi*); and he brought a complaint to the king against Bodhisatta on false charges (I. 199ff).

These few words read with the allusion to a pious headman in another place who stopped the sale of strong drink in his estate (IV. 115) lead to a strong presumption that the headman either himself

1. In the *Digha Nikāya* there is a stock passage which seems to indicate *prima facie* that the royal fiefs carried with them administrative power. "Now at that time so and so the Brāhmaṇa was dwelling at such and such place, a place teeming with life with much grassland and woodland and water and corn, on a royal domain granted him by so and so the king as a royal gift *with power over it as if he were the king*" (*rājabhoggaṃ raññā dinaṃ rājadāyaṃ brahmadeyyaṃ*, III. i. 1; IV. i. 1; XII. i. 1). The fief from the description seems to be not a settled village but a large tract of irrigated and cultivated soil with fenland and pasture fit for animal farming; and the concluding phrase permits the interpretation that the usufructuary right and titular ownership of the king were transferred to the assignee along with the land.

maintained breweries in the village—those crime-centres and plague-spots of rural life, or he enjoyed the excise dues thereon whether within or outside the revenue transferred by royal assignment. The fines undoubtedly went to his pocket. For he adjudicated rural cases. To a question why a certain headman had fallen from better days a king replies: "That village headman used once to deal justice indifferently, so that men were pleased and delighted wth him; and in their delight they gave him many a present (*bahupannākāram āhariṃsu*). This is what made him handsome, rich and honoured. Now he loves to take bribes (*pana lañcavittako hutvā*), and his judgment is not fair; so he is poor, miscrable and jaundiced. If he judges once again with righteousness he will be again as he was before. He knows not that there are kings in the land. Tell him that he must use justice in giving judgment (*dhammena aṭṭaṃ vinicchinituṃ* II. 309).

There is a sharp demarcation between the legitimate dues and the illegal gratifications of the headman. But a judge who can accept presents from litigants without any sense of wrong, must be prone to count these tips among his dues as much as the judicial fines and to allow his decisions to be bought all the more when they are not assisted by a jury or a folk moot of any *sort*[1] and when there appears to have been no appeal against them. The vaunted prerogative of interference claimed by the king was certainly no common occurrence in those days of disorder and insecurity, of decentralised government and undeveloped communication.[2] It was asserted only on grave issues or when the king's revenue was at stake.

---

1. The village affairs discussed in the public hall bore on civic amenities, co-operative labour and state of crops but there is no authority to assume that they include judicial matters except in the republics. In the foregoing passage the headman's justice is undivided. Kauṭilya's ordinance of a fine of 24 paṇas for a headman who expels from a village anyone except a thief and an adulterer (*Artha-śāstra* III. X) presumes untrammelled exercise by the headman of his judicial powers. There is no sufficient data for the assumption that in Naurya times he carried on the village administration and judicial business in consultation with the *grāmavṛddhas* or elders. For this view see Thomas in *Cambridge History of Ancient India,* vol. I and Ray Choudhuri, *Political History of Ancient India*: 3rd Edition, p. 199.

2. The evidence of the *Kulāvaka Jātaka* and of the *Gāmani Canda Jātaka* just quoted leads a scholar to think that "administration of justice was one of the essential links that bound the scattered villages to the central organisation of the state" and that in this matter final authority rested with the king. He relies further on the custom referred to in the latter by which any one could challenge a disputant to come to the king's officer by picking up a potshered or stone. But the village concerned is not a *bhogagāma*. Such central control in normal administration of justice in rural areas under influential lords goes against the cumulative evidence of the Jātakas and the possibilities of the times. See B.C. Sen in *Journal of Letters* vol. XX, p. 107.

Without doubt the headman was a big man of opulence and position whose wrongs could not be held in check by any lesser authority than the king. In the Kulāvaka Jātaka referred to above we find him for once heavily chastised by the king for falsely bringing grave charges of treason against the whole body of villagers. He has power to prohibit slaughter of animals for sacrifice within his area (IV. 115). He dares to commit adultery with a *gahapati's* wife and when caught and thrashed by the husband, none other than Bodhisatta would have ventured on similar method of exacting 'damages', he expostulated saying 'I am the headman' (*gāmabhojako'mhiti* II. 135). Elsewhere a headman conspires with brigands to carry off the taxes collected for the king: and here for the second time we see him feel the heavy hand of an overlord (I. 354).

The last intance implies the existence of another kind of headman besides the one who enjoyed the village revenue from royal grant, a semi-official entrusted with the collection and despatch of the king's share of produce. Whether he was king's nominee or elected by the rural constituency or whether he held a hereditary post is impossible to ascertain beyond dispute. That the zemindaries were hereditary admits of no doubt. In the Mahāsutasoma Jātaka "headship of a single village" (*ekagāmabhojanaṃ*) is spoken of in contrast with the "Office of Commander-in-chief and similar posts" (*Senāpatiṭṭhānādini* V. 484) the suggestion being that the head was a king's officer. There is no example in the birth stories or any contemporary evidence to warrant the conclusion that he was the "elected chief of the village *community*."[1] That he stood in certain relations with the king is attested by many passages (IV. 310). As noticed above he could seek justice in king's court whenever there was trouble in his affairs. It is probable that he discharged certain vague undefined functions as an intermediary between the king and the freeholders.

Thus the headman is a 'persona grata' with the king as with his tenants. He is aparently the sole and final judge of the small village causes. He collects the king's tithe and sends it to the treasury unless the revenue is assigned to him by royal writ. The judicial fees and fines and the returns of liquor houses or excise dues are among his perquisites. He is the agricultural bank 'par excellence'. He may have had other incomes lawful or otherwise[2] for his assets are in

1. For this view see Fick's *Die Sociale Gliederung im Nordöstlichen Indien zu Buddhas Zeit*, pp. 105-6.
2. The words *gāmabhojaka* and *gāmabhojana* suggest not usufructuary title over land but enjoyment of all possible revenue derivable from the village.

cases guaged at eighty crores. In one of these he is described as a landowner (*asītikoṭivibhaoo kuṭumbika*, IV. 370). In another he is the King's chaplain and hoards up the sum apart from his office (*purohitaṭṭhānena saddhiṃ asītikoṭidhanaṃ chaddetvā*, IV. 484)—presumably from the 'revenue village' (*bhogagāmaṃ*) which he visits from time to time (IV. 473). The landholder Sujāta at Benares lodges in his park and ministers tofive hundred ascetics (V. 465) and the multimillionaire Anāthapiṇḍika frequently beats therecord. Giving due allowance for the tendency of folktales towards exaggeration these figures show that the landlord might occasionally rise to the topmost rung of economic ladder and rank with the plutocracy of Brāhmaṇa and Seṭṭhi magnates who basked in the sunshine of court and whose wealth is often estimated in the same fabulous figures.

Whether absorbed in the luxuries and money transactions of urban-life or settled in his rural estate, the headman has little to do with the communal life of the village and he owes no responsibility either to the king or to a village council for rural welfare. In the numerous famine scenes we invariably miss him. Once only he is found giving an old ox to hungry cultivators under the grip of scarcity on condition of repayment after two months from the next harvest (II. 135) and this must be regarded as part of his ordinary lending business than of a benevolent distribution of *dole.*[1]

In the Vedic texts village headmen (grāmani, grāmika) are styled Rājakartṛ and Ratnin aiding in the consecration of the king among certain other functionaries and are consulted by the king along with the ministers. The Mahāvagga gives the important reference that the gāmikas of Bimbisāra, 80,000 in number, used to be summoned in a great assembly (V.I. 1ff). In those days when kingship had not yet outgrown the tribal stage, the village chiefs were communal representatives and exerted a wholesome check on royal absolutism. But later records which synchronise with the growth of a centralised monarchy fortified by a bureaucratic machine, strike a different note. The periodical assemblies of *gāmikas* seem to have fallen into disuse with the rise of Maurya imperialism: they gradually sank down from the headship of autonomous villages to sleeping landowners with irresponsible powers and vested privileges or were

1. Kauṭilya exhorts villagers to accompany the grāmika by turns whenever he "has to travel on account of any business of the whole village." From evidences already adduced it may be argued '*a fortiori*' that this business was personal (*i.e.* related to his own income) rather than corporate and administrative (*Arthaśāstra*, III. X).

transformed into king's officers and absorbed into an official hierarchy. The Jātakas exhibit the headman in both these capacities. Even in later Upaniṣadic literature we find the king appointing *adhikṛtas* over *grāmas*;[1] such appointment tallies with the conception of civil polity and paramount sovereignty implied in the honorific '*Samrāt*'. In the Arthaśāstra, the *grāmabhṛtakas* are king's servants and the *grāmikas* are subordinate to the *gopas, sthānikas* and still higher officers. The bureaucratic system is perfected in the law-codes (*Āpastamba* II. 26. 4-5; Viṣṇu III. 7-15; Yājñavalkya I. 337) and Manu lays down a detailed official gradation. The *grāmikas* appointed by the king are not to take cognizance of crimes and decide according to their free will but report all cases to lords of ten villages, they in turn to the next superior officers and so on (VII. 115-117). In the *Sukranītisāra* the headman is a king's deputy (ii. 343) "intoxicated by drinking the vanity of office" (ii. 227). In the Śaka and Gupta inscription as well, side by side with land charters issued to royal favourites, the *grāmikas, bhojakas* etc. are found fitted in an elaborate framework of civil administration. Thus the upholder of popular rights and duties who loomed large in Vedic and early Buddhist social economy is no longer the representative of free village corporations and fades out into a leisurely landlord or is stereotyped into an official automaton.

1. *Praśna-Upaniṣad*, III. 4. Quoted in Ray Choudhuri, *Political History of Ancient India*, 4th Edition, p. 141, f.n. 4.

Chapter - 31
On the 'Buddhacarita' of Asvaghoṣa

Sukumar Sen

The 'Buddhacarita,' as edited by E.B. Cowell (in the *Anecdota Oxoniensia* series), is a very interesting work, forming the earliest extant specimen of artificial epic poetry (*kāvya*) in Sanskrit. In this brief note I shall discuss the language of the published text, which far from being complete and is overstrewn with early interpolations and scribal errors as well as emendations. I must add here that I have not here considered the last four spurious cantos. The eleven *ślokas* in Canto 9 which do not occur in Cowell's text but which were recovered by Mm. Haraprasad Sastri (JASB., 1909) have not been utilised in this paper, although they are genuine.

There are only three notable Prakritisms: *khela* ($\sqrt{}$ *krīḍ*), 2. 31 and 7. 36; *ābhāsura* (〈 *ābhāsvara*), 12.53; and *vaṅka* (〈 *vakra*), 11. 46.

Two wrong *sandhis* occur: *ubhe 'pi* (for *ubhe api*), 9. 21; and *saujasvi* (for *sa ojasvi*), 8. 3. There is also a shortening of quantity of the long vowel ā for metrical purpose: gato *'ryaputraḥ* (for *gata āryaputraḥ*), 8. 34.

Anomalous nominal forms are very few: *loka* has once been used as neuter, e.g. *lokāni hi trīṇi*, 'the three worlds,' 10. 81; añjanā for añjana 'collyrium,' 8. 21; *sahīyā* for *sahīyasī*? 10. 26; *vasthānam* for *avasthānam*, 4. 55; *dharman* for *dhrama*, 5. 77, 11. 20. Once the verb in plural has been construed with the nominative in singular (this is no doubt scribe's blunder): *nypo'pi ca prāpur imaṃ giriṃ vrajan* 'the king too, walking, reached the hill,' 11. 73.

A remarkable feature is the abundant use of the cognate accusative, especially with verbs meaning 'to speak'. Thus *puṣ padrumāḥ svaṃ kusumam puphulluḥ* 'the flowering trees put on their blossoms,'1. 44; *tapāṃsy atapta* 'practised penances,' 2, 49; *vacāṃsy uvāca* 'spoke words,' 1, 59; *vākyam abravīt* 'spoke the word,' 4.3; *vacanaṃ cedam uvāca* 'spoke this speech', 5. 29; *brūvan vākyam idaṃ tasthau* 'stood speaking this speech', 6.13; *giram ity uvāca* 'this speech he uttered', 7. 37, etc.; *abravīd vacaḥ*, 9. 62; *vaco babhāṣe*, 13. 3; *nanāda siṃhanādam* 'roared the lion's roar', 5. 84.

The preposition *prati*, in various senses, governs the accusative; 1. 73 (twice); 1. 81; 2. 57; 4. 24; 6. 43; 7. 12, 45; 8. 54; 9. 14, 67; 11. 50. 62; 13. 16. The accusative is also governed by desiderative adjectives, but the genitive occurs with *didṛkṣā*, e.g. *didṛkṣā śākyakuladhvajasys* 'for the desire of seeing the banner of the race of the Sākyas', 1. 63; etc. In the compound *vanabhūmididṛkṣayā* 'for the desire of seeing the forest tract', 5.2, however, it governs the accusative. The accusative has also been used with the compound *vibhī*: *sukhaṃ vibhīr mām apahāya* 'afraid of pleasure, (and) leaving me', 8. 64. Peculiar is the accusative in: *dharmanadīṃ pādysti jīvalokaḥ* 'living beings would drink of the river of *dharma*', 1. 76. The instrument with the compound *vinākṛta* 'separated' occurs frequently: 8. 21, 37, 78, etc.; also the instrumental is construed with the conjunctives and derivatives of *vi-yuj*; e.g. *viyujyamāne' pi tarau puṣpair api phalair api* 'in the tree, also, when divorced from flowers and from fruits', 4. 61. In the following instance the instrumental has been used absolutely: *śarīra-cittavyasanā-tapais tair evaṃvidhais taiś ca nipātyamānaiḥ / naivāsanāc chākya-muniś cacāla svāṃ niścayaṃ bandhum ivopaguhya* 'inspite of those penances of body and mind, and heat, and inspite of these thus assailing him, the Śākya sage did not move from his seat, hugging his own resolve, as it were a friend', 13. 42.

The dative is regularly construed with verbs meaning 'to tell, to send, to show' etc., but in a few instances the dative has been replaced by the genitive; e.g. *tato' bravīt sārathir asya* 'then the charioteer spoke to him', 3. 42; *babhramur darśayantyo'sya śroṇīḥ* 'they rambled showing their hips to him,' 4. 34; *tad bravīmi suhid bhūtvā taruṇasya vapuṣmata idaṃ na pratirūpaṃ te* 'so being a friend I say to you who are young and well-shaped, this is not fitting for you', 4. 66. See also verse 2. 44, *infra*. The following instance of ablative of comparison is noteworthy: *dharmasya tasyāśravaṇād ahaṃ hi manye vipattiṃ tridive' pi vāsaḥ* 'living in heaven I consider to be an evil worse than not listening to that *dharma*', 1. 82. In the following instance the genitive absolute implies no sense of *anādara*: *iti paśyata eva rājasūnor idam uktvā sa nabhaḥ samutpapāta* 'while the king's son was thus looking on, he, saying this, flew up in the sky' 2. 20.

The 'Buddhacarita' agrees with the epics in having the locative used in the various case relations. Thus: *d'śyatāṃ strīṣu māhātmyam* 'let the excellence of women be noted', 4. 50; *yadi tvāṃ samupekṣyeyaṃ na bhaven mitratā mayi* 'if I spurn you I would not have any friendship (for you)', 4. 65; *prayatasvātamahite jagaddhite ca* 'strive for your own and for world's welfare', 5. 78; *api nairguṇyam asmākaṃ vācyaṃ narapatau tvayā* 'you should also speak to the king about my worthlessness', 6. 24; *bodhiprāptau samartho' bhūti* 'he was successful in winning perfect knowledge', 12. 109.

One compound formation should be noted: *suhṛdbrūva* 'one who speaks himself as a friend', 8. 35.

The author appears to have been very fond of desideratives,— nouns, adjectives and verbs. These are: *didṛkṣā* 'desire of seeing', 1.63, etc.; *jijīviṣā* 'desiring of living', 8.12; *cikīrṣā* 'desire of doing', 10.39; *jighāṃsā*, 'desire of killing', 13.66; vivakṣā 'desire of going out', 10.22; *vivatsā* 'desire of dwelling', 7.42; *niścikramiṣā* 'desire of going out', 5.66; *niścikramiṣu* 'desirous of going out', 5.37; *vijighāṃsu*, 'desirous of slaying', 5.43; *mumukṣu* 'desirous of emancipation', 9.61, etc.; *amumukṣu* 'not desirous of emancipation', 8.77; *nirmumukṣu* 'desirous of emancipation', 5.39; *yiyāsu* 'desirous of going' 5.79, etc.; *vijijñāsu* 'desirous of knowing', 7.11, etc.; *bubhuku* 'desirous of food, hungry', 8.63; pipāṣa 'desirous of drink', 8.80; *tirtīrṣu* 'desirous of fording or crossing over water', 9.5, etc., *didṛkṣu* 'desirous of seeing', 9.9, etc.; *jihīrṣu* 'desiring of taking', 11.15; *śuśrūṣu* 'desirous of hearing', 12.82; *prepsu* 'desirous of getting', 12.86, etc.; *jigīṣu* 'desirous winning', 13.4; *jighṛkṣu* 'desirous of taking' 13.27; *jighāṃsu* 'desirous of slaying', 13.4; *didhakṣu* 'desirous of burning;, 13.50; *rirakṣiṣant* 'desiring to protect', 2.55; *ārurukṣant* 'desiring to climb, 2. 48; *yiyāsanti* 'they wish to go', 7. 53; *parīpsanti* 'they wish to attain', 7.53 etc; *jigīṣanti* 'they wish to win', 11.12; *cikārṣant* 'desiring to do', 13.18; *jighṛkṣati* 'he wishes to catch', 8.64; *na cājihīrṣīd balim aparvattam na cācikīrṣīt paravastu abhidhyām/ cāvivakṣīd dviṣatām adharmaṃ na cādidhakṣīd hṛdayena manyum* 'he did not desire to take contributions not forthcoming; he did not desire the contemplation of (appropriating) other's property; he did not desire to teach the wrong to the enemies (even); nor did he desire to entertain anger at heart': 2.44. This beats even the 'Bhaṭṭikāvya.'

Only one adnominal verbal formation occurs: *karuṇāyamānaḥ* 'feeling pity', 3.45 and 13.61.

Simple perfect has been used with about 145 roots and about 645 times. Periphrastic perfects have been formed from about 22 roots,—with *as* 20 occurrences, with *kṛ* 7, and with *bhū* 5. The following three instances, where the cognate accusative parts have been separated from the main verbal form by the instrusion of other words, are noteworthy: *mātṛṣvasā mātṛsamaprabhāvā saṃvardhayām ātmajavad babhūva* the mother's sister, with a mother's authority nursed (him) like her own son,' 2. 19; *divyair viśeṣair mahyāṃ ca cakruḥ* '(the gods) honoured (him) with divine preparations', 6.58; *pratyarcayāṃ dharmabhṛto babhūva* '(he) worshipped the pious ones in return', 7.9. A similar construction occurs twice in the 'Raghuvaṃśa': *taṃ pātayām 'prathamam āsa papāta paścāt,* '(it) first felled him and then fell itself', 9.61; *prabhraṃśayām yo nahuṣaṃ cakāra* 'who caused Nahuṣa to fall', 13.36.

Simple aorist occurs with 11 roots and about 25 times: these roots are: *adhi-i, gam, car, tap, bhū, yaj, vac, śak, śī and hā*. The reduplicated aorist occurs with *ky*, *chid*, *jval*, *bhid*, and *han*, and only once with each. The aorist with desiderative stems occurs only 4 times; see verse 2. 44, *supra*. The ratio between the perfect and the aorist is about 20:1. This in the main agrees with Kālidāsa. The number of imperfect forms is less than that of the aorist. The present form with *sma* has been used as equivalent to the perfect not infrequently. Constructions with the passive participle in *-ta* is anything but rare, while that with *-ta-vant* is very scarce; e.g. *na yaṃ vaśiṣṭhaḥ kṛtavān aśaktiḥ* 'what Vaśiṣṭha, lacking power, did not do', 1.47.

There are only two occurrences of the periphrastic future: *kim eṣa doṣa bhavitā mamāpi* 'is it that this evil would happen to me even?', 3.32; *na punar ahaṃ kapilāhvayaṃ praviṣṭā* 'but I shall not again enter the (city) named Kapila', 5.84. Note the absence of *asmi* in the last instance. The conditional mood occurs in one verse only: *yadi hy aheṣiṣyata bodhayañ janaṃ khuraiḥ kṣitau vāpy akariṣyata dhvanim / hanusvanaṃ vā 'janayiṣyad uttmaṃ na cābhaviṣyam mama duḥkham īd śam* 'had (the horse) neighed, waking the people, had it raised noise with its hoofs (beating) on the ground, had it made good noise with its jaws, such misery would not have accrued to me', 8.4. The precative occurs once only, in 1.53.

Peculiar as well as interesting is the following instance where the finite verbal form *asmi* 'I am' has been used for the regular pronoun *aham: mā bhūn matis te nṛpa kācid anyā niḥsaṃśayaṃ tad yad avocam asmi* 'may you have no other apprehension, O king: certain is what I have said', 1.72. Mallinātha under 'Kirātārjunīya' 3.6. says, on the authority of the 'Gaṇavyākhyāna', that *asmi* is also an indeclinable in the sense of *aham*, and quotes the parallel: *dīse kṛtāgasi bhavaty ucitaḥ prabhūṇāṃ iti sundari nāsmi dūye* 'a kick to the slave who has committed an offence, is proper for masters, hence, O beautiful one, I do not grudge.' This is probably not an interpolation as the author uses *asmi* very frequently with past participles in *-ta*. To this can be compared the periphrasic future forms such as *dātāsmi* and *dātāham* (the latter frequently occurs in the 'Mahābhārata'); cf. also, *na punar ahaṃ kapilāvayam praviṣṭā,* supra. The Prakrit future forms like *dāhaṃ-dāsyāmi* are based on periphrastic forms like *dātāham* and not on the *-sya-* future: cf. S.K. Chatterji, 'Origin and Development of the Bengali Language', 1926, p. 549.

A few anomalous verbal forms occur: *supet* ($\sqrt{}$ *svap*, 4.59; *sisiñcire* for *sisiñcuḥ 8. 26; niṣīdatuḥ* for *niṣedatuḥ*, 9.11; 12.3; *samupekṣeyam* for *samupekṣeya*, 4.65; *vijigāya* for *vijigye*, 1.28 ff.; the right from has been used in 2.34; *upatasthuḥ* for *upatasthire*, 5.45 (the right form has been used in 10.19); *vivarjayitvā, paripālayitvā* for *vivarjya, paripālya*, 11.29.

The following perfect participles occur: *ūcivāṃs* 3.43; 5.36; *upeyivaṃs* 3.8; *sameyivāṃs* 5.20; *upajagmivāṃs* 12.2; *tasthuṣī* 4.36; *lelihāna* 13.13.

A chain of conjunctives occurs in one verse: *niḥśvasya dīrghaṃ sa śiraḥ prakampya tasmiṃś ca jīrṇe viniveśya cakṣuh/ tāṃ caiva dṛṣṭvā janatām saharṣāṃ vākyaṃ sa saṃvignam idaṃ jagāda* 'heaving a long (sign), shaking the head, rivetting (his) eyes on the old (man), and looking at the rejoicing crowd, he uttered this sorrowful speech', 3.25. In quite a number of instances the conjunctives have been used incorrectly: *tam preksya kasmāt tava dhīra bāṣpaḥ* 'why, O calm one, your tears on seeing him ?' 1.68; *ato me dhyānāni labdhvāpy akṛtārthataiva* 'hence, through finding meditations, my lucklessness', 1.82; *puruṣasya vayaḥsukhāni bhuktvā ramaṇīyo hi tapovanapraveśaḥ* 'of man, after enjoying youthful pleasures, entering the forest is really befitting', 5.53; *evaṃ ca te niśeayam etu buddhir dṛṣṭvā vicitraṃ vividhapracāram* 'having seen various ways let your mind come to determination', 9.34; *devena vṛṣṭe'pi hiraṇyavarṣe dvīpān samudrāṃś caturo' pi jitvā/ śakrasya cārdhāsanam apy avāpya māndhātur āsīd viṣayaeṣv atiptiḥ* 'notwithstanding the God raining gold, notwithstanding (his) conquering the continents and the four oceans, and inspite of (his) occupying half of Śakra's throne, Māndhātṛ had insatiety in enjoyment', 11.13; *kratoḥ phalaṃ yady api śāśvataṃ bhavet tathāpi kṛtvā kim upakṣayātmakam* 'even if the result of sacrifice be permanent, what is the good of suffering?" 11.65.

The infinitive has been used incorrectly in: *jīrṇaṃ naraṃ nirmamire prayātum* they fashioned a decrepit man to go', 3.26; *tad vijñātum imaṃ dharmaṃ pramam bhājanam bhavān* 'so you are the best person for knowing this *dharma*', 12.9.

When reading the 'Buddhacarita' one cannot help noting that the author was unusually fond of finite verbs. I quote here some passages which can easily pass for extracts from the grammatical epic, the 'Bhaṭṭikāvya': *cacāra harṣaḥ praṇanāśa pāpmā* jajvāla dharmaḥ *kaluṣah śaśāma* 'joy prevailed, sin died out, *dharma* blazed forth, evil abated', 2.16; *śame 'bhireme virarāma pāpād bheje damaṃ saṃvibabhāja* 'he rejoiced in peace, desisted from evil, practised abstinance, and honoured the pious', 2.33; *nādhyaiṣṭā duḥkhāya parasya vidyāṃ jñānaṃ śivaṃ yat tu tam adhyagīṣṭa* 'he did not learn other's knowledge (which comes) for sorrow, but acquired the knowledge which is good', 2.35; *ekaṃ vininye sa jugopa sapta saptaiva tatyāja rarakṣa pañca/ prāpa trivargaṃ bubudhe trivargaṃ yajñe dvivargaṃ prajahau dvivargaṃ* 'he subordinated the one, he nurtured the seven; he gave up the seven, he kept the five; he acquired the triad, he perceived the triad; he knew the couple, and he rejected the couple', 2.41.

Aśvaghoṣa apparently wrote in quite good Sanskrit, although his standard is not that of Pāṇini. It is nevertheless an authoritative form of Sanskrit which is also found in the epics and the 'Purāṇas', and is based largely on the spoken usage of the centuries immediately preceding the birth of Christ.